HOW TO KILL A TIGER TANK

UNPUBLISHED SCIENTIFIC REPORTS FROM THE SECOND WORLD WAR

CRAIG MOORE

FONTHILL

Fonthill Media Language Policy
Fonthill Media publishes in the international English language market. One language edition is published worldwide. As there are minor differences in spelling and presentation, especially with regard to American English and British English, a policy is necessary to define which form of English to use. The Fonthill Policy is to use the form of English native to the author. Craig Moore was born and educated in London, England; therefore, British English has been adopted in this publication.

Fonthill Media Limited
Fonthill Media LLC
www.fonthillmedia.com
office@fonthillmedia.com

First published in the United Kingdom and the United States of America 2021

British Library Cataloguing in Publication Data:
A catalogue record for this book is available from the British Library

ISBN 978-1-78155-858-4

Typeset in Minion Pro 10pt on 13pt
Printed and bound in England

CONTENTS

ACKNOWLEDGEMENTS

Herbert Ackermans, Bob Barlow, Adrian Barrell, Jason Belgrave, Pierre-Oliver Buan, Lauren Child, Jeremy Churchill, Rob Cogan, Joshua Collins, Eddie Coleman, Arnaud Deporspo, Alexis Dours, Hilary Louis Doyle, Len Dyer, Daniel Enriquez, Joris Fareu, David Fletcher, Massimo Foti, Andrew Hills, Marcus Hock, Jonathan Holt, John Kantek, Patrik Krista, Pierre Garnier de Labareyer, Robert Livingston, Pavel Medek, Russell Moore, Sue Moore. Steve Osfield, John Osselaer, Yuri Pasholok, John Pearson, Walter J. Spielberger, Steve Tatham, Ed Webster, John D. Webster, and Ian Wilcox.

Deutsches Panzermuseum, Imperial War Museum, Kubinka Tank Museum, Musée des Blindés (French Museum of Armour, Saumur), National Archives at Kew, U.S. Army Armor & Cavalry Collection at Fort Benning, Australian Armour and Artillery Museum, and the Tank Museum, Bovington.

Captured Tiger tank 131 photographed in North Africa prior to shipping to Britain. (*STT*)

GLOSSARY

Annulus	the region between.
AFV	armoured fighting vehicle.
AP	armour-piercing shell.
APC	armour-piercing capped shell.
APCBC	armour-piercing capped ballistic cap shell.
APCBCHE	armour-piercing capped ballistic cap high-explosive shell.
APDS	armour-piercing discarding sabot shell.
AT	anti-tank.
Azimuth	It is an angular measurement in a spherical coordinate system. The vector from an observer to a point of interest is projected perpendicularly onto a reference plane; the angle between the projected vector and a reference vector on the reference plane is called the azimuth. An example of azimuth is the angular direction of a star in the sky. The star is the point of interest, the reference plane is the local horizontal area, and the reference vector points north. The azimuth is the angle.
Brinell Hardness Test	a widely used and standardised hardness test in engineering and metallurgy.
Broadside	length wise, full length exposed.
Buffs	The Buffs (Royal East Kent Regiment).
Burster Boards	sheets of wood suspended in the air at set heights that when hit by a shell explode to simulate an air burst.
Butt	a protected pit with three raised sides used in test firing weapons or a part of a gun that rests against a soldier's shoulder.
cm	centimetre (1 cm = 0.39 inch).
cwt	hundredweight.
DAK	*Deutsches Afrika Korps.*
DS	discarded sabot.
DTD	Department of Tank Design, also Directorate of Tank Design (the terms were used interchangeably).
Dunkelgelb	dark sandy yellow.
Dunkelgrau	dark grey.
FCS	full service charge.
f.s. or ft. sec.	feet per second.
FVPE	Fighting Vehicle Proving Establishment.
Fahrgestell-Nummer Serie	hull/chassis number.
Flammenvernichter	flame suppressor exhaust mufflers.

Glacis plate	the sloped armoured plate at the front of the tank hull.
HC	high capacity.
HE	high-explosive shell.
Hispano	a 20-mm cannon and armour-penetrating ammunition.
Kampfwagenkanone	tank gun.
Kugelblende	ball mount for a machine gun.
l	litre (1 l = 0.26 US gallon/0.22 imperial gallon).
lb	pound weight, i.e. 1 lb (1 lb = 0.454 kg).
Louvre	a set of angled slats fixed at regular intervals.
Mantlet	bulletproof screen around a gun.
Mk	mark or version.
mm	millimetre (1 mm = 0.039 inch).
MQ armour	British machinable quality armour.
Nahverteidgungswaffe	smoke grenade, signal flare, and fragmentation grenade launcher.
Nearside	left-hand side.
Normal	head-on attack at a right angle.
Offside	right-hand side.
Olivegrün	olive-green.
oz	ounce (one-sixteenth of an imperial pound).
Pannier	British armour term for the part of the hull along the side that projected over the tracks. It could sometimes be used for stowage.
Panzer	abbreviation for tank (lit. armour).
Panzerkampfwagen	tank (lit. armoured battle vehicle).
Panzerschürzen	skirt armour.
pdr	pounder—the weight of a shell also used as a gun designation.
PIAT	projector, infantry, anti-tank hand-held weapon.
Poldi Hardness tester	a piece of equipment that measures the hardness of armour and produces Brinell Hardness scale figures.
Pz.Kpfw	abbreviation for *Panzerkampfwagen* (lit. armoured battle vehicle).
Pz.Kw	British version of abbreviation *Panzerkampfwagen* (lit. armoured battle vehicle).
RHA	Royal Horse Artillery.
Rohrausblasevorrichtung	gun gas extractor fan.
Rotbraun	reddy-brown.
Round	one piece of ammunition—a shell or bullet.
rpm	revolutions per minute.
Schnelllauffähige Kette für Kraftfahrzeuge	fast running track for motor vehicles.
Schürzen	skirt (armour).
schwimmende Bolzen	swimming/rotating bolt.
Splash	fragments of ammunition.
Stahlguß aller Legierungen	steel castings of all alloys.
SV	shell velocity.
Tarnlampe	headlights.
Tenon	tenon joint used in carpentry to interlock two pieces of wood. Also used on the panther tank armour plate.
Trockenbolzen-Scharnierkette	dry single-pin track.
Turmzielfernrohr	turret binocular gun sight.
Witness Card	paper or card used to detect weapon penetration inside a tank.
W/R limit	If the shell velocity is slower or the armour angle higher than the stated amount, the shell would not perforate (R) or total penetrate (W) the armour.
Yard	three feet (91.44 cm).
Zahnradfabrik	gear factory.

INTRODUCTION

This poor-quality photograph of the front of a captured Panzer VI Tiger tank was reproduced as part of a collection of tank recognition images contained in a briefing document circulated to British and Commonwealth troops before D-Day. (*649th ENGR. BN. May 1944*)

When the Panzer VI Ausf. E Tiger tank first arrived on the battlefield, it started the Allied and Soviet intelligence race to discover everything they could about this new threat. The British Army quickly needed to know how to knock it out, then communicate that information back to the troops that had to face this new German metal monster either by official means or via newspapers. This is not a typical book on the Tiger tank. It tries to show the reader what the British and Commonwealth forces knew about the Tiger tank during the war and the results of scientific firing trials. Unpublished Second World War original documents, discovered in different archives, have been transcribed and reproduced along with any existing photographs found in those official secret reports.

The Tiger was not designed as a reaction to events on the Eastern Front. Its development started long before the 22 June 1941 start date of Operation Barbarossa, the invasion of the Soviet Union. The first documented mention of the requirement for a heavy tank was found in a German Army Weapons Agency (*Heeres Waffenamt*, HWA) report dated

30 October 1935. It was written by General Liese and titled *Offensive Abwehr von Panzerwagen* ('Offensive defence for armoured vehicles') and covered the type of weapons needed to deal with French heavy tanks, like the Char B1 bis.

A few things need to be explained so you can better understand the information contained in the scientific reports. The *Panzerkampfwagen* Tiger Ausf. E was often just referred to as the 'Tiger' in wartime documents. It was only when the Panzer VI Ausf. B Tiger II, known by the British as the 'King Tiger' tank, arrived on the battlefield that the 'Tiger' tank was given the name 'Tiger I'. The German word '*Panzerkampfwagen*' literarily translates to 'armoured combat vehicle' (tank) and is often abbreviated to Panzer, Pz.Kpfw., or in most of the British scientific reports as Pz.Kw, or in a few reports, PZ.KPFW V.

The original imperial feet and inches measurements found in the official reports have been kept. There are twelve inches in a foot and three feet in a yard. Metric measurements have not been added to the transcribed text of the original documents as they were not included at the time (1 inch = 2.54 centimetres, 1 foot = 30.48 centimetres, and 1 yard = 91.44 centimetres).

The imperial weight measurement ounce (oz and ozs) are used in the report (1 oz = 28.3495 g). The British used the approximate weight of the shot fired in a round from a gun as a form of designation. This is a Royal Navy tradition from the days of the old wooden fighting sailing ships of the line. An armour-piercing 2-pounder (2-pdr) shell projectile weighed 2 lb (980 g). An armour-piercing 6-pdr shell projectile weighed 6 lb 5 oz (2.86 kg). A high explosive 6-pdr shell weighed approximately 6 lb 10 oz (3 kg). An APCBC 17-pdr shell projectile weighed 17 lb (7.7 kg). The metric equivalents are approximate and not exact.

During the firing trials, 'Witness Cards' were used to assess damage inside the tank. These were made from cardboard or just white paper. They were placed inside the tank in front of vulnerable positions, like the water-cooling radiators, to be able to count how many pieces of shrapnel would have pierced the internal equipment after a shell was fired at the tank.

The term 'Normal' is often used in British wartime scientific data records of the live firing trials. It means the shell was fired at the armour plate at a 'right angle'—90 degrees to the metal. Imagine a British Sherman Firefly tank was in a village street in Normandy, near a 'T' junction and a Tiger tank passed in front of it, going from left to right. If the Firefly tank fired at the side of the Tiger, the 17-pdr AP shell would hit the side hull armour at a 90-degree angle. This angle is referred to as 'Normal'. If the Tiger tank had turned left and headed straight towards the Sherman Firefly tank and the British crew fired their 17-pdr gun at the front armour of the Tiger 'head-on,' that angle would also be called 'Normal'. The shell would hit the front armour at a 'right angle'—90 degrees to the metal. The scientists also use the adjective 'normal' in their observations to describe what they see as being typical or expected. This can be confusing.

The British scientists also use the terms 'offside' and 'nearside'. The British drive on the left side of the road. British cars and tanks are 'right-hand drive', meaning the driver sits on the right side of the vehicle. The 'nearside' of a vehicle is the side nearest to the kerb when it is being driven on a British road. This is the left side of the vehicle. The 'offside' is the side of the vehicle furthest away from the kerb. That is the right side of the vehicle. The navy terms 'starboard' and 'port' are also used. The right-hand side of the tank is the 'starboard' side and 'port' is the left-hand side.

The British scientists also used a brief compact notation grammar style. It was not shorthand, but it does make reading their notation hard to understand sometimes. It was done to keep the comment section short, their findings condensed and succinct.

The story of the capture of Tiger 131, now on display at the Tank Museum in Bovington, and the first British tank battles with Tiger tanks in North Africa are not covered in this book. Several accounts of what happened have already been published in other books. The official reports on the battlefield firing trials on knocked-out Tiger tanks in Tunisia (19 May 1943 and 30 October 1943) are covered in Chapter 6.

The Tank Museum in Bovington's military historian and archivist, David Fletcher, reproduced the detailed wartime School of Tank Technology (STT) instructional book called 'Report on PzKw VI (Tiger) Model E Parts I–IV' in his book, *Tiger! The Tiger Tank: A British View*. The original record of the scientific examination of a Tiger tank and report on the findings that were used to write the STT instructional book is the subject of Chapter 10. The STT instructional book on the Tiger tank has not been reproduced as David Fletcher has already done that in his book.

Unfortunately, many of the photographs that formed part of the scientific wartime live-firing trials reports were out of focus. There is only so much image sharpening you can do on scans of period monochrome photographs that are out of focus before the clarity deteriorates.

This poor-quality photograph of the rear of a captured Panzer VI Tiger tank was reproduced as part of a collection of tank recognition images contained in a briefing document circulated to British and Commonwealth troops before D-Day. *(649th ENGR. BN. May 1944)*

POST-WAR TIGER TANK RESEARCH HISTORY

This section has been included to give the reader a better understanding of how information about the Tiger tank's development was obtained and how some errors, by accident, were introduced into the tank's story. We have a lot to thank these pioneer post-war military historians for; they discovered and published the information they found in the archives for all to read.

Dr F. M. von Senger und Etterlin served in 24th Panzer Division and later as adjutant to General von Schweppenburg at the German High Command (OKH). In the post-war German military *Bundeswehr*, he rose to the rank of general commander in chief of Allied Forces Central Europe. He published many books on armoured fighting vehicles, including the influential *Die Deutschen Panzer 1926–1945*, which was first published in German in 1959. It was intended to be a historical reference book for new soldiers. It was not widely known in England or North America.

As a young engineer in the early 1960s, Hilary Louis Doyle and PR manager Chris Ellis established 'Bellona Publications'. Bellona published the very first accurate drawings of armoured vehicles, including the Tiger tank, that were based on actual surveys. They would conduct their research in the archives at the Imperial War Museum, the Public Record Office (now the National Archives at Kew), and the Tank Museum, Bovington. The majority of the wartime documentation available at that time in Britain was Allied, not German. Hilary also worked with Peter Chamberlain, who would become a highly respected military vehicle history author. He used to work as a volunteer at the Imperial War Museum archives.

By the mid-sixties, this work had attracted the attention of Walter J. Spielberger, one of the foremost German Panzer historians. As a schoolboy in Germany, Walter already had a deep interest in vehicles. He was sent on a school-release programme to the tank design and assembly firm Alkett in Berlin. Then followed years of front-line and technical experience with Panzers. Most of his collection of tank material was lost at the end of the war. He was a prisoner of war until 1947. In the late 1950s, he began to work with several close friends to document and put some order on what little Panzer information was available at that time.

His articles were published in the magazine *Feldgrau* (trans. field grey) and then incorporated in the history section of the second edition of *Die Deutschen Panzer 1926–1945* by Dr F. M. von Senger und Etterlin in 1965.

Walter had a significant network of military contacts from his Panzer days, but as a senior executive of Volkswagen (VW) on the west coast of the USA, he was a friend of American military vehicle historian and author Richard Pearce Hunnicutt. Research at the US National Archives and Records Administration (NARA) was becoming easier. As more and more original German documents were being released, it was becoming clear that Allied wartime documents had to be considered secondary sources as they contained many errors. The information in military vehicle history books had to be changed and revised editions published. New books were published based on this newly discovered information.

When the German Federal Archives (*Bundesarchiv*) opened for research, Hilary initially travelled there on his own. In 1973, Walter returned to Europe and became PR manager for the military defence section of the German manufacturing company Krauss-Maffei, which was involved in the production of military vehicles, such as the Leopard tank. Walter was now able to conduct more comprehensive research among his expanding network. He also worked with the *Bundesarchiv* as many now declassified documents had been returned to Germany from the American NARA archives.

In the same year, Hilary was one of the joint founders of the German Nixdorf Computer company in Ireland. *En route* to Nixdorf meetings, Hilary would visit Walter in Munich to collect copies of the research. Hilary and Walter seldom went on joint research trips because their diaries did not match. Both men were extremely busy, having many work commitments. They decided to divide up research tasks: Walter searched for and analysed wartime German documents while Hilary concentrated on physical surveying and photographing surviving vehicles to enable him to produce scaled, accurate drawings.

Walter used to stop over in Ireland during business trips to Europe and visit Hilary. For nearly forty years, Walter and Hilary worked together publishing a vast range of books on armoured fighting vehicles. Walter was responsible for more than forty large books and continued to write and incorporate the latest research in his *Militaerfahrzeuge* series (*Motorbuch*) until 1998 when his health failed.

In the early seventies, while researching in the German *Bundesarchiv* in Koblenz, Hilary met Thomas L. Jentz who was still in the US Army and preparing a book on the battles in North Africa during the Second World War. In due course, Tom moved to Washington, DC, adjacent to the NARA. After that, Tom and Hilary went on many research trips together, stopping off at Munich to swap the finds with Walter.

At the end of the nineties, to find a new way of presenting the combined research, Tom and Hilary founded 'Panzer Tracts'. To date, almost sixty volumes of research have been published based on primary source material. The data in their books only came from original German wartime documentation found in the archives, not Allied or Soviet documents that may have been inaccurate through a lack of available information during the war. They continued to examine surviving vehicles, take measurements, photograph them, and collect wartime photographs, so Hilary could produce more scale drawings.

All the surviving Tiger tanks are missing parts and equipment or have had post-war alterations. They, therefore, could not be relied upon for accuracy. Tiger tanks were not photographed from every angle as they left the factory gates. Thus, an accurate wartime photographic record does not exist of all the different features that changed over time. The primary source archive documents provided accuracy. This is why the German documents kept in different archives are so important.

Walter Spielberger and Hilary Louis Doyle are standing next to the Irish Army's Landswerk L-60 tank. The photograph was taken in 1977. The tank was designed and built in the mid-1930s by the part-German-owned Swedish company called AB Landsverk. German tank designer Otto Merker joined the staff to assist with this new tank project, gaining valuable experience. (*Hilary Louis Doyle*)

There is a common misconception that covers both the Panzer VI Ausf. E Tiger I and the Panzer VI Ausf. B Tiger II heavy tanks that needs to be cleared up. All tank turrets fitted on the prototype Porsche Tiger I tank hulls and the Henschel production Tiger I and the Tiger II tank hulls were designed by Krupp. Tiger I turrets were assembled at Fried Krupp A.G. Essen, Dortmund Hoerder Huttenverein (DHHV), and at the Wegmann Factory. The terms 'Porsche turret', 'Porsche turm', 'Henschel turm', or 'Henschel Turret' are wrong. Neither Porsche nor Henschel designed a turret for a Tiger tank.

These names were incorrectly used in the influential 1969 military history book, *German Tanks of World War II* by Dr F. M. von Senger und Etterlin. This was an English translation of the original 1958 German-language book *Die Deutschen Panzer 1926–1945*. It appears the translator misunderstood what he was reading, and for brevity describes the King Tiger tanks fitted with Krupp-designed turrets, which were part of the 'Porsche project' as 'Porsche turret King Tigers' in the English version of the book. The later-production King Tiger tanks then became wrongly known as the Henschel turret King Tiger. This incorrect information was repeated in subsequent books on German tanks, as the editors trusted the information contained in Dr von Senger und Etterlin's book was correct and believed that the translation was word perfect. The error was not spotted for many years.

When researchers gained access to more declassified documents in the *Bundesarchiv* in Koblenz, Germany, it was discovered that Allied wartime reports were sometimes inaccurate. The mistranslation in the English version of *Die Deutschen Panzer 1926-1945* was also discovered. The errors were corrected in later books. Unfortunately, the damage had been done. The incorrect designations 'the Porsche turret Tiger tank', 'the Porsche turret King Tiger', and 'the Henschel turret King Tiger' were still being printed in books published in 2020 by major publishing companies.

David Willey, curator of the Tank Museum, Bovington, in a 2019 video suggested that the correct term for the surviving prototype King Tiger they have in their collection should be the 'pre-production King Tiger'. The first fifty tanks fitted with the curved-front Krupp-designed turret are best described as early-production King Tiger tanks. The Tank Museum refers to the version with the near-vertical slab front Krupp-designed turret as the 'production King Tiger tank'.

The 1958 German-language book *Die Deutschen Panzer 1926–1945* contained the correct Tiger tank turret terminology. The 1969 English translation of the original book was called *German Tanks of World War II*. It contained the translation error and used the wrong names for the Krupp-designed Tiger tank turrets due to a misunderstanding by the German to English translator.

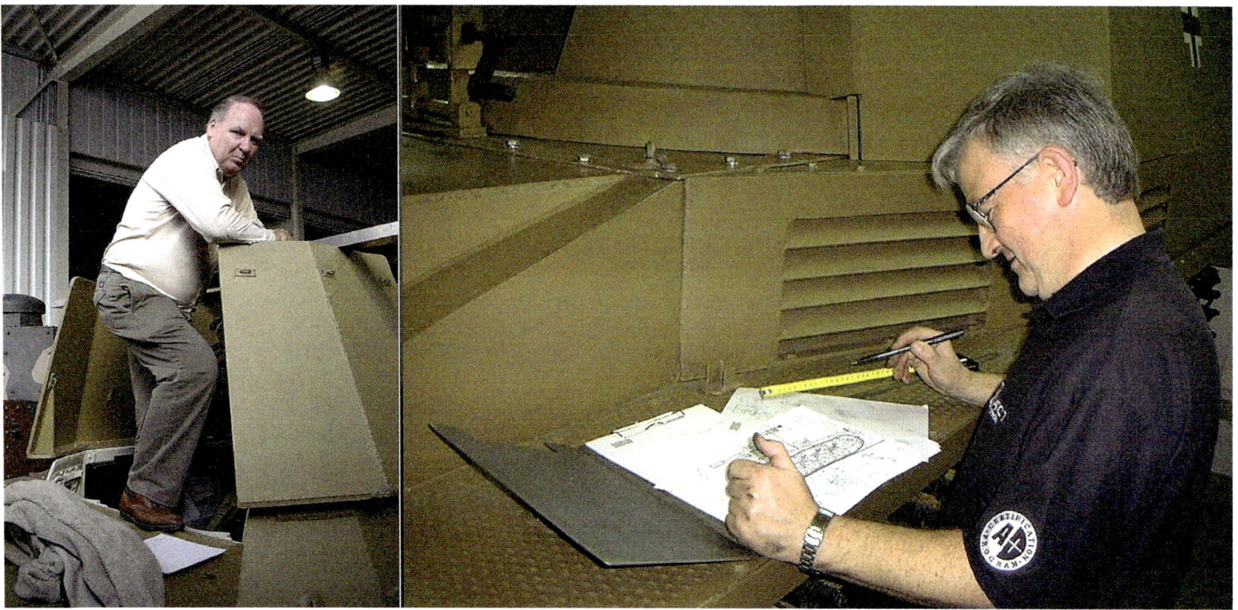

Thomas L. Jentz and Hilary Louis Doyle at the Scientific Collection of Defence Engineering Specimens (WTS) in Koblenz, Germany, in 2001. (*Hilary Louis Doyle*)

NEW RESEARCH

New, unpublished wartime documentation continues to be found by accident. This happens when archivists do not know what they are looking at and file documents, reports, and photographs wrongly. They do not record the correct title, department name, subject heading or fail to add relevant keywords like 'tank', 'panzer', 'Tiger', or 'German' to the digital entry on the archive database.

Most of the firing trials reports reproduced in this book were found at the National Archives at Kew, but if you tried to find them using sensible keywords like 'German Panzer VI Tiger tank' on the archive database, they would not appear in the results page. I found the first one by accident while looking for information on British tanks. This enabled others to be located. More wartime documents are waiting to be re-discovered in archives around the world, but it is hard to find them because many have been mislabelled.

Panzerkampfwagen Tiger Ausf. E. (*STT*)

1

TIGER TANK DEVELOPMENT AND PRODUCTION

Captured Tiger tank 131 photographed in North Africa prior to shipping to Britain. Notice the early-production drum-shaped cupola, rubber-rimmed road wheels, and smoke dischargers. (*STT*)

This chapter covers some of the major changes made during the production run of the Tiger tank, first highlighted by those six pioneering researchers—von Senger und Etterlin, Chamberlain, Doyle, Ellis, Jentz, and Spielberger.

There were over 100 significant external alterations made to the Tiger tank during its production run and many internal changes. When the tank was in operational service, the local units made their own modifications. These included brackets for additional track links attached to the front of the tank hull and turret sides. Some had steps and handles welded onto the vehicle to make it easier to climb on and off. The early Tigers did not have external stowage bins. Crews salvaged stowage bins from other types of tanks and fixed them to tank's turret. Later factory-designed bespoke stowage bins were fitted. Some crews carried bundles of wood on the side of the tank; this was not designed to add additional protection from enemy armour-piercing shells. The bundles were for use as wooden roadways to put under the tracks to give the tank extra grip in muddy, waterlogged open country or to help them get out of a ditch.

When a vehicle was damaged, it was repaired with whatever parts were available at the maintenance depot. This is why some tanks were photographed fitted with both early rubber-rimmed road wheels and later metal-rimmed road wheels. Many new features were retrofitted to earlier Tigers when they went back to the factory or a large maintenance workshop for an overhaul.

Due to all the changes made to the Tiger tank during its production run, terms such as early-production Tiger, late-early-production Tiger, mid-production Tiger, early-late-production Tiger, and late-production Tiger tank are used in other books, websites, and on social media. This can be very confusing when trying to identify when a tank was built. To try and simplify the situation, this book just uses the term 'early-production Tiger tank' when referring to a tank with rubber road wheels and drum-shaped cupola and 'late-production Tiger tank' for one with metal-rimmed road wheels and a dome-shaped cupola, while pointing out other changes.

DESIGN AND DEVELOPMENT

The weapons manufacturers Henschel and Porsche competed to design the hull for the new heavy tank for the German Army. Both companies built prototype hull designs. The competition culminated in the German *Waffen Prüfen* 6 (Wa Prüf 6), the Tank Design Office of the German Army Ordnance Department, awarding the contract to Henschel on 6 July 1941, to build three hulls to be used for development trials. They were given the designation VK 45.01 (H) *Versuchs-Fahrgestell* (experimental hull) with the hull numbers V1, V2, and V3. They would be fitted with the 8.8-cm KwK 36 L/56 armed Krupp-designed turret. The letter 'H' was an abbreviation for Henschel.

In April 1942, after successful trials, Henschel was given a further contract to build 200 VK 45.01 (H) hulls fitted with the Krupp turret. The tank would be given the designation *Panzerkampfwagen* Tiger (8.8-cm) *Ausfuehrung*.E (Sd.Kfz. 181). This order would continually be increased until a total of 1,346 were completed. The Fgst.Nr. hull numbers ranged from 250001 to 251346.

THE NAME

The Tiger tank had several different names used on official Henschel factory and government documents during its development. In 1941, it was referred to as VK 45.01 then Pz.Kpfw.VI Ausf. H1 (VK 4501). In 1942, this was abbreviated to VK 4501 (H) but then six different designations were used in documents: Tiger H1 (VK 4501—*Aufbau für* 8.8-cm KwK Krupp-Turm); Pz.Kpfw.VI (VK 4501/H) Ausf. H1 (Tiger); Pz.Kpfw. 'Tiger' (H); Pz.Kpfw.VI, VK 4501 (H), Tiger (H) Krupp-Turm *mit* 8.8-cm KwK. L/56 Ausf. H1; *Panzerkampfwagen* VI H (Sd.Kfz.182); Tiger I; and then Pz.Kpfw VI H Ausf. H1 (Tiger H1).

In 1943, it was referred to as Pz.Kpfw VI H Ausf. H1 and then changed to *Panzerkampfwagen* Tiger Ausf. E. Notice the number six (VI) was dropped in this later designation. It was only referred to as the Tiger I after the *Panzerkampfwagen* Tiger (8.8-cm) *Ausfuehrung*.B (Sd.Kfz. 182), described by the Allies as the King Tiger tank or Tiger II appeared on the battlefield.

MAIN GUN

The high-velocity 8.8-cm KwK 36 L/56 anti-tank gun was the main armament mounted in the Tiger's turret. The tank could carry ninety-two rounds of armour-piercing (AP) and high-explosive (HE) ammunition, usually in the form of 50 per cent Pz.Gr.39 APCBC-HE-T (armour-piercing capped, ballistic capped, high explosive, tracer), which had a small explosive filler, and 50 per cent Spr. Gr. (high explosive). Most were stowed in five racks in the hull panniers above the track. There were also five smaller racks nearer the turret basket.

As tank guns used by the German Army became more powerful, they required different methods of managing the strong gun recoil when a shell was fired. An increase in recoil can be countered with stronger spring and hydraulic systems. The problem with this method is that this can take up valuable space in an already crowded fighting compartment. The solution the designers implemented was to add a muzzle brake at the end of the Tiger's 8.8-cm gun barrel.

A muzzle brake helps reduce the gun recoil by deflecting the propellant gases from a fired shell to either side of the muzzle through the openings of the brake, called baffles. The baffles act as an air brake, using the propellant gas to slow the gun's recoil to the rear. This pushes the gun barrel forwards, away from the tank, and in so doing lessens the recoil action. It is estimated that this reduced the Tiger's main gun recoil by around 70 per cent. The original muzzle brake was replaced by a lighter one during the production run. This new version had been designed for the more powerful and longer gun being fitted to the King Tiger tank.

The Tiger was armed with a high velocity 8.8-cm KwK 36 L/56 anti-tank gun. It is fitted with 'transportation' tracks, and the side track skirt has been removed as if it was ready to drive on to a railway flat wagon. (*Musée des Blindés, Saumur, France*)

The 8.8-cm KwK 36 L/56 anti-tank gun was fitted with a muzzle brake to help reduce the gun's recoil by deflecting the propellant gases on either side of the muzzle. (*Musée des Blindés, Saumur, France*)

MACHINE GUNS

Secondary armament consisted of a 7.92-mm *Maschinengewehr* 34 (7.92-mm MG 34) mounted coaxially on the right of the main gun. It was operated utilising a floor-mounted firing pedal and had a maximum depression and elevation of -8 to +15.

The Tiger had a second 7.92-mm MG 34, fitted in a ball-mount, on the right side of the front hull. It was capable of a 15-degree traverse left and right (total arc of fire was 30 degrees) and an elevation of -7 to +20. On late-production Tiger tanks, a 7.92-mm MG 34 was later mounted onto a circular piece of metal welded to the top of the commander's cupola. This was intended for use against low-flying enemy reconnaissance and ground-attack aircraft.

SMOKE GRENADE LAUNCHERS

Starting in August 1942, instructions were given that six 95-mm diameter smoke grenade launchers (*Nebekwurfgeraet*), in two sets of three, were to be mounted on the side of the Tiger's turret. They could fire Nb.K.39 90-mm smoke generator grenades to produce a smokescreen that made it harder for the enemy to target the tank while it changed position. The mounting brackets and wiring holes were completed in the factory, and crews had to fix the launchers when they became available from the manufacturer. Starting in October 1942, the complete unit was attached to the tank before it left the factory.

In June 1943, an instruction was issued to stop fitting the smoke grenade launchers. A report from the Eastern Front stated that the smoke generator grenades had exploded when they were hit by small arms fire, while still in the launchers on the side of the tank. On a calm day with little wind, the smoke covered the tank, temporarily choking and blinding the crew.

‹ A 7.92-mm *Maschinengewehr* 34 (MG 34) was fitted in a ball-mount on the right side of the front hull. (*Musée des Blindés, Saumur, France*)

› A 7.92-mm MG 34 was mounted coaxially on the right of the main gun. (*Musée des Blindés, Saumur, France*)

‹ On late-production Tiger tanks, a 7.92-mm MG 34 was mounted onto a circular piece of metal welded to the top of the commander's cupola. (*Musée des Blindés, Saumur, France*)

› This replica Tiger tank has a 7.92-mm MG 34 mounted onto a circular piece of metal welded to the top of the commander's cupola. (*Musée des Blindés, Saumur, France*)

Smoke grenade launchers were fixed to the turret of early production Tiger tanks. After June 1943, they were no longer fitted. (*No. 2 Army Film and Photo Section, Army Film and Photographic Unit*)

S-MINE DISCHARGERS

The front coaxial machine gun on the turret could not hit enemy troops hiding close to the sides and rear of the tank. Starting in January 1943, early versions of the Panzer VI Ausf. E Tiger were fitted with a self-defence system designed to kill enemy infantry approaching and climbing onto the tank. They were called *Minenabwurfvorrichtung* (a S-mine discharger system). Five dischargers were fitted to the side and rear of the tank. Command tanks only had four.

The S-mine was quite large: 15 cm tall without its sensors and 10 cm in diameter. Its body was a steel cylinder that had a steel rod protruding from the top. This rod held the main fuse with its striker and percussion cap, attached to three metal prongs and a plunger.

When the mine was fired upwards into the air and away from the tank, after a very slight delay, the main charge detonated. It released about 360 steel balls, scrap metal fragments, or short steel rods into the surrounding area at very high velocity. These would kill or severely maim any enemy infantry near the tank. The main problem was that it could not be reloaded from inside the tank. In early October 1943, orders were issued to stop fitting them to Tiger tanks on the production line as plans were made to replace them with a single swivelling, close-defence weapon mounted in the turret roof called the *Nahverteidigungswaffe*.

‹ The S-mine was also called the *Splittermine*, *Springmine*, or *Schrapnellmine*. The Allies called the S-mine a 'Bouncing Betty'. The official designation was SMi-35 and SMi-44 depending on their first year of production. There were only minor differences between the two models. (*Eben-Emael Fortress*)

› A reconstruction of a Tiger tank S-mine discharger has been added to this model. It is in the bottom right of the photograph. It looks like a coffee mug lying on its side.

On 5 November 1944, the 2nd Armoured Replacement Group, Royal Armoured Corps conducted experiments with captured tank S-mine dischargers. They recorded their findings in a report marked 'Top Secret'. It was given the number G/100/12. Three tanks were driven to the firing point. They were surrounded by 6-foot-high hessian screens, 10 feet away from the tanks. Officers from different regiments were invited to watch the live firing. They were positioned in trenches while others sat in the tanks and observed what happened through the tank periscopes. After firing the S-mines, the visitors were invited to inspect the damage caused to the hessian screens by the lethal shrapnel, so they could get an impression of the 'beaten zone'. At the end of the invitation to this event, there was a typically British comment: 'Point 7. On conclusion of the trial tea will be available at the car park'.

The results of this trial were published on a page marked Appendix B G/100/12.

S-Mine Discharges

1. The mines jump approximately 1 foot out of the dischargers.
2. The mine has a danger area of 50 × 50 yards to 100 × 100 yards (45.72 × 45.72 m to 91.44 × 91.44 m).
3. Mines fired from one side of the tank have little effect on the other.

4. Impractical to the front of tank owing to damage to periscopes; therefore, front not covered.
5. External items of stowage may be damaged.
6. Mines did not explode when exposed to small arms fire, but this is not considered always to be the case.

NAHVERTEIDIGUNGSWAFFE (CLOSE DEFENCE WEAPON)

Starting from March 1944, after a delay, the *Minenabwurfvorrichtung* (S-mine discharger system) was replaced with a *Nahverteidigungswaffe* (close defence weapon). It could fire signal flares, smoke grenades, and anti-personal grenades in all directions. A big advantage was that it could be reloaded from inside the tank.

The *Nahverteidigungswaffe* was mounted at an angle of 50 degrees, in a hole in the turret roof. It looked like a large flare pistol and could be traversed 360 degrees. It fired a small explosive shell, called a *Sprenggranate Patrone* 326 Lp, between 7–10 metres away from the tank. This fragmentation grenade would explode above the ground, killing or injuring enemy infantry up to 100 m away. The shrapnel would not damage the Tiger tank or hurt any of the crew who were safely behind the tank's armour plate. The crew could also use this weapon to fire smoke shells for concealment or coloured smoke for signalling.

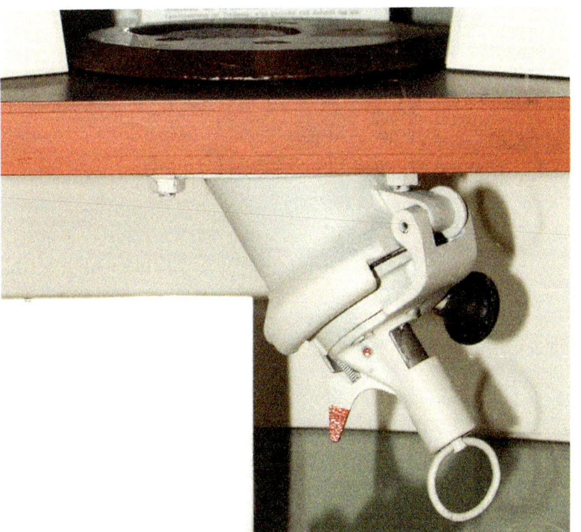

‹ *Nahverteidigungswaffe* (close defence weapon). (*Deutsches Panzermuseum*)

› *Nahverteidigungswaffe* exit point on the roof of the Tiger tank turret. (*Musée des Blindés, Saumur, France*)

THE ENGINE AND TRANSMISSION

Only the first 250 Tiger I tanks were powered by the Maybach HL 210 TRM P45 V12 water-cooled 21-litre petrol/gasoline 650-hp at 3,000-rpm engine. From May 1943 onwards, the others were fitted with the slightly more powerful Maybach HL 230 TRM P45 V12 water-cooled 23-litre petrol/gasoline 690–700-hp at 3,000-rpm engine. The Maybach HL 210 engine had an aluminium engine block as opposed to a cast-iron engine block that was fitted to the later Maybach HL 230 engine. The letters 'HL' were an abbreviation for *Hochleistungsmotor* (high-performance motor). The three letters 'TRM' stood for *Trockensumpfschmierung mit Schnappermagne* (dry sump lubricant with impulse magneto). The letter 'P' in front of the number 45 was for *Panzermotor*, indicating that the engine was specifically designed as a tank engine.

The Maybach-designed Olvar 40 12 16 Getriebe (OG 40 12 16) hydraulically-controlled pre-selector gearbox and semi-automatic transmission was installed in the Tiger I. It had eight forward and four reverse gears. Drive was transmitted to each of the front drive sprockets by spur reducing and epicyclic gears inside the sprockets. The final drive was manufactured by Henschel.

‹ Maybach HL 210 TRM P45 V12 water-cooled 21-litre petrol/gasoline 650-hp at 3,000 rpm engine. (*AACC*)

› Here is an air filter on the Maybach HL 210 P45 engine. (*No. 2 Army Film and Photo Section, Army Film and Photographic Unit.*)

EXHAUST SYSTEM HEAT SHIELDS

Early-production Tiger I tanks were fitted with an exhaust system that had two silencers (mufflers) fixed to the rear armour plate. Two curved-cast armoured covers protected the junctions where the exhaust pipes came out of the armour plate. The design of these covers was not changed during the production run.

Crews noticed that when the exhaust silencers became hot, they glowed red. This was particularly noticeable in the snowy winter conditions on the Eastern Front and at night in the desert. It made the tank easy to see by enemy forward artillery spotters who would call down an artillery barrage. Units in the field started to construct exhaust silencer heat shields out of bent sheet metal that would hide the glowing silencer from view. In January 1943, factories were instructed to fit them. They also added an exhaust flame deflector that comprised of a circular metal cover supported by five rods fixed above the end of the exhaust pipe.

‹ Two curved cast-armoured covers protected the junctions where the exhaust pipes came out of the armour plate. The left one has been removed for restoration. You can see the exhaust outlet. (*AACC*)

› The back of this replica Tiger illustrates what the field modification exhaust silencer heat shields would have looked like. They were made out of bent sheet metal and designed to hide the glowing red silencer/muffler from the enemy.

SUSPENSION AND TRACK

The Tiger was very heavy. To reduce the amount of ground pressure it exerted and to stop the tank from sinking in wet, muddy ground, wide tracks were fitted. An interleaved road wheel system was used to maintain pressure evenly across the width of the track. The drive sprocket was at the front of the tank. The suspension used 55-mm diameter torsion bars. They ran the complete width of the hull. The two front and two rear torsion bars were slightly wider at 58 mm in diameter. Each torsion bar was connected to three road wheels.

The early-production Tigers had rubber-rimmed road wheels. Several changes were made during production to increase the strength of the wheels mainly by the addition of extra securing bolts and additional welding. As the supply of rubber was reduced, the rubber-rimmed road wheels were replaced, from January 1944 onwards, with metal-rimmed rubber cushioned steel road wheels. It used a small amount of synthetic rubber in an internal ring bolted between the inner wheel disc and the outer solid steel wheel rim. The synthetic rubber helped decrease vibrations. It was not uncommon to see Tiger tanks with a mixture of early-production rubber-rimmed road wheels and late-production steel-rimmed road wheels.

In October 1942, Tiger tanks were fitted with Kgs 63/725/130 cross-country tracks. The first twenty tanks produced had tracks specifically designed for either the right or left side of the tank. The new tracks could be used on either side of the tank. The standard 725-mm-wide operational track (*Marschkette*) made the Tiger too wide for train transportation. The outer four wheels from each side had to be removed, and the wide track replaced by a slimmer 520-mm transportation track (*Verladkette*). In October 1943, the design of the tracks was changed to incorporate anti-skid chevrons cast onto the track face.

The idler wheel was at the rear of the tank and was used to help tension the track. Starting in February 1944, after the introduction of steel road wheels, a smaller diameter idler wheel was fitted. The early one was 700 mm, and the new one was 600 mm in diameter.

In March 1943, a new style of track pin was introduced because the original pins had a habit of working loose. These new track pins were secured by a metal ring and a small securing pin. The side of the hull still had a track pin return bump in case the new metal securing ring failed. Each time a loose track pin went past the bump, it would be knocked back in place. In May 1944, following the introduction of a smaller diameter idler wheel, the track pin return bump was widened and mounted at an angle.

Above left: Early-production Tigers had rubber-rimmed road wheels. Each torsion bar was connected to three road wheels that were interleaved to maintain pressure evenly over the wide track. (*AACC*)

Above right: From January 1944 onwards, they had metal-rimmed, rubber-cushioned steel road wheels. (*Musée des Blindés, Saumur, France*)

Right: The Tiger tank's track was wider than the three sets of interleaved road wheels. This helped reduce the amount of ground pressure produced by the weight of the tank on soft ground. (*Patriot Park, Kubinka, Russia*)

The Tiger tank's transportation tracks were not as wide as its standard tracks. The wide tracks needed to be changed to the slimmer tracks every time the tank was transported by rail. This was because the total width of the vehicle was too wide to go through tunnels or travel past railway signals and trackside furniture. (*Musée des Blindés, Saumur, France*)

ARMOUR

For the main armour plates, the Tiger used rolled homogeneous armour, which had a consistent hardness throughout its thickness. It was not fitted with face-hardened armour which was used on other German tanks. Homogeneous armour plates had a high content of chromium and molybdenum, but also carbon (an impurity that makes welding more difficult).

A British report dated September 1943, gave the findings of the examination of the armour on captured Tiger tanks. The scientists concluded that the Tiger's armour quality was similar to Allied machineable quality armour plate of the same thickness. They noted that the method of construction used a combination of keyed, overlapping, and stepped-interlocking plates of armour.

The manufacturing process resulted in armour plate having slightly different thicknesses. These tolerances could vary by a few millimetres. The driver and hull machine gunner sat behind a protective frontal armour plate that was 100 mm thick set at a 9-degree angle from vertical. In front of this was the sloping glacis plate, which was 60 mm thick set at an angle of 80 degrees from vertical. The lower front armour plate was 100 mm thick angled at 25 degrees from vertical. The belly plate armour was 25 mm thick. The rear armour was 80 mm thick angled at 90 degrees from vertical. The lower side hull armour was vertical and 60 mm thick. The upper side hull superstructure armour was again vertical but 80 mm thick. The rear engine deck was 25 mm thick. A number of the joints used dovetailing to interlock the plates before welding, which improved the strength of the joints.

The turret side and rear armour that was bent into a horseshoe shape were 80 mm thick. The vertical armour plate in the front of the turret behind the gun mantlet was 57 mm thick. The gun mantlet thickness ranged from 70–145 mm thick. The turret roof armour was in two parts, and both were 25 mm thick. An inserted piece of metal at the front of the tank's turret roof was 40 mm thick. The armour on the commander's cupola was 15 mm thick.

The Tiger tank turret had 80-mm-thick armour on the side and rear. The turret roof was 25 mm thick. (*AACC*)

CAMOUFLAGE

Most of the 1,350 Tiger tanks built were painted in *Dunkelgelb* (RAL 7028). Some early-production Tigers left the factory painted *Dunkelgrau* (RAL 7021). Those that were being sent to North Africa were painted in a two-tone sandy 'tropical' colour scheme. Instructions were given on 17 March 1941 that equipment destined to be sent to North Africa was to have two-thirds of the surface painted in *Gelbbraun* (RAL 8000) and one-third in *Gelbgrün* (RAL 7008). This can be seen on the preserved Tiger tank at the Tank Museum, Bovington. Central and southern Russia was considered a 'tropical' zone. Tigers issued to units serving in those locations received tanks painted in the 'tropical' paint scheme. In February 1943, instructions were issued to factories that all new tanks were to be painted *Dunkelgelb* (RAL 7028).

From photographic evidence, it looks like twenty-five Tigers were delivered to their new units in *Dunkelgrau*. In 1942, nine were issued to s.Pz.Abt.502 deployed near Leningrad (St Petersburg) in the north of Russia. A further seven arrived in February 1943. Nine grey Tigers were issued to 2nd Company of s.Pz.Abt.502 also based in Leningrad, but they were redeployed south towards Rostov. Twelve more were issued to training schools and testing grounds. There are no records or photographs available that can confirm what colour these tanks were painted.

When Tigers arrived in their units painted *Dunkelgelb*, they would receive a bespoke camouflage scheme as per the instructions of the unit commander. Additional paint colours would be *Olivegrün* (RAL 6003) and *Rotbraun* (RAL 8017). In the winter, many of the Tigers fighting in Russia were painted with whitewash to help them blend in with the snow.

PRODUCTION FIGURES

In 1942, seventy-six Tiger I tanks left the factory gates. In 1943, a further 647 were produced, and in 1944, a final batch of 623 was manufactured. The total number of Tiger I production tanks built between August 1942 and August 1944 was 1,346 (some other sources state 1,354).

PRODUCTION CHANGES

During the production run, different modifications were made. Some of these changes were introduced to rectify problems found during combat, to add protection, or to increase firepower. Others were made to simplify production or to overcome material shortages. Damaged or broken-down tanks would be fixed using parts available in the stores. These could be new spare parts or older parts salvaged from knocked-out tanks.

Track Guards

The wide cross-country tracks extended beyond the pannier sides. The crews found that mud, dirt, dust, and debris was slung up on top of the tank. Periscopes, vision ports, hatches, and turret rings would get covered.

In May 1942, bent sheet metal track guards were fixed on hinges at the front of the Tiger. A metal frame was welded to the hull to support the rear track guards.

In November 1942, four removable sheet metal mudguards were bolted to the pannier sides. They would be removed along with the wide tracks when the Tiger was transported by rail. The front and rear track guards were replaced with a new design that incorporated a hinged side extension that could be folded up for rail transport.

In December 1942, instructions were given to mount the four side mudguards in a straight line and not to follow the bend in the lower edge of the upper hull side. In May 1943, a redesigned three-piece hinged rear track guard with a cut out for the convoy light was introduced.

In May 1942, bent sheet metal track guards were fixed on hinges at the front of the Tiger. A metal frame was welded to the hull to support the rear track guards. In November 1942, four removable sheet metal mudguards were bolted to the pannier sides. (*Patriot Park, Kubinka, Russia*)

Turret Pistol Ports and Escape Hatch

Early-production Tiger turrets had two pistol ports at the rear. These were small holes with an armoured cover that could be used to point the barrel of a handgun or *Maschinenpistole* 40 (MP 40; trans. sub-machine gun) through and kill enemy troops who were near the rear of the tank or who had climbed onto the engine deck. The port was opened by rotating an internal lever. In December 1942, the one on the right rear was replaced with a large circular emergency escape hatch, but the one on the back left was retained until October 1943 when it was deleted from production requirements.

Turret Roof

On early-production Tigers, the hull deck and turret roof were 25 mm thick, although the leading edge was 40 mm thick. After analysis of combat damage and reports from the battlefield, the 25-mm-thick turret roof was considered insufficient to protect the crew from artillery shells and fire from ground-attack aircraft. Starting in March 1944, the thickness of the armour was officially increased to 40 mm. In May 1944, a British report examining a knocked-out Tiger found the roof to be 45 mm thick. Vehicles were retrofitted to this standard when they were returned to the factory for repair. This roof modification required the commander's cupola to be changed. To accommodate for the thicker roof, the loader's hatch was replaced with one initially designed for the Tiger II. It was therefore possible to have an early-production Tiger tank hull with a later-production-style turret.

‹ This is the large circular turret escape hatch. Below it is the turret ring guard welded to the hull deck. (*Musée des Blindés, Saumur, France*)

› Underneath the larger armoured louvre, the fuel tanks were sloped to enable air to flow over the radiators at the back of the tank. (*Musée des Blindés, Saumur, France*)

Additional Fuel Tank and Radiator Protection

One of the weak spots in the Tiger tank's armour was the engine deck. Artillery high explosive fragmentation shell splinters could penetrate the armour plate and the armoured louvres. The tank had two fuel tanks mounted to the left and right of the engine but behind the radiators. The side nearest the rear of the tank was sloped to enable air to flow over the radiators. An 8-mm-thick armoured plate protected the fuel tank. A wire mesh screen in a frame was bolted to the outside of the armoured grill on the engine deck. This was not enough protection. From April 1944, a wooden decking cover was installed over the fuel tanks and inside the air inlet ducts, to catch shrapnel or bullet fragments hitting the metal ducts and ricocheting into the nearby unprotected engine radiators.

Spare Track

Racks for carrying extra track links were fitted to the lower front armour plate, adding some slight additional protection. Spare track links were also carried on the side of the turret and on the near-vertical armour plate that protected the driver and hull machine gunner. These were field modifications. Each unit came up with its own solution to spare track stowage.

Not all tanks had these brackets fitted. Starting in mid-April 1943, the factory fitted brackets for five spare track links on the left side of the turret between the pistol port and the vision slit. Brackets for three additional track links were welded onto the right side of the turret between the escape hatch and the vision port. In April 1943, this was reduced to two track holder brackets on the right side.

‹ Spare track was added to the lower front armour. The addition of this retaining bar and step was a field modification, not a feature added by the factory. Notice the driver's visor periscope holes have been sealed shut following the February 1943 order stopping the fitting of the KFF 2 periscopes. (*Ian Wilcox Tiger Day, The Tank Museum, Bovington*)

› Track links were also added to the side of the Tiger tank's turret. On early-production Tigers, this was a battlefield modification, not a factory fitting. (*STT*)

Gunsight

Early-production Tiger tank turrets were fitted with a T.Z.F.9b binocular sight to the left of the main gun. This required two holes to be drilled into the gun mantlet, one for each lens. It was later replaced by the cheaper but no less effective T.Z.F.9c monocular sight. The gun mantlet had to be redesigned to only have a single hole in late production Tigers.

The pair of holes in the early production gun mantlet created a weak point. A recess was ground out at the rear, leaving only 70 mm of armour. When the monocular sight was introduced, this problem was rectified. At least twelve different types of Tiger gun mantlets from different manufacturers are known. They cannot be used to accurately date a tank as they are often damaged by enemy fire and were repaired or replaced with newer or older gun mantlets.

‹ Early-production Tiger tank turrets were fitted with a T.Z.F.9b binocular sight to the left of the main gun. This required two holes to be drilled into the gun mantlet, one for each lens. (*Patriot Park, Kubinka, Russia*)

› Late-production Tiger tanks were fitted with a T.Z.F.9c monocular gun sight and only required one hole to be drilled in the gun mantlet. (*Musée des Blindés, Saumur, France*)

Turret Ring Guard

Starting from February 1944, an 80-mm-thick turret ring protector that was capable of deflecting a 7.5-cm high-explosive shell was fitted to new Tigers in the factory. The problem had been identified as a source of concern. In January 1943, Wa Prüf 6 (weapons testing office number 6) ordered a study into an effective solution. It took over a year to design and implement the new modification.

Driver's Visor and Loaders Periscope

On the early-production Tiger tanks, the driver could see forward through a shuttered visor on the front of the near-vertical 100-mm-thick armoured plate. During combat, the protective armoured shutters could be closed by a hand wheel to the right of the vision block inside the tank. He could then use a pair of KFF 2 periscopes to see where he was driving. Starting in February 1943, these periscopes were no longer fitted to the tank. If the two holes had already been drilled in the armour, they were plugged with weld. The frontal armour on late production vehicles no longer had these holes above the driver's visor. Vision blocks made of laminated glass 70 × 240 × 94 mm thick were introduced. If they got damaged by shrapnel or small arms fire, the driver could close the shutters quickly, fit a replacement spare block and then reopen the shutter. Starting in March 1943, the loader was given a single, fixed position periscope facing forwards in the turret roof in front of his hatch. It was protected by an armoured cover.

‹ Early-production Tiger tank driver's visors had two holes drilled above it to facilitate the mounting of the KFF2 periscopes. When the visor was shut during combat, the driver looked through the periscopes. The visor was protected by a 'splash guard' fitted in front of it on the glacis plate. It was designed to prevent shrapnel from shattered bullets hitting the armoured glacis plate and ricocheting into the driver's vision slot.

› Late-production driver's visors did not have two holes drilled above them. The KFF2 periscopes were not fitted after February 1943. The driver was protected by thick glass prisms fitted behind the vision slit. The driver also had access to the periscope mounted in the hull deck above his head. The armoured periscope cover can be seen on the top right of this photograph. (*Musée des Blindés, Saumur, France*)

Commander's Cupola

Early-production Tiger tanks had a drum-like commander's cupola fitted onto the roof of the turret. The sides of the cupola were nearly vertical. It had five vision ports. Each one of the slits cut into the side of the armour had a 90-mm-thick laminated glass block behind it. The hinged hatch opened upwards and could be locked into position. In July 1943, the commander's cupola was changed to a new low-profile cast dome-shaped cupola that had seven periscopes. The hatch, when unlocked, pivoted sideways to help maintain a low profile.

Stowage Bins

The design of the early-production Tiger tanks overlooked the crew's need to store personal equipment, food, tools, and spare parts. They left the factory without stowage bins fitted to the turret. Some units provided their tanks with stowage bins similar to those used on the Panther III. There are photographs of a Tiger tank, with the turret number 100, equipped with rectangular stowage bins on each side of the turret. Starting in August 1942, Panzer III stowage bins were fitted to the rear of the turret at the factory as a temporary solution. Starting in late January 1943, Tiger tanks were equipped with a much larger stowage bin at the factory. It was shaped to fit the rear of the turret and matched the curvature of the armour. It ended 20 mm from the escape hatch opening.

❮ Early-production Tiger tank turrets were fitted with a drum-shaped commander's cupola. (*AACC*)

❯ Starting from July 1943, Tiger tank turrets were fitted with a lower profile dome-shaped commander's cupola with seven periscopes. (*Musée des Blindés, Saumur, France*)

❮ Early-production Tiger tanks left the factory without a stowage bin fitted to the rear of the turret. Some were added as battlefield modifications later or retrofitted with factory-built bins. Late-production Tiger tanks were fitted with large turret stowage bins in the factory.

❯ Starting in August 1943, *Zimmerit* was applied in the factories to Tiger tanks. (*Musée des Blindés, Saumur, France*)

Zimmerit

In the Second World War, the Germans developed magnetic anti-tank mines. They believed that the Soviets would also deploy similar magnetic mines. Starting in August 1943, factories producing Tiger tanks were instructed to apply a coating of *Zimmerit* paste. In January 1944, Panzer divisions operating in the field were ordered to apply a layer of *Zimmerit* to their tanks.

It was applied to the surface of the tanks in such a way as to break up the surface into a series of small ridges and troughs, producing a very uneven coating. It would reduce a magnet's ability to cling to the armoured plate of a tank. The paste was made from PVA glue, pine sawdust, pebble dust, zinc sulphide, barium sulphate, ochre, and pine crystals dissolved in benzene.

The instructions on how to apply *Zimmerit* were precise, but each factory used a different method to make the ridges and troughs in the paste. This has provided a quick way for military historians to identify what company manufactured a specific tank that appears in a photograph.

Some battlefield reports stated that the *Zimmerit* paste caught fire when enemy shells hit the tank. Intelligence reports also highlighted the fact that Soviet infantry were not using magnetic anti-tank mines, contrary to expectations. Applying *Zimmerit* paste took time. On 9 September 1944, to increase the production of armoured vehicles and because of the previous two issues, instructions were given to stop applying *Zimmerit* paste.

Feifel Air Filters

The early-production Tiger tanks drew in air through the armoured openings on the engine deck. The Maybach's integral air filters were deemed to be inadequate to cope with the sand, dust, and girt of the North African desert. In November 1942, the Tiger's engines were modified by the addition of an external Feifel air filter system. Mounting plates were already being installed for the filters in October 1942. Two pairs of filters, also called pre-cleaners, were mounted on the rear corners of the tank. Air was taken through the filters via tubes that rested on the engine deck. The untreated air entered the Feifel air filter system at the bottom of the unit. Clean, filtered air was sent back across the engine deck from a tube that came out the top of the unit. This clean air was then fed into the engine compartment. In March 1943, the design of the Feifel air filters, with a simplified upper chamber, was introduced.

In October 1943, instructions were given to the factories to discontinue fitting Fiefel air filters. The welded mounting points on the rear hull plate were still provided on new Tigers for about three more months. The air intake slit used by the system's tubes in the forward end of the engine deck was now protected by an elevated plate. The North African campaign ended in February 1943. This complex air filtration system was considered not necessary for tanks on the Eastern Front. This instruction may have been a mistake because in the summer, the dust clouds produced on unmade roads in Russia were as bad if not worse than anything in North Africa. Karl Tutschek remembers his grandfather, *Oberscharführer* Karl Tutschek, who served with the 2e *Waffen-SS Das Reich* in Russia, saying that had they had oil bath filters, to keep their engines free of dust, they would have reached Moscow a month sooner.

Many crews did not use them. The tubes had to be removed to gain access to the engine compartment. They caused overheating and were susceptible to damage. Crewmen found it was easier to use the standard filters and regularly take them out and bash the accumulated dirt out of them. Not fitting the Fiefel air filter system simplified production. It reduced costs and enabled more tanks to be produced faster.

The external pre-cleaner Feifel air filter system was discontinued in October 1943.

The external pre-cleaner Feifel air filter system had two large filters fitted on the rear of the Tiger tank, one each side of the exhaust silencer/muffler heat shields. (*Ian Wilcox Tiger Day, The Tank Museum, Bovington*)

Crew Compartment Heater

Starting in December 1942, tanks sent to the frigid Eastern Front were fitted with a crew compartment heater. A large sheet metal boat hull shaped cowling was installed on top of the rear engine deck over the warm air outlet grill. It redirected the warm air to the wading snorkel inlet and into the crew compartment. It was only used when temperatures were cold.

These are just a few of the more visible modifications.

SPECIFICATIONS	
Length overall	8.45 m
Length hull	6.31 m
Width	3.70 m
Height	3 m
Combat weight loaded	57 tonnes
Rail transport weight unloaded	52.5 tonnes
Main Gun	8.8-cm KwK 36 L/56
Secondary armament	7.92-mm MG34 machine gun
Crew	5 (commander, gunner, loader, driver, radio operator/ hull machine gunner)
Radio	Fu 5 and Fu 2 Intercom
Early production Engine	Maybach HL 210 TRM P45 V12 water-cooled 21-litre petrol/gasoline 650-hp at 3,000 rpm
Late production Engine (after Fgst.Nr 250251)	Maybach HL 230 TRM P45 V12 water-cooled 23-litre petrol/gasoline 690-hp at 3,000 rpm
Transmission	8 forward, 4 reverse, Olvar 40 12 16 Getriebe (OG 40 12 16)
Maximum Speed	45 km/h (28 mpg)
Average Road Speed	20 km/h (12 mpg)
Cross Country Speed	15 km/h (9 mpg)
Range on Road	125 km (77 mpg)
Range Cross Country	80 km (50 mpg)
Trench Crossing	2.3 m
Fording Depth	160 cm
Drive	Front sprocket
Suspension	Torsion bars
Track	Kgs 63/725/130 dry pin
Track links per side	96
Armour: Front superstructure	100 mm (angled at 9 degrees from vertical)
Armour: lower front plate	100 mm (angled at 25 degrees from vertical)
Armour: Upper glacis plate	60 mm (angled at 80 degrees from vertical)
Armour: Upper side hull superstructure	80 mm (angled at 0 degrees from vertical)
Armour: Lower side hull superstructure	60 mm (angled at 0 degrees from vertical)
Armour: Turret side and rear	80 mm (angled at 9 degrees from vertical)
Armour: Behind Gun mantlet	57 mm (angled at 0 degrees from vertical)
Armour: Gun mantlet	70–145 mm (angled at 0 degrees from vertical)
Armour: Front turret roof	25 mm (angled at 85 degrees from vertical) later 40 mm
Armour: Rear turret roof	25 mm (angled at 90 degrees from vertical) later 40 mm
Armour: cupola	15 mm (angled at 90 degrees from vertical)
Armour: Engine deck	25 mm (angled at 90 degrees from vertical)
Armour: Rear	80 mm (angled at 9 degrees from vertical)
Armour: Belly	25 mm (angled at 90 degrees from vertical)
Total built	1,346

2

OPERATIONAL DEPLOYMENT

The first batch of Tiger I tanks left the factory in August 1942 and were immediately sent to the Eastern Front, south of Leningrad (Saint Petersburg), to counter the menace of the Soviet T-34 and KV-1 tanks. They first saw action on 16 September 1942. As with all new tank designs, the tank crews and maintenance personnel discovered mechanical and reliability issues to be overcome and fixed. The accurate, powerful, long-ranged gun of the Tiger was particularly suited to the relatively flat, open farmland of this part of northern Russia. The Tiger could knock out enemy tanks at long range without being in danger of return fire penetrating its armour.

In 1942, the Panzer III was still the main German tank with the Panzer IV being the support tank used to fire HE shells. When it was introduced in 1942, the Tiger was intended to be used as a heavy support tank for breakthrough operations against enemy defences. They usually fought in packs as part of a heavy tank battalion (*schwere Panzer-Abteilung* or s.Pz. Abt.) and not as a lone wolf, as portrayed in the Hollywood movie *Fury*.

Most Tiger tanks were issued to one of the ten different heavy tank battalions. They were numbered s.Pz.Abt. 501 to s.Pz. Abt. 510. Some were sent to three different SS heavy tank battalions—s.SS-Pz.Abt. 101, s.SS-Pz.Abt. 102, and s.SS-Pz.Abt. 103.

The *Kriegstärkenachweisung* (K.St.N) was the officially authorised structure of a military unit. It must be remembered that the *Kriegstärkenachweisung* was a guideline. Many units failed to maintain their established strength of vehicles, people, and equipment due to combat losses, mechanical breakdowns, and problems with resupply. There would be reserve tanks. Unit strength reports submitted by battalion staff for High Command were not always accurate. If they had received a surplus of Panzer III or IV tanks over the authorised strength, this would often not be reported.

Two *Kriegstärkenachweisung* instructions detail the combat strength establishment of the 1942 Heavy Tank Company (*Schwere Panzer-Kompanie*): HQ Company (*StabsKompanie*) K.St.N. 1150b and Heavy Tank Company (*Schwere Panzer-Kompanie*) K.St.N. 1176d. These instructions were modified as the availability of Tiger tanks increased. The early version contained the following data:

HQ COMPANY (*STABSKOMPANIE*)

2 × Tiger Command tanks, 1 × Panzer III, 1 × Platoon (*Züg*) 5x Panzer III tanks.
1st Company Troop (*1.Kompanietrupp*) 1 × Tiger 2 × Panzer III tanks.
1st Platoon (*1.Züg*) 1 × Tiger, 2 × Panzer III, 1 × Panzer IV tanks.
2nd Platoon (*2.Züg*) 1 × Tiger, 2 × Panzer III, 1 × Panzer IV tanks.
3rd Platoon (*3.Züg*) 1 × Tiger, 2 × Panzer III, 1 × Panzer IV tanks.
4th Platoon (*4.Züg*) 1 × Tiger, 2 × Panzer III, 1 × Panzer IV tanks.
2nd Company Troop (*2.Kompanietrupp*) 1 × Tiger 2 × Panzer III tanks.
1st Platoon (*1.Züg*) 1 × Tiger, 2 × Panzer III, 1 × Panzer IV tanks.
2nd Platoon (*2.Züg*) 1 × Tiger, 2 × Panzer III, 1 × Panzer IV tanks.
3rd Platoon (*3.Züg*) 1 × Tiger, 2 × Panzer III, 1 × Panzer IV tanks.
4th Platoon (*4.Züg*) 1 × Tiger, 2 × Panzer III, 1 × Panzer IV tanks.

HQ Company (*Stabskompanie*):
1st Company Troop (*1.Kompanietrupp*)
1st Platoon (*1.Züg*)
2nd Platoon (*2.Züg*)
3rd Platoon (*3.Züg*)
4th Platoon (*4.Züg*)
2nd Company Troop (*2.Kompanietrupp*)
1st Platoon (*1.Züg*)
2nd Platoon (*2.Züg*)
3rd Platoon (*3.Züg*)
4th Platoon (*4.Züg*)

A revision was made to the Heavy Tank Company (*Schwere Panzer-Kompanie*) K.St.N. 1176d instructions because more Tiger tanks became available. The Panzer IV was removed from each platoon and replaced with a Tiger.

In 1944, the official establishment of a heavy Tiger tank battalion (*schwere Panzer-Abteilung 'Tiger'*) was increased to forty-five Tigers. Each heavy tank battalion consisted of three companies, which were subdivided into three platoons, issued with four Tiger tanks. The additional tanks were used as command vehicles and as reserves. The official establishment figures often did not match the tanks that were available for combat use. These numbers were reduced due to mechanical failure and battle losses.

On 5 March 1943, order K.St.N. 1150e changed the authorised establishment of a heavy Tiger tank battalion (*schwere Panzer-Abteilung 'Tiger'*) to the following vehicles:

HQ COMPANY (STABSKOMPANIE)

3 × Tiger Command tanks.
1st Company Troop (*1.Kompanietrupp*) 2 × Tiger tanks.
1st Platoon (*1.Züg*) 4 × Tiger tanks.
2nd Platoon (*2.Züg*) 4 × Tiger tanks.
3rd Platoon (*3.Züg*) 4 × Tiger tanks.
2nd Company Troop (*2.Kompanietrupp*) 2 × Tiger tanks.
1st Platoon (*1.Züg*) 4 × Tiger tanks.
2nd Platoon (*2.Züg*) 4 × Tiger tanks.
3rd Platoon (*3.Züg*) 4 × Tiger tanks.
3rd Company Troop (*3.Kompanietrupp*) 2 × Tiger tanks.
1st Platoon (*1.Züg*) 4 × Tiger tanks.
2nd Platoon (*2.Züg*) 4 × Tiger tanks.
3rd Platoon (*3.Züg*) 4 × Tiger tanks.

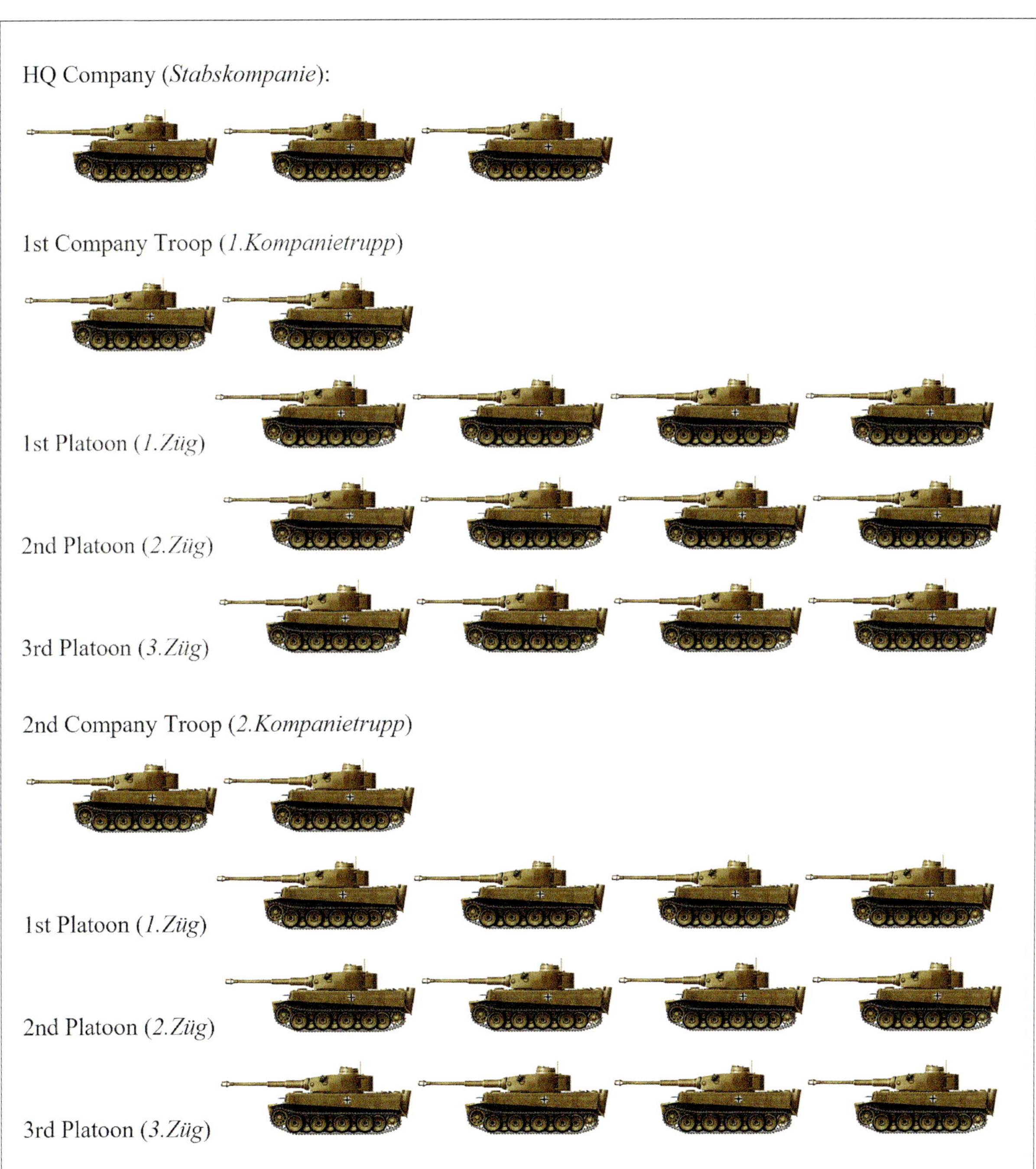

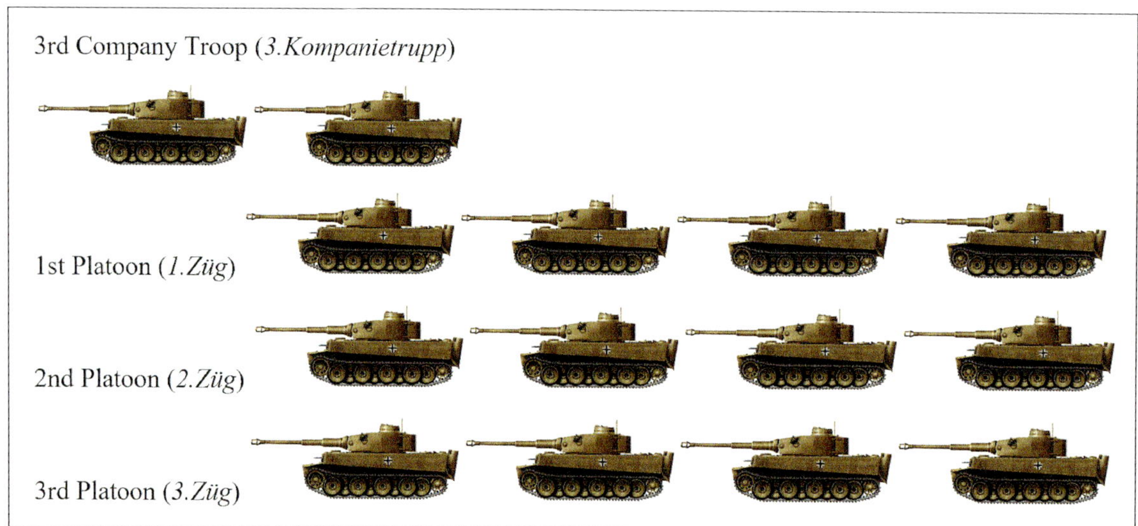

Starting in early 1944, the system changed. The term *Freie Gliederung* (free organisation, though better translated as 'independent unit') began to be used on *Kriegstärkenachweisung* (K.St.N) instructions. Different non-frontline combat units, like transportation, were no longer shown at company level but allocated at battalion or regimental level. The number of platoons (Züg) per company was reduced from four to three.

HEAVY TANK COMPANY 'TIGER' (INDEPENDENT UNIT)

schwere PanzerKompanie 'Tiger' (freie Gliederung) (Schw.Panz.Kp. 'Tiger')
K.St.N 1176, dated 1 June 1944
Group Leader (*Gruppenführer*): 2 × Tiger Command tanks.
1st Platoon (*1.Züg*) 4 × Tiger tanks.
2nd Platoon (*2.Züg*) 4 × Tiger tanks.
3rd Platoon (*3.Züg*) 4 × Tiger tanks.

An instruction dated 1 November 1944, removed one Tiger tank from the authorised HQ company strength. The company platoon (*Züg*) strengths were the same.

The Tiger I tank first saw combat during the invasion of the Soviet Union but also saw action in the deserts of North Africa, Sicily, Italy, and in Normandy following the 6 June 1944 D-Day landings. In December 1944, they took part in the Ardennes offensive, the Battle of the Bulge, and then the defence of Germany. Tiger I tanks were still in service at the end of the war.

3

EARLY 1943 SOVIET ARMY TIGER TANK PAMPHLET

On 9 November 1942, the British military mission in the Soviet Union obtained a German document that listed new models of German armoured fighting vehicles. It was dated 7 October 1942 and recorded the Pz.Kpfw.I Ausf. C, Pz.Kpfw. II Ausf. G, Pz.Kpfw.II Ausf. J, and Pz.Kpfw. VI. Other than the names on the list, there were no more details about the vehicles. The British surmised that a new tank called the Pz.Kpfw. VI would be larger and heavier than the Pz.Kpfw.III and Pz. Kpfw. IV. They passed this information on to London and formally requested the Soviet authorities update them with any more details about the Pz.Kpfw. VI if one should be sighted or captured. This is believed to be the first information the Allies obtained about the construction of the Tiger tank.

The Soviet Army, just like the British Army, needed to inform its men about the vulnerabilities of the new German menace. They produced a pamphlet at the beginning of 1943, before the Battle of Kursk, showing the Tiger tank's weak spots. A newer version was issued after the battle that contained more up-to-date information. The Soviet Army was the first to capture and inspect German Panther and Tiger tanks. They shared the information they obtained with their allies in the west.

Part of the data used to construct the pamphlet came from Soviet military observations, battlefield reports, measurements and test firing results on captured Tiger tanks. On 17 January 1943, Panzer VI Ausf. E. Tiger tank turret number 121 (serial number 250004) of the German 502nd Heavy Tank Battalion (1/502 s.Pz.Abt.) near to Leningrad suffered engine and radiator mechanical problems and could not move. The German tank crew set off charges inside the tank before abandoning it. Tiger 121 was recovered by Soviet troops and later transported to the live firing range at the Kubinka Army Base outside Moscow. It was here that the strength of its armour was tested and the search for weak spots began.

On 17 January 1943, Panzer VI Ausf. E. Tiger tank turret number 100 (serial number 250009) was also abandoned by its crew in the same area. It had rolled off the road and could not get out of the ditch. It was transported to Gorky Park in Moscow and put on display with other captured German weapons and vehicles. Tiger 121, after the live firing trials, complete with holes, was also exhibited in Gorky Park so the public could see that some Soviet armour-piercing shells could penetrate the Tiger tank's armour. They remained on display until 1948 when they were scrapped.

Documents record that two other Tiger tanks were recovered that day; one was totally burnt out, and the other was damaged and partly burnt out. These two tanks were salvaged for spare parts and used to cut out sections of armour plate for testing.

These Tiger tank drawings formed part of a 1943 Soviet Army pamphlet to illustrate the weak spots in the tank's armour. (*Russian Archives*)

The right side of *Panzerkampfwagen* VI. Ausf. E Tiger tank turret no. 121 of the German 502nd Heavy Tank Battalion (502 s.Pz.Abt.) before the firing trial. (*Russian Archives*)

The left side of *Panzerkampfwagen* VI. Ausf. E Tiger tank turret no. 121 of the German 502nd Heavy Tank Battalion (502 s.Pz.Abt.) before the firing trial. (*Russian Archives*)

This is what the left side of *Panzerkampfwagen* VI. Ausf. E Tiger tank turret no. 121 looked like after the firing trial. (*Russian Archives*)

‹ The front view of *Panzerkampfwagen* VI. Ausf. E Tiger tank turret no. 121 of the German 502nd Heavy Tank Battalion (502 s.Pz.Abt.) before the firing trial. Notice the battalion icon on the upper right section of the front hull armour. (*Russian Archives*)

› This is what the front of *Panzerkampfwagen* VI. Ausf. E Tiger tank turret no. 121 looked like after the firing trial. (*Russian Archives*)

‹ The captured *Panzerkampfwagen* VI. Ausf. E Tiger tank turret no. 100 of the German 502nd Heavy Tank Battalion (502 s.Pz.Abt.) on display at Gorky Park in Moscow in 1943. (*Russian Archives*)

› Inspection by senior Soviet Army officers of the captured Panzer VI. Ausf. E Tiger tank turret no. 100 of the German 502 s.Pz.Abt. on display at Gorky Park in Moscow in 1943. (*Russian Archives*)

EARLY BRITISH INTELLIGENCE REPORTS ABOUT THE TIGER TANK

The British War Office was aware that it needed to provide information to its forces about the threats they would have to deal with on the battlefield. As information became available about new enemy weapons, it was quickly disseminated.

In late 1942 and early 1943, the British War Office Ministry of Intelligence, Section 10 (MI10) started to receive information about a new German heavy tank from sources outside the Soviet Union. MI10 was responsible for weapons and technical analysis during the Second World War. It later became part of the British Secret Intelligence Service (SIS), commonly known as MI6.

MI10 gathered as much data as possible. This enabled them to produce these diagrams. In April 1943, it was sent to as many units on the front line as possible. No information about weak spots or advice on methods of attack was given. This example was issued to the 6th Battalion, Lincolnshire Regiment and was found in the regimental papers.

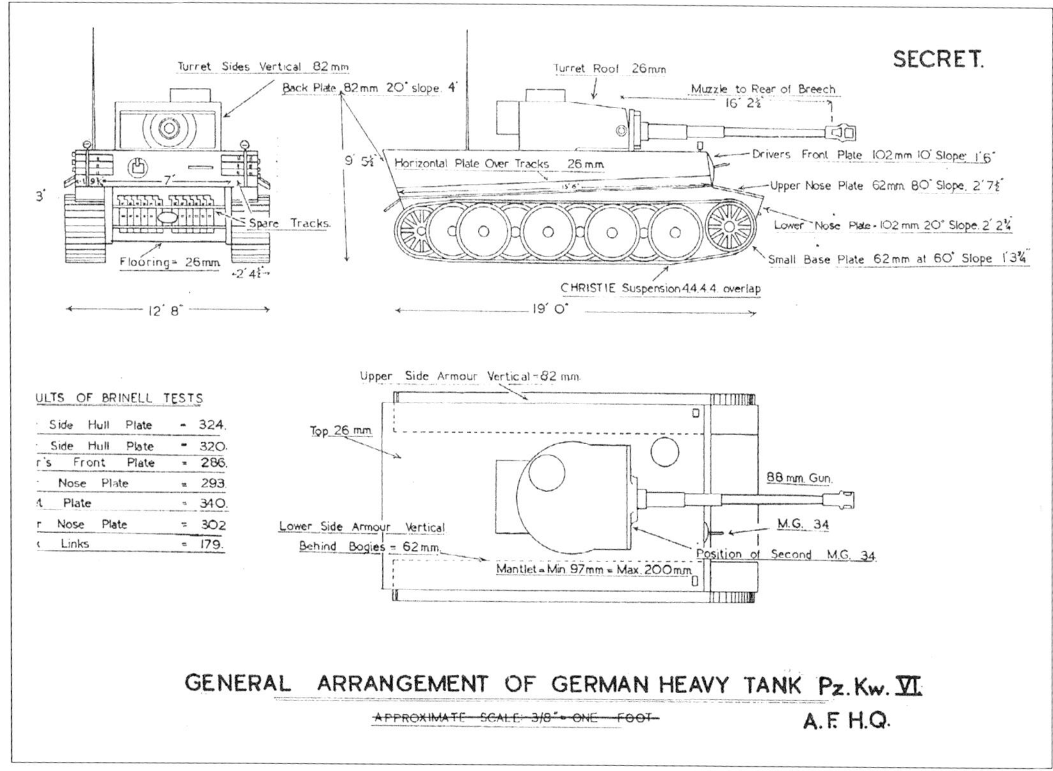

These plans of the Panzer VI Ausf. E Tiger tank are dated April 1943. (*Regimental Collection of 6th Battalion of the Lincolnshire Regiment.*)

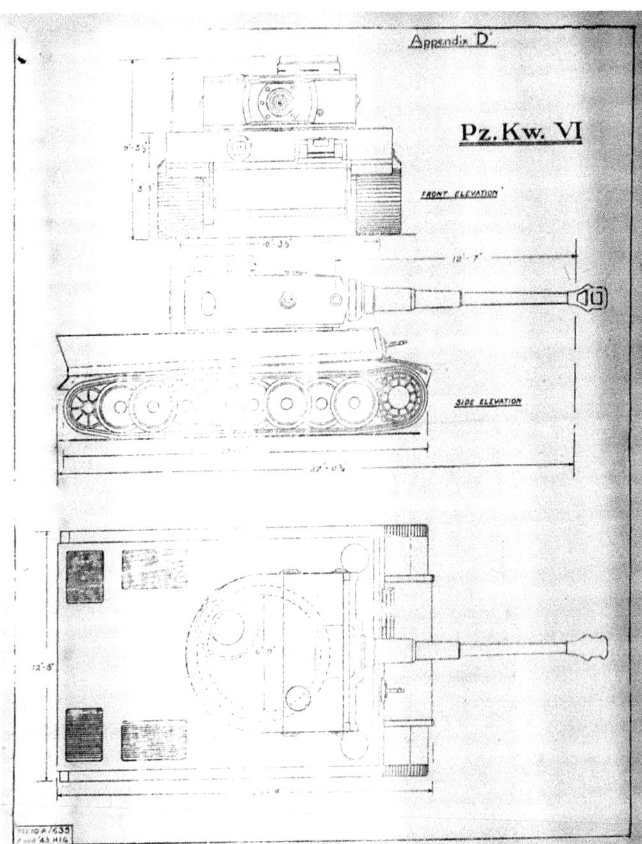

This was the early British drawings of the Panzer VI Ausf. E Tiger dated April 1943 sent to the military headquarters of Canada and America, the Allied Forces HQ, as well as British Army units in the UK and North Africa. (*MI10 A/535 April 1943 H.I.6*)

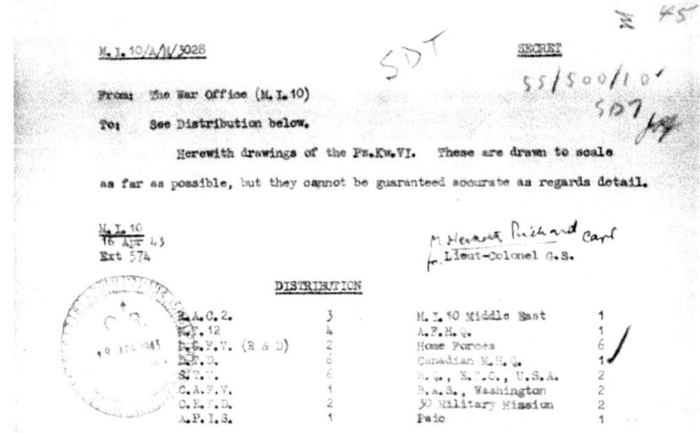

M.I.10/A/M/3028

SECRET

From: The War Office (M.I.10)

To: See Distribution below.

Herewith drawings of the Pz.Kw.VI. These are drawn to scale as far as possible, but they cannot be guaranteed accurate as regards detail.

M.I.10
16 Apr 43
Ext 574

for Lieut-Colonel G.S.

DISTRIBUTION

R.A.C.2.	3	M.I.10 Middle East	1
M.T.12	4	A.F.H.Q.	1
D.G.F.V. (R & D)	2	Home Forces	6
D.T.D.	6	Canadian M.H.Q.	1
S.T.T.	6	H.Q., N.T.C., U.S.A.	2
C.A.F.V.	1	B.A.S., Washington	2
C.E.F.D.	2	30 Military Mission	2
A.P.I.S.	1	Paic	1

This is a scan of a message marked 'secret', sent by the War Office Intelligence Department MI10 giving the distribution list of an early drawing of the Panzer VI Ausf. E Tiger tank. It was sent to the military headquarters of Canada and America, the Allied Forces HQ, as well as British Army units in the UK and in North Africa. This message was dated 18 April 1943. (*MI10/A/M/3028*)

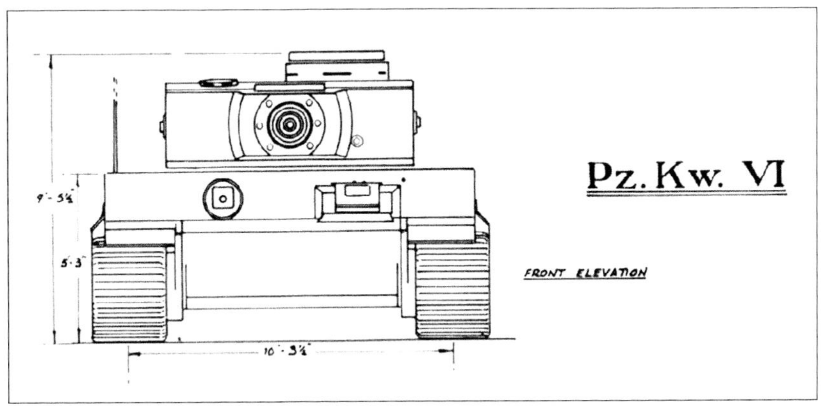

(*MI10 A/535 April 1943 H.I.6*)

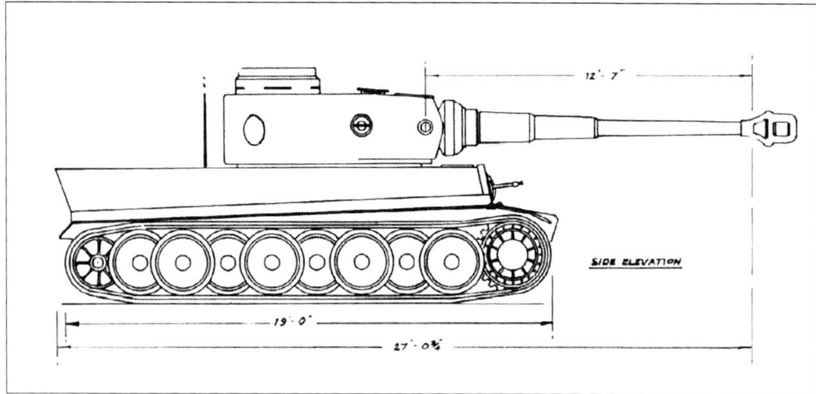

(MI10 A/535 April 1943 H.I.6)

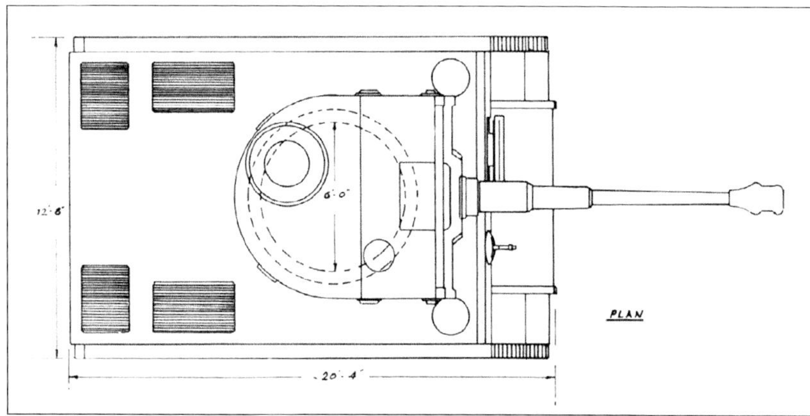

(MI10 A/535 April 1943 H.I.6)

Early rumours of a new German heavy tank were included in a coded MI10 telegram circulated to officers in charge of government departments that were involved in tank development and intelligence. The message contained a few abbreviation spelling mistakes. It also wrongly assumed that the reason for not calling the new heavy tank *Panzerkampfwagen* V, but instead calling it the Panzerkampfwagen VI was that the large 1936 Neubaufahrzeug tank that saw service in the occupation of Norway in 1940 had the designation for the Pz.Kpfw. Nb.Fz.V. At the time the memo was written, the British did not know about the Panzer V Panther tank. The wrong assumption about the reason for the number jump from Panzer IV to Panzer VI may have put the British Intelligence Service off the hunt for a new German tank called the Panzer V. The abbreviation AFV is short for 'armoured fighting vehicle'. The memo said:

SECRET

MI10 [MI10.a/3008]

Secret Cipher Telegram 1/65667 of 29 October from Middle East has reported the identification from a captured German Document, equivalent to British ACIs, of the following AFVs not hitherto identified.

A new type known as K.PFW.VI. This confirms that as expected, a new heavier than III or IV is being built. The absence to any reference to Pz.Kpwf.V suggests that this nomenclature was probably applied to the heavier type first reported in 1937/38. Later seen in Norway and in German Propaganda papers, and since discarded.

We have asked both Middle East and the Mission in Moscow to take urgent steps to obtain precise information on the characteristics of the Pz.Kpfw. VI.

SGD. Shallard
Major
For Lieut:Col:G.S.
MI10.
3 Nov 1942
Extn 230

The Directorate of Military Intelligence (DMI) was a department of the British War Office. It issued an intelligence briefing on the new German heavy tank in November 1942. The information was limited, and it does not reveal its sources:

MOST SECRET

ENEMY WEAPONS

New German Super-Heavy Pz.Kw.VI tank

The following information has been received from a delicately placed, reliable source. It may be communicated, at your discretion, to those whose work is *immediately* affected by it, but it must NOT be generally circulated or reproduced in a summary.

Weight 57 tons

Dimensions

Length 20 feet 3 inches

Width 11 feet 8 inches

Armour Source does not know but thinks about 100 mm

Armament 8.8-cm KwK

Performance

Trench Crossing

Step Source is endeavouring to obtain details.

Water Forded

Maximum Gradient

No details of the 8.8-cm KwK are known. KwK is the normal nomenclature given to guns mounted in AFVs as distinct from those on field or self propelled mountings.

The above information has been given to ACIGS, DAFV, DRA.

Nov. 42

for D.M.I.

What follows is a transcription of a message by MI10, sent to General MacNaughton in the Canadian Military Head Quarters (CMHQ). The message is dated 9 February 1943 and gives an update on the information received on the new *Panzerkampfwagen* VI Ausf. E Tiger:

SECRET

MI10.a./M.1895

C.M.H.Q. (For General MacNaughton)

The particulars of the Pz.Kw.VI so far received from Allied Forces Head Quarters (AFHQ) are attached. More information is expected, and the full report will be published in our technical intelligence summary.

Meanwhile, certain points may be noted:

(i). The drawing issued with our summary No. 97 is substantially correct so far as it goes, but the gun is fitted with the usual German type of muzzle brake.

(ii). The 8.8-cm ammunition is apparently the same as for the 8.8 cm Flak gun, and therefore AP and HE performance will no doubt be the same.

(iii). The suspension details are not yet known, but it seems clear now that the large wheels are mounted in the overlapping arrangement common on German semi-tracked vehicles, and it is probable that the discs of these wheels are armoured.

(iv). No spaced armour is fitted.

(v). Press reports of armour thickness of 10 inches have proved incorrect. The maximum is in fact about 4 inches.

(vi). AFHQ have reported that our 6-pdr AP shot has penetrated the turret armour of this tank at about 500 yards.

(vii). Homogeneous plate is used throughout. This suggests that supplies of face hardened plate are reserved for the less heavily armoured tanks.

S.O.M. Shallard. Major. G.S.

For Lieut. Colonel. G.S.

MI10 9 Feb 43

On 11 December 1942, a photograph of Tiger tank 142 of 501st Heavy Tank Battalion (s.Pz.Abt.501) driving through the streets of Tunis, North Africa, was published in the German newspaper called *National Zeitung*. MI10 obtained a copy of the newspaper and studied the photograph. In early January, a copy was sent to the School of Tank Technology and the Department of Tank Design. A technical draftsman was commissioned to make a scale drawing of the tank from the photograph. From that diagram, the dimensions of the new metal beast were calculated. It was fitted with the smaller 'transportation tracks' as the tank had just driven off a tank landing craft onto the beach. The muzzle brake was not fitted. On 15 January 1943, MI10 released this briefing note:

TECHNICAL INTELLIGENCE SUMMARY NO. 97

War Office (MI10)
15 January 1943
New Heavy Tank

Reference summary 94 para. 4, a photograph showing a new type of German tank, said to be passing through Tunis has recently been published in the Continental Press. This photograph forms the basis of the drawing at Appendix C.

It is considered that the tank shown is almost certainly the Pz.Kw.VI with 8.8 cm KwK.36 mounted in the turret.

Scaling from the photograph, rough estimates for dimensions are:

Overall height about:	9 feet 6 inches
Overall length about:	21 feet
Overall width about:	10 feet to 10 feet 9 inches
Width of track plates:	nearly 2 feet
Diameter of road wheels:	3 feet (Approx.)

The suspension is not at all clearly shown in the photograph. Thus while it is clear that the bogie wheels are of the large armoured disc type, it is not clear whether they are arranged in a straight line or interleaved as in the suspensions of German semi-tracked vehicles. In the drawing, the suspension is provisionally shown as being of the latter type.

Many typical German features will be observed from the drawing. For example:- the conventional German type of gun mounting on the front of the superstructure; the cupola; and the design of the front of the hull which is not unlike that of the Pz.Kw.IV Model G though the glacis plate is shorter.

It will be noted that the superstructure overhangs the full width of the tracks and in this way, no doubt helps to solve the problem of stowage for the 8.8-cm ammunition. This ammunition will possibly be of the Q.F. separate loading type.

Technical diagram based on a newspaper photograph of a Tiger tank in Tunis. (*MI10 A/545 Jan 1943 H.I.6*)

As more accurate information became available MI10 circulated it to the heads of departments that needed to know. Interestingly, the word 'Tiger' is not being used. This information may not have been known.

Further to our minute of 3 November 1942 (MI10.a/3008) on the subject of new AFVs and our minute of 4 January on the Pz.Kw.VI., the following particulars of this tank have now been obtained from a document captured in North Africa:

Weight	56 tons
Length	20 feet 4 inches
Length inc. gun	27 feet 0.75 inches
Width	10 feet 11.75 inches
Height	9 feet 5.5 inches

A disabled Pz.Kw.VI, which it was not possible to recover, has been examined, and the particulars will be sent to you as soon as they are received here.

MI10.

On 5 February 1943, the British press quoted the Reuters battle report of the fight between British forces and German Tiger tanks on the road towards Robaa on 20 January 1943. The press and the British War Office were keen to inform the public that the new German heavy tank was not unstoppable with headlines like, '6-pounder beats new Nazi tank.' It was a public relations gift for the Allies. The Reuters' war correspondent story was run in most Allied newspapers to show that the Tiger could be stopped.

On 15 February 1943, Brigadier T. Lyon Smith, attached to the Royal Artillery HQ staff, submitted a brief composite summary report of all the information he had managed to obtain. The news report did not give details on how far away from the British 6-pdr guns the Tiger tanks were before they were engaged and knocked out. This was the essential detail that military intelligence wanted to know.

SECRET

RA/0/2/5
H.Q.R.A
6th Armd. Div.
15 Feb. 43

I have sifted all possible information and questioned all witnesses concerning the encounter between 2 Troops A/72 A/Tk Regt R.A. and the German Tank Force on the Robaa Road on 20 Jan 1943.

I have also studied the southern half of the ground.

I am satisfied that the leading tank (Mark VI) was not engaged at any time at a range less than 500 yards. This tank was hit on the *side* mainly.

The 2nd Mark VI tank was hit and disabled at not less than 800 yards. It was also chiefly engaged by *frontal fire.*

I thought these factors are of sufficient importance to warrant a thorough investigation, as they prove conclusively (to me anyhow) that the 6-pr. A/Tank gun can deal most effectively with the Mark VI tank. I hope I may not be proved at a later date to have been wrong.

I believe 16 other tanks were seen following behind—these withdrew. They, in turn, were followed very closely by the Panzer Regt (Inf) in armoured carriers or TCVs. They were seen to be sitting smartly to attention until engaged by 12 RHA. They then dismounted hurriedly, and delivered a most determined attack on the Buffs.

Yours
(Brig. T. Lyon Smith)

Knocked-out Tiger tanks in the deserts of North Africa were examined and makeshift firing trials, including using anti-tank mines, were conducted in the field. An official report that contained an assessment of the tank with specifications was quickly sent back to London. This report is reproduced in David Fletcher's book *Tiger! The Tiger Tank: A British View.* Pieces of armour plate from the wrecked Tiger tanks were sent back to Britain. The information obtained was used to help produce briefing sheets that were then circulated to Allied forces.

5

THE ARMOUR CODE

Throughout the British scientific data recording sheets attached to the reports on the firing trials on captured Tiger tanks, code letters were used to indicate how much damage was inflicted on the test vehicle. This was called the 'Armour Code', and a brief explanatory sheet was included in an appendix in each report. In March 1945, the School of Tank Technology printed a booklet to help explain the armour code to students attending courses. What follows is a transcript of that booklet. It will help you understand the information contained in some of the reports covered in the following chapters of this book.

COVERING MEMO

Restricted
Armour Section, School of Tank Technology.
Prepared for Students of the School of Tank Technology. March 1945.
The subject matter of this pamphlet has been arranged in a manner suitable for its ultimate direct inclusion in a new edition of 'Armour for Fighting Vehicles.' The numbering of sections and illustrations conforms to the plan agreed upon for this type of publication. Definitions considered necessary for present use are included at the end of the pamphlet.

CHAPTER 2: THE ARMOUR CODE

2.1. It is first necessary to learn certain terms relating to the perforation of armour, and it is proposed to define these in the present chapter.

Fig. 2.1a illustrates the processes which take place when an armour piercing AP shot strikes a plate of machineable quality (MQ) armour at zero impact angle (normal) and with different values of strike velocity (SV).

At (i) the shot has had insufficient remaining velocity (RV) to strike the plate with any appreciable SV.

At (ii) the SV has been sufficient to produce only a small dent in the surface.

Conditions (i) and (ii) are defined in Ordnance Board Proceeding (O.B.Proc.) No. 24, 782, dated 20 September 1943, by the code letter A, and by the symbol ⊙ for the purpose of a graphical representation.

At (iii) the SV has been sufficient to produce a deep impression, defined as B damage, and symbolised as ⊙.

In the above instances no damage has occurred at the back of the plate. In (ii) and (iii) the shot would rebound, leaving the front damage available for inspection and coding as A or B. In practice code A is confined to damage caused by small arms S.A. ball ammunition where little more than lead splash has occurred.

2.2. In the discussion which follows in Paras 2.2–2.5 it should be assumed that the shot remains undamaged and does not lodge in the plate.

When the SV is raised the damage becomes greater and can be observed at the back of the plate. Examples are shown in Fig. 2.2a (i), (ii) and (iii) and Fig. 2.3a, with equivalent codes as defined as follows

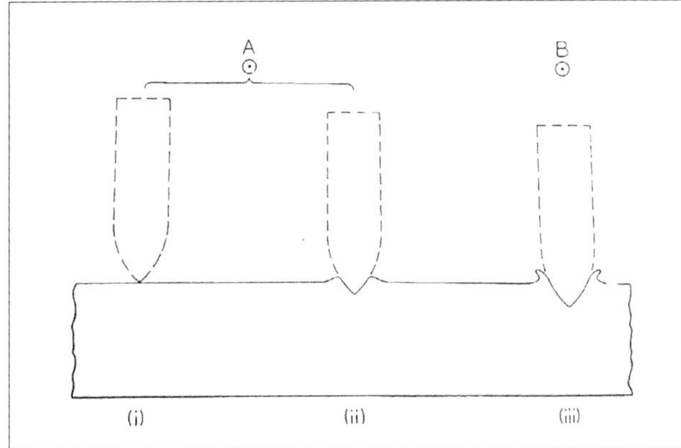

Fig. 2.1a. (*Armour Section, School of Tank Technology*)

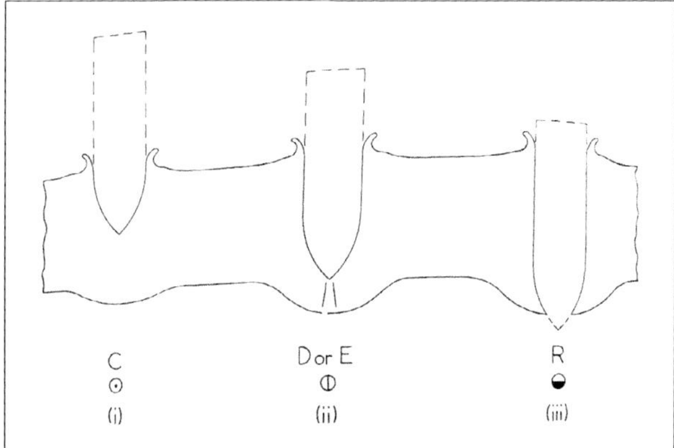

Fig. 2.2a. (*Armour Section, School of Tank Technology*)

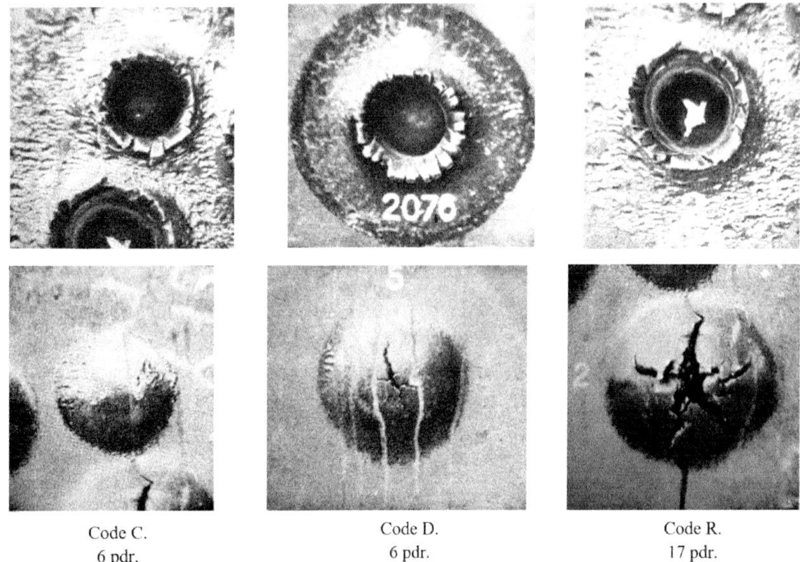

Code C.
6 pdr.

Code D.
6 pdr.

Code R.
17 pdr.

Fig. 2.3a. (*Armour Section, School of Tank Technology*)

Code C: Back bulge which has not cracked.

Code D: Back bulge which has cracked, but insufficiently to allow the passage of daylight.

Code E: As for D, except that cracking is sufficient to allow the passage of daylight.

Code R: Is best explained by reference to Fig. 2.3a. The hole at the back of the plate is too small to allow the shot to pass through, but it geometry has been determined chiefly by the nose of the shot.

With the proviso that the shot remains undamaged no missile will have passed through the armour in the cases so far considered. Let the SV be raised until a hole is made through the plate and the shot passes through undamaged.

Code W: represents the above condition, and is illustrated in Fig. 2.3b.

2.3. It is now opportune to discuss the examples of Figs 2.3a and 2.3b in more detail. During examination of the photographs, care should be taken to differentiate between lacquer applied for anti-erosive purposes and other plate surface effects.

(a) Front Damage: All examples show that some metal has been forced towards the gun in the form of 'front petals.' Surrounding them is a zone which has bulged slightly above the main plate surface. The ultimate boundary of the mechanically disturbed zone is the approximate circle where the oxide scale of the plate surface has not been dislodged. In the USA, front petals are sometimes called spurs.

Fig. 2.3b. (*Armour Section, School of Tank Technology*)

(b) Impression, Penetration, Perforation: The term 'impression' implies that the shot has not succeeded in pushing its way through the back of a plate, and applies up to E damage. 'Penetration' means that a hole has been made but that it is too small to have allowed the shot to pass through. 'Perforation' means that the hull is of sufficient size to allow the passage of the complete shot. The equivalent American term is 'complete penetration'.

(c) Back Damage:

Codes D, E: Sometimes, daylight illumination is insufficient to distinguish between D and E. This can then be done by placing a lighted candle or torch behind the bulge and viewing from immediately in front. When the cracks radiate from a centre of origin, the damage may be annotated as 4- star or 5-star according to their number.

Code R: In the example of Fig 2.3a the bulge has divided into five 'segments', also called 'back petals'.

Code W: In the 2-pdr example of Fig. 2.3b the segments have bent back to allow the passage of the shot, but remain firmly attached to the plate. In the 6 pdr and 17 pdr examples the segments became detached during the perforation and acted as missiles. Such damage would be annotated as 'segments broken off'. The mechanically disturbed zones can be seen again as areas of oxide scale removal.

2.4. In the examples discussed so far, the shot has defeated the plate only at W damage, and has passed through, with or without the accompaniment of segments as missiles. The letter code W may be remembered easily as being a WIN for the shot. Similarly, the letter code R might be a REBOUND or REJECT, implying a failure on the part of the shot. Figs. 2.3a and 2.3b are characteristic of good MQ armour.

2.5. Other types of damage which may occur are flaking and plugging.

Flaking: Fig 2.5a shows the method by which flaking may take place, the photographic examples are given in Fig 2.5b. DTD's description is: 'Severe Flaking—Poor bulging takes place with the appearance of a circumferential crack on a large diameter before any radial cracks are developed.

In the worst cases, the bulged metal or flake is completely detached before any radial cracks appear, in other cases radial cracks of comparatively small dimensions may be formed before the flake is separated from the plate. (Damage should be described as 'flake off in one piece', giving maximum dimensions. In summarising back damage the term 'flaking' should be used and the lowest SV, at which the flake started, quoted).' When a flake is of approximately circular shape, it is often called a 'disc', and further examples are shown in figs. 2.5c and 2.5d. The armour code suffix is (F).

In the photograph of back damage note the central convex burnished area, followed by two zones in which failure has taken place in tension and shear respectively.

Tendency to flake: Is intermediate between severe flaking and normal damage and is illustrated in Fig. 2.5e. DTD's description is: 'Tendency to Fake—Moderate bulging takes place with the development of radial cracks but accompanied by the appearance of a circumferential crack around the bulge, on a diameter usually about twice the calibre of the shot. As penetration proceeds,

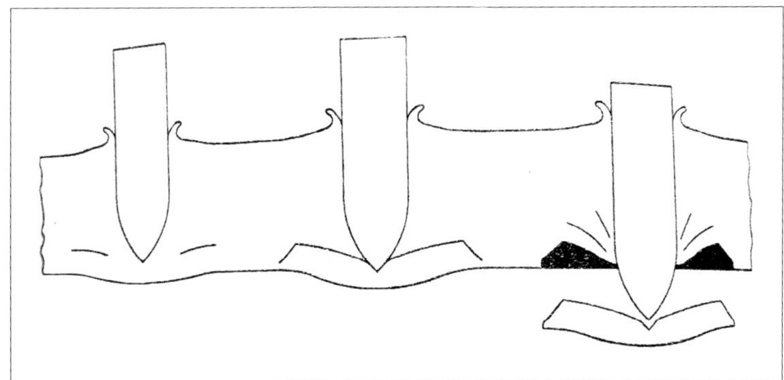

Fig. 2.5a. (*Armour Section, School of Tank Technology*)

Code R -
flake off

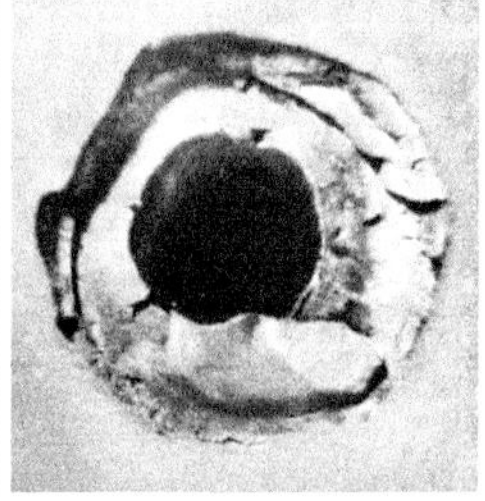

Code W -
flake off shot through

Fig. 2.5b. (*Armour Section, School of Tank Technology*)

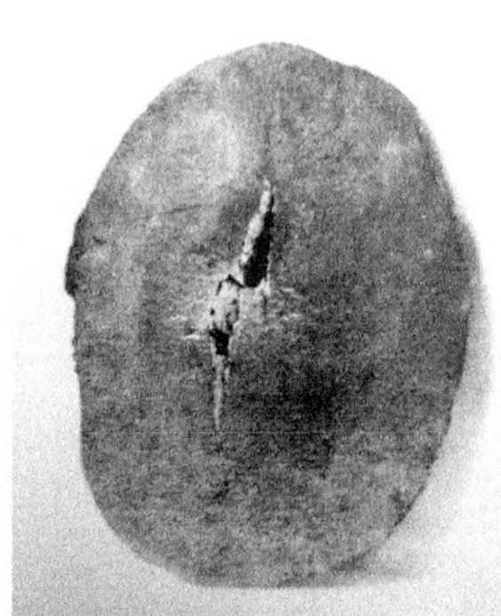

Disc.

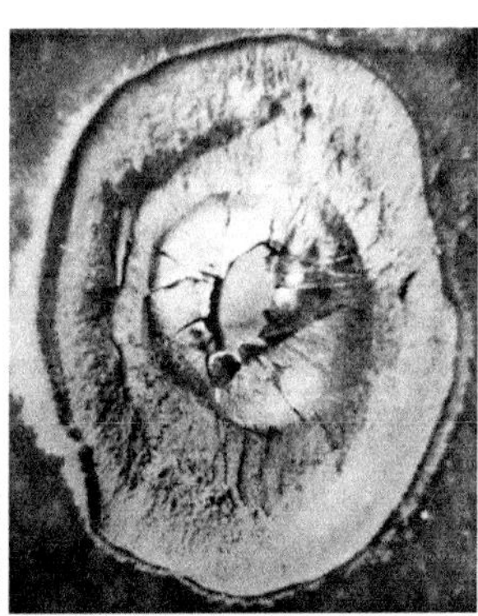

Plate back-damage.

Fig. 2.5c. (*Armour Section, School of Tank Technology*)

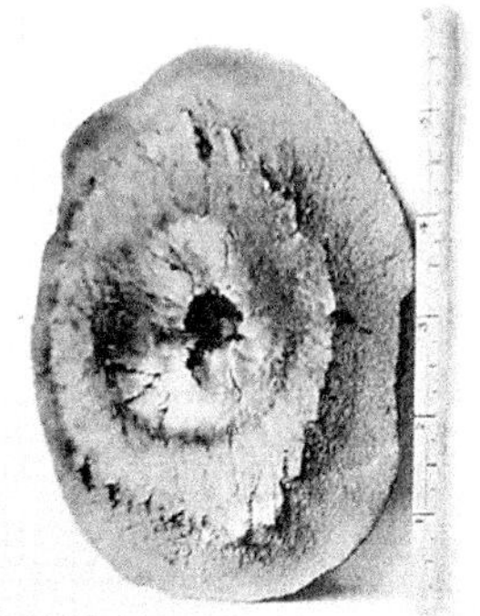

Further views of disc shown in Fig. 2.5c.

Fig. 2.5d. (*Armour Section, School of Tank Technology*)

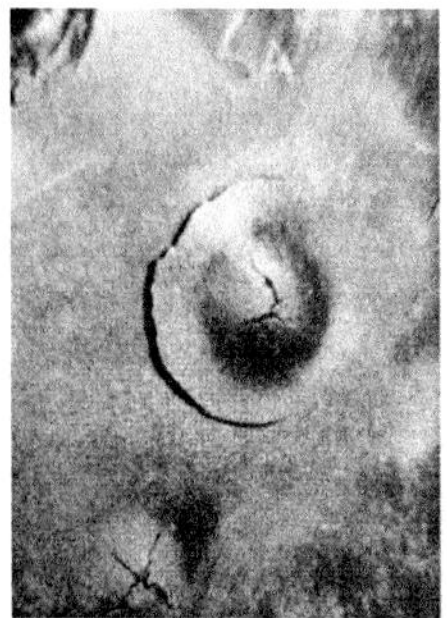

Code D.
Moderate bulge
with circumferential
fracture.

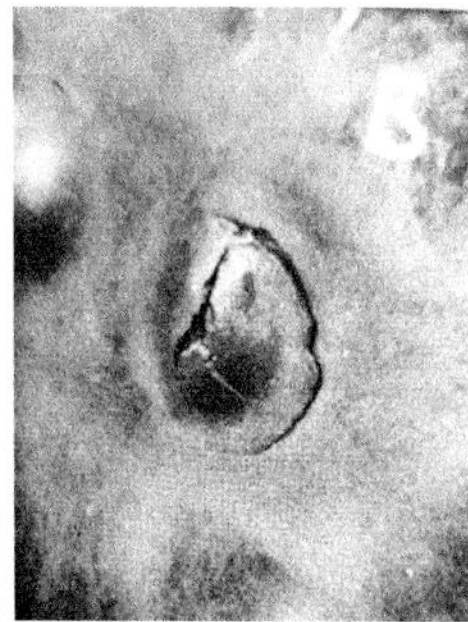

Code E.
Extension of
previous damage.

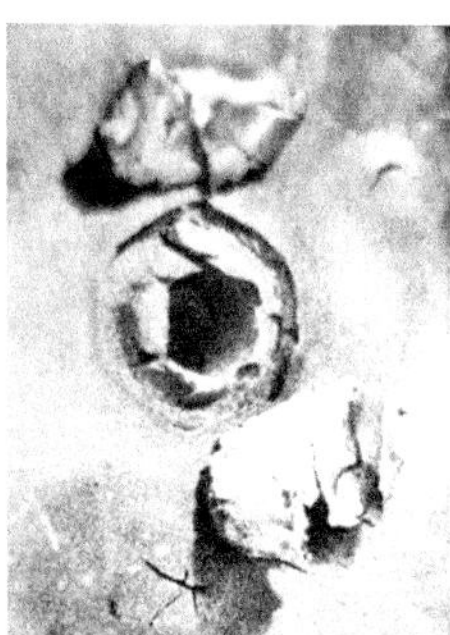

Code W.
Metal off in two
pieces. Shot through.

Fig. 2.5e. (*Armour Section, School of Tank Technology*)

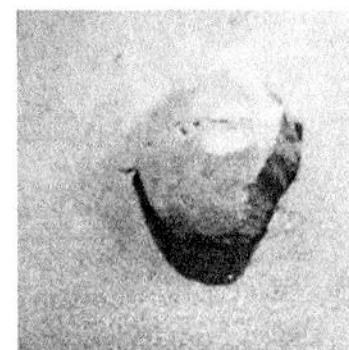

Code D.
Plugging started.

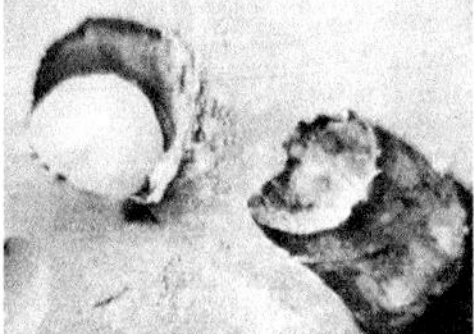

Code R.
Plug out & shot not through.

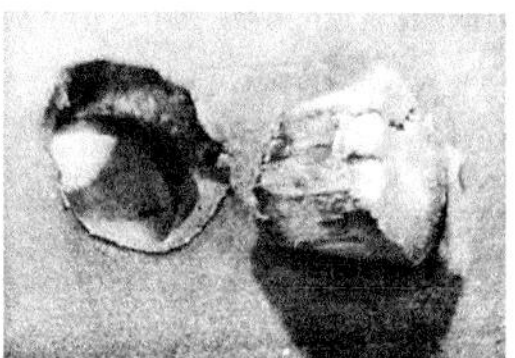

Code W.
Plug out & shot through

Fig. 2.5f. (*Armour Section, School of Tank Technology*)

the separation of the bulged metal into normal segments goes on, but almost simultaneously, the increased tension causes complete fracture around the circumference of the bulge. Under these circumstances, the displaced metal is usually broken into two or more segments. (Damage should be described as "Normal, segments broken off", giving maximum dimensions of metal off. In summarising the back damage on armour of this type, the description, "Tendency to Flake" should be added).'

Plugging: It is quite different from the types of damage so far considered and is illustrated in Fig. 2.5f. DTD's description is: 'Severe Plugging—Pressure of shot causes separation by pure shear of an approximately cylindrical plug. The plug usually bears a deep impression of the shot nose and maybe, in length, from ⅓ to ¾ of the plate thickness. Its maximum diameter is usually from 1 ¼ to 1 ½ times the shot calibre. Only slight bulging of the plate is apparent before separation, with small cracks in the centre of the bulge. The plug is usually projected rearwards at angles to the plate. (Damage should be described as "Plug out", giving maximum dimensions of hole and depth of shear. In summarising back damage the term "Severe plugging" should be used, and the lowest SV. At which plugging occurs, quoted).' When comparing R and W (Fig. 2.5f), it should be noted that irrespective of apparent hole size, the conditions at R were such that the shot rebounded while at W it passed through.

Tendency to Plug: Is intermediate between severe plugging and normal damage, and is illustrated in Fig. 2.5g. DTD's description is 'Tendency to Plug—Separation by pure shear, but commencing after deeper penetration than in severe plugging. Taper of plug more acute with corresponding increase in bulging and consistent crack development. Maximum diameter may be from 1 ½ times to nearly twice the calibre of the shot, and it is usual for the plug to break into two or more segments on separating from the plate. Such segments may be projected to the rear at angles of from 35 to 45 degrees to the line of fire. (Damage should be described as "Plug out, in pieces", giving maximum dimensions of hole. In summarising back damage the term "Tendency to Plug" should be used).'

2.6. Lodging of shot: When an undamaged shot is held in the plate after penetration it is said to be 'lodged', and the condition is denoted by the suffix (L). The suffix does not necessarily indicate how far the shot has penetrated, and if accurate information is required in this respect, it is usually added as a separate note. The condition is illustrated in Fig. 2.6a.

2.7. Code E—Lodged: The definition of code E stipulates that light must be able to pass through the cracked bulge. When the penetration is filled with a lodged shot however, it becomes obvious that this condition cannot be complied with. In this case, a careful examination of the rear cracking is made, and the damage is reported as code E(L) if any portion of the shot can be seen through the interstices of the cracked bulge, as in Fig. 2.8a.

Code D.
Plugging started.

Code R.
Plug out in pieces.

Code W.
Plug out in three pieces.

Fig. 2.5g. (*Armour Section, School of Tank Technology*)

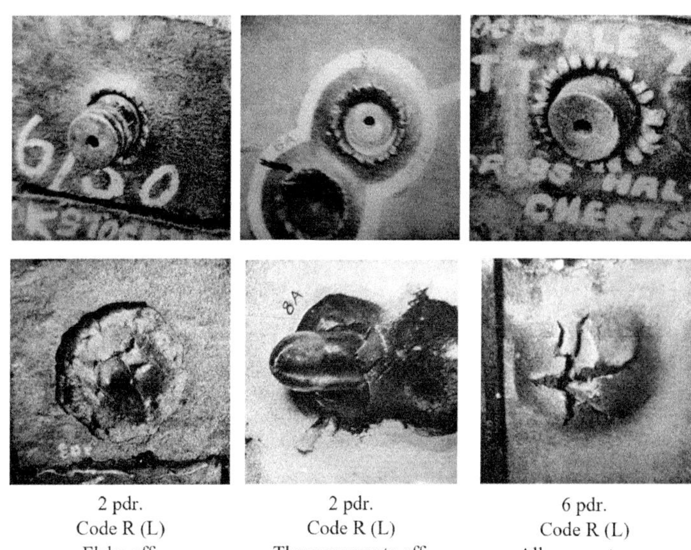

2 pdr.
Code R (L)
Flake off.

2 pdr.
Code R (L)
Three segments off.

6 pdr.
Code R (L)
All segments on.

Fig. 2.6a. (*Armour Section, School of Tank Technology*)

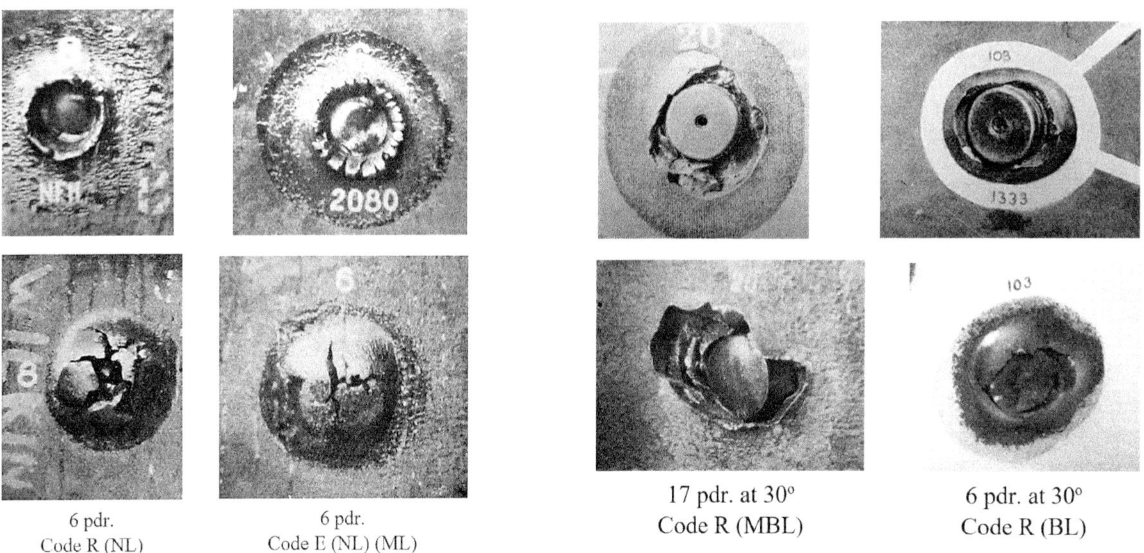

6 pdr.
Code R (NL)

6 pdr.
Code E (NL) (ML)

Fig. 2.8a. (*Armour Section, School of Tank Technology*)

17 pdr. at 30°
Code R (MBL)

6 pdr. at 30°
Code R (BL)

Fig. 2.8b. (*Armour Section, School of Tank Technology*)

2.8. Shot which break up: In the previous discussion, care was taken to stipulate that the shot remained undamaged. However, it sometimes happens that the shot breaks up into a number of pieces, which might be fitted together again to resemble the original projectile. This phenomenon is important in the assessment of R and W damage, and will be discussed by an examination of the examples shown in Figs. 2.8a and 2.8b.

Nose lodged (NL): the pieces which are lodged in the plate is the nose only, a term which covers the portions up to the complete head of the shot. The definition implies that the middle and base have rebounded. In the example shown the head is broken into a number of pieces which can be checked on the actual plate from the fact that the nose can be moved about, while the lower proportion of the head is fixed firmly in the penetration.

Nose lodged, middle lodged (NL) (ML): implies that the base only has rebounded. In the example shown, the damage is assessed as code E since on actual examination, the shot nose can be seen through the interstices of the cracked bulge. When (NL) is included in the suffix it may usually be assumed that no proportion of the shot has succeeded in passing through the plate as a missile

The examples shown in Fig. 2.8b. Illustrating (MBL), (BL) described below, are strikes of 30 degrees impact angle. The angle of impact may be neglected for present purposes of definition.

Middle and base lodged (MBL): Usually indicates that the nose has succeeded in passing through the plate as a missile or missiles.

Base lodged (BL): usually indicates that the nose and part of the body have succeeded in passing through the plate as a missile or missiles.

Middle lodged (ML): (no example shown) the middle proportion only lodged.

2.9. Influence of breakup on assessment at R and W: The definitions of R and W apply to conditions other than those considered for undamaged shot. At present, it suffices to say that examples (MBL) and (BL) of Fig. 2.8b would be defined as W for specific purposes.

2.10. Other designations in the armour code: Other conditions, including a bleak attack and shot shattering, which will be considered later, are included in the armour code.

2.11. Definitions:

AP shot: A solid armour-piercing shot without additional modifications such as piercing and ballistic caps.

Machineable quality armour: Armour which is still sufficiently soft to be machined when assembled in the vehicle.

Impact angle: The angle between the plate and the line of flight of the projectile on impact. In British service, the angle is measured from the normal to the plate surface.

Striking velocity: The velocity with which the projectile strikes the armour.

Remaining velocity: The velocity of the projectile at any specified point on its trajectory.

Ordnance Board Proceeding: The Ordnance Board is an advisory board consisting of representatives of the three services, and scientific associations. The board publishes certain of its transactions in the form of Ordnance Board Proceedings (secret).

Missile: Is used here in a special sense. The definition includes any object which is projected freely through or from the back of the armour was sufficient velocity to be capable of inflicting wounds or damage. The term 'freely' has been included to imply that any proportion of a projectile which remains lodged, irrespective of its distance of protrusion, is not counted as a missile. In a fighting vehicle, the term 'object' is very wide in definition and may include various materials from shot and armour debris to the interior paint substance, which latter may be capable of producing eye wounds.

TUNISIA FIRING TRIALS REPORTS

Unfortunatly, many of the original photographs contained in these reports were of poor quality and some were out of focus. The information in this chapter has been transcribed from original wartime documents. The report format and brief notation style has been kept.

TUNISIA FIRING TRIALS REPORT 19 MAY 1943

Appendix 'B' to Special Report On German Pz.Kw.VI 'Tiger' Dated 5 June 1943

Report of Preliminary Firing Trial Carried Out on German Pz.Kw. VI 'Tiger'

Object of Trial: To investigate the resistance of the side armour of Pz.Kw.VI to attack by 75-mm APCBC 6-pdr AP, and 2-pdr AP shot.

Place of Trial: Beside main road from BEJA to SIDI N'SIR.

Date of Trial: 19 May 1943

Range: 100 yards.

Equipments and ammunition used:

1. 75-mm M.3 Gun in Sherman Tank firing APCBC M61 shot (new gun -5 EFC)
2. 6-pdr Mk III (worn gun) in Churchill tank firing AP shot, Low-Velocity charge. Cartridge stamped ECC Lot 349, 1942, on base.
3. 2-pdr Mk X (worn gun) in Churchill Tank firing AP shot High-Velocity charge.

1. Introduction

The hull allocated for this trial could not be moved from the place where it was found and firing was restricted by the presence of live minefields. It lay at an angle of 5 degrees to the horizontal, which could not be altered. In order to get a 100[x] point, a 50[x] [In order to get a 100-yard range point, a 50 yard] safe lane had to be made in a minefield which involved detecting and blowing up a number of mines which were in an extremely dangerous condition. The hull itself was beside a main road; a railway and second road were just beyond. Considerations of time and safety made it impossible to extend the range.

2. Account of Trial

Shoot 1: 75-mm APCBC M61 Shot from new 75-mm M.3 Gun.

The equipment used was in a new condition, only 5 EPC having been fired. The striking velocity at 100 yards was therefore probably about 2,020 f.s.

Against the 62-mm lower side plate one round was fired at 30 degrees. A complete penetration was obtained, with a flake dislodged from the back (photos 1 and 2).

Against the 82-mm side structure firing was opened at 30 degrees. This gave a scoop with a very slight bulge at the back (photo 3). The angle was progressively reduced until a 16.5-degree complete penetration was obtained.

At 18.5 degrees one round was fired which failed to penetrate, giving 'D' damage (photos 4, 5, 6, 7).

Thus the W/R limit of this plate at 17.5-degree angle of impact is about 2,020 f.s.

On the outside of the plate or displaced metal sheared away leaving a very jagged and irregular entry hole for shot. (Note photo 4). The metal displaced from the back of the overmatching round at 16.5 degrees was 11 × 6 inches.

Shoot 2: 6-pdr AP shot from 6-pdr Mk III gun (worn) with low-velocity charge.

The gun used was well worn, but it was not possible to make accurate wear measurements. It is not likely that the muzzle velocity would be much less than 2,500 ft. sec. nor more than 2,600 ft. sec. This puts the striking velocity at 100 yards between about 2,520 and 2,430 ft. sec.

Attack was commenced at 30 degrees on the 82-mm plate, the same as in shoot 1. The shot shattered, the usual shattering dents being found on the outside of the plate. The angle of impact was reduced to 20 degrees, 15 degrees, and then to 5 degrees, but the same result was obtained—shot shatter. Due to a tilt of the vehicle of 5 degrees, shooting at less than this angle of impact was impossible.

Shoot 3: 2-pdr AP shot from 2-pdr. Mk X (worn) with high-velocity charge.

This gun was also well worn. The muzzle velocity with this ammunition would probably be between 2,650 and 2,750 ft. sec. giving a striking velocity of between about 2,540 and 2,640 ft. sec. at 100 yards.

The 62-mm plate was attacked at Normal horizontal angle, the angle of tilt being 5 degrees. The first round passed through three bogies before hitting the plate which it failed to penetrate.

The second round was a fair hit clear of all bogie wheels and lodged hole in the plate. A flake was displaced from the back, the damage being an R/L.

3. Observation.

(1) The actual thickness of the plates could not be measured so that they may vary from the 82 mm and 62 mm found in similar models.

(2) The tank had had a small fire in the base, but the ballistics of the armour were not impaired as was shown by the 2-pdr AP shot which failed to score a complete penetration through the 62 mm plate.

(3) The shattering of the 6-pdr AP shot against the 82-mm plate at all angles down to 5 degrees suggest that some surface hardening was present. Shatter is extremely unlikely to occur against homogenous plate at this velocity, at this low angle of impact. The jagged holes produced by the 75-mm APCBC shot tend to confirm this, though indicate flame hardening rather than true case hardening, since no actual flaking occurred on the outer surface.

(4) The resistance of both plates to penetration appears considerably higher than that of the British Machinable Quality Armour. The W/R of the 82-mm plate at 17.5 degrees was about 2,020 f.s. against American 75-mm M61. A thickness of about 92 mm of British armour would be expected to have this limit.

The 62-mm plate was not completely penetrated by the 2-pdr AP shot at 5 degrees at a striking velocity probably about 2,500 f.s. Yet about 82 mm of British Machinable Quality Armour to I.T. 80 D would be expected to have a W/R limit at this velocity and angle.

Detailed Firing Results

Shoot 1: 75-mm APCBC M61 shot versus 62-mm and 82-mm side plates. Striking velocity approximately 2,020 f.s.

No. of Rounds	Horizontal angle of attack	Angle of impact including tilt of 5 degrees	Code damage	Description	Photo Illustrating
62-mm plate					
	30 degrees	30 degrees	W	Complete penetration. Flake off back. Crack 10 inches long extending to the right of the hole (photo 1).	1 & 2
82-mm plate					
1	30 degrees	30 degrees	C	Scoop 4.5 × 3.75 inches, 0.75 inches deep. Smooth bulge at back.	3
2	20 degrees	21 degrees	D	Scoop 6 × 4.5 inches, 2.5 inches deep. Shot rebounded. Displaced metal sheared off.	4
3	20 degrees	21 degrees	C	Scoop 5 × 4.5 inches, 1.5 inches deep. Displaced metal sheared out.	4

4	15.5 inches	16.5 inches	W	Complete penetration. Shot recovered whole from inside tank. Flake dislodged. Metal off back 11 × 6 inches. On front displaced metal sheared off in irregular fashion leaving jagged entry hole. Photos 5 and 6 show front and 7 the rear damage	5, 6 & 7
5	17.5 inches	18.5 inches	D	Scoop 5.5 × 4.5 inches, 2.5 inches deep. Displaced metal sheared out leaving very irregular outline of scoop.	5

Shoot 2: 6-pdr AP shot versus 82-mm side plates. Striking velocity approximately 2,420 f.s. and 2,520 f.s.

No. of Rounds	Horizontal angle of attack	Angle of impact including tilt of 5 degrees	Code damage	Description	Photo Illustrating
1	30 degrees	30 degrees	NFH	Shot scooped top of plate.	8
2	30 degrees	30 degrees	C	Shatter dent 3.5-inch diameter 1.5 inches deep. Shot shattered.	8
3	30 degrees	30 degrees	C	Shatter scoop 3.5 inches diameter 1.25 inches deep. Shot shattered.	8
4	20 degrees	21 degrees	C	Shatter scoop 4 × 3.5 inches, 1.25 inches deep. Shot shattered.	9
5	15 degrees	16 degrees	C	Shatter scoop 4.75 × 4 inches, 1.5 inches deep. Shot shattered.	9
6.	Normal	5 degrees	C	Hit edge of 75-mm shot scoop but again produced a shatter scoop. Pieces of shot remained embedded in plate	None

Shoot 3: 2-pdr AP shot versus 62-mm side plates. Striking velocity estimated to be between 2,540 f.s. and 2,640 f.s.

No. of Rounds	Horizontal angle of attack	Angle of impact including tilt of 5 degrees	Code damage	Description	Photo Illustrating
1	N	5 degrees	NFH	Shot penetrated 3 bogies before striking plate. Only small impression produced.	
2	N	5 degrees	RCL	Shot lodged holed. Flake off back. Front displaced metal sheared off.	10

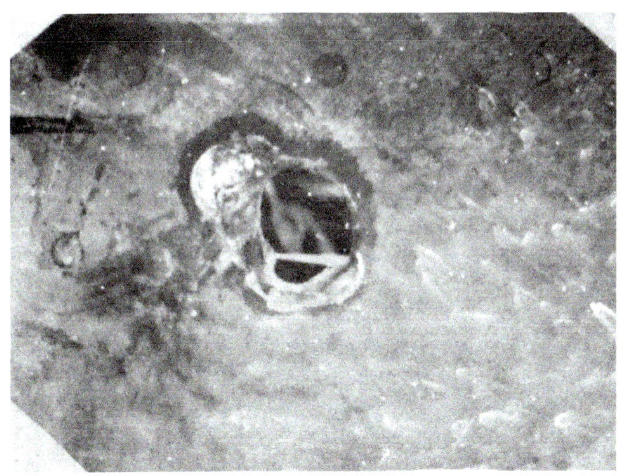

❮ 75-mm APCBC M61 shot *v.* 62-mm side plates of a Tiger. Complete penetration. Flake off back. (*DTD*)

❯ 75-mm APCBC M61 shot *v.* 62-mm side plates of a Tiger. Complete penetration. Flake off back. (*DTD*)

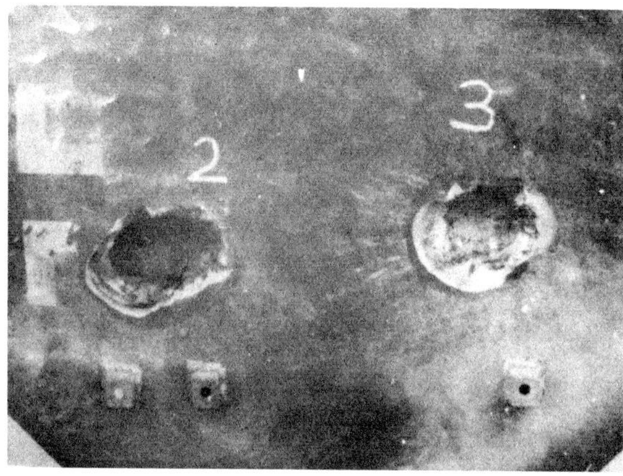

‹ 75-mm APCBC M61 shot *v.* 82-mm side plates of a Tiger. Scoop 4.5 × 3.75 inches, 0.75 inches deep with a smooth bulge at the back. (*DTD*)

› 75-mm APCBC M61 shot *v.* 82-mm side plates of a Tiger. Round No. 2: Scoop 6 × 4.5 inches, 2.5 inches deep. Shot rebounded. Displaced metal sheared off. Round No. 3: Scoop 5 × 4.5 inches, 1.5 inches deep. Displaced metal sheared out. (*DTD*)

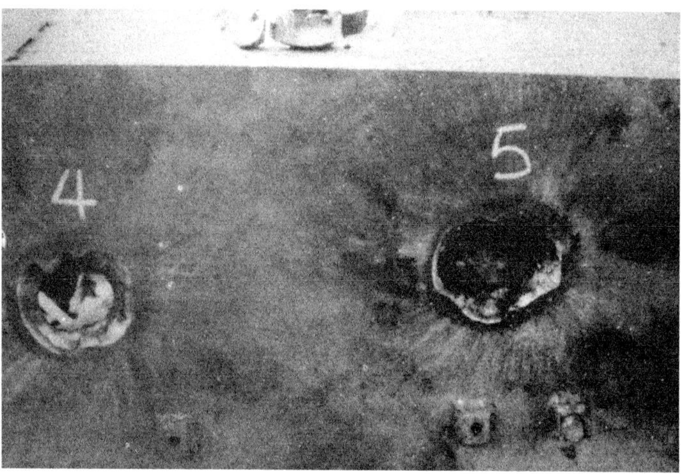

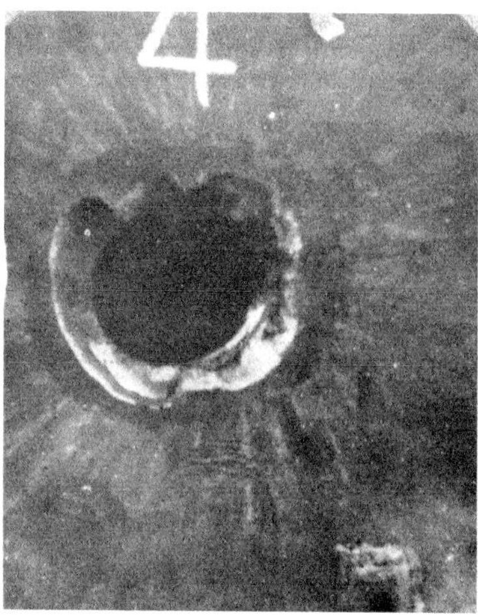

‹ 75-mm APCBC M61 shot *v.* 82-mm side plates of Tiger. Round No. 4: complete penetration. Shot recovered whole from inside tank. Round No. 5: scoop 5.5 × 4.5 inches, 2.5 inches deep. Displaced metal sheared out leaving very irregular outline of scoop. (*DTD*)

› 75-mm APCBC M61 shot *v.* 82-mm side plates of a Tiger. Round No. 4: complete penetration. Shot recovered whole from inside the tank. (*DTD*)

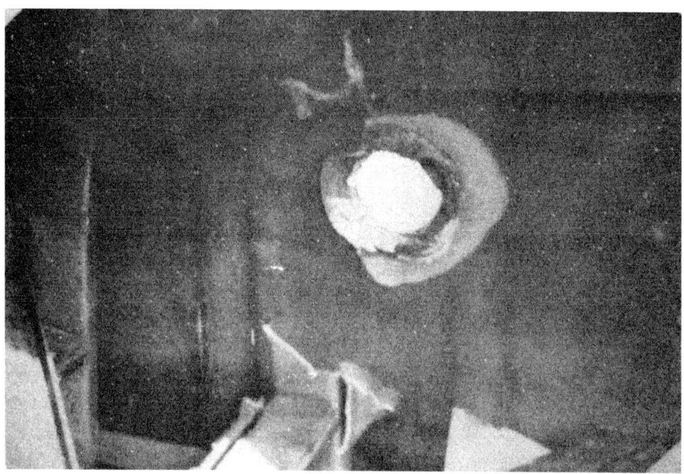

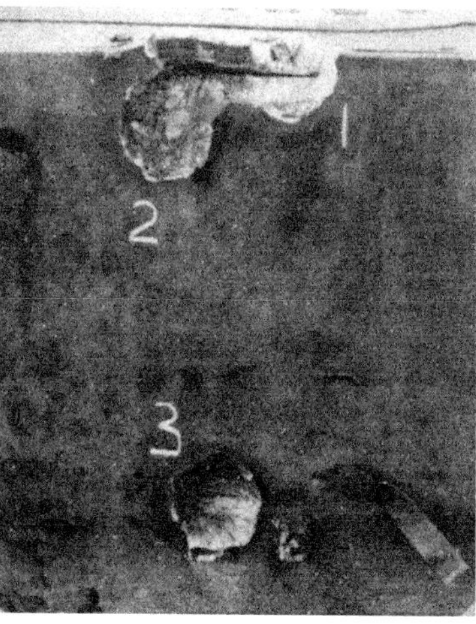

‹ 75-mm APCBC M61 shot *v.* 82-mm side plates of a Tiger. Round No. 4: complete penetration. Shot recovered whole from inside the tank. (*DTD*)

› 6-pdr AP shot *v.* 82-mm side plates. Round No. 1: shot scooped from the top of the plate. Round No. 2: shatter dent 3.5 inches diameter, 1.5 inches deep. Shot shattered. Round No. 3: Shatter scoop 3.5 inches diameter, 1.25 inches deep. Shot shattered. (*DTD*)

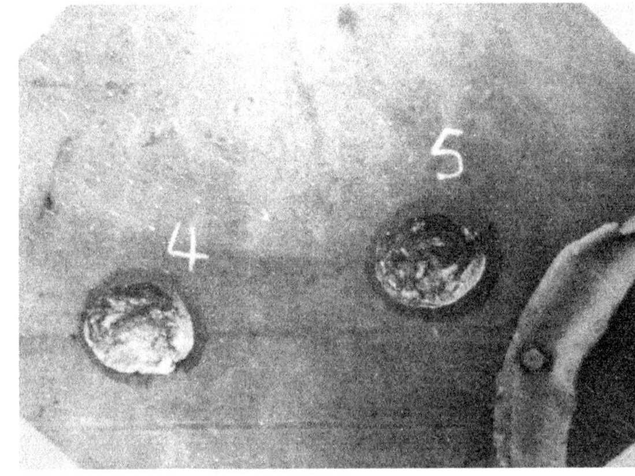

‹ 2-pdr AP shot versus 62-mm side plates. Shot lodged holed. Flake off back. Front displaced metal sheared off. (*DTD*)

› 6-pdr AP shot versus 82-mm side plates. Round No. 4: Shatter scoop 4 × 3.5 inches, 1.25 inches deep. Shot shattered. Round No. 5—Shatter scoop 4.75 × 4 inches, 1.5 inches deep. Shot shattered. (*DTD*)

Tunisia Firing Trials Report: 30 October 1943

Photo No. 1: This photograph shows what the Tiger tank hull used in the firing trails in Tunisia in October 1943 looked like before the trials started. (*Department of Tank Design*)

Secret
Report No. M6816a/4 No. 1.
Department of Tank Design
Materials Division
Armour Branch

Subject
Firing trial in Tunisia against the hull of a Pz.Kw. VI.

Remarks
The armour tested in this trial was all of homogeneous machinable type, but, as it was pointed out in DTD Experimental report M. 6816A/2 No. 1, the composition of samples of similar plates, taken from other tanks, tested in this country was such as to allow of flame-hardening.

The quality of the armour was variable and not up to the high standard of the samples of thinner German homogeneous armour taken from the Pz.Kw. III and IV. The ballistic resistance was, in general, comparable to that of British MQ type the German armour behaved very badly under overmatching. All the plates plugged severely, some flaked and some cracked, while one plate broke up.

The 6-pdr projectiles used in the trial behaved moderately well, but the behaviour of the 17-pdr. AP was disappointing.

Future Action

It is recommended that armoured plates should be produced in this country, some tempered and some flame-hardened, according to German practice, and that trials should be carried out on an adequate scale to determine the most efficient projectiles for attacking both the Tiger and Panther tanks. It is tentatively suggested that the trials may bring out the superiority of APBC over all other projectiles as long as the German armour remains of the same type found on the Pz.Kw. VI.

(A.T. Bowden)
Assistant Director (Armour)
(A.A.M. Durrant)
Director
30. 10. 1943.
M. 440 (o)
ID.

INDEX AND SUMMARY

1. Introduction: object of trial.
2. Conduct of trial.
3. Details of guns, projectiles and adjusted charges.
4. Target details, including details of battle damage.
5. Details of trials.
6. Summarised table of vulnerable ranges and ballistic view of the various German plates.
7. Summarised table of results from previous trials and of damage in battle.
8. Assessment of German armour. All the plates were of machinable quality, appreciably harder than British armour of the same type. The ballistic quality of the armour proved to be variable: in general, it had a ballistic resistance comparable to that of the British MQ armour. When overmatched, the German armour failed more suddenly and more disastrously. It plugged badly and showed both flaking and cracking tendencies. One plate proved to be of outstandingly bad quality. Two plates have broken up in trials.
9. Behaviour of 6-pdr AP and APC shot. The AP shot behaved moderately well. A few rounds shattered unexpectedly: all the rounds shattered at 30 degrees against the 82-mm plates. This was not unexpected.

   Two rounds of APC fired at 30 degrees also shattered.

   At normal attack against the same plate, the AP had an advantage of some 350 yards over the APC.

   The 6-pdr AP, MV 2,925 f.s., will defeat the driver's plate (102 mm at 10 degrees) at about 650 yards, but it is unlikely ever to defeat the nose plate (102 mm at 25 degrees).
10. Behaviour of 17-pdr AP shot. This was disappointing. The shot broke up constantly though it defeated the nose plate at about 1,800 yards.
11. Recommendations.

   A series of trials against specially produced British plates is recommended, with a view to finding the most efficient projectiles against the two heavy German tanks, the Tiger and the Panther.

Appendix A: round by round firing trial reports.
Appendix B: photographs.

1. Introduction

The trial was carried out to investigate the quality of the armour in the German Pz.Kw.VI tank and determine its resistance to British and American projectiles. Only the hull of the tank was available trial. The present report brings forward Captain Martin's and discusses the results obtained.

2. Conduct of Trial

Place: Bon Ficha, Tunisia.
Date: 30 July to 3 August, 13 August 1943.
Present: Lt. Col. W.J.C. Hayward W.T.S.F.F., Capt. A.R.F. Marin AFV(T), Capt. C.A. Rock, 2 Calibration Troop R.A.

3. Guns Used

(1) 6-pdr Mk II, No. L.22472.
(2) 17-pdr Mk I L/192/FL6106
(3) 75-mm M.3 in Sherman Tank M4A1.

The 6-pdr and 17-pdr were provided by the 81st A/Tk Regiment R.A. Both were new guns, the 6-pdr having fired 26 EFC rounds and the 17-pdr unknown, but fewer, EFC rounds. The Sherman tank was provided by the 2nd Tk. Group of the United States Army. The gun was stated to have fired less than 10 EFC rounds.

Charge Weights

The charges for the 6-pdr and 17-pdr were adjusted by extracting propellant through the primer holes. This process could not be carried out with the 75-mm ammunition because of the fixed primers. A number of rounds were broken down by Ordinance at Tripoli and made up into a series of specified charges.

Shot

The 6-pdr and uncapped shot and the 17-pdr uncapped shot were of mixed batches and makers. Details of each round fired are given at Appendix A.

4. TARGET DETAILS (SEE PHOTO 1 GENERAL VIEW)

This consisted of a Pz.Kw.VI (Tiger) tank, without turret, recovered from a workshop. It had been fitted with bogies and narrow road tracks, but all internal fittings had been removed. A few small brackets were found welded to the site superstructure on the outside of the tank. The tank had not been burnt out or damaged by fire.

Battle damage to the tank from AP and HE attack was found entirely on the port flank. (See photo 2)

Photo No. 2: Damage received in battle. Strikes by at least two HE rounds (note the cracks) with one AP hole. (*Department of Tank Design*)

Details of damage are:

(a) Hole in port side superstructure, 3.5 by 2.25 inches, with flake off, 8.5 inches in diameter 3 radial cracks extended some 15, 14 and 7 inches from the hole. Rust made it difficult to assess the exact fate of the round, but it was considered that no perforation [had] taken place. The report does not say what calibre of shot had caused the damage.

(b) Cracking and surface scoring from HE shell, probably 25-pdr, on the port side superstructure. There were two strikes from HE about 12 inches apart. The plate was extensively cracked over about 4 feet, the cracks going right through the plate. No metal had come off. Fittings might have been dislodged by the shock of the impacts, but there would have been no other internal damage.

(c) A strike from a 6-pdr AP shot between the bogies started a plug, some 3-inch diameter, without quite dislodging it.

The tilts of some of the plates were measured by means of an optical protractor, working to the true horizon. The angles were as follows:–

Front lower plate	25 degrees
Driver's visor plate	10 degrees
Rear plate	10 degrees

5. Details of Trials

A. Target: Starboard side superstructure, 82-mm Plate, Brinell Probably About 330

(a) 6-pdr AP At normal.

Estimated B.L. = 1,922 f.s.

Estimated W/R limit = 1,963 f.s.

The plate did not stand up well to overmatching of 6 rounds at SVs of 1,956 f.s. and over 3 dislodged flakes of some 6–7-inch diameter, while the other 3 dislodged metal, presumably in the form of segments, to a diameter of 4.5–5 inches.

The shot behaved reasonably well: 3 rebounded whole; 2 lodged whole; one of them showing a circumferential crack 2 inches from the shoulder; 2 perforated hull. A round at high SV (2,622 f.s.) also perforated but was found broken in the tank.

(b) 6-pdr AP at 30 degrees

Four rounds, at SVs 2,397, 2,487, 2,667, 2,635 f.s., shattered harmlessly on the plate. The scoops were from 0.125 to 1-inch deep and 4.5 inches diameter. The third round caused the cracks some 12 inches long from the scoop to the top edge of the plate.

(c) 6-pdr APC at normal

Estimated W/R limit = 2,233 f.s.

The plate behaved as against the AP shot. Only one round perforated, and this dislodged metal to a diameter of 4 inches. A round which holed but lodged, not off a flake of 9-inch diameter: while around at SV 2,119 f.s. started a flake of some 6-inch diameter. This shot rebounded whole.

(d) 6-pdr APC at 30 degrees

Two rounds at SVs 2,440 (estimated) and 2,688 f.s. shattered harmlessly, the latter failing to blow a hole in the plate even know it was a double hit on the previous scoop. (for effects of 6 pounder attack, see photos 3 and 4)

(e) 75-mm APCBC, M61, at normal

Estimated W/R limit 1,810 f.s.

A piece some 4 feet long had been kept clear on the plate for this attack. 2 rounds hold, the plate failing by plugging. The metal dislodged was of some 4.5-inch diameter. A round at SV 1,792 f.s. started a plug and a crack about 1 foot long in the plate. The seventh round knocked out a piece of plate 2 × 1 foot, not near the point of impact. The next round in large the fracture to an area of 3 × 1 foot approximately. 2 rounds rebounded whole. (See photo 5 for damage)

Photo No. 3: Starboard side superstructure (82-mm) back damage, rounds 1–6: 6-pdr AP at normal. Note flake at round 6. Plugs and detached segments at previous rounds. (*Department of Tank Design*)

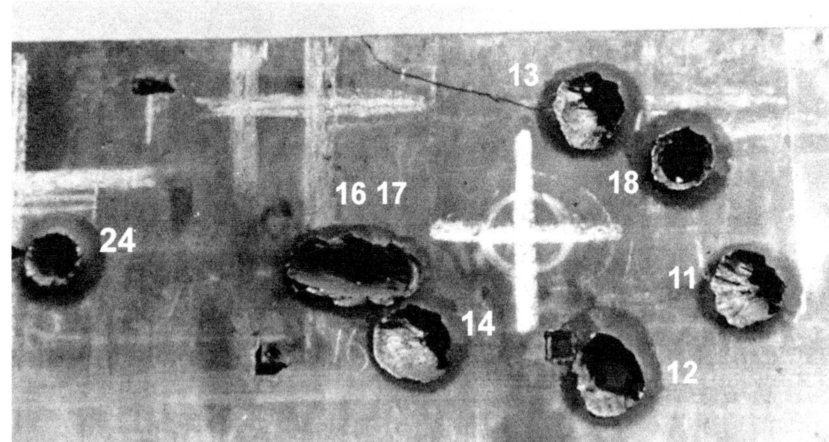

Photo No. 4: Starboard side superstructure (82-mm) front damage. Rounds 11–14: 6-pdr AP shatter scoops; rounds 16–17: 6-pdr APC shatter scoops; round 18 at normal: 6-pdr APC cracked bulge (E); and round 24 at normal: 6-pdr AP cracked bulge (D) (Scoop of Rd 12 perforated in later shot). (*Department of Tank Design*)

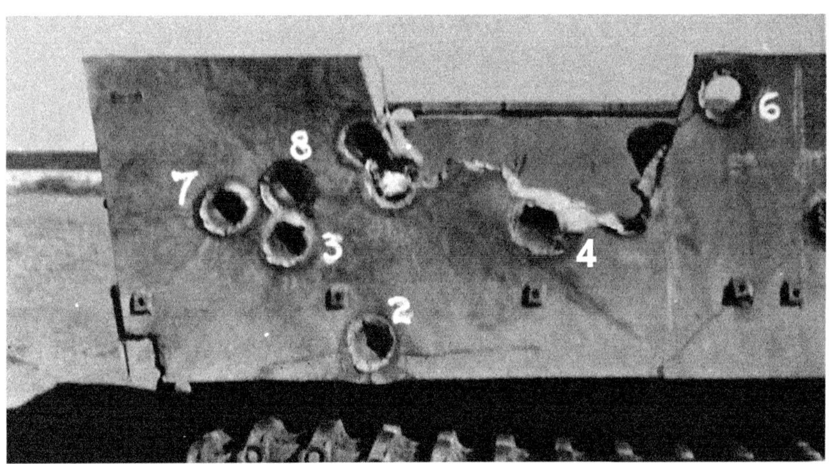

Photo No. 5: Starboard side superstructure. Front damage. 75-mm M.61 (rounds 1–8). Crack caused by round 4 fracture followed rounds 7–8. (*Department of Tank Design*)

B. Target: Port side superstructure. 82-mm plate. Brinell probably about 330.

(a) 6-pdr AP at normal

Estimated (roughly) W/R limit = 1,706 f.s.

This plate behaved very badly indeed. 6 of the 7 rounds fired dislodged flakes off the back, these varying from 7 to 10 inches in diameter. The largest was from a round at SV 1,633 f.s., much damage would have been caused inside the tank at ranges above that regarded as critical (W/R limit).

Only one round is reported to have been found intact inside the tank, while one round rebounded whole. One round, with the marking E. 35B, U.l.O. 1/42, shattered at SV 1,962 f.s.

(b) 6-pdr AP at 30 degrees

One round only, at SV 2,162 f.s. was fired. This shattered completely, the dent caused being only 0.5 inches deep. (For damage see photos 6 and 7)

C. Target: Rear plate, 82-mm thick, tilted at 10 degrees

6-pdr AP at 17 degrees in the horizontal plane: angle of impact 20 degrees

Estimated B. L. = 2,068 f.s.

Assessed W/R limit = 2,116 f.s.

This plate seemed slightly more resistant than the starboard side plate and behaved better under overmatching. Only one flake, of some 4-inch diameter, was dislodged there was one plug at 2,086 f.s and 1 incipient plug at 2,050 f.s. (estimated).

The shot also behaved reasonably well. One round shattered at 2,123 f.s. And one round was recovered inside the tank, slightly distorted and cracked. 2 rounds were recovered whole after rebound and one was found intact and undistorted inside the tank. Another of the E. 35B, U.L.D.4 rounds was fired at SV 2,050 f.s.: This did not shatter. (See photos 8 and 9)

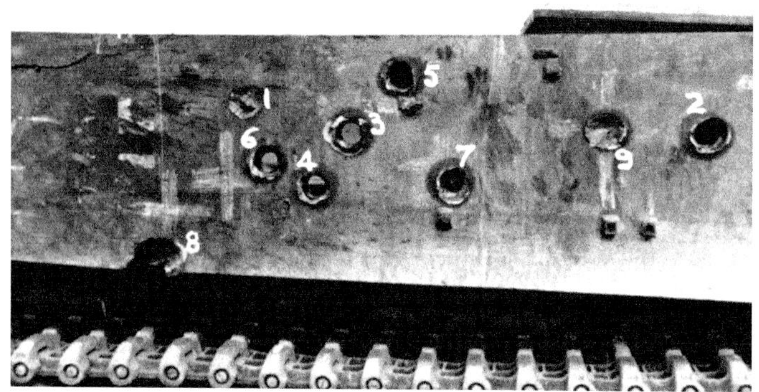

Photo No. 6: Port-side superstructure (82 mm). Rounds 1–7: Front damage, 6-pdr AP at normal and round 9: Front damage, 6-pdr AP at 50 degrees. Note slight surface flaking rounds 3 and 6. Crack at left-hand corner—battle damage (see Photo No. 2). (*Department of Tank Design*)

Photo No. 7: Port-side superstructure (82 mm). Rounds 3–7: Back damage, 6-pdr AP at normal. Note flaking, especially round 7 (R at SV 1,633 f.s.). (*Department of Tank Design*)

Photo No. 8: Rear plates (82 mm at 10-degree tilt). Rounds 1–7: Front view general, 6-pdr AP at 20 degrees. Note: Round 5's shatter scoop SV 2,123 f.s. and round 2's slight surface flaking. (*Department of Tank Design*)

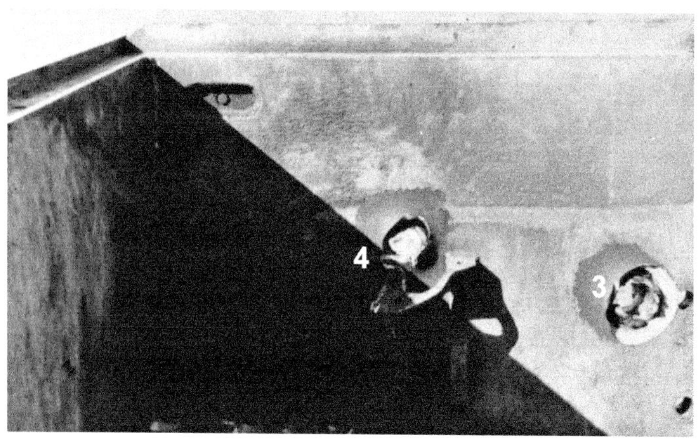

Photo No. 9: Rear plate (62 mm at 10-degree tilt). Rounds 3–4: Back damage, 6-pdr AP at 20 degrees. Note: Flaking at round 3 (W at SV 2,145 f.s.) and plugging at round 4 (R at SV 2,086 f.s). (*Department of Tank Design*)

D. Target: Driver's Visor Plate, 102-mm Thick, Tilted at 10

6-pdr AP from direct ahead: angle of impact 10

Estimated B.L. = 2,264 f.s.

W/R limit = 2,380 f.s.

The plate behaved reasonably well. Only one perforation was scored, this being accompanied by a plug of some 3-inch diameter. There were no signs of flaking or of cracking. The shot behaved somewhat inconsistently. Two rebounded whole, one undistorted and one slightly distorted. Another broke up (not shattered) ineffectively at SV 2,382 f.s. A fourth lodged hole at SV 2,403 f.s. (See photo 10)

Photo No. 10: (a) driver's visor plate (102 mm at 10 degrees). Rounds 1–8: Front view, 6-pdr AP from direct ahead; note fair petalling. (b) Front nose plate (102 mm at 25 degrees). Rounds 6–7: Front view: 6-pdr AP from direct ahead and rounds 1–5:17-pdr AP from direct ahead; note absence of petalling and 6-pdr shatter from round 7 (SV 2,600 f.s. approx.). (*Department of Tank Design*)

E. Target: Lower Front Plate, 102-mm Thick, Tilted at 25 Degrees

(a) 6-pdr AP from direct ahead: angle of impact 25 degrees

Only 2 rounds were fired. One at 2,531 f.s. gave D and rebounded severely distorted and with nose broken off at the shoulder. The second at 2,620 f.s. (estimated) shattered, leaving a scoop 1 inch deep.

(b) 17-pdr AP from direct ahead: angle of impact 25 degrees

Estimated B.L. = 1,862 f.s.

Estimated W/R limit = 1,975 f.s.

This plate plugged badly but showed no flaking tendency. Plugs were knocked out at velocities down to 1,905 f.s. The round themselves broke up into large fragments. One round rebounded and was recovered in 3 large pieces. (For damage see photo 10)

6. Vulnerable Ranges and Worth of Plates

The following table summarises the results in terms of vulnerable ranges, and the values of the plates in terms of British MQ armour.

Plate	Gun	Projectile	Angle of attack	Muzzle Velocity in f.s.	Vulnerable ranges in yards		Approximate value in mm of British MQ Plate	
					BL Level	WR Level	BL Level	WR Level
1. Starboard side super-structure 82 mm	6–pdr	AP	Normal	2,925 2,675	1,300 975	1,250 925	86	80
	6–pdr	AP	30 degrees	Four shatter failures at SVs 2,397–2,667 f.s.				
3. Starboard side super-structure 82 mm	6–pdr	APC	Normal	2,900 2,650	– –	875 525	– –	85 (OB43/CV/2)
4. Starboard side super-structure 82 mm	6–pdr	APC	30 degrees	Two shatter failures at SVs 2,400 (estimated) and 2,688 f.s.				
5. Starboard side super-structure 82 mm	75 mm	M. 61 (USA)	Normal	2,050	–	900	–	–

6. Port side super-structure 82 mm	6–pdr	AP	Normal	2,925 2,675	–	1,650 1,300	– –	65 –
7. Port side super-structure 82 mm	6–pdr	AP	30 degrees	Shatter failure at 2,162 f.s.				
8. Rear plate 82 mm at 10 degrees	6–pdr	AP	20 degrees	2,925 2,675	1,100 750	1,050 700	85 –	82 –
9. Driver's visor plate 102 mm at 10 degrees	6–pdr	AP	10 degrees	2,925 2,675	800 500	650 350	102 –	102 –
10. Lower front plate 102 mm at 25 degrees	6–pdr	AP	25 degrees	Normal failure at 2,513 f.s. Shatter failure at 2,620 f.s.				
11. Lower front plate 102 mm at 25 degrees	17-pdr	AP	25 degrees	2,900	2,050	1,800	Perhaps 103 mm	

7. Summaries of Other Trials and Battle Damage

Plate	Gun	Projectile	Angle of Attack	Range or SV	Remarks
(a) Lower nose 102 mm	6-pdr Mk II	AP unknown make	21 degrees	300 yards	Firing trial NE. Two rounds failed to perforate. Plate fractured. No shatter of shot.
(b) Turret side 82 mm	6-pdr	Unknown probably AP	30 degrees (?)	650 yards (?)	Battle damage. One round holed (It is thought that the angle of attack is much overestimated)
(c) superstructure side 82 mm	6-pdr	Unknown probably AP	15 degrees (?)	650 yards (?)	One round holed
(d) superstructure side 82 mm	6-pdr	Unknown probably AP	25–30 degrees (?)	650 yards (?)	Two rounds almost through. Plate flaked.
Reference	6-pdr	Unknown probably AP	35–45 degrees (?)	650 yards (?)	3 rounds scooped harmlessly.
(Reference for (a) to (e):		Report by Col. Barlow W.T.S.F.F. About March 1943, brought forward in DTD Experimental Report M. 6816A/1 No. 1)			
(f) superstructure side 82 mm	6-pdr Mk III (worn) L.V. charge	AP	From 5–30 degrees	100 yards (SV 2,400–2,500 f.s.)	Firing trial Shatter of all 6 rounds. Plates thought to be face hardened.
(g) superstructure side 82 mm	75-mm	M. 61 APCBC	From 16–30 degrees	100 yards (SV 2,020 approx.)	Success at 16 degrees. Failures at bigger angles
(Reference for (f) to (g):		Special report issued by Brig Blagden with AFV Technical Report No. 14. Preliminary trial carried out by Captain Martin in May 1943 (in M.E.)			
(h) Driver's visor 102 mm	6–pdr	AP Hadfields	Normal	SV 2,294 f.s.	One round on a piece 12 × 15 inches scored a smooth (c)
(i) Lower front	6–pdr	AP Hadfields	Normal	SV 2,458 f.s.	One round on a piece 13 × 15 inches fractured the piece in two.
(Reference for (h) to (i): DTD Report M. 6816A/2 No. 1)					

8. Assessment of German Armour

(a) 82-mm Plates

Two other specimens, one the turret, the other a superstructure side plate, have been metallurgically examined in this country. (See DTD Experimental Report M. 6816A/2 No. 1 of 3.6.43) The Brinell hardness figures were of the order of 320–340.

In the present trial, 3 plates of this thickness were attacked. There was no evidence to confirm the suspicion raised after the preliminary trial (Section 7f) that the plates were face hardened.

In that they were vulnerable to the 6-pdr at about the same range, 2 of the plates reacted much as one would expect average quality British MQ armour to react. However, as might be expected with the harder German plates, the mode of failure was both more sudden and more disastrous than with the softer British plate. With the latter it needs, in general, some 140 f.s. More striking velocity to pass from the ballistic limit level of plate failure to the W/R (50 per cent perforation) level of failure. With these two German plates increases of 41 and 48 f.s. only were needed.

All three plates flaked to a greater or lesser extent, and all plugged badly. They all tended to crack and one broke up after 6 rounds of heavy attack. (75-mm M 61)

The port side superstructure plate was outstandingly bad. Its ballistic resistance was low, being equivalent to that of only 65 mm of average I.T. 80 D armour, and it flaked severely.

In general, the more indefinite evidence at section 7 confirms this assessment of the armour. Some flaking and a fracture under 6-pdr attack were reported.

(b) 102-mm Plates

Two specimens, one of visor plate, the other a nose plate, have been metallurgically examined (see report M. 6816A/2 No. 1) The first was of Brinell 285/288, the other of Brinell 295/300.

The plates in the present trial provided no more resistance than British MQ plate of the same thickness. There was no evidence of flaking, but there was severe plugging. Failure against the 6-pdr was so sudden as on the 82-mm plates, but it was fairly sudden against the 17-pdr. This again is in accord with the hardness figures. The plate showed a tendency to crack.

Two pieces of another nose plate have been attacked by the 6-pdr, one piece in Africa and one small piece in England. Both fractured (section 7 (a) and (i)).

A piece of visor plate has also been attacked by the 6-pdr in England. The one round fired gave evidence of (1) high ballistic quality, (2) no flaking and (3) no cracking tendency. (DTD Report M6816A/2 No. 1)

Such evidence as is available shows that these plates are also variable in quality.

General

If the armour tested so far is typical of recent German production, the outlook is distinctly encouraging. There is nothing like the same consistently high quality that was found in the specimens of the thinner German machinable quality armour taken from the Pz.Kw.III and Pz.Kw.IV. The hardness of the thicker plate does not materially increase their ballistic resistance above that of softer British armour, hence there is no compensation for the worse behaviour of the German plates when overmatched.

9. Behaviour of 6-pdr Shot

This is summarised as follows:

AP *v*. 82-mm plates

One round at SV 1,962 f.s. shattered at normal attack.

One round at SV 2,123 f.s. shattered at 20-degree attack.

All five rounds at SVs 2,162, 2,397, 2,487, 2,667, 2,635 f.s. shattered at 30-degree attack.

AP *v*. 102-mm plate at 10 degrees

None of the rounds fired shattered, but there was some distortion and break up. One round broke up badly at SV 2,382 f.s.

AP *v*. 102-mm plate at 25 degrees

One round, at SV about 2,600 f.s., shattered. A second round at SV 2,531 f.s. Rebound it, distorted and broke.

APC *v*. 82-mm plate

None of the 3 rounds fired at normal shattered. Both rounds fired at 30 degrees, at SVs 2,440 and 2,680 f.s., shattered.

In the preliminary trial (section 7) all the AP Shot that, fired at 100 yards range and F.S.C., shattered on the 82-mm Superstructure armour at all angles of attack from 30 degrees down to 5 degrees.

In this present trial the 6-pdr AP shot that behaved moderately well, though a few rounds shattered unexpectedly. The shot would be just likely to shatter against a British 82-mm MQ Plate at 30 degrees or against a 102-mm plate at 25 degrees.

As has been stated above, and uncapped shot would be expected to shatter against 82 mm of homogeneous armour at 30 degrees, but the Shot would be expected to defeat it without shatter. Against the German plate, the 2 Shot fired shattered harmlessly. This is a most disappointing result.

The following results have been obtained in the last 12 months in Ordnance Board trials AP 46, 51, 52, 53 and 72 against British homogeneous armour at 30 degrees. Some 80 per cent of the 6-pdr APC Rounds that use were of N.C.F. make and some 20 per cent were of Hadfield's make.

(1) *v.* 80-mm plate:
3 out of 21 rounds, fired at SVs from 2,150 to 2,700 f.s., Shattered.
(2) *v.* 89-mm plate:
2 out of 15 rounds, fired at SVs from 2,073 to 2,867 f.s., Shattered.
(3) *v.* 100-mm plate:
1 out of 9 rounds, fired at SVs from 2,642 to 2,996 f.s., Shattered.

That is, against these British plates, less than 1 in 7 of the rounds shattered. The 2 rounds that shattered against the German 82-mm plate at 30 degrees were of NCF manufacture, dated October and November 1942.

10. Behaviour of 17-pdr AP

The behaviour of the 17-pdr uncapped shot against the relatively easy target of 102 mm at 25 degrees attack was disappointing. All 5 rounds fired broke up into large fragments. Illogically enough two the rounds probably did more damage than a good shot would have done. These two rounds, at SVs 1,905 f.s. and 1,957 f.s., lodged in the plate, but the nose went through, and the bases broke off. Good shot which kept together would, with one round certainly and with both rounds possibly, have lodged whole and nothing would have gone through.

With shot of the quality used in this trial, break up in shatter will be still more prevalent and deleterious against relatively harder targets. In particular the front of the tank will be vulnerable over an arc of fire a good deal smaller than it should be.

11. Recommendations

It is felt that the probable success of the 6-pdr against the Pz.Kw.VI Tiger is so restricted and yet so important that the most affected projectile or projectiles should be immediately available, whether the armour remains of the present machinable type or becomes of a face-hardened type. Similarly, there is an urgent necessity for the development and supply of the most effective 17-pdr projectile against both the Pz.Kw.VI Tiger and the Panther tanks.

It is submitted that extensive trials are needed for comparison to be made between the various possible projectiles, and the following recommendations are made accordingly.

1. Failing an adequate supply of typical German armour, British MQ plates, 60, 80 and 100 mm thick should be produced, these plates being tempered to about the same hardness as those of the corresponding German plates, that is, about 330 and 300 Brinell respectively,

2. An attempt should be made to produce flame hardened armour in thicknesses from 3 to 6 inches, as nearly similar as possible to the type produced by the Germans at 50-mm thickness.

3. Representative lots of 6-pdr AP, APC and APCBC shot, past proof and taken from the biggest maker of each type, should be fired at various angles against the plates at (1) and (2). Polar diagrams for each type of shot against each thickness should then be drawn. (Report author's note: see next paragraph)

4. If the AP shot, judged in terms of striking velocity, is not markedly inferior to the other 2 types, then a 6-pdr APBC shot should be produced and tested, together with the best possible AP, APBC and APCBC, against the 80-mm and 100-mm plates, comparisons to be made by the method of polar diagrams.

(It is pointed out that the slight decrease in MV due to the extra weight of the ballistic will be very slight as compared with that of the AP and that the degradation in perforation performance will probably also be very slight. Hence the APBC will not start with the initial handicaps of the APCBC against MQ Plate)

5. Similar trials should be carried out with respective lots of 17-pdr AP, APBC and APCBC Against the plates at (1) and (2), comparisons to be made by the method of polar diagrams. Again, there may be a case for the development of APBC.

6. The preliminary reports on the type, thickness and tilts of the armour on the Panther should be confirmed as soon as possible. (The hull front plate, for instance, is said to be about 80 mm, at 55 degrees) The trials with the 6-pdr and 17-pdr projectiles should then be extended to plates of the appropriate thickness at the appropriate angles of attack. It is submitted that there have been far too few trials carried out at these very oblique angles.

7. The conditions under which the various projectiles shatter against the plates at (1) and (2) should be carefully investigated, to determine whether these conditions differ appreciably from those obtained against softer British MQ plates.

H. Harris Jones, Major, R.A.
O. i/c Ballistics Section.
M. 407 (s)
rmp

APPENDIX A

Detailed Firing Results

Shoot 1: 6-pdr AP verse Starboard Side Superstructure at Normal

No. of rounds	Batch No.	Shot manufacture	Mk of shot	Wt. of charge removed	Striking velocity	Code damage	Description
å2	E117Q	NCN 7/42	V11T	ozs. 13	NR	E	Cracked bulge 4-inch dia. 1-inch lift. 5 star cracks. Shot recovered whole and undistorted after rebounding. On front wall developed petals.
24	E199M	BSJC 9/42	V11T	12 ½ (HV)	1,898	D	Cracked bulge 4-inch dia. 1 inch high 1 inch. Shot rebounded and was recovered whole.
5	E117Q	NCN 7/2	V11T	12	1,946	E	Cracked bulge 4-inch dia. 1 inch high 1 inch open. Shot rebounded and was recovered whole
4	E118A	NCN 6/42	V11T	11	NR	L sv	Star cracked bulge 1.25 inches open at centre. Tip of shot showing.
25	E199M	BSJC 9/42	V11T	11 (HV)	1,956	R.L.	Flake off 6-inch dia, shot base level with front surface of plate. Circumferential crack in shot 2 inches below shoulder.
6	E121B	NCFG 7/42	V11T	11	1,970	W	Flake off 7-inch dia. Shot recovered whole and undistorted.
1	E117Q	BSNCH 7/42	V11T	11	NR	W	Failure from star cracked bulge. Metal off 4.5 inches dia.
5	E118A	NCFG 6/42	V11T	10	2,067	W	Failure from star cracked bulge. Metal off 3 × 4.5 inches. 2 segments still on.
9	E121B	NCFG 7/42	V11T	10 ½	2,119	W	Flake off 6-inch dia. Shot recovered whole.
10	E140B	BSJMBH 8/42	V11T	0	2,622	W	Failure from star cracked bulge. Metal off 5-inch dia. Shot recovered but base had broken off

Assessed W/R limit: 1,963 f.s.
Estimated Ballistic Limit: 1,922 f.s.
Rounds 7 and 8 at full charge were not fair hits.

Shoot 2: 6-pdr AP *v*. Starboard Side Superstructure at 30 Degrees
High-Velocity Charge

No. of rounds	Batch No.	Shot manufacture	Mk of shot	Wt. of charge removed	Striking velocity	Code damage	Description
11	E119M	BSJC 9/42	V11T	ozs. 5	2,397	Cal	Shatter scoop 4.5-inch dia. 0.125 inches deep
12	E119M	BSJC 9/42	V11T	3	2,487	C	Shatter scoop 4.5-inch dia. 1 inch deep. Smooth bulge 4-inch dia. 0.125 inches high.
13	E119M	BSJC 9/42	V11T	0	2,667	C	Shatter scoop 4.5-inch dia. 1 inch deep. Smooth bulge 4-inch dia. 0.125 inches high. Crack developed in plate 12 inches long to top edge.
14	E140M	BSJMBH 9/42	V11T	0 (LV)	2,635	C	Shatter scoop 4.5-inch dia. 1 inch deep

Shoot 3: 6-pdr APC *v*. Starboard Side Superstructure at 30 Degrees

16	E214H	NCFG 10/42	V11T	4	NR	C	Shatter scoop 4.5-inch dia. 1 inch deep.
17	E214H	NCFG 11/42	V11T	0	2,688	NRH	Double hit on round 16. Shatter scoop. No penetration.

Shoot 4: 6-pdr APC *v*. Starboard Side Superstructure at Normal

18	E214H	NCFG 10/42	V11T	10	2,119	E	Star cracked bulge. 4 star cracks. Flake started 3-inch radius over 90-degree segment. 0.125 inches lift. On front displaced metal sheared off. Shot rebounded and was recovered whole less.
21	E214H	NCFG 11/42	V11T	8	2,205	RL.	Flake off 9-inch dia. Base of shot level with outer face of plate.
23	E214H	NCFG 10/42	V11T	7	2,242	W	Failure developed from a star cracked bulge. Metal off 4-inch dia.

Rounds 19, 20 and 22 were not fair hits. Striking earlier damage or scooping off the edge.
Estimated W/R limit: 2,223 f.s.

Shoot 5: 6-pdr AP *v*. Port-Side Superstructure 82-mm Thick at Normal

High-Velocity Charge

No. of rounds	Batch No.	Shot manufacture	Mk of shot	Wt. of charge removed	Striking velocity	Code damage	Description
1	E35B	ULD4 1/42	V11T	ozs. 11 (LV)	1,968	C	Shatter dent 4-inch dia. 0.125 inches deep
2	E35B	ULD4 1/42	V11T	12 (LV)	1,927	W	Flake off 8-inch dia. On front displaced metal sheared off.
3	E211A	BSJMBH 12/42	V11T	13	1,990	W	Flake off 7-inch dia. 2 inches thick recovered in one piece. Shot found whole and undistorted in tank. On front displaced metal sheared off and flake off 1 inch wide round half circumference.
4	E211A	BSJMBH 12/42	V11T	14 ½	1,835	W	Front displaced metal sheared off, no flaking. Back Flake off 8.5-inch dia.
5	E211A	BSJMBH 12/42	V11T	16	1,803	W	Flake off 8-inch dia. Radial crack 6 inches long.
6	E211A	BSJMBH 12/42	V11T	17 ½	1,776	W	Flake off 7.5-inch dia. Small Flake off front (see photo 5)
7	E211A	BSJMBH 12/42	V11T	19	1,633	R	Flake off 10-inch dia. in one piece. Shot rebounded whole.

Estimated W/R limit: 1,706 f.s.

Shoot 6: 6-pdr AP *v*. Port-Side Superstructure at 30 Degrees

9	E211A	BSJMBH 12/42	V11T	9	2,162	C	Shatter scoop 4-inch dia. 0.5 inches deep.

Round 8 was not a fair hit, scooping off the lower edge.

Shoot 7: 6-pdr AP *v*. Rear Plate 82-mm Tilted at 10-degree HV Charge

Angle in horizontal plane 17 degrees. Angle of impact 20 degrees.

No. of rounds	Batch No.	Shot manufacture	Mk of shot	Wt. of charge removed	Striking velocity	Code damage	Description
2	E199M	BSJC 9/42	V11T	ozs. 10	2,049	D	Bulge 4-inch dia. 1 inch high. Horizontal crack 2 inches long. On front Flake off 2 inches wide 1 inch deep 4 inches long. Displaced metal sheared off. Shot rebounded and was recovered whole.
4	E199M	BSJC 9/42	V11T	9 ½	2,086	R	Plug out. Metal off 2.75-inch dia. Hole 2 × 1.75 inches. Shot rebounded.

5	E199M	BSJC 9/42	V11T	9	2,123	C	Shatter scoop 5 × 4 inches, 1.5 inches deep.
3	E199M	BSJC 10/42	V11T	9	2,145	W	Flake off 4-inch dia. On front displaced metal sheared off. Shot recovered slightly distorted with crack 0.75 inches round circumference 3.5 inches from the base.
1	E199M	SSJC 9/42	V11T	8	2,180	W	Failure from star cracked bulge. Metal off 4-inch dia. Shot recovered whole and undistorted from tank.
7	E35B	ULD 4 1/42	111T	9 ½ (LV)	No result 2,050 expected	E	Plug started 3-inch dia. 2 inches lift. Shot rebounded
6	E35B	ULD 4 1/42	111T	0 (LV)	2,611	W	Failure from a star cracked bulge. Mortal off 4-inch dia. Shot not found but there were no signs of shatter.

Assessed W/R limit: 2,116 f.s. Estimated Ballistic Limit: 2,068 f.s.

Shoot 8. 6-pdr AP *v*. Driver's Visor or Plate 102 mm at 10-Degree Tilt

Attack from dead ahead. High-velocity charge.

3	E199M	BSJC 9/42	V11T	7	2,200	NFH	Hit supported by roof. Crack 6 inches long to top edge
4	E199M	BSJC 9/42	V11T	7	2,238	D	Cracked bulge 4-inch dia. 0.75 inches high. 4 star cracks 0.125 inches open. One front fair petalling, one petal starting to shear off.
5	E199M	BSJC 9/42	V11T	6	2,290	ESL	Cracked bulge 4-inch dia. 3 star cracks 0.25 inches open. Shot rebounded and recovered whole and undistorted.
1	E199M	BSJC 9/42	V11T	5	2,356	W	Plug out. Metal off 3-inch dia. Front fair petalling. Shot recovered whole but slightly distorted.
6	E199M	BSJC 9/42	V11T	5	2,382	C	Smooth bulge 4-inch dia. 0.5 inches high. Deep impression 3-inch dia. 2.5 inches deep. Shot had broken up, a small part of the tip embedded in plate. Part of nose recovered in front of plate.
8	E40U	BSAP RCC 6/42	IV T	3 ½	2,403	RL	Cracked bulge. 3 segments plug out, one still on. Metal off 3 × 2 inches. Shot base level with front surface of plate.

Rounds 2 and 7 were not fair hits, glancing off top of plate.
Estimated W/R limit: 2,380 f.s. Estimated ballistic limit: 224 f.s.

Shoot 9: 6-pdr AP *v*. Front Lower Plate 102 mm Thick

Tilt 25 degrees attack from dead ahead. Low-velocity charge.

No. of rounds	Batch No.	Shot manufacture	Mk of shot	Wt. of charge removed	Striking velocity	Code damage	Description
6	E40U	BSAPRCC 6/42	IVT	ozs. 2	2,531	D	Cracked oval bulge. Horizontal crack 1 inch long, 0.125 inches open. Shot recovered severely distorted with nose broken off at shoulder.
7	E40U	BSAPRCC 6/42	IVT	ozs. 2	No result 2,620 expected	C	Shatter scoop 4-inch dia. 1 inch deep.

Shoot 10: 17-pdr AP *v*. Front Lower Plate 102 mm Thick Tilted 25 Degrees

Attack from dead ahead. Low-velocity charge.

No. of rounds	Batch No.	Shot manufacture	Mk of shot	Wt. of charge removed	Striking velocity	Code damage	Description
4	E.3.G.	JMB 9/42	IIIT	lb 3.5	1,818	D	Bulge 4-inch dia. 1 inch lift. 1 vertical crack 3 inches long. Shot rebounded and broke up into 3 large pieces.
2	E.3.G.	JMB 9/42	IIIT	3	1,905	RL	Plug out 4-inch dia. 3.5 inches thick recovered in one piece. Shot lodged broken up. Nose broken off at shoulder and entered tank. Base broke off and rebounded.
3	E.3.G.	JMB 9/42	IIIT	2.75	1,957	RL	Plug out 3.5-inch dia. Shot lodged broken up. Base broke off outside and tip inside the tank.
5	E.3.G.	JMB 9/42	IIIT	2/625	2,014	R	Plug out 3.75-inch dia. About 25 per cent of shot through. Base found outside tank.
1	E.3.G.	JMB 9/42	IIIT	2.5	2,023	W	Plug out 3.5-inch dia. 3.5 inches thick found in one piece in the tank. Shot broke up. Pieces including base found inside the tank.

Assessed W/R limit: 2,018 f.s. Estimated ballistic limit: 1,862 f.s.

Shoot 11: 75-mm AP *v*. Starboard Side Superstructure 82 mm Thick

At Normal. Ammunition lot No: 6951-KOP-74.

No. of round	Charge weight (lb oz)	Striking velocity	Code damage	Description
1	1.6	1,484	C	Smooth bulge 3-inch dia. 0.25 inches lift. Front displaced metal sheared off. Shot rebounded whole.
2	1.8	1,590	NFH	Hit supported by floor of Tank
3	1.10	1,687	C	Bulge 4.5-inch dia. 0.5 inches high. Shot rebounded whole. On front displaced metal sheared off.
4	1.12	1,792	D	Bulge 4.5-inch dia. 1 inch high. Plug started 0.25 inches lift. Crack 1 ft long to top of plate.
7	1.12	No record	D	Bulge 4.5-inch dia. Piece of plate knocked out 2 ft × 1 ft not near impact. (See photo 10).
8	1.13	No record	E	Cracked bulge. Irregular vertical crack 2 inches long 0.5 inches open. More plate knocked off enlarging area out to 3 ft × 1 ft.
6	1.13	1,828	W	Plug out. Metal off 4.5-inch dia. Shot not recovered.
5	FSC	No record	W	Plug out. Damage ran into that of round 7.

W/R limit: 1,810 f.s.

7

PAMPHLET ON ATTACK ON PANTHER Pz.Kw.V AND TIGER Pz.Kw.VI

The information in this chapter has been transcribed from original wartime documents. The report format and brief notation style has been kept.

SECRET

Prepared for the use of Students of the School of Tank Technology
April 1944 (Copy number B8727)

Amendment No. 1

The issue of an amended RV curve for 6-pdr APCBC has made it necessary to revise the figure for this projectile. New half-tone pictures and polar diagrams have been prepared and are enclosed herewith.

The examination of the one Panther that has so far reached this country has supplied slightly different figures for the armour thicknesses and angles to those given on page 2 of the pamphlet. It is not considered that these differences are sufficient to call for a revision of the figures for the other weapons quoted in the pamphlet until other specimens of Panther had been examined in detail. In any case the errors involved are less than those which will be introduced by inaccuracies in the estimation of range, angle of presentation and the actual M.V. of the guns under operational conditions. The new figures for the 6-pdr APCBC have been based on the increased thickness and angle data.

SECTION 1

1. This paper is an attempt to define the conditions under which Panther (Pz.Kw.V) and Tiger (Pz.Kw.VI) may be attacked successfully by British and American A/T guns. The information is given in the form of marked photographs and polar diagrams. It is limited to the attack of certain prominent plates on each vehicle, and in making the necessary calculations the conditions stated in paragraphs 2, 3 and 4 have been assumed.

2. Armour on Tiger

The armour is assumed to be of rolled machineable quality of a standard similar to that required for British machineable quality plate, and of the following thickness and tilts.

Plate	Thickness	Tilt
Driver's visor	102 mm	10 deg.
Front of turret	102 mm	5 deg.
Side of turret	82 mm	Vertical

Rear of turret	82 mm	Vertical
Hull, side superstructure	82 mm	Vertical
Hull side, below mudguard	62 mm	Vertical
Rear of hull	82 mm	8 deg.

3. Armour on Panther

The armour is assumed to be of rolled machineable quality of the standard similar to that required for British machineable quality plate, and of the following thicknesses and tilts.

Plate	Thickness	Tilt
Glacis plate	85 mm	57 deg.
Front of turret	102 mm	Vertical
Side of turret	45 mm	25 deg.
Rear of turret	45 mm	25 deg.
Side of hull	45 mm	Vertical
Hull, side superstructure	45 mm	42 deg.
Rear of hull	45 mm	30 deg.

4. Guns and Projectiles

The data refer also only to the following guns and projectiles with muzzle velocities as stated below. The following approximate corrections for muzzle velocity are suggested.

Gun	Type of Projectile	Weight of Projectile	Muzzle Velocity
37-mm	APCBC (M51)	1.92 lb	2,900 f.s.
6-pdr Mk IV	APCBC	7.19 lb	2,725 f.s.
75-mm M3	APCBC (M61)	14.36 lb	2,030 f.s.
3-inch	APCBC (M62)	14.89 lb	2,600 f.s.
17-pdr	APCBC	17.00 lb	2,900 f.s.

5. A small difference in the weight of a projectile will not have a marked influence on its performance. On the other hand the performance decreases somewhat rapidly as the muzzle velocity decreases.

	MV Correction	Projectile
	50 f.s.	37-mm APCBC
Decrease each range by	40 f.s.	6-pdr APCBC
100 yards for a fall	30 f.s.	75-mm APCBC
In muzzle velocity of:-	30 f.s.	3-inch APCBC
	30 f.s.	17-pdr APCBC

6. The information is given primarily in the form of a set of seven marked photographs for each combination of the projectile and tank. The photographs have been chosen to represent typical orientations at which enemy tanks may be found. The relationship of gun and observer and the general appearance of Tiger at these presentations are given below. The arrow indicates the direction in which the tank is moving and is also the normal to the front (or rear) of the tanks, in the horizontal plane the hatched line indicates the normal to the side.

It should be realised perfectly that, because the turret of a tank can rotate, photographs and diagrams given must be regarded as being in two distinct parts, one for the turret and the other for the hull. To take the extreme case, the photograph and diagram for attack on the rear (Fig. 7) will apply to the hull only. Those for the head-on position (Fig. 1) will apply to the turret. Similarly, if a tank has halted broadside to a gun and is firing at it, the broadside photograph and diagram (Fig. 4) will apply to the hull: the head-on photograph and diagram (Fig. 1) will apply to the turret, and so on for other combinations.

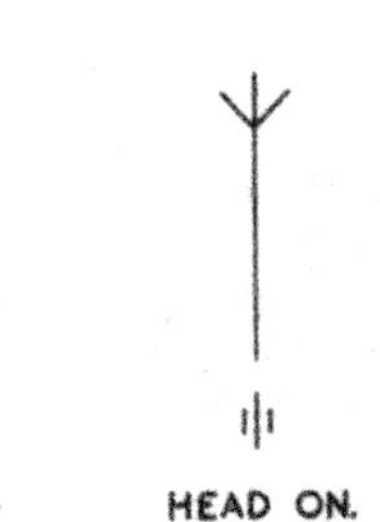

Fig. 1. Head-on. Angle of Impact in Horizontal Plane—Front Normal. (*School of Tank Technology*)

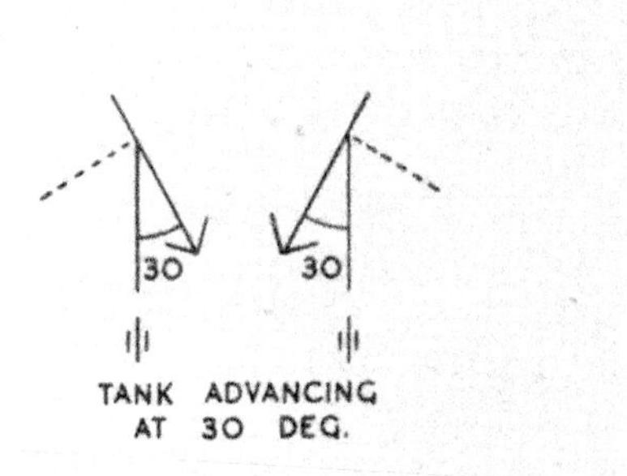

Fig. 2. Tank advancing at 30 degrees. Angles of Impact in Horizontal Plane—Front 30 deg. Sides 60 deg. (*School of Tank Technology*)

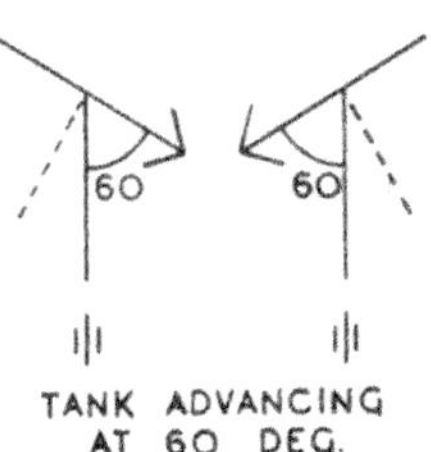

Fig. 3. Tank advancing at 60 deg. Angles of Impact in Horizontal Plane—Front 60 deg. Sides 30 deg. (*School of Tank Technology*)

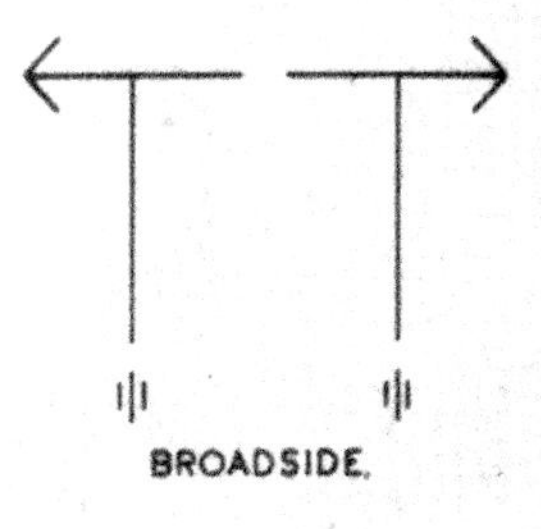

Fig. 4. Broadside. Angle of Impact in Horizontal Plane—Sides Normal. (*School of Tank Technology*)

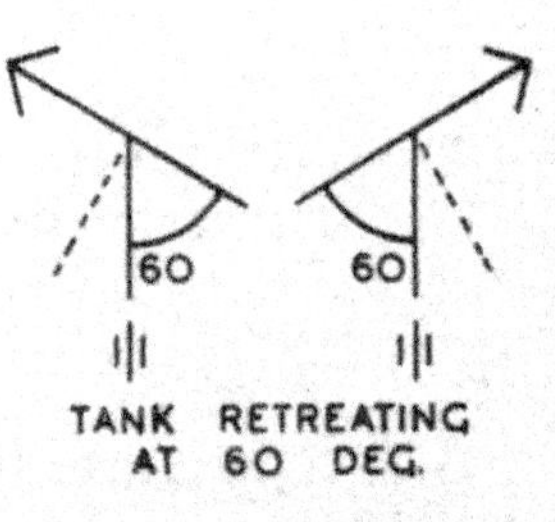

Fig. 5. Tank retreating at 60 deg. Angles of Impact in Horizontal Plane—Sides 30 deg. Rear 60 deg. (*School of Tank Technology*)

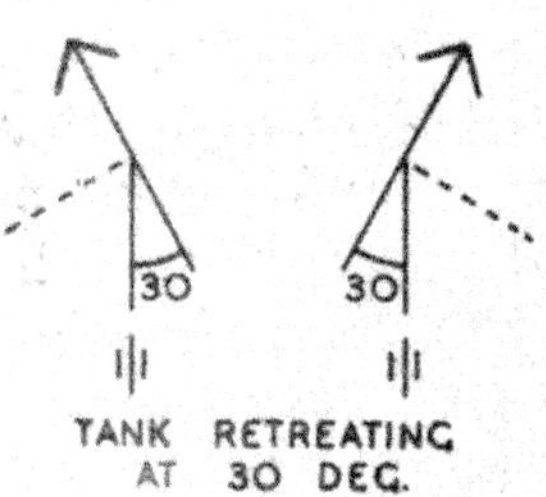

Fig. 6. Tank retreating at 30 deg. Angles of Impact in Horizontal Plane—Sides 60 deg. Rear 30 deg. (*School of Tank Technology*)

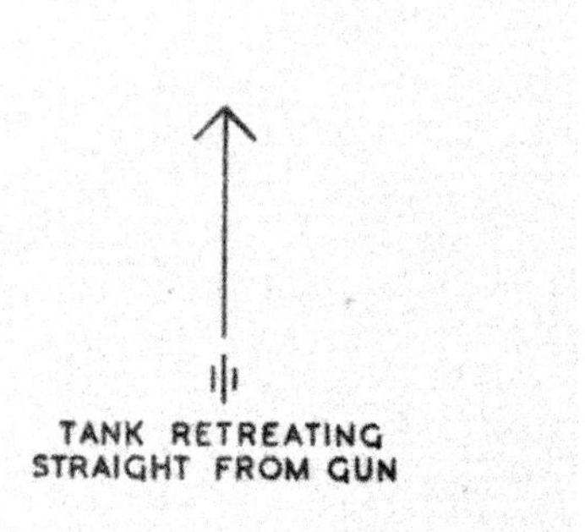

Fig. 7. Rear Angle of Impact in Horizontal Plane—Rear Normal. (*School of Tank Technology*)

Some Notes on the Attack of Enemy Tanks
Explanation of Photographs and Diagrams
Section II

9. Damage to enemy tanks can be divided into two classes:
   (a) Primary, where a main plate is holed.
   (b) Secondary, where damage is done to the tracks and suspensions, the turret is jammed, etc., but the projectile does not enter the tank.

10. The data supplied refer only to primary damage. It does not follow that when a shot is shown as failing against the main plate under a given set of conditions that it is useless to fire at the tank. While it is unlikely that the shot will enter the tank if it strikes fairly on the main plate, a certain number of hits will do secondary damage and may even violently dislodged fittings inside the vehicle.

Nonetheless, it is always better, if circumstances allow, to wait until the conditions are such that there is a reasonable probability of hitting and of the hit penetrating a main plate.

11. The quality of German plate varies considerably and that of our shot is not consistent. It is, therefore, impossible to do more than indicate conditions under which average shot are likely to prove successful against plate of average quality. If the shot are rather poor and the plate is exceptionally tough, the ranges stated may have to be shortened, perhaps by 200 yards or more. On the other hand if there is a favourable combination of shot and plate the tank may be defeated at ranges longer by perhaps 200 yards or more than those indicated.

12. The performance figures have been produced on the assumption that the tank is standing on level ground and that fire is in the horizontal plane, that is angle of descent and angle of site have been neglected. With high velocity guns at short ranges the angle of descent will always be small and will usually be negligible in comparison with the angle of site. The corrections are usually quite small and cannot be made without introducing complications. The general effect, however, can be indicated.

Thus, if the tank is on level ground and the gun is firing downhill at it, the driver's visor plate of the Tiger, which is tilted back at an angle of 10 degrees, will be struck at an angle of less than 10 degrees (unless the gun is very high indeed) and will prove more vulnerable than usual. The same will be true if tank and gun are at the same height and with the tank coming downhill towards the gun. (The tank is here tilted forwards towards the gun). In the above cases, the increase in effective range will not be large, perhaps not more than 200 yards with 6-pdr APCBC.

If the plates on the tank have a considerable backward tilt, conditions such as those indicated above will be relatively more favourable to the gun, the contrary conditions, however, being relatively less favourable. The greater the tilt of a plate, the greater the change in resistance caused by a small change in the angle of impact.

The further away from the condition of horizontal fire and the more the tank is off an even keel, the more difficult it is to get through a vertical plate, but the effect is again usually small under ordinary practical conditions.

13. Attack on Turret Fronts

The resistance of the armour on the front of a turret varies from point to point and is difficult to assess. The ranges given are those at which performance or severe secondary damage should be obtained, but it must be realised that an occasional hit under the conditions defined may be almost ineffective. On the other hand, a hit at a longer range will sometimes put the tank out of action.

When a tank has a turret front and a main front hull plate, of approximate the same thickness and tilts, as on the Tiger, a hit on the main plate will probably prove the more effective.

When the gun mantlet is curved, as on the Panther, the vulnerability of the turret front depends still more on the point of strike, and any range must still more be taken only as a general guide. The hull front on the Panther, however, is so strong that the gunner's best chance in a head-on attack is to go for the turret.

14. Attack on the Turret Sides

When the turret side is straight or nearly straight, as on the Panther, the ranges given hold, with the usual reservations. When the side is curved however, as on the Tiger, the ranges refer to the area halfway between the mantlet and turret rear. When the turret is broadside to the gun a hit in any other position will only perforate at a shorter range. On the other hand, when the turret is not square to the gun, as when the tank is advancing or retreating at 60 degrees, there will be a small area round about the centre of the target as presented, where a hit near normal and favourable to the gun can be obtained on the turret. Thus as the ranges given for the above conditions refer to the real mid-position, and not to the apparent mid-position, they will be somewhat pessimistic when applied to the special area.

15. Remarks on Attack on Tiger

(a) The nose plate is thick (100 mm), tilted forward (25 degrees) and is often covered with shoes. The 6-pdr will almost invariably fail against it, and it is definitely a less promising target than the visor plate for the 17-pdr or M10.

(b) When the tank is broadside there is a small area of vertical plate 62 mm thick on the hull side just above the track and below the superstructure. This can be perforated quite easily by the 75-mm and 6-pdr at moderate ranges even at unfavourable angles. However, as a target this area is very small. A hit still lower on the side of the tank will strike the bogies. Whether shot will enter the hull or not will then depend to a considerable extent on the exact point of strike, but sometimes the wheels will add only slightly to the resistance of the main armour which is still the vertical plate only 60 mm thick.

(c) The various fittings on the rear of the hull and turret add little to the resistance of the main plates.

(d) When the visor plate seems to be as long as the hull superstructure side plate, the tank is advancing at slightly more than 30 degrees, when the rear and side superstructure appears to be of equal length the tank is retreating at about 30 degrees.

16. Remarks on Attack on Panther

(a) The armour on this tank is out of balance, the hull front being very strong and the turret front being an awkward target, but all the other plates on the tanks have only a moderate resistance. It follows therefore that the flanks and rear of this tank should be engaged wherever possible. It should be noted, however, that a lucky hit at quite long ranges low down on the turret front may result in a ricochet through the roof of the hull.

(b) The hull side superstructure is tilted back at the awkward angle of 42 degrees, but the plate is comparatively thin (45 mm). It follows that although the side superstructure is very resistant to a small gun its resistance to a gun of moderate size, such as the 6-pdr, is not good, and that the 17-pdr, is able to perforate it under a wide range of conditions.

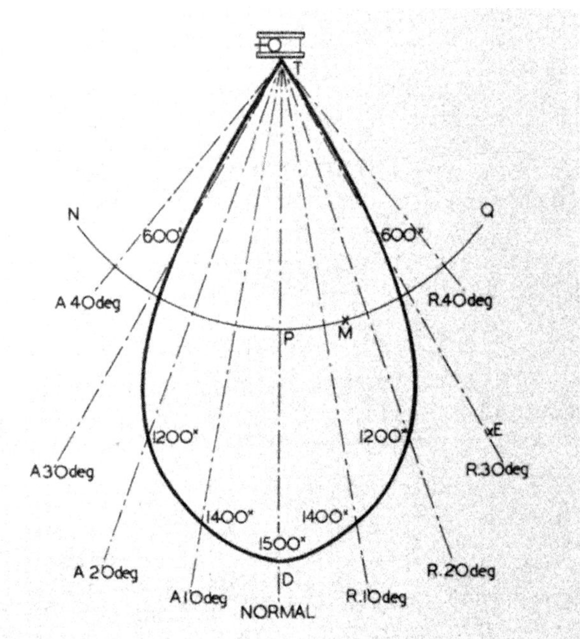

Fig. 8. Polar Diagram—Illustrated attack on side of tank with APCBC shot. (*School of Tank Technology*)

17. Explanation of a Polar Diagram

The polar diagram is simply a crude map of the ground. Unlike the ordinary map, the ruling direction is not north, but the direction at right angles to the front, side or rear of the tank, as the case may be. Instead of all distances being measured from an agreed and stationary datum point, they are measured from the tank, and mixed co-ordinates, arrange and in angle, are used instead of the ordinary rectangular co-ordination.

18. Fig. 8., A scale diagram to express the attack on the side of the tank using APCBC Shot illustrates. The line, DT, is the ruling direction and is the normal to the side of the tank. The vehicle would be broadside to an observer standing at any point along TD, and would appear as in Fig. 4. The rays coming out from the tank are at intervals of 10 degrees and give the angle of attack on the side plates. Thus to an observer standing somewhere on the R30 degree ray along the TE the tank would appear to be retreating at 60 degrees and would appear as in Fig. 5. A shot fired from a gun along this Ray would strike the side at 30 degrees. The tank would appear to an observer along the A30 degree ray to be advancing at 60 degrees. (Fig. 3) but a shot from a gun sited along this ray would again strike the side at 30 degrees. In other words, from the point of view of striking the side, there is no material difference between the rays at A30 degree and R30 degree.

19. Ranges on the diagram can be represented by arcs of circles with their centres at the tank. Thus in Fig. 8., NPQ is the arc representing a range of 800 yards. These arcs are used in the construction of a diagram but, as they become unnecessary and tend to confuse the finished map, often they are later removed. In an alternative form of a diagram, the arc representing the principal ranges are left in, but the ranges in yards at which the plate can be perforated at particular angles are then not stated numerically.

20. In illustration of how the position of a point with respect to a tank can be defined in terms of range and angle, consider point M. M is clearly 800 yards, R15 deg., and any position on the ground in front of the side of the tank can be stated in this a similar manner.

21. The performance of a gun against a plate depends on the range and angle as well as on the nature of the ammunition used. The effective range decreases as the angle of attack increases, the change sometimes being a very fast. It is possible by using the polar diagrams system to show this somewhat complicated connection between range and angle. Thus for a particular gun firing APCBC, The relationship which might be much as shown in Fig. 8. If the gun is square to the side of the tank, the tank will appear to the gunner as in Fig. 4, the gun will be along TD, and if the range is less than 1,500 yards, the gun will be successful. If the range is longer than 1,500 yards the gun will fail to do primary damage. If the gun cannot hit the tank quite squarely as at 10 degrees, the critical range shortens to 1,400 yards. In this particular case there is a further small decrease in effective range to 1,200 yards as the angle increases to R20 degrees, but the effective ranges halved as the angle increases from R20 degrees to R30 degrees and disappears altogether at about R35 degrees.

At R30 degrees the tank will appear as in Fig. 5. An area, or wing, is obtained by joining these critical positions. When the gun is inside the area, it can defeat the tank: when outside, it will fail. Thus, every hit will probably perforate if the gun is at M while it is unlikely that a gun cited at E will ever be successful.

22. While the general shape of the polar diagram remains fairly constant, the actual ranges and angles depend very much on the size and muzzle velocity of the projectiles, the thickness of the target, and on other factors. If, however, the gunner is supplied with information, perhaps in the form of marked photographs, telling him how his shot will perform against a particular tank at certain definite angles (e.g. broadside, advancing at 60 degrees, advancing at 30 degrees), and this information is supplemented by one or two polar diagrams typically of particular plates on the tank, he can usually tell with reasonable accuracy what the critical ranges are at other angles of attack.

For example, a marked photograph may tell him that he can get through the side of the tank at 1,200 yards provided the tank presents itself squarely. Another may tell him that if he can hit the side only at 30 degrees, his shot will probably fail at any range. In the absence of a polar diagram, a special photograph would be required to state the position at 20 degrees attack but a polar diagram of a plate of about the same thickness gives the information that in this special case the effective range does not change very much from normal up to perhaps 20 degrees. When this critical Angle is past, his chances of holing the plate at any range are small. If, however, the plate on the front of the tank is much thicker than that on the side, the polar diagram for the side will be useless as a guide to the behaviour of the shot against the front of the tank and a more suitable diagram would have to be used.

23. The polar diagram differs from an ordinary map but only as stated in para.17, but also in another very important aspect as explained below. The vulnerable area or wing of the diagram is a property of the tank and not of the ground. As the tank shown in Fig. 8 moves to the left, so does the wing move with it. As the tank turns, so does the wing turn. The wing, indeed, may be regarded as an imaginary shadow attached to the tank. When the wing or shadow falls over the gun, then a hit from the gun will perforate the tank. Thus an A/T gun at N (Fig. 8) is not under the wing and therefore will not be able to do the side of the tank primary damage. But if the tank moves left, it will carry its shadow with it: N will then be covered and the gun can win. In exactly the same way, if the tank does not advance but swings round clockwise to retreat, the wing will again swing over the gun, which can then succeed.

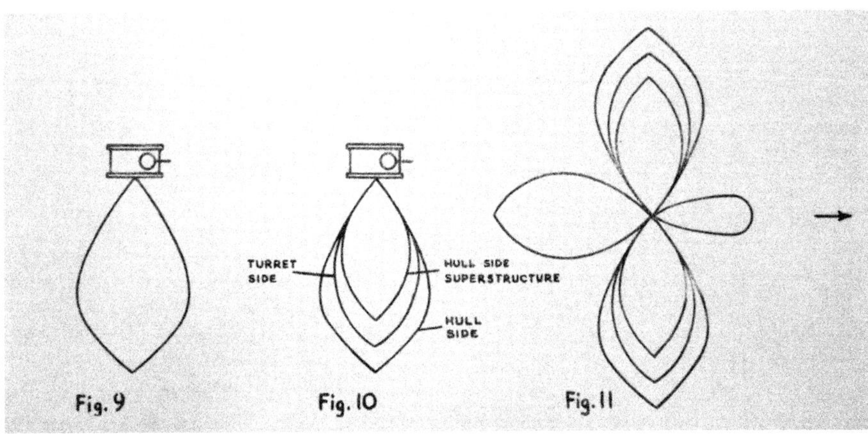

Polar diagrams. *(School of Tank Technology)*

24. A single polar diagram, as Fig. 9, can apply only to a single plate. However, the aspect of the tank may consist of several plates, each of a different resistance, and each requiring a polar diagram for itself. Thus the side (hull and turret) of Panther has three main plates, each 45 mm thick, but of different resistance to horizontal fire, because they are mounted on the tank at different tilts—namely, hull side vertical, hull side superstructure, at 42 degrees, and turret side at 25 degrees. These can be shown as a family of polar diagrams as in Fig. 10.

Further, a family such as that given in Fig. 10, is required for each aspect of the tank, front, sides and rear. These can be assembled as in Fig. 11 to give a 'butterfly' which gives an idea of the vulnerability of the tank as a whole. In Fig. 11, the arrow indicates the direction in which the tank is moving. As the areas often overlap, the tank must be shown to scale (i.e. as a point) and not of grossly exaggerated size as in Figs. 9 and 10.

Alternatively, the 'butterfly' can be simplified by taking the most prominent or strongest or weakest plate to represent a particular aspect. It should be realised clearly that the polar diagram as given define only the conditions under which a hit will be successful. They say nothing about the probability of a hit being obtained. In order to obtain a complete picture of the attack on a tank the two factors, the probability of a hit and the probability of a hit perforating, must be considered together. It is obvious that the probability of a hit will increase as the range shortens. The lesson seems to be moderately short range squarely as possible to the aspect of the tank under attack.

26. In the polar diagrams prepared, the vulnerable and in vulnerable areas are shown as being separated by lines. It would be more correct to replace the lines by bands, the inner side of the band representing the attack of worst British shot on best German plate, and the outside that of best British shot on worst German plate. The lack of data does not permit this to be done.

As the available Soviet firing-trial results only cover a small fraction of the conditions which must be defined, much of the data used in the construction of the diagrams has had perforce to be obtained indirectly by calculation and assessment, and unsatisfactory process at best. An attempt has been made to put the lines through the centre of the bends. That is, if a gun is sited on, and is firing shot of average quality against plate of average quality, it is calculated that 50% of the hits under the conditions set out in para.12 above will be through is. A small error in a calculation, particularly as the loss in energy of APCBC. Projectiles with increasing range is not marked, may result in a substantial error in the position of the line and its displacement from the centre of the band. Further, the vulnerable areas will swell or contract pending on whether the ground level favours or does not favour the gun (see para. 12).

For these reasons, the data given both on the photographs and in the form of polar diagrams can at best be accepted only as a crude guide.

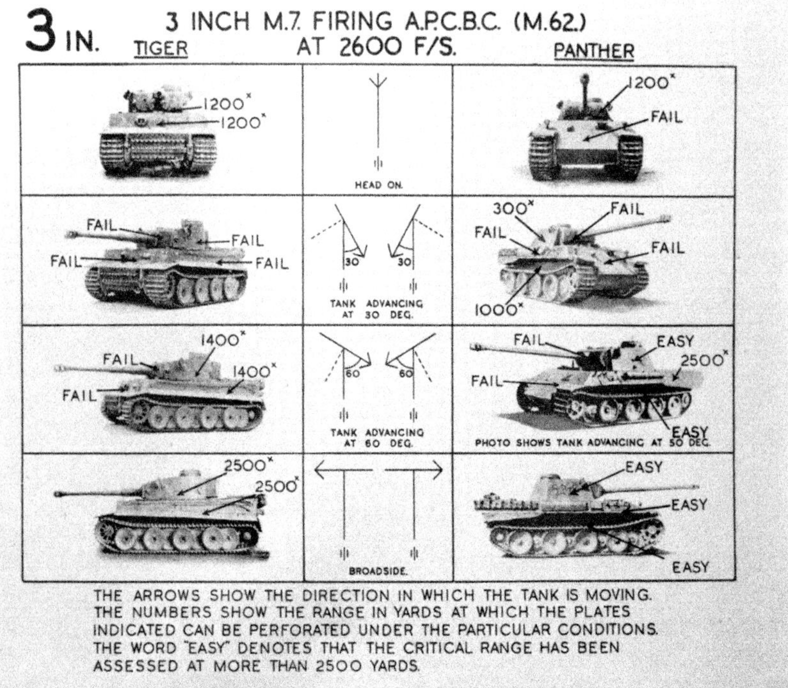

(School of Tank Technology)

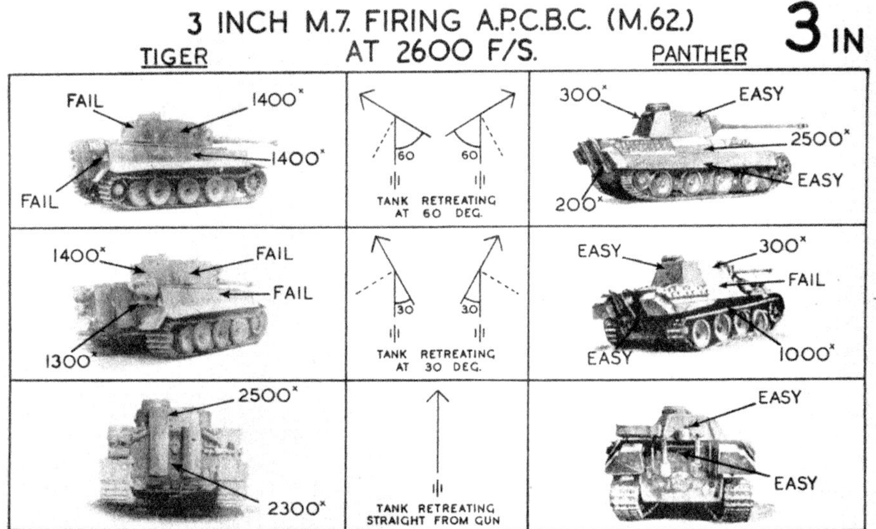

(*School of Tank Technology*)

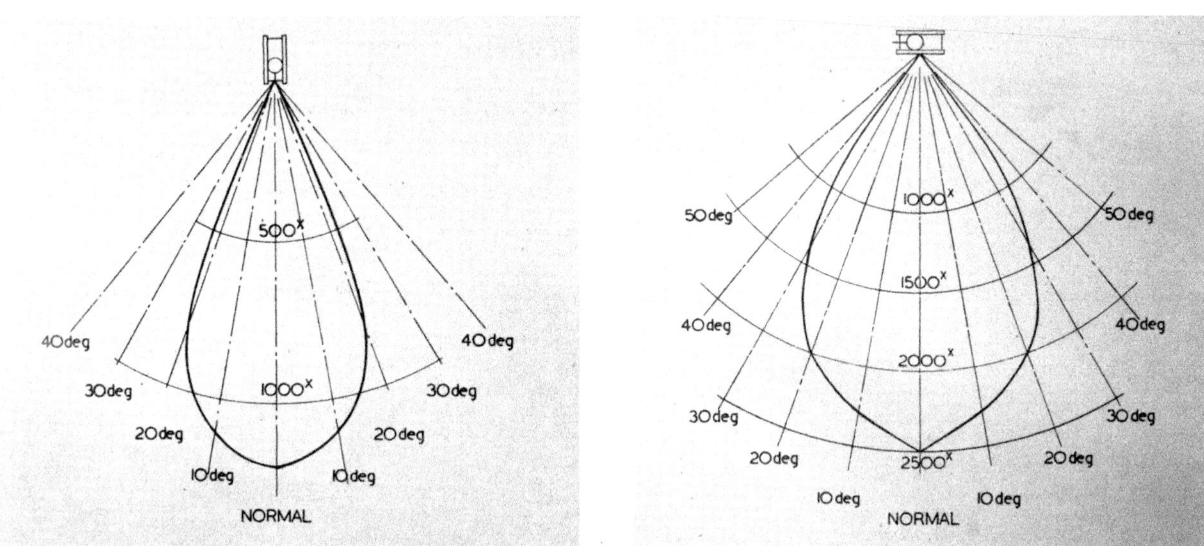

‹ Polar diagram: 3-inch M7 Gun (M62 APCBC) at 2,600 f.s. *v.* vision plate of Tiger (Pz.Kw.VI) and turret front of Tiger and Panther (Pz.KW.V). This projectile is not expected to succeed against the glacis plate of Panther. (*School of Tank Technology*)

› Polar diagram: 3-inch M7 Gun (M62 APCBC) at 2,600 f.s. *v.* hull-side superstructure of Tiger (Pz.Kw.VI). This diagram applies also to the rear hull of Tiger provided all ranges are shortened by 200 yards. (*School of Tank Technology*)

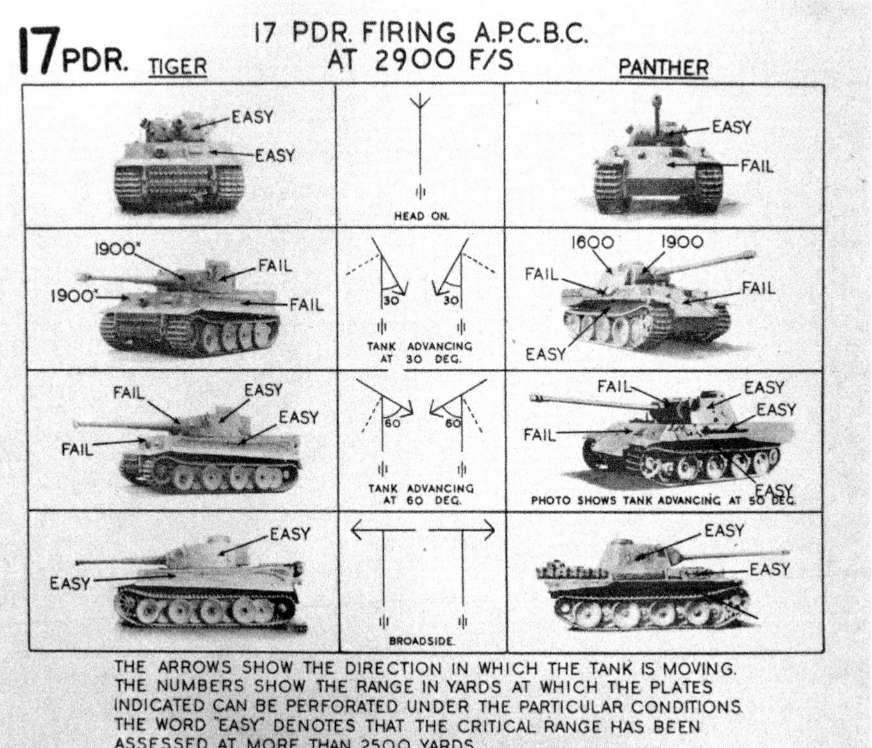

(*School of Tank Technology*)

27. No attempt has been made to estimate performances at ranges over 2,500 yards. If it is judged that the projectile will succeed under the stated conditions at a longer range, the plate on the photographs is marked 'Easy', and the polar diagram is left open. The fact that the diagram is open means no more than this, and in these cases it will not normally be possible to estimate the critical range at normal from the information given.

28. Changes in the armour of the enemy AFV's may cause the information to become obsolete and misleading. For example, there is at the time of writing a report that the Tiger has been strengthened, but what plates are affected and the amount of the strengthening, is not yet known.

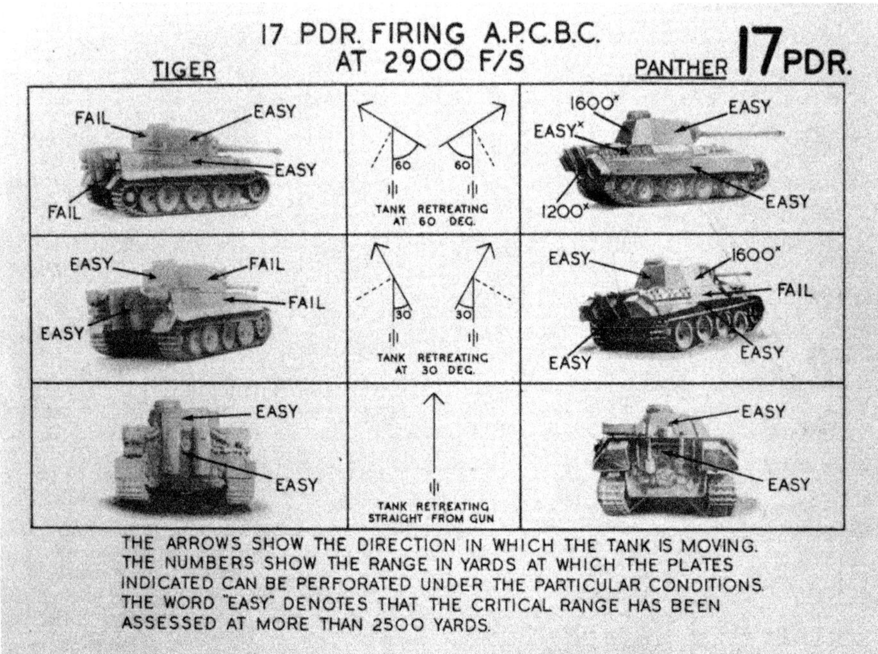

(*School of Tank Technology*)

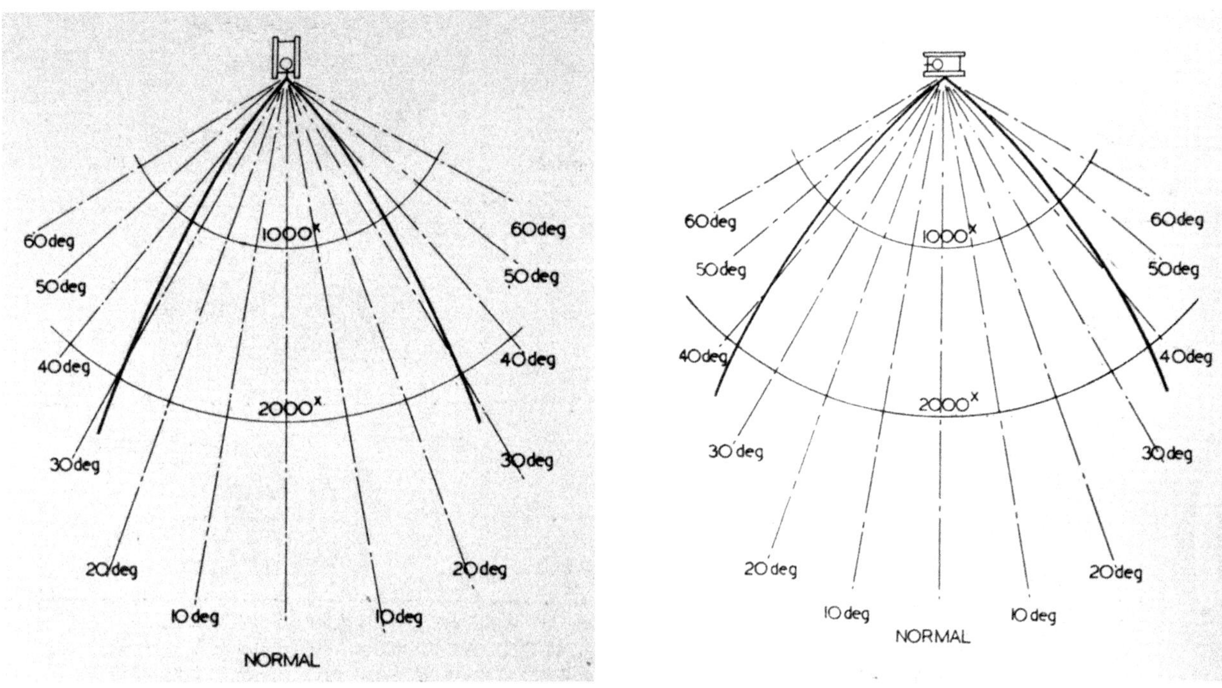

❮ Polar diagram: 17-pdr firing APCBC at 2,900 f.s. *v.* turret front of Tiger (Pz.Kw.VI) and Panther (Pz.Kw.V). Also driver's visor plate of Tiger. The 17-pdr is not expected to succeed against the glacis plate of Panther. (*School of Tank Technology*)

❯ Polar diagram: 17-pdr firing APCBC at 2,900 f.s. *v.* hull-side superstructure and side and rear of the Tiger (Pz.Kw.VI) and Panther (Pz.Kw.V). This diagram applies with reasonable accuracy to the hull and rear of the Tiger. (*School of Tank Technology*)

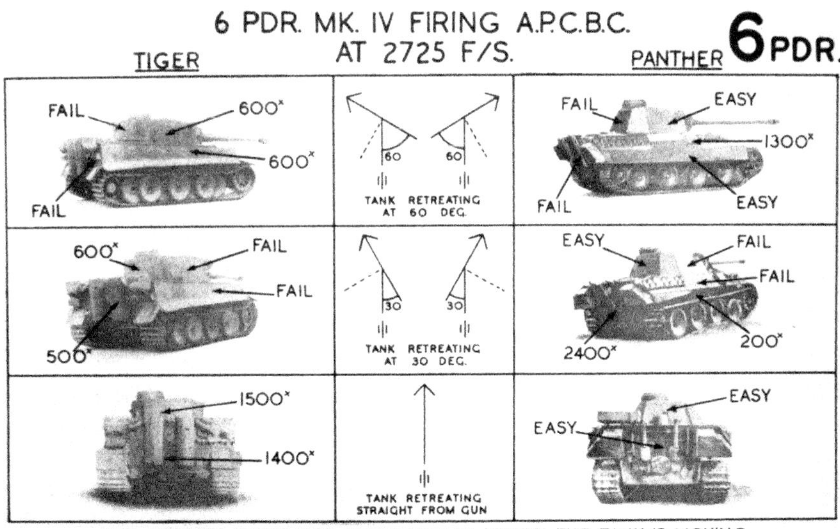

(*School of Tank Technology*)

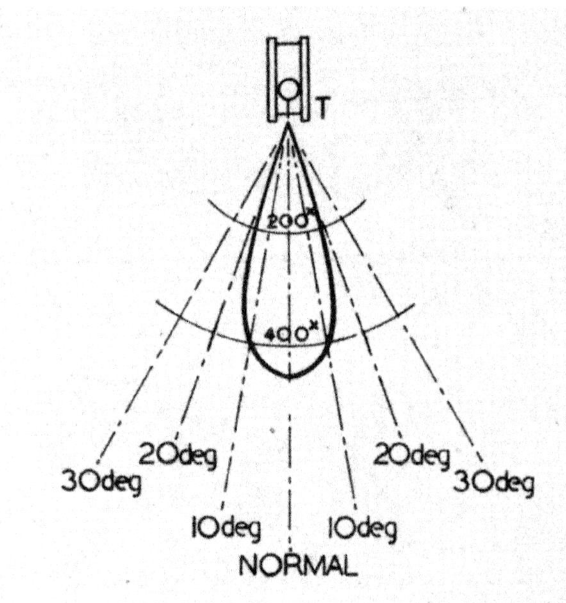

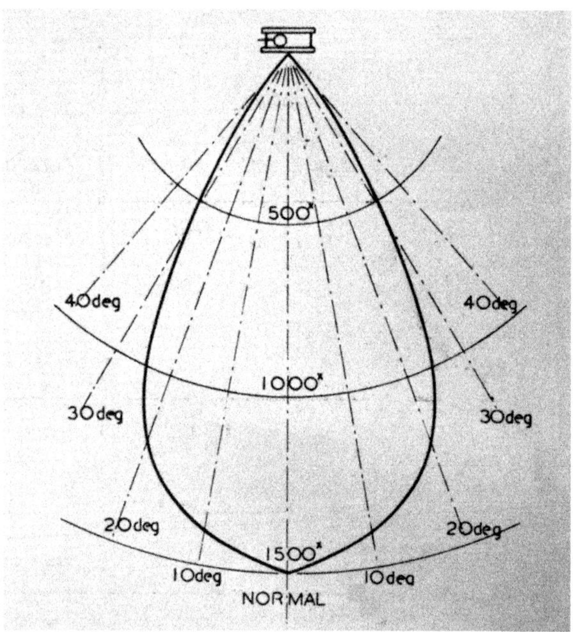

‹ Polar diagram: 6-pdr Mk IV firing APCBC at 2,725 f.s. *v.* driver's visor plate and front of the turret of the Tiger (Pz.Kw.VI). Note: this diagram for this projectile applies to the front of the turret of Panther Pz.Kw.V. The shot cannot be expected to succeed against the glacis plate of the Panther. (*School of Tank Technology*)

› Polar diagram: 6-pdr Mk IV firing APCBC at 2,725 f.s. *v.* side of the hull superstructure and side and rear of the turret of the Tiger (Pz.Kw.VI). Note: this diagram applies with slight modifications to attack on the rear hull of the Tiger. (*School of Tank Technology*)

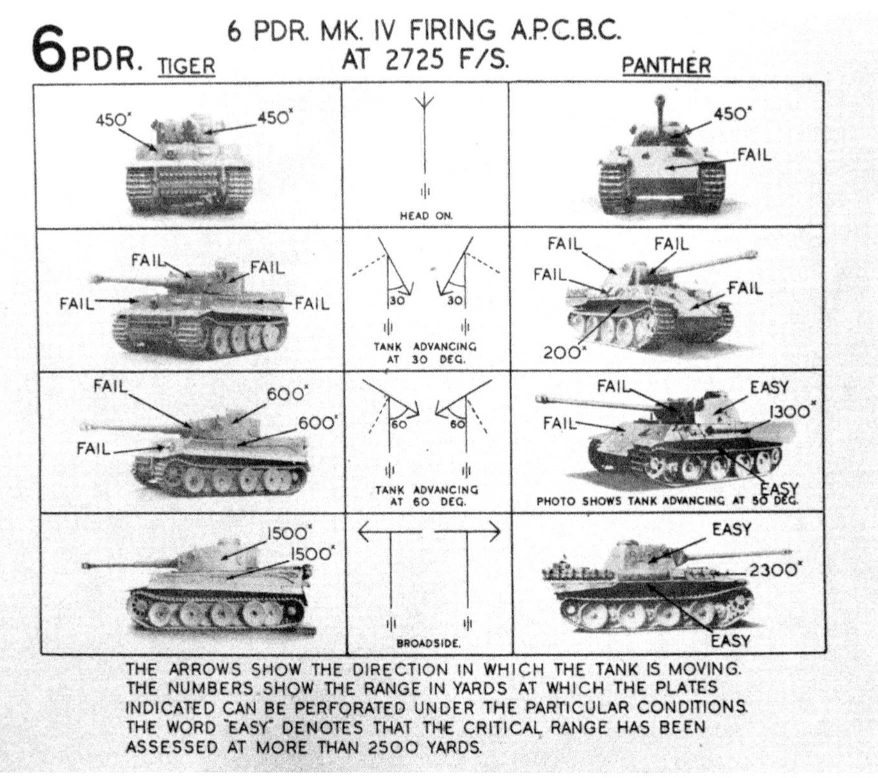

(*School of Tank Technology*)

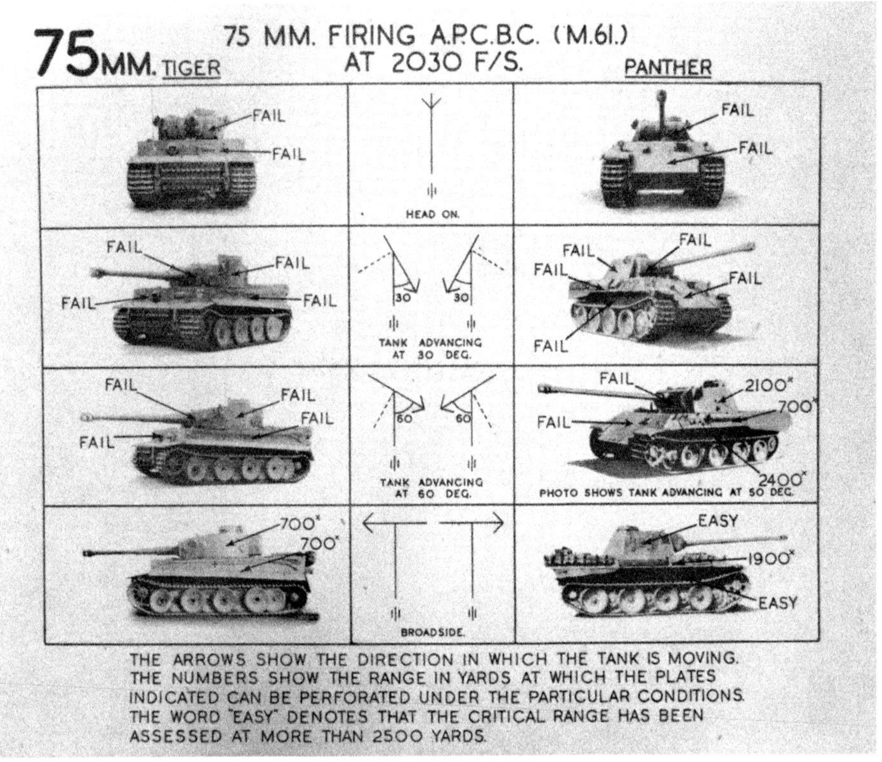

(*School of Tank Technology*)

(*School of Tank Technology*)

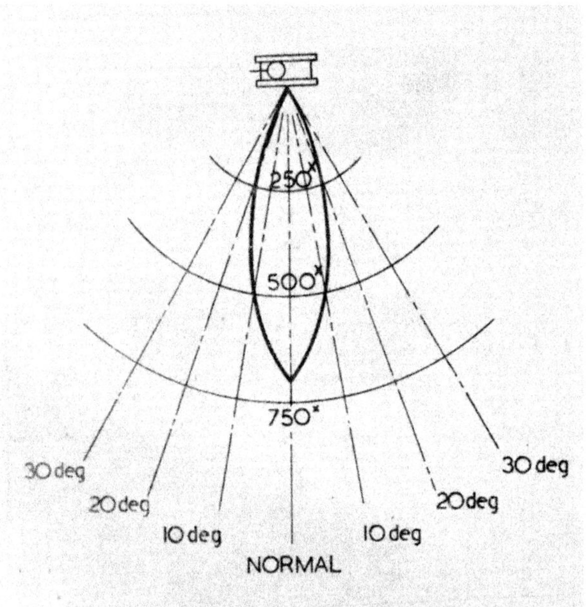

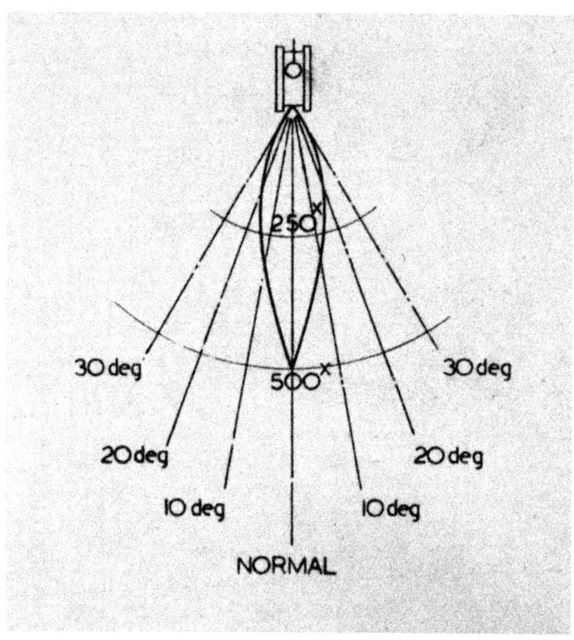

‹ Polar diagram: 75-mm M61 APCBC at 2,030 f.s. *v.* turret side and rear and hull side superstructure of the Tiger (Pz.Kw.VI). It is not expected that the projectile will succeed against the front of either hull or turret of either the Tiger or the Panther. (*School of Tank Technology*)

› Polar diagram: 75-mm M61 APCBC at 2,030 f.s. *v.* rear hull of the Tiger (Pz.Kw.VI). (*School of Tank Technology*)

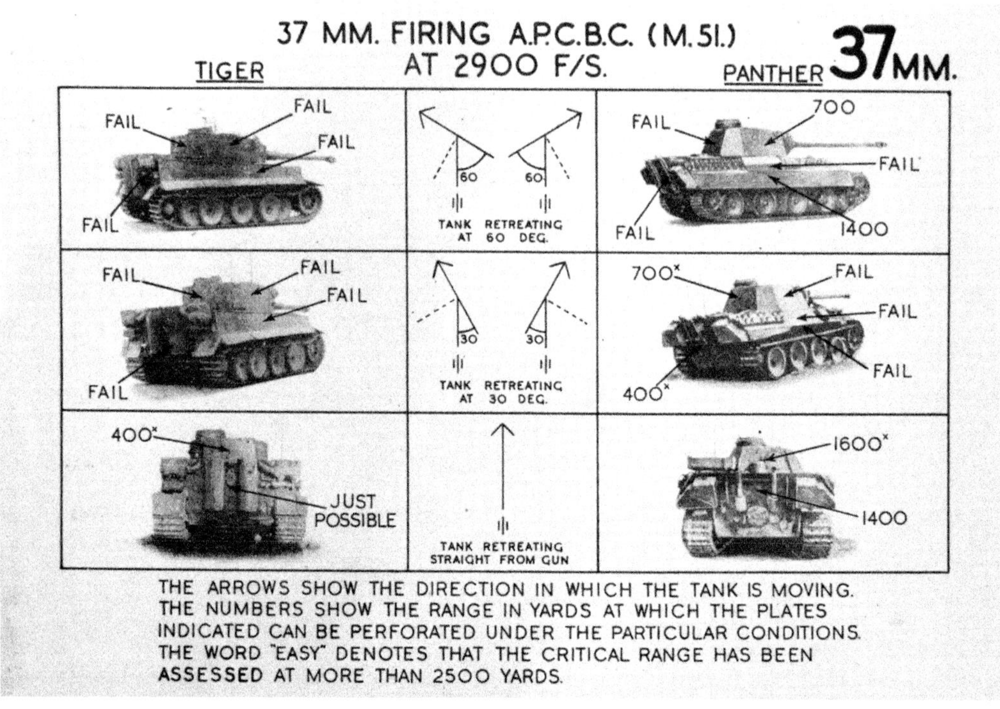

(*School of Tank Technology*)

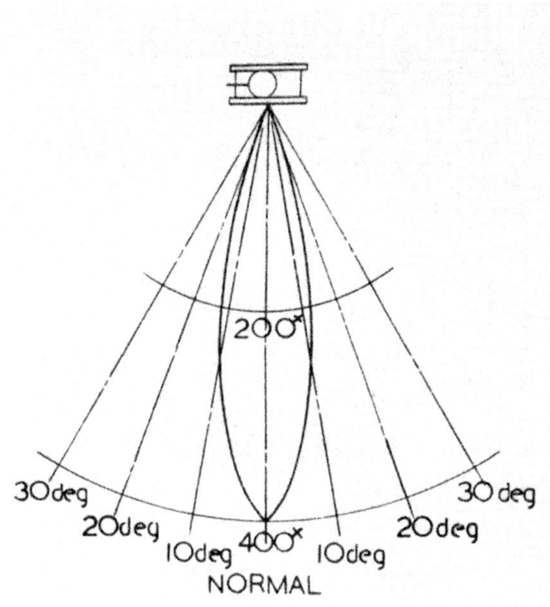

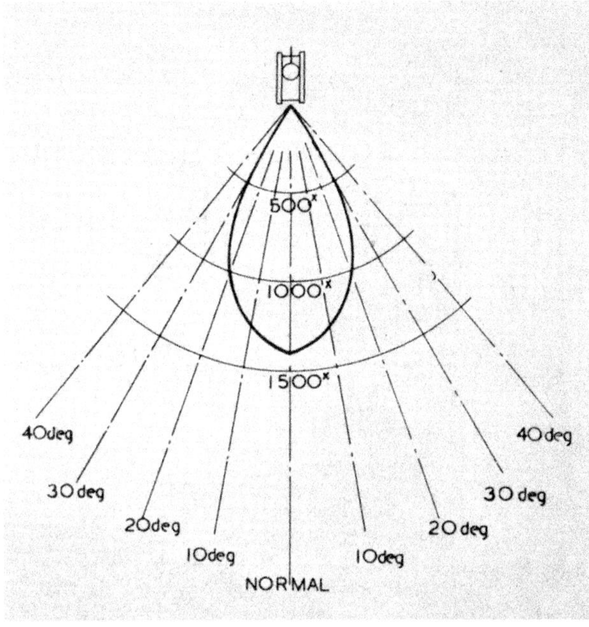

‹ Polar diagram: 37-mm M51 APCBC at 2,900 f.s. *v.* hull side superstructure and rear of the turret of the Tiger (Pz.Kw.VI). The projectile has a small chance against the hull side superstructure and the side and rear of the turret, but only at very short ranges and angles very near to normal. It has a similar, though smaller, chance against the rear of the hull. It is unlikely to perforate either the front of the turret or the front of the hull of this tank. There is a small strip between the side superstructure and the top of the bogie wheels where the shot will succeed at about 1,300 yards when the tank is broadside to the gun and at 500 yards when the tank is advancing or retreating at 60 degrees, but as a target, this area is very small. (*School of Tank Technology*)

› Polar diagram: 37-mm M51 APCBC at 2,900 f.s. *v.* rear hull of the Panther (Pz.Kw.V). (*School of Tank Technology*)

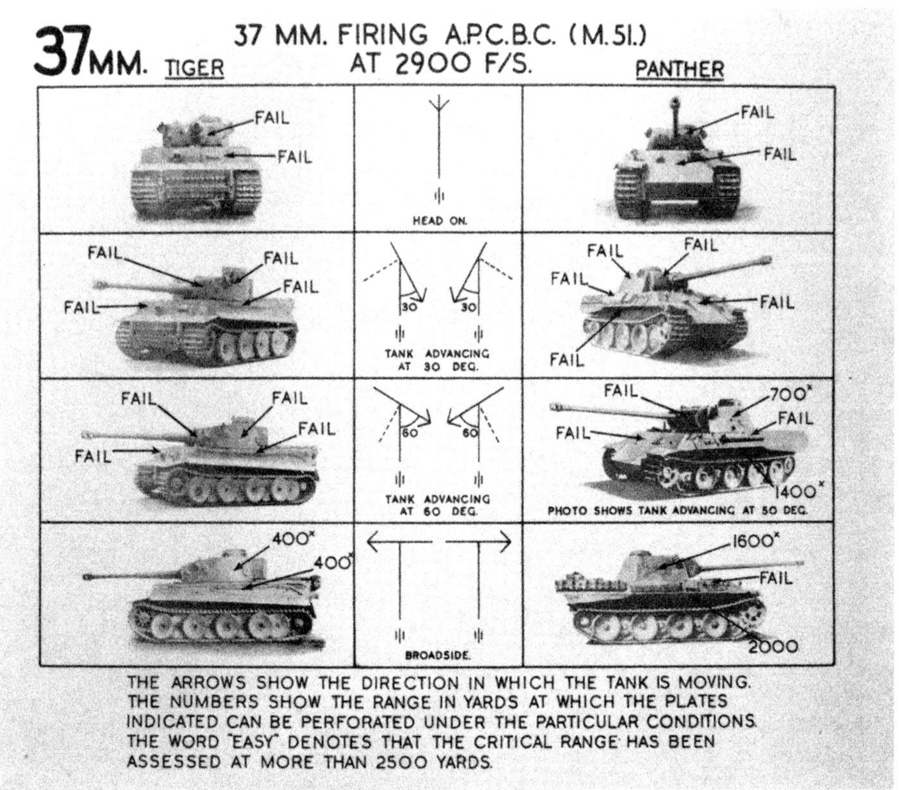

(*School of Tank Technology*)

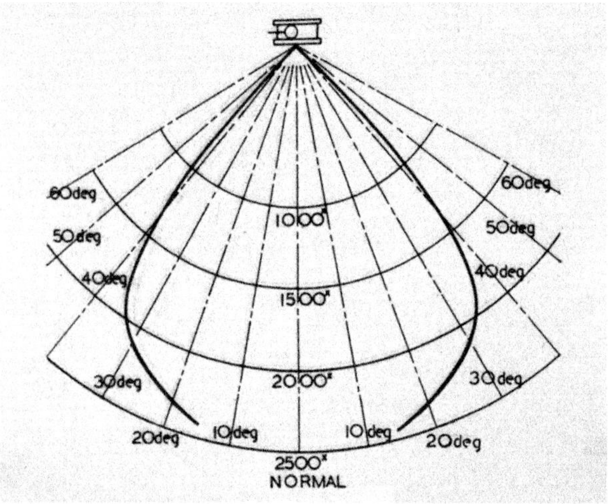

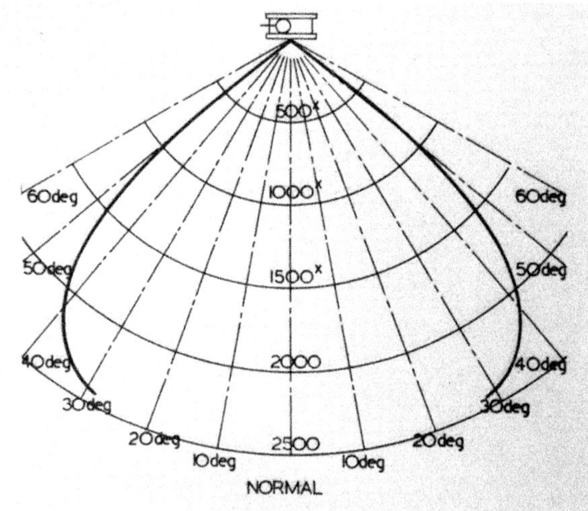

❮ Polar diagram: 75-mm M61 APCBC at 2,030 f.s. *v.* the side and rear of the turret of the Panther (Pz.Kw.V). (*School of Tank Technology*)

❯ Polar diagram: 75-mm M61 APCBC at 2,030 f.s. *v.* the hull side of the Panther (Pz.Kw.V). (*School of Tank Technology*)

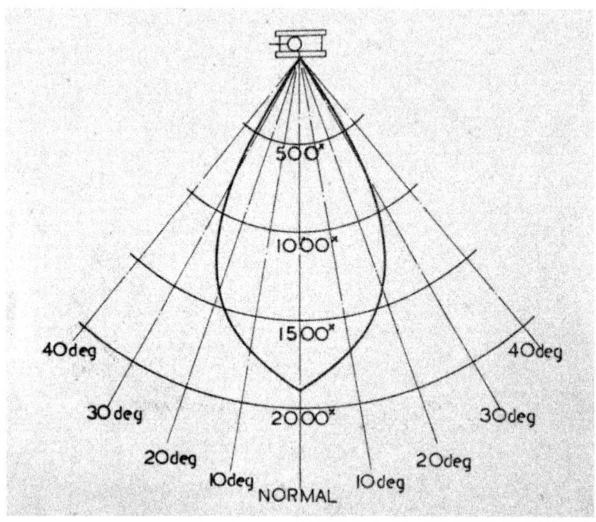

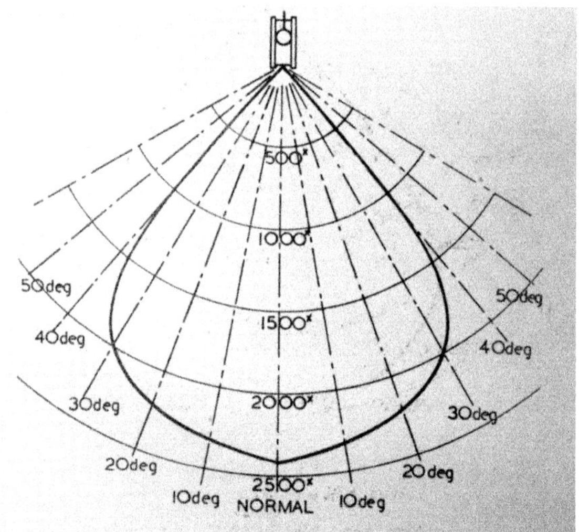

❮ Polar diagram: 75-mm M61 APCBC at 2,030 f.s. *v.* the hull side superstructure of the Panther (Pz.Kw.V). (*School of Tank Technology*)

❯ Polar diagram: 75-mm M61 APCBC at 2,030 f.s. *v.* rear hull of the Panther (Pz.Kw.V). (*School of Tank Technology*)

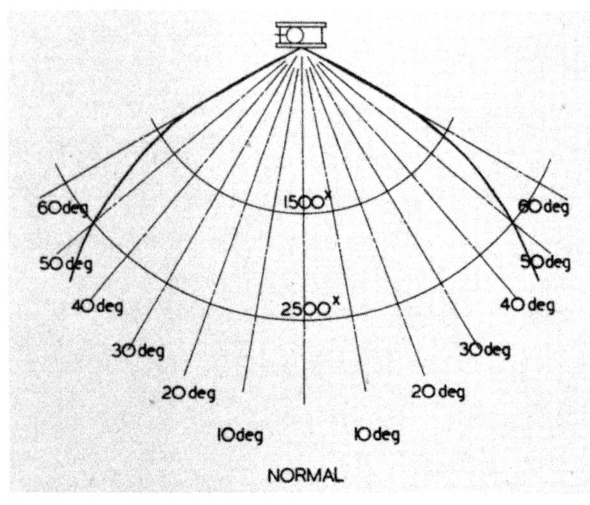

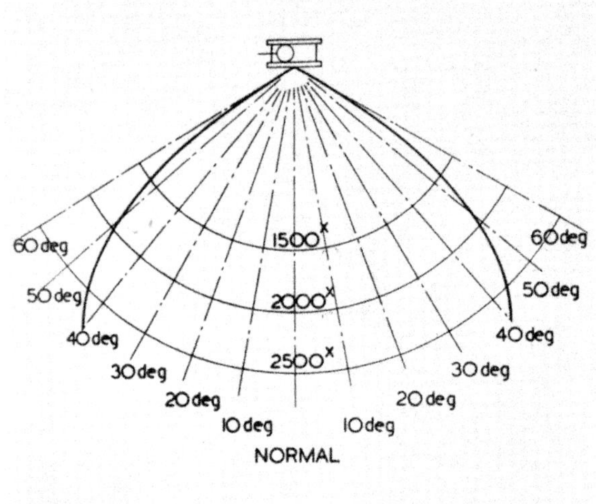

Bottom of previous page:

❮ Polar diagram: 3-inch M7 Gun M62 APCBC at 2,600 f.s. *v.* the hull side of the Panther (Pz.Kw.V). (*School of Tank Technology*)

❯ Polar diagram: 3-inch M7 Gun M62 APCBC at 2,600 f.s. *v.* the side and rear of the turret of the Panther (Pz.Kw.V). This diagram applies reasonable accuracy to the attack of this projectile on the rear hull of the Panther. (*School of Tank Technology*)

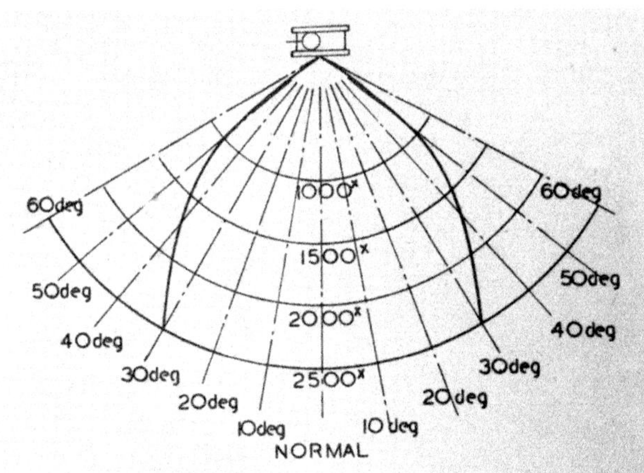

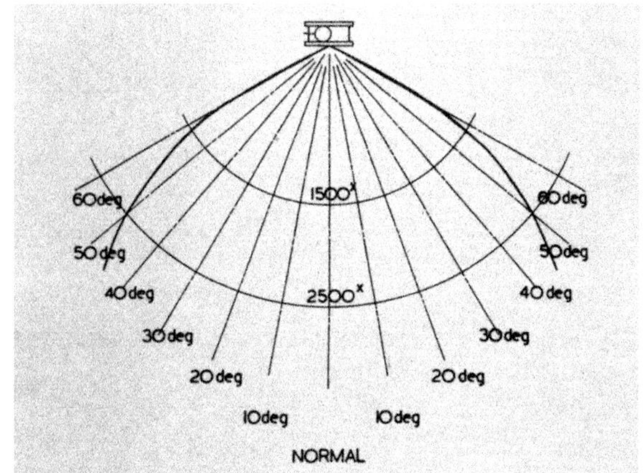

❮ Polar diagram: 3-inch M7 Gun M62 APCBC at 2,600 f.s. *v.* the hull side superstructure of the Panther (Pz.Kw.V). (*School of Tank Technology*)

❯ Polar diagram: 3-inch M7 Gun M62 APCBC at 2,600 f.s. *v.* the hull side of the Panther (Pz.Kw.V). (*School of Tank Technology*)

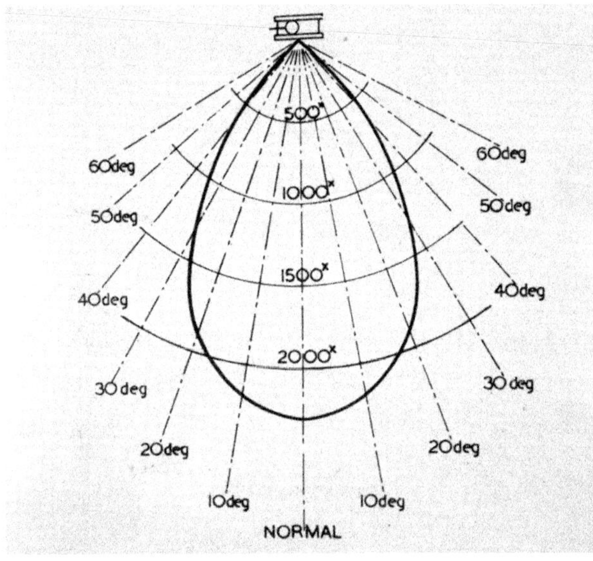

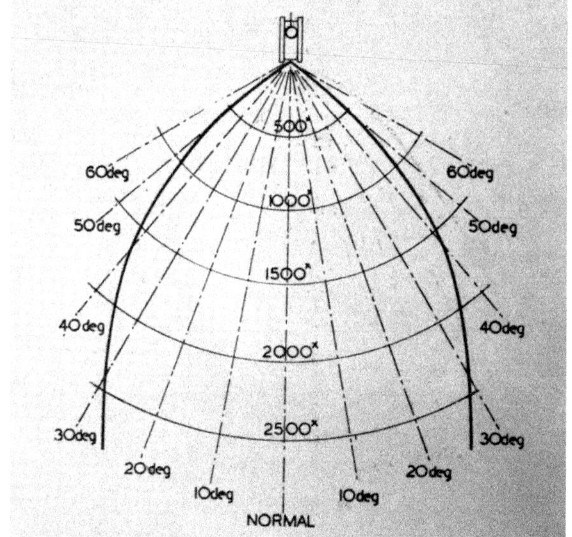

Above left: A 6-pdr Mk IV firing APCBC at 2,725 f.s. *v.* the hull side superstructure of the Panther (Pz.Kw.V). (*School of Tank Technology*)

Above right: A 6-pdr Mk IV firing APCBC at 2,725 f.s. *v.* rear hull of the Panther (Pz.Kw.V). (*School of Tank Technology*)

Right: A 6-pdr Mk IV firing APCBC at 2,725 f.s. *v.* the side of the turret of the Panther (Pz.Kw.V). (*School of Tank Technology*)

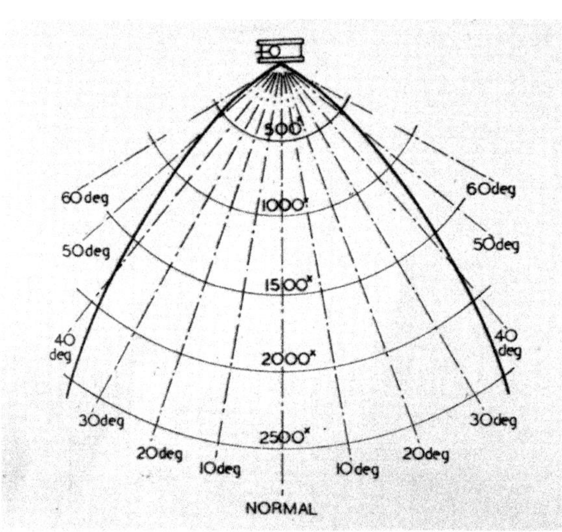

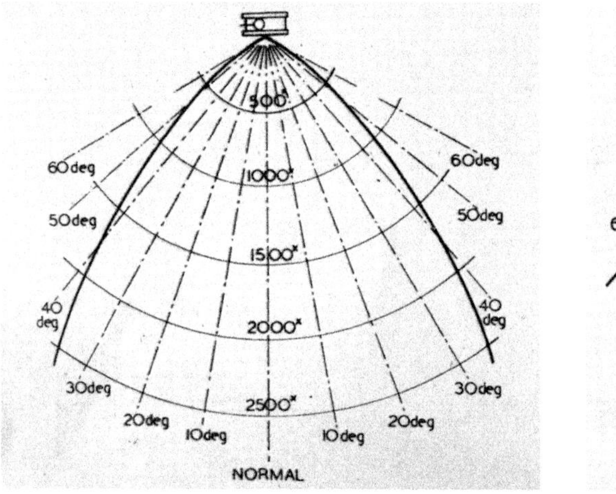

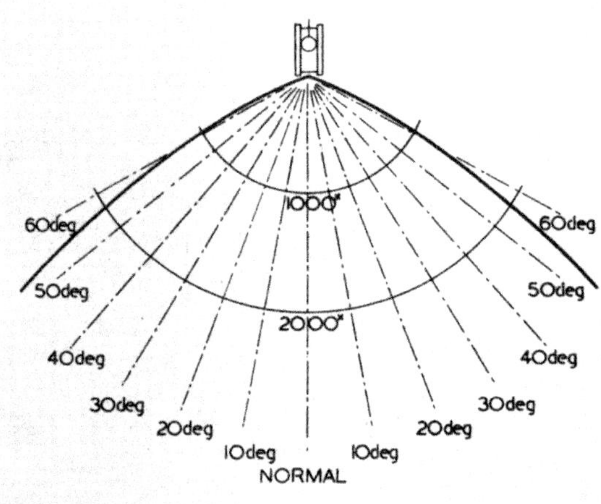

◀ A 6-pdr Mk IV firing APCBC at 2,725 f.s. *v.* the hull side of the Panther (Pz.Kw.V). (*School of Tank Technology*)

▶ A 17-pdr firing APCBC at 2,900 f.s. *v.* rear hull of the Panther (Pz.Kw.V). (*School of Tank Technology*)

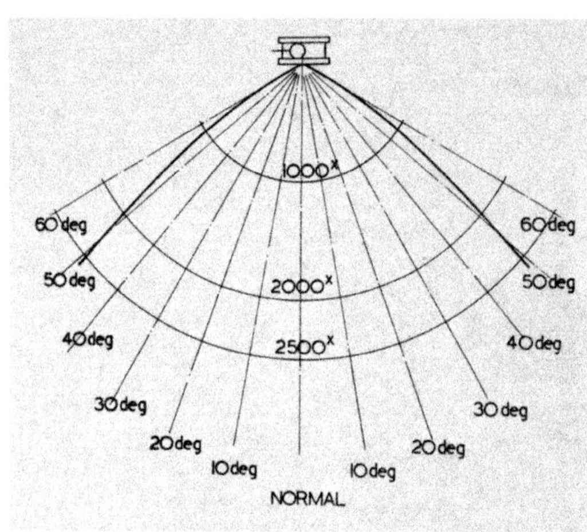

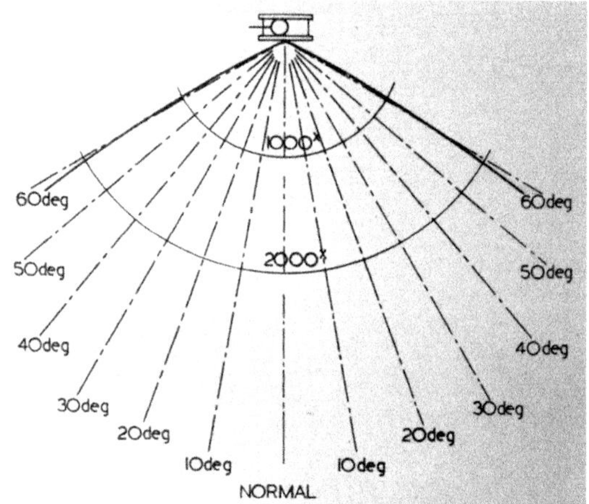

◀ A 17-pdr firing APCBC at 2,900 f.s. *v.* hull side superstructure of the Panther (Pz.Kw.V). (*School of Tank Technology*)

▶ A 17-pdr firing APCBC at 2,900 f.s. *v.* side and rear of the turret of the Panther (Pz.Kw.V). It is expected that against the vertical hull side of Panther the diagram will be similar, but that the 17-pdr will always fail at 70 degrees and will succeed against it at 60 degrees at any range at least up to 2,500 yards. (*School of Tank Technology*)

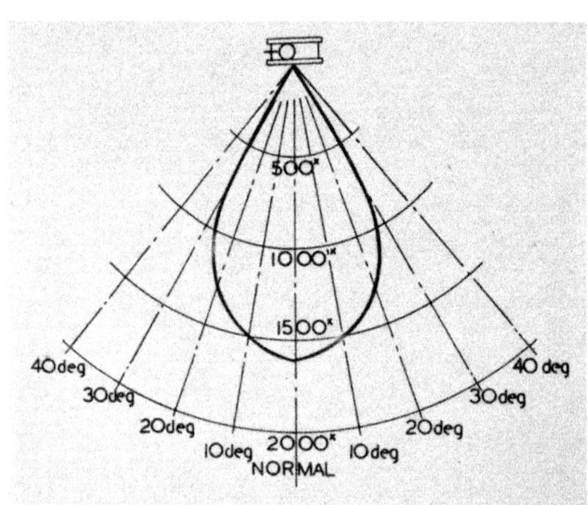

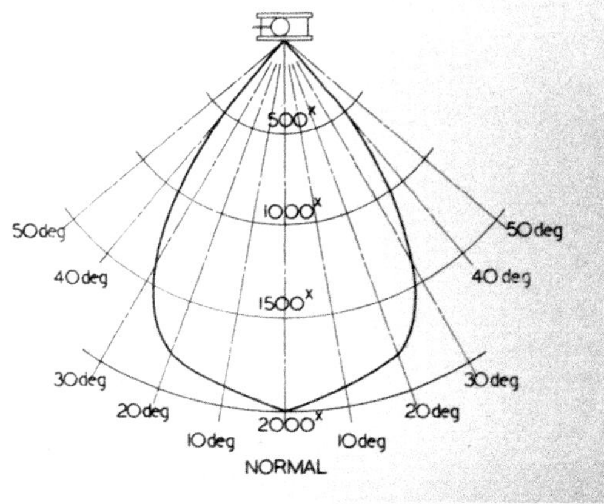

◀ A 37-mm M51 APCBC at 2,900 f.s. *v.* side and rear of turret of the Panther (Pz.Kw.V). (*School of Tank Technology*)

◀ A 37-mm M51 APCBC at 2,900 f.s. *v.* hull side of the Panther (Pz.Kw.V). This projectile is most unlikely to defeat either the glacis plate or the front of the turret of the Panther, neither is it expected to succeed against the hull side superstructure. (*School of Tank Technology*)

8

BRITISH INTERCEPTS OF GERMAN CODED MESSAGES

An Enigma machine on display at Bletchley Park, Buckinghamshire, England.

THE ENIGMA CODE

Just after the end of the First World War, German engineer Arthur Scherbius invented the Enigma machine. It was capable of sending coded messages and looked like a typewriter. Various models were produced over the following twenty-five years. The German military used it. The Enigma machine was built around a series of interchangeable rotors that rotated every time a key was pressed on the keyboard. This meant that the cypher kept changing continuously. It was linked to a plugboard on the front of the machine where pairs of letters were transposed. There were around 103 sextillion possible code settings to choose from. The German armed forces believed that the Enigma code was unbreakable and relied upon it to send classified messages.

In 1932, the Polish military broke the German Enigma code but kept that fact a secret. In 1939, the threat of war with Germany was close. The Poles decided to inform the British of what they had accomplished and how. The German's improved their system, which made it more complicated to decipher. The British set up the Enigma Research Section at Bletchley Park, a nineteenth-century mansion in Buckinghamshire, 50 miles north-west of London. In January 1940, this was where the first wartime Enigma messages were decoded. Enigma traffic continued to be routinely intercepted, and the code deciphered at Bletchley Park for the remainder of the war.

Most mornings, copies of the deciphered messages were sent to Prime Minister Winston Churchill. He used a red pen to make notes or comments on the messages and often wrote his initials 'WC' instead of using a signature. His right-hand man, Commander of the Imperial General Staff (CIGS) 1st Viscount Alan Brooke KG, GCB, OM, GCVO, DSO & Bar, used a green pen and usually just signed any note with the letter 'C' (The designations 'M' and 'Q' are used in James Bond 007 films, as titles for the head of departments in British Security Service MI6).

Alan Brooke was the professional head of the British Army during the Second World War and was promoted to field marshal in 1944. As chairman of the chiefs of staff committee, Brooke was the foremost military advisor to Winston Churchill, the British Prime Minister, and had the role of co-ordinator of the British military efforts in the Allies' victory in 1945. After retiring from the army, he served as lord high constable of England during the coronation of Queen Elizabeth II in 1953. His war diaries attracted attention for their criticism of Churchill and for Brooke's forthright views on other leading figures of the war.

FIRST MENTION OF A TIGER TANK

On 26 November 1942 at 8.37 a.m., a German coded message was intercepted and decoded at Bletchley Park. It was sent to Churchill and classified as 'Most Secret'. It had been sent in the morning of 25 November 1942 by German Luftwaffe Commander Albert Kesselring, who was working with Field Marshal Erwin Rommel in North Africa, to General Walther Nehring, who commanded the German contingent in Tunisia.

It read 'I call your attention to the view of the Führer concerning the use of Tiger Tanks for turning the tide of battle. (text for Commands Abroad to follow T26).'

This document is historically significant. It pinpoints the exact date that Winston Churchill first learnt of a new German tank called the Tiger. He has circled the words 'Tiger Tank' in his red pen and then written 'GIGS What are these? WC.'

On 28 November 1942, in a two-page letter, Chief of the Imperial General Staff (CIGS) Sir Alan Brooke replied:

MOST SECRET
CIGS/PM/340
War Office, Whitehall, London, S.W.1.
Prime Minister.

On the accompanying report (CX/MSS/1731/T2) you ask the nature of the German 'Tiger' tanks. These have been mentioned from time to time in MSS reports, and we originally thought that they were captured Russian tanks of some 50 tons wait. We now know them to be the same as the new Pz.Kw. VI super-heavy German tank of which the particulars are given below:

Weight: 57 tons in fighting trim
Dimensions:
Length 20 feet 3 inches
Width 11 feet 8 inches
Armour: Believed to be about 100 mm (3.9 inches)
Armament: 8.8-cm (3.46-inch) tank gun. The name of this gun (KwK 36) suggests that it is not substantially different in performance from the 3.46 in. multi-purpose gun (Flak 36).

Speed & Performance: No details are available. A most secret report speaks of a 'Tiger Squadron' of six Tigers and six Pz.Kw. III 'escort tanks': the German tank squadrons are always mixed but the term 'escort tank' is new and might suggest a certain lack of speed and manoeuvrability in the Pz.Kw. VI.

CIGS Sir Alan Brooke
28 November 1942

REQUEST FOR INFORMATION ON THE TIGER

This intercept may have delayed the intelligence search for the Panzer V Panther tank. The leap from IV to VI in the official German tank designation was confusing. The British conclusion that the Panzer V name had already been used for the 1936 Pz.Kpfw. Nb.Fz.V *Neubaufahrzeug* tank seemed sensible.

MOST SECRET

TO BE KEPT UNDER LOCK AND KEY AND NEVER TO BE REMOVED FROM THE OFFICE
THIS FORM IS TO BE USED FOR AIR INTELLIGENCE MESSAGES ONLY.

A.M. FORM No. 1479

GR. No. OFFICE SERIAL No.

TIME OF RECEIPT TIME OF DESPATCH SYSTEM

CX/MSS/1731/T2.

M E D I T E R R A N E A N.

FROM KESSELRING TO XC AK, GENERAL NEHRING VERY EARLY ON 25/11: -

I CALL YOUR ATTENTION TO THE VIEW OF THE FUEHRER CONCERNING THE USE OF TIGER TANKS FOR TURNING THE TIDE OF BATTLE.

(TEXT FOR COMMANDS ABROAD TO FOLLOW T 26).

B/W HYD/AHW/NC 0837/26/11/42.

RD A TO.

TIME OF ORIGIN SIGNATURE OF ORIGINATOR. NOT TO BE TELEPRINTED OPERATOR'S RECEIPT

The red pen is Winston Churchill asking Chief of the Imperial General Staff (CIGS) Alan Brooke 'What are these?' Tiger tanks. (*National Archives, Kew in London ref HW 1/1169, War office reference CX/MSS/1731/T2*)

MOST SECRET

Secret Cipher Telegram 1/65667 of 29 October from Middle East has reported the identification from a captured German document? Equivalent to British A.C.Is of the following AFVs not hitherto identified.

A new type known as PZ.KPFW.VI. This confirms that as expected, a new tank, heavier than III or IV is being built, the absence of any reference to PZ.KPFW V suggests that this nomenclature was probably applied to the heavy type first reported in 1937/38, later seen in Norway and in German propaganda papers, and since discarded.

We have asked both Middle East and the mission in Moscow to take urgent steps to obtain precise information on the characteristics of the PZ.KPFW.VI.

MI10
3 Nov 1942
EXTN 230
SGD. Shallard
Major
For Lt.Col: GS

GERMAN *DAK* DAILY REPORT: 22 DECEMBER 1942 BRITISH INTERCEPT

Most army units send daily reports to headquarters about the current strength available for combat operations. On 22 December 1942, British codebreakers at Bletchley Park managed to intercept and decode a very long German DAK day report that gave information on troop and tank strengths. This report is interesting in that it does not mention Tiger tanks even though three had arrived in North Africa on 23 November 1942. It may have been the Tiger tanks were not operating in the area of North Africa covered by the report, or they wanted to keep their arrival secret. The following translated intercept was sent to Prime Minister Winston Churchill. This report was transcribed from the National Archives in Kew, London (HW1/1251).

MOST SECRET

To be kept under lock and key: never to be removed from the office. This form is to be used for air intelligence messages only.
CX/MSS/1857/T11.
QT/9321.

MEDITERRANEAN

Day report No. 35824 22/12 issued by Otto Tiger (Panzer Army Rommel, Ia) at 2100/22/12:

1). In the course of the day the British reconnaissance forces did not feel their way any further forward against our rear-guards. Air reconnaissance revealed no significant change in the British dispositions. The British air force restricted its activity to isolated fighter-bomber attacks on troops in the forward area and principally, to maintain a fighter screen over his L. of C. area. German air reconnaissance reported moderate column traffic on the Via Balbia (road) between Arco del Filent and Nofilia. From this it can be concluded that the enemy is continuing to build up his supply base at Nofilia. This is also confirmed by V.N. reports. Enemy sabotage detachments carried out further raids in the area of Gheddahia and to the south-west. As counter measure, a German reconnaissance ABT. is being moved to the area Beni Ulid.

2). The intentions of Panzer Army for 23/12 are unchanged.

3). The following are so far operating in the Buerat positions, in the sector 15 km south south east of Gheddahia to the coast:

XX A.K. with Bettelmonench (164 Infantry Division): Young Fascists Division with Spezia Division, Raubvogel (Brigade Ramcke) and Pistoia Division.

In addition, the southern flank of the position is being covered by an Italian Garrison Force in Bungem and by the Battle Group Ariete 20 km south of Gheddahia.

In all, there are thus operating:

a). On the right wing:

aa). Bu Gnem: 2 Battalions with 7 light Italian batteries.

bb). Battle Group Ariete with 22 medium tanks, 12 armoured cars, 3 coys, 7 anti-tank guns 4.7 cm, 4 Flak 2 cm.

b). In the positional front roughly 60 km in breadth:

Under XX A.K.

aa). Bettelmoench with 4 Battalions

5 anti-tank guns 5 cm.
10 anti-tank guns 7.5 cm.
3 infantry guns.
7 Flak 2 cm.
3 light field howitzers. 10.5 cm.
24 Flak 2 cm.
7 Flak 8.8 cm.

bb). Young Fascist Division with 6 Battalions.

63 anti-tank guns 4.7 cm.
6 Flak 2 cm.
26 guns 6.5 cm.
20 guns 7.5 cm.
8 howitzers, 10 cm.

cc). Corps Artillery:
17 guns 10.5 cm.
Under XXI A.K.
aa). Spezia division with 9 Battalions
60 anti-tank guns 4.7 cm.
12 Flak 2 cm.
30 guns 6.5 cm.
26 guns 7.5 cm.
bb). Raubvogel with 4 battle groups.
13 anti-tank guns 5 cm.
12 Flak 2 cm.
30 Flak 2 cm.
6 Flak 8.8 cm.
cc). Pistoia division with 8 Battalions.
35 anti-tank guns 4.7 cm.
11 Flak 2 cm.
9 guns 6.5 cm.
23 guns 7.5 cm.
15 howitzers 10 cm.
dd). Corps Artillery:
17 guns 10.5 cm.
8 guns 8.7 cm.
19 guns 15 cm.

In addition, elements of Nikolaus (19th Flak Division) are already operating in the Buerat position in the anti-aircraft and/or ground role.

The German motorised formations are at present ready for defence in the area Sirte-Buerat and southwards.

4). The strained fuel situation continues to make mobile operations and the employment of motorised formations against an enemy envelope in movement to the south for the present still impossible. Up to the present only the withdrawal of the motorised formations now east of the Buerat position into the position itself, together with the most essential supply traffic is assured.

5). Tank situation of Felsbrock (D.A.K.), Serviceable:

Tanks III	2
Tanks III/long	15
Tanks IV	11
Tanks IV/long	30
Command vehicles	2

Total 58 tanks, 2 command vehicles.

(Bletchley Park—Reference the above the following was passed at 23.27hrs 23 December 1942 as QT/9321/CO/AL/WD/PK)

ROMMEL'S CHRISTMAS PRESENT

On 25 December 1942, Rommel's DAK received more Tiger tanks. They were shipped from Italy to Tunisia by two tank landing craft and successfully beached on the North African coast at La Goulette, the port of Tunis, capital of Tunisia. On 23 December 1942, the British intercepted, decoded and translated this German Navy message. The report was transcribed from the National Archives in Kew, London (HW1/1251).

MOST SECRET

To be kept under lock and key: never to be removed from the office. This form is to be used for air intelligence messages only.
CX/MSS/ZTPGM/5975(1858/5)
QT/9339.

MEDITERRANEAN

Time of Despatch 23/12/1942

Compiled from document seen by source on 23/12/42 from German Naval Command Italy to German Naval Command Tunisia.

'Ventun Aprile and Carlo Zeno (see QT/9236) now to arrive La Goulette 1500 hours 25th 'probably' with two landing-craft carrying Tiger tanks above according to Germans evening 23rd.'

Passed at 0407/Z/24/12/42 AS:

QT/9339 CO/AL/MA/NC/PK.

TIGER TANKS ON THE PROWL

On 1 March 1943, Bletchley Park intercepted and decoded a German DAK message that gave the strength of Tiger tanks operating in the northern sector. Fifteen were on the prowl, two had been knocked out, and one was being repaired. This was sent to Prime Minister Winston Churchill:

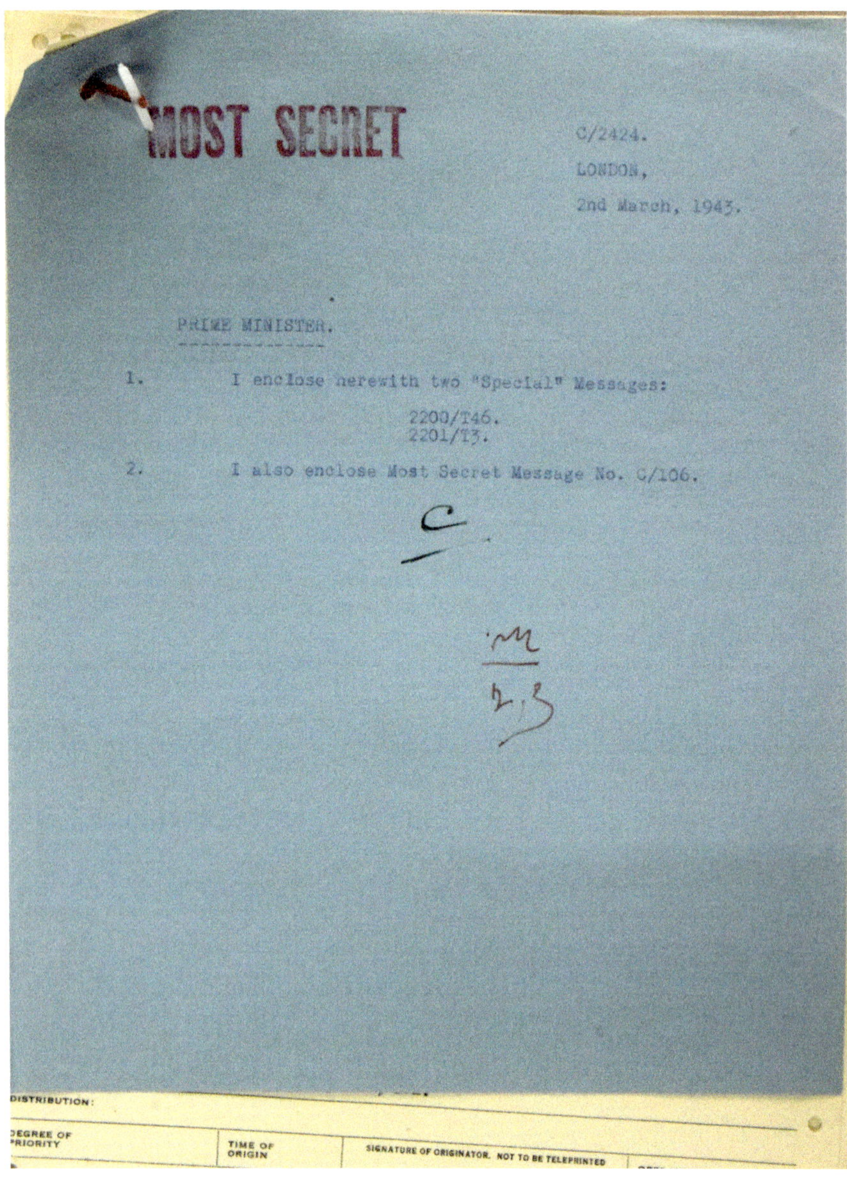

MOST SECRET

C/2424.
LONDON,
2nd March, 1943.

PRIME MINISTER.

1. I enclose herewith two "Special" Messages:

2200/T46.
2201/T3.

2. I also enclose Most Secret Message No. C/106.

C

DISTRIBUTION:

DEGREE OF PRIORITY | TIME OF ORIGIN | SIGNATURE OF ORIGINATOR. NOT TO BE TELEPRINTED

This is the front cover containing secret messages sent to Prime Minister Winston Churchill on 2 March 1943. It contains a report on Tiger tanks on the prowl. Churchill signed the front of the cover in a red pen to indicate he had seen it. CIGS Alan Brooke used a green pen to write the letter 'C' to indicate he had seen it. (*National Archives, Kew in London ref HW 1/1415, War office reference C/2424. C/106. 200/T46. and 201/T3*)

MOST SECRET

To be kept under lock and key: never to be removed from the office. This form is to be used for air intelligence messages only.

CX/MSS/2200/T46.

VM/5363.

MEDITERRANEAN

Document sent to Army group Africa by Panzer Army 5 Ia on 1 March 1943, has been seen by source.

No. 436.

(a) In workshop 1 Tiger.

(b) 15 operating in the Northern Sector, two totally destroyed

(c) Nil return.

Note: Above is the reply to Army Group Africa's request reported in CX/NSS/2197/T 21

TIGER TANKS AND SPARES IN ITALY

At 2 p.m. on 1 May 1943, Bletchley Park intercepted, decoded, and translated a German DAK message requesting Tiger tank spare parts held in Italy be sent to units in North Africa as soon as possible. This was sent to Prime Minister Winston Churchill. This report was transcribed from the National Archives in Kew, London (ref. HW 1/1668).

MOST SECRET

To be kept under lock and key: never to be removed from the office. This form is to be used for air intelligence messages only.

CX/MSS/2522/T30.

ML/1064.

MEDITERRANEAN

From Panzer Army 5 Ia to A.O.C. in C. South ops. Abt. on 1/5:-

The further serviceability of Tiger tanks here, which, under certain circumstances, could be decisive in the coming fighting, depends on the speediest possible supplying of the following spare parts:

1). Complete ventilator(s) with sliding couplings '*Rutschkupplungen*' and oil pipes.

2). At least one engine (HL 23210).

3). Track assembly parts.

4). At least 1 complete steering mechanism.

5). Two 8.8 gun barrels.

6). One radiator.

7). All small spare parts in stock in Naples. In Trapani there are also spare parts of Panzer Abt 501 and 504, these could be loaded as additional freight on ferries. We also request the dispatch of the 2 tanks VI of Abt. 2/501 and the complete 2/504 which are also in Trapani. An answer is requested.

Following passed with T.O.O. To 2231/4/5/43Z

REMAGEN BRIDGEHEAD

At 9 p.m. on 12 March 1945, the British codebreakers at Bletchley Park intercepted and translated a message sent by General-Major Zimmerman regarding the possibility of Tiger tanks going to the aid of German troops at Remagen. US forces had captured the Ludendorff bridge over the river Rhine at Remagen on 7 March 1945. It was brought to the attention of Prime Minister Winston Churchill. The town of Erpel is on the eastern side of the Ludendorff bridge. The German tank company referred to in this message never got there. There was a counter-attack by Tiger II tanks from Sennelager at the end of the month near Paderborn.

TOP MOST SECRET ULTRA

To be kept under lock and key: never to be removed from the office. This form is to be used for air intelligence messages only.

T.O.O. 2100/12/3/45

CX/MSS/T487/36.

BT 71041064.

WEST EUROPE

No. 616 part (Roman) II, from C. in C, West (Roman) Ia, liaison officer, signed Gen.-Major Zimmerman, at 2100/12/3

To Army Group B: –

Ref. No. 616 from C. in C, West (Roman) Ia, liaison officer,

Four tanks, of 11/3:-

Subject: Heavy Pz. Abt.506

With the approval of OKW the Tiger Coy of SS Pz. Abt 501, after handing over its tanks to a Coy of heavy Pz. Abt 506, is to be sent off again to Sennelager. As already ordered the Coy is to be employed with the necessary staff and staff elements of heavy Pz. Abt 506 at the Erpel (F62) Bridgehead.

The bringing up of additional tigers is not to be expected for the time being. General of Pz. Troops West has already issued the appropriate orders for the dispatch and the handing over of the tanks.

Note: Not seen by source. SS Pz. Abt 501 known to have been loading earlier this month, (T484/64), but source had not identified any of its elements in the West front area.

9

1943 NEWSPAPER REPORTS ON THE NEW TIGER TANK

Surprisingly, the British government did not censor the news that the Germans had developed a new heavy tank called the Tiger, which had very thick armour and a big gun. They allowed the press to print reports of the Tiger in action even though there was a risk this could demoralise the public and the armed forces. It was a good day for British government public relations when the press later reported the first formidable Tiger tanks being knocked out. Providing the British press with after-battle reports and intelligence data was another way the government relayed information to its armed forces that the feared Tiger tank was not invincible. The press then continued to report incidents of other Tiger tanks being stopped or destroyed and how this was done.

On 30 January 1943, the *Daily Mail* reported that the German Army in Tunisia had a new 62-ton monster Tiger tank equipped with a dual-purpose 88-mm gun. The journalist Alan Humphreys used First World War terminology to describe the new tank. He referred to it as a 'Land Battleship' and remarked that although it was a similar size to the Panzer IV, it was around twice the weight because of the additional armour. He informed his readers that 7 inches of armour plate protected the turret, 8-inch thick armour was used on the front of the tank, and that the side armour was 5 inches thick. These thicknesses were very inaccurate: 7 inches converts to 178 mm; 8 inches are 203 mm, and 5 inches equals 127 mm. The correct data was that the armour at the front of the Tiger was 100 mm thick, the turret was 80 mm thick, and the sides were protected by 60-mm-thick armour. Allied tank crews reading this inaccurate newspaper article would be shocked. On the plus side, he did report that three of the Tiger tanks had been stopped when French anti-tank mines blew off the tank's tracks.

On 5 February 1943, *The Daily Telegraph*, *Daily Record*, and the *Daily Mirror* reported that British 6-pdr guns penetrated the armour of a Tiger tank near Robaa in North Africa and knocked it out. They stated that the Mark VI tank's armour had been pierced four times from a range between 400 and 500 yards. With obvious glee, they reported that the legend of the Tiger tank's 'invulnerability had been completely dissipated.' *The Daily Telegraph* incorrectly reported that the Tiger had 7-inch (178-mm) armour plates with an extra 1-inch (25 mm) shield in the front. The *Daily Mirror* stated that the Mark VI tank carried an 88-mm gun and looked like a field gun with caterpillar wheels.

On Wednesday, 10 February 1943, the *Liverpool Evening Express* newspaper reported a verbal disagreement in the House of Commons following the public release of the physical specifications of the new German Tiger tank. Mr Stokes MP asked Sir Andrew Duncan, minister of supply, if there was a British tank currently in production that was equal to the German Tiger tank. Sir Andrew replied that it was not in the public interest to make that sort of information public knowledge. Mr Stokes was not happy with that reply and suggested that the government was embarrassed that they did not have a tank that could deal with the Tiger tank and did not want to tell the truth. He also suggested that it was time for a debate on the 'tank situation'. In reply, Sir Andrew reaffirmed the government's position that it would be disadvantageous to the public interest to make this information public.

Mr Shinwell, Labour MP for Seaham, then stood up and asked the same type of question, demanding to know if the British government were at last producing a tank 'equal to the best the enemy have got.' Sir Andrew did not reply as many other members in the House of Commons shouted, 'No' and 'Don't answer.' Mr Shinwell then continued stating that he was not asking for details, but the rest of his question was drowned out by shouts of 'Order, Order'. Although there were no tanks in production at the time these questions were asked, there was a lot of work being carried out on how to fit a high-velocity 17-pdr gun that could knock out a Tiger tank into an armoured vehicle. This design work produced the Archer, 17-pdr SP M10 Achilles self-propelled guns, Sherman Firefly, A30 Challenger, A34 Comet, and Centurion tanks.

On Wednesday, 24 February 1943, the *Yorkshire Evening Post* quoted the military correspondent of *The Times*'s description of the Tiger tank being used by the Germans in Tunisia. This was a short piece that educated its readers on what type of vehicle British troops were fighting against. There was no editorial comment. 'Its size is governed by the weight of the 88-mm gun [1.5 tonnes] and the size and weight of the ammunition.' The reporter then gave details about the thickness of the Tiger's armour, which was much more accurate than the earlier exaggerated reports printed in other newspapers. 'The amour in front is 4in. thick and on the side 3 ¼ in. [101 mm and 82 mm]'. The reporter also added details about the width, height, and length of the tank.

On Wednesday, 24 February 1943, the *Yorkshire and Leeds Intelligencer* reported on the success of 'light batteries' knocking out Tiger tanks at nearly point-blank range as the tanks tried to negotiate winding mountain roads following the defeat and retreat of Allied forces at the Kasserine Pass in North Africa. The paper stated that fourteen German tanks had been destroyed and many others damaged in this action.

On the same page, in a different report, a journalist described a British Guards unit's defence of the town of Thala in North Africa. It commanded a defile leading down to the plain across which ran the Tebessa–Bou Arda railway, which was a vital Allied supply line. The British repulsed the German attack but sustained heavy casualties. What is interesting about this report is that it was prefaced by the observation that the British Armoured Guards unit was equipped with the same type of Churchill tanks, armed with 6-pdr guns, which had successfully knocked out the 'monster Mark VI in previous engagements in Tunisia'.

On 4 March 1943, the *Liverpool Evening Express*, using country sports shooting terminology, reported that Churchill tanks 'bagged a Tiger' and described the enemy tank as 'the monster German Mark VI'. The reporter stated that this action happened in the Béja-Mateur sector of Tunisia.

On Tuesday, 9 March 1943, the *Hull Daily Mail* reported how British artillery kept Rommel's panzers, including Tiger tanks, at bay near the Mareth Line in North Africa during the previous weekend. The 25-pdr bombardment was so successful that it was unnecessary to send British tanks into action. The attack was halted, and the enemy withdrew.

On Thursday, 23 March 1943, the headline in the *Nottingham Evening Post* was: 'Tigers Knocked Out'. It published a report from the Reuters correspondent with the American forces on the Gafsa Front in Tunisia, North Africa. The article covered Rommel's counter-attack against the US Army's flank below the Gafsa–Gabes road, which was 15 miles east of El Guettar. The attack was spearheaded by Panzer III, Panzer IV, and 'giant "Tiger" Mark VI Tanks'. An American artillery barrage knocked out a 'few of the "Tigers"'. During the battle, it was reported that ten German tanks were destroyed with twenty more knocked out. This showed the readers that the Tiger tank could be stopped by artillery guns.

On Saturday, 10 April 1943, Alan Humphreys, Reuter's correspondent in North Africa submitted a report on the capture of the Axis port of Sfax in Tunisia, and the two tank engagements fought on Thursday, 8 April 1943. It was printed in a number of newspapers, including the *Liverpool Echo*. He reported that Rommel's Tigers had advanced cautiously across the rolling fields that sweep down from the hills towards the plans of Sfax. This was an effort to hold up the British Eighth Army while their 'soft-skinned columns' retreated from the western end of the Wadi Akarit line. He informed his readers that he had watched British cruiser and Sherman tanks half-hidden in the fields of barley waiting to be given the signal to engage the enemy.

At 3 p.m., an artillery barrage of high-explosive fragmentation shells fell on the German tank position. This was followed by the shellfire from anti-tank guns. He saw that two of the Tiger tanks had been knocked out by AP rounds fired by the anti-tank guns. At the same moment, the British tanks raced across the barley fields, 'smashing down the tall crops.' Rommel's panzers, 'did not stay long' and 'turned and ran heading for the black ridge of hills to the north-east.' South African Boston and American Mitchell bombers were directed to drop their bombs on the fleeing German tanks. Readers learnt from this article that Allied anti-tank guns could knock out a Tiger tank.

Not every piece of intelligence about the Tiger tank was shared with the public. On Tuesday, 13 April 1943, the *Liverpool Evening Express* reported a response to a question about the Tiger tank. 'Sir James told Mr Granville (Ind. eye): "It is not in the public interest to disclose the date on which information about the German Tiger tank was first received by the War Office"'.

On 23 April 1943, the *Aberdeen Evening Express* reported that three battalions of German infantry and forty tanks including many Tiger tanks had attacked from the direction of Goubellat in Tunisia, North Africa. The article reported that many enemy tanks were knocked out by the 'murderous fire from 25-pounder' artillery guns, 'shooting over the open sights the gunners knocked out tank after tank'. This was soon followed by a counter-attack by British tanks, who used their machine guns to kill the supporting German infantry. The battle went on for four hours and resulted in a German defeat.

On Thursday, 6 May 1943, *The Scotsman* reported the repulse of a counter-attack east of Medjez al Bab, west of Tunis in Tunisia, two days earlier. The enemy attacked with seventeen tanks but one Mark III tank, nine Mark IV tanks, and two Mark VI Tiger tanks were knocked out.

When Churchill visited North Africa, the Media followed. He was photographed and recorded on film when he inspected captured and knocked-out Tiger tanks. Churchill's examination of Tiger tank 131 (which is now at the Tank Museum, Bovington) is the most widely known example, but Pathé News also showed film footage in cinemas of Churchill's entourage stopping by a badly damaged Tiger tank 121 of 1./s.Pz.Abt.504 taken on 29 May 1943. He is surrounded by senior officers who give the prime minister a walk-around tour of the tank. Although later photographs showed it had three holes in the side armour caused by AP shells, it may have been destroyed by its crew who had to abandon it due to a mechanical breakdown and the wreck was used for target practice.

On 11 May 1943, the *Aberdeen Press and Journal*, on its front page, reported that a German anti-tank gun, captured by British troops in Tunisia, complete with ammunition, was used to knock out a Tiger tank at a point-blank range of 5 yards. The photograph that appeared in the newspaper showed three British soldiers manning a German 7.5-cm Pak 97/38 anti-tank gun.

On Monday, 7 June 1943, the *Aberdeen Press and Journal* published an article stating how German propaganda was praising the strength of the new Tiger tank on the Eastern Front but then the Soviets countered with reports that it had vulnerabilities. The Soviets admitted that it had exceptional heavy armour and a very powerful gun but stated that the weight of the Tiger was too heavy. The tank's tracks and road wheels were very vulnerable to shells. This was the sort of message the British government wanted the public and their armed forces to hear.

On Wednesday, 7 July 1943, the *Dundee Courier* reported that Tiger tanks were used for the first time on the Soviet front during their attack in the Orel-Kursk sector. The article stated that Soviet long-range guns badly mauled the Tigers and forced them to turn back to their starting point. During the counter-attack, the Germans lost half their forces, including ten Tiger tanks.

On 13 July 1943, the *Birmingham Daily Post* emphasised that the feared Tiger tank was 'not an insoluble problem'. They quoted Soviet *Pravda* reporters' accounts of Tigers being set ablaze by hand grenades and incendiary bottles—the famous Molotov Cocktail. Both these weapons would be thrown on the back of the engine deck. Shrapnel from the fragmentation grenades and flaming petrol would enter the engine compartment through the armoured air intake and exhaust louvres, causing severe damage. The *Pravda* reporters also claimed that the Tiger was 'quite vulnerable' to Soviet guns and anti-tank rifles. This last bit was not true. The 14.5-mm Soviet anti-tank rifles could not penetrate the side armour of the tiger tank. They could penetrate the side armour on the Panzer III, Panzer IV tanks, and Stug III.

On Wednesday, 28 July 1943, the *Liverpool Evening Express* reported that Moscow radio had announced that 160 German Tiger tanks had been destroyed around Byelgorod. This report broke Moscow's silence about what was happening on the Leningrad front.

On 4 August 1943, the *Nottingham Evening Post* reported that the Germans had abandoned tanks on Eastern Front battlefields, some of them undamaged. Early-production Panther and Tiger tanks suffered mechanical failures. If they could not be recovered, they were often scuttled by the crew by setting off explosive charges inside the tank before heading back for their own front line. Some crews did not do this and sometimes the explosive charges failed to work. This sort of information would again help deflate the invulnerable Tiger tank myth. The account stated, 'roads and forests are littered with abandoned German material including guns and tanks—often in good condition. Among the abandoned tanks are several practically undamaged Tigers'.

On 5 August 1943, the *Liverpool Daily Post* reported that a small number of Mark VI Tiger tanks, with other tanks, were used in an attack against British infantry in North Africa. British and Commonwealth anti-tank gunners managed to stop the attack. One Tiger and two other tanks were abandoned by the Germans when they withdrew.

On 11 October 1943, the *Nottingham Journal* reported that Britain had a new anti-tank gun that could kill a Tiger tank at 1,000 yards called the 17-pounder. This seems a strange thing to make public. The Germans would obtain this information and plan accordingly. The reasons for the official censor letting this military secret become public knowledge is unclear. The possibility that good news would raise the spirits of the public and armed forces alike could have been a major influence.

The *Nottingham Journal* column stated that the 17-pdr gun could 'knock out the most heavily armoured enemy tanks at up to 1,000 yards range'. The journalist then accurately wrote about the foresight in the War Ministry—that they concluded there would be a requirement for a more powerful anti-tank gun in the future, even though 'the 2-pounder and 6-pounder anti-tank guns were a match for all the existing German tanks'. They believed that the enemy would pin their hopes on a very heavily armoured tank, a slow-moving tracked fortress, with an immensely powerful big gun.

The article then went on to cover battlefield reports of the 17-pdr in action in North Africa. In the spring of 1943, one gun apparently knocked out an enemy tank at a range of 1,500 yards and blew the turret off. In late April, it was reported that one 17-pdr stopped three tanks with three rounds. A later report stated that one 17-pdr gun knocked out six tanks, including two Mark VI Tigers.

On Friday, 27 August 1943, the *Yorkshire Post and Leeds Intelligencer* published a poor-quality photograph of a knocked-out Tiger tank by the side of a road in Sicily. They reported that it weighed 56 tons and was armed with an 88-mm gun.

THE SCOTSMAN

31,182. EDINBURGH, THURSDAY, MAY 6, 1943. PRICE

Nottingham Evening Post

TERED FOR TRANSMISSION IN THE UNITED KINGDOM] WEDNESDAY, AUGUST 4, 1943.

The Yorkshire Post

and Leeds Mercury

No. 29,965—ESTAB. 1754 LEEDS, FRIDAY, AUGUST 27, 1943 DAILY—ONE PENNY

10

SCHOOL OF TANK TECHNOLOGY Pz.Kw. VI (TIGER) REPORT No. 19

This report was one of the early assessments of the Tiger tank, its capabilities, weaknesses, and design disadvantages. Future instructional wartime booklets used the information contained in this report. The information in this chapter has been transcribed from original wartime documents. The report format and brief notation style has been kept.

FOREWORD

This vehicle is a well armoured tank of sound construction designed to carry an 8.8-cm gun in a fully traversing turret. It has deep wading facilities and a limited underwater performance to a depth of approximately 15 feet. This feature is worthy of special note as it is an essential part of the basic vehicle design.

The introduction of a plate interlocking in addition to the normal stepped jointing is a distinct development in German armoured fighting vehicle construction. It must, however, be remembered that up to now no German vehicle has carried armour of greater thickness than 50 mm, whereas the bulk of armour of the Pz.Kw. VI is of 62, 82, and 102 mm thickness.

Against the tank's tactical advantages, derived mainly from its armament it incorporates some important disadvantages, the most outstanding being the restriction on transportation due to its width and weight, and its limited climbing ability due to the small height of the centre line of the front sprocket above the ground.

A further serious disadvantage is its restricted radius of action, due to its small petrol tank capacity and heavy consumption, stated by the enemy to be 2.75 gallons per mile on normal cross-country running. Against this must be offset the feeling of the crew, who have a good sound tank, able to out range any it has met, roomy, and with comfortable positions for all. Driving, in particular, is a pleasure and the gunner's layout as convenient as you could wish.

Front cover of the November 1943 Preliminary Report No. 19 on the Tiger tank. (*School of Tank Technology*)

PRELIMINARY REPORT ON Pz.Kw. VI MODEL 'H'

(Note the letter 'H' denoted the manufacturer Henschel later changed to Ausf. E)

(STT/8/2/11 Ex North Africa)
Examined at Chobham. D.T.D Project No. 3016, November 1943
Examiner: Major A.D. Lidderdale, A.M.I. Mech.E., R.E.M.E.

General Specifications

Type Pz.Kpf.Wg. VI H. Model H.1.
Tank No. 131. hull No. 250122. Turret No. 230639.
Armament One 8.8-cm tank gun KwK. 36 and one 7.92 MG 34
Co-axial in turret.
One MG 34 in superstructure front plate.
One 9 mm machine carbine stowed.

Armour	26–102 mm (There is local thickening of the gun mantlet to 110 mm).	
Weight	As received on narrow tracks: 50 tons 5 cwt. (Less crew of five, their kit and rations, and with petrol tanks half full and half complement of ammunition). Estimated weight in battle order is therefore 56 tons.	
Max speed	No accurate figure available but 18 mph recorded.	
Crew	Five: Commander, Gunner, Loader, Hull gunner/wireless operator, Driver.	
Dimensions	Length (excluding gun)	20 feet 8.5 inches
	Length (including gun at 12 o'clock)	27 feet 9 inches
	Width (overall)	12 feet 3 inches
	Height	9 feet 4.75 inches
Ground Contact	12 feet 6 inches	
Track Centres	9 feet 3.5 inches	
Engine	Maybach V12 cyl. 650 metric HP (642 British B.H.P)	
Gearbox	Maybach Olvar—Preselector—hydraulically operated.	
Steering	Controlled differential—hydraulically operated by steering wheel. For emergency steering—steering levers operate vehicle breaks independently.	
Drive	Front sprockets.	
Suspension	Torsion bar. Sixteen single and 4 twin bogies on each side giving a total of 24 tyres. When narrow track is fitted—8 twin and 4 single bogeys on each side.	
Tracks	Manganese steel 4/4 lugs.	

CONDITION

The general condition of the vehicle is reasonably good both structurally and mechanically. Heavy frontal attack is in evidence at the front of the vehicle. An oblique hit which registered at 12 o'clock on the superstructure top plate has fractured the lateral weld along the centre of the plate. The round struck the turret ring joint damaging the pneumatic ceiling tube and jamming the turret traverse. The blow on the top front plate also resulted in the complete disintegration of the wireless set.

There are no penetrations of the armour although the vehicle has been subject to heavy fire, the front of vertical plate and the turret front being considerably scarred. Apart from a minor defect in the starting apparatus the vehicle was in good mechanical condition when received in this country.

1. GENERAL CONSTRUCTION

Hull

The construction of the hull departs from the familiar German practice in that the front and rear superstructure are in one unit and it is welded to the lower hull. Interlocking stepped joints secured by welding are used in the construction of both the lower hull and superstructure. This space is continued from the front of vertical plate to the tail plate.

The top front plate covers the full width of the panniers thus providing a horizontal seating 10 feet 4 inches wide upon which the turret ring is mounted. It is this exceptional width that enables the turret ring of 6 feet 1 inch internal diameter to be fitted. The belly of the hull is formed of one 26-mm plate measuring 5 feet 11 inches × 15 feet 10.25 inches.

The hull is divided into 4 compartments. The forward compartment on the nearside accommodates the driver and his controls. A centrally disposed gearbox to the front of which the steering unit is mounted, separates the driving compartment from the offside forward compartment in which the hull gunner is seated.

The third compartment, the fighting chamber, occupies the central portion of the hull and is separated from the rear engine compartment by a bulkhead and from the forward compartments by an arched cross member. The floor of the fighting compartment is suspended from and rotates with the turret.

Turret

The turret is centrally mounted between the hull side plate with the centre of the turret ring approximately 6.5 inches to the rear of the transverse centre line of the vehicle.

The vertical sides and rear are formed of the bending into horseshoe form of a single 82-mm plate. The toe of the horseshoe forms the rear of the turret whilst the extremities at the front are tied in by two 100-mm rectangular section bars which are dovetailed and welded to the main plate. The upper and lower edges of the sides converge towards the front in order to allow movement of the gun mantlet when the gun is elevated or depressed.

The roof of the turret consists of a single rolled plate of 26 mm bent slightly forward of the centre line to suit the taper of the side plate at the front. The roof plate is recessed into and welded to the turret wall.

The main trunnions which are of a spherical type are mounted in the turret sides and carry an external robust cast steel mantlet and the gun cradle. Removal of the complete mantlet and gun cradle can be affected by the removal of four set bolts. The mantlet projects over the side plates and affords adequate protection for the open front of the turret. The trunnions are extended outwards to form lifting lugs for the removal of the turret. A further lug is provided at the rear of the turret on the vertical centre line, thus providing correctly balanced three-point slinging.

Cupola

A circular fixed cupola is mounted in the turret roof—the cupola has an inside diameter of 20 inches and is offset to the extreme nearside.

2. ARMOUR

	Armour	Basic	Extra	Angle
A.	Cupola top	15 mm		90 degrees
B.	Cupola front and sides	50–80 mm		0 degrees cylindrical
C.	Turret top front	26 mm		81 degrees
D.	Turret top rear	26 mm		90 degrees
E.	Turret sides	82 mm		0 degrees
F.	Turret rear	82 mm		0 degrees
G.	Turret front		local thickening	5 degrees
H.	Gun mantlet	100–110 mm		Moving
J.	Front vertical plate	102 mm		10 degrees
K.	Front glacis plate	61 mm		80 degrees
L.	Front nose plate	102 mm		24 degrees
M.	Front lower nose plate	63 mm	(approx.)	63 degrees
N.	Side superstructure	80 mm		0 degrees
O.	Pannier floor	26 mm		90 degrees
P.	Side hull plate	63 mm		0 degrees
Q.	Top front plate	26 mm		90 degrees

R.	Top rear plate	26 mm	90 degrees
S.	Top rear engine cover plate	26 mm	90 degrees
U.	Belly plate	26 mm	90 degrees
W.	Tail plate (upper)	82 mm	8 degrees

[The 'Angle of plate' given is the angle between the plate surface and the vertical, which is equal to the 'Angle of impact' for horizontal attack.]

The cast front plate of the gun mantlet has a thickness of 92 mm over the full height and breadth. Measured through the gunsight borings, the thickness is 100 mm. In the centre portion where the front plate is reinforced around the gun, the thickness is increased to 200 mm. There is no spaced armour or the provision for fitting it. The stowage of a spare length of track on the front nose plate adds to the effectiveness of the armour at this point.

There is no face hardened armour. The thin horizontal plates, 26 mm thick, range from 298–343 Brinell and the thick vertical or near vertical plates range from 257–310 Brinell. The bulk of the plate is comparable with British standard machinable quality.

Except for the fact that the front of vertical plate projects slightly above the top front plate and may afford some protection to the turret ring and the hatches on either side of the top plate, there is no splash protection for the turret ring joint. This is interesting in view of the fact that a pneumatic rubber sealing ring is fitted in this joint. Deflector bars are fitted at either side of the driver's visor or and on the glacis plate immediately in front of it.

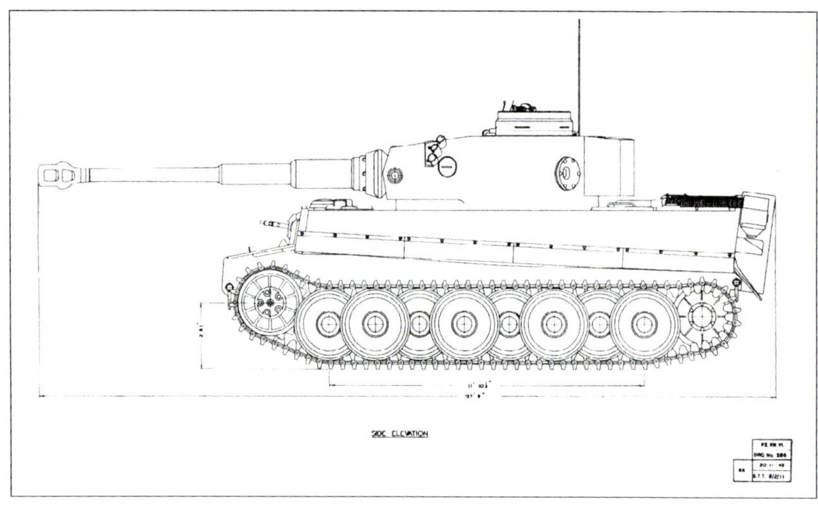

This side elevation drawing of the Panzer V Ausf. E Tiger tank was included in the report and dated 10 November 1943. (*School of Tank Technology*)

3. ARMAMENT

One 8.8-cm Tank Gun KwK 36)
One 7.92-mm MG 34) Co-axial in turret
One 7.92-mm MG 34) In ball mounting on offside of front vertical plate
One 9-mm Machine Carbine

8.8-cm Tank Gun

The 8.8-cm gun is approximately 17 feet in length, of which 7 feet overhangs the hull, and it is fitted with a double baffle muzzle brake. The breech, which is of the semi-automatic vertical-falling-block-type, is actuated by the lever breech mechanism at the right of it. It is electrically fired from a control incorporated in the elevating hand wheel. An electrical safety device identical to that fitted in the Pz.Kw III and IV is provided which prevents firing if the breech is not closed, the gun not fully run out, or the buffer not full. An extension to the rear of the gun carries a canvas sack for receiving the ejected cases. A recoil indicator is fixed on the left arm of the frame and shows a maximum normal working recoil of 580-mm Buffer and recuperator are of orthodox pattern.

The unbalanced weight to the gun is counteracted by a system of levers from the mantlet to a compression cylinder located in the starboard wall of the turret, with a smaller secondary cylinder forward of it.

Sights

To the left of the gun a mounting is provided in the mantlet for the binocular sight which consists of two articulated telescopes to permit adjustment of intraocular distance. To allow elevation and depression, the graticule box, which moves with the gun mantlet, is hinged to the body of the sight and the eyepiece end is suspended from the turret roof on the hinged link.

A hand lever causes the rotation within the sight of a circular scale, graduated both for 8.8-cm gun and machine-gun, in metres. The rotation of the figures on this scale to coincide with a fixed point at 12 o'clock brings about the raising or lowering of the three arrow heads, which remain level with each other whatever their position vertically in relation to the figures around the circumference of the scale. Thus for any given range the site gives a correct adjustment of elevation for each gun without the gunner losing sight of his target, and requiring only the use of his free left hand.

Elevation

Elevation of the turret guns is by hand wheel on the right of the gunner.

Maximum elevation	17 degrees approx.
Maximum depression	6.5 degrees approx.

On the right of the gunner is a Clinometer incorporating an illuminated bubble, the graduation giving 400 mils (22.5 degrees) elevation, and 100 mils (5.625 degrees) depression shown in red. There are in addition, meter graduations from 0–8,000 metres.

Traverse

The turret may be traversed through 360 degrees by power or hand. The hand operated lock in the form of a spring-loaded plunger which engages co-incident holes in the fixed and moving members of the turret ring locks the turret at 12 o'clock, 6 o'clock or 11.30 o'clock.

The 'hour' of traverse is indicated by the now familiar turret position indicator which registers on the dial on the left of the gunner and on a toothed annular ring in the cupola.

Power Traverse

The turret is rotated by engine power, through a hydraulic coupling in which is incorporated the gunner's control for direction and speed of rotation. A small universally jointed shaft driven by a gear in constant mesh with the gearbox input shaft conveys power to a shaft in the base junction. A cone clutch mounted on the shaft is controlled by a lever mounted at the rear of the gearbox on the hull gunner's side. This lever also controls the engagement of the bevel gear in this junction by means of which the power is taken up the vertical centre line of the turret, and so through another pair of bevels to the horizontal input shaft of the hydraulic coupling. A further position of the lever engages the bilge pump, (see para. 19 'Submersion Arrangements'). A hand lever on the hydraulic coupling controls the engagement of a dog clutch on the input shaft. The hydraulic coupling consists of a large cylindrical oil reservoir with filler, level and drain plugs, and containing in separate compartments two eccentric vane oil motors. The rotor on the input side is driven through the shaft and gearing described, whilst the body has horizontal motion from the fully eccentric position on one side to the fully eccentric position on the other (i.e., completely reversing the flow of oil through the assembly). This movement is controlled by a treadle operated by the gunner's foot.

The inlet and outlet flow of oil passes through separate passages in a central stationary spindle which passes through to the other compartment where it forms the centre spindle of the similar eccentric vane motor on the output side. The rotor on the output side is connected through a universally jointed shaft to the turret traverse gearbox. The body of the output motor has a similar horizontal motion giving either the fully eccentric position on one side or a position on the same side but with one half the amount of eccentricity (i.e., two speeds of rotation). This movement is controlled by a lever on the output end of the casting. An overload clutch is incorporated in the traverse gearbox.

It will be observed that all the hydraulic mechanism is carried in the turret and with the removal of the turret no disconnection is required as the vertical driveshaft incorporated dog clutch at its upper end leaving the base junction in position on the hull floor.

Co-axial Machine Gun

This is a MG 34 mounted to the right of the 8.8-cm gun in a cradle fixed in a bracket bolted to the rear of the mantlet. It is fired automatically by a foot operated trigger at the gunner's right foot.

Auxiliary Machine Gun

The weapon is a MG 34 and is carried in a ball mounting with internal moving mantlet, on the offside of the front vertical plate. The sighting of the gun is by telescope of orthodox German design. The gun is fired by hand by its own trigger.

Smoke

Six smoke candles are carried, three each side of the turret, each in a discharger cup 9 cm diameter by 15 cm long. The front discharger cup is pointed forward and slightly outwards, 2 and 3 are set on progressively lower elevation and progressively greater angles. They are fired electrically by 3 buttons in a small box set in the turret roof each side of the commander's seat.

4. AMMUNITION CARRIED

8.8 cm

Two types of ammunition are found in this vehicle, APCBCHE and HE. Both have electric primers. The cartridge cases are marked '8.8-cm Flak 18' and '8.8-cm 398T' respectively.

A total of 92 rounds of 8.8 cm can be stowed as follows:

Fighting Compartment	Rounds
Stowed horizontally into bins forward at each side each holding 16 rounds	64
Stowed horizontally on floor into bins at each side each holding 4 rounds	16
Stowed horizontally in bin under floor	6
Stowed in bin pannier alongside driver	6
Total	92

7.92 mm

Details of the quality and disposition of the SAA carried will be given in a subsequent report.

5. OBSERVATION

Cupola

The commander is provided with five horizontal slits giving all round vision. The slits are equally spaced around the cupola and measure 7.25 × 0.625 inches. No shutters are provided for these visors—a sighting strip is fitted to the foremost visor.

Turret

In addition to the gun sight the turret gunner's vision comprises a vision slit at 10 o'clock in the nearside turret wall. No external BP flap is provided. A similar vision slit is provided in the offside wall of the turret at approximately 2 o'clock for use by the loader.

Hull

The driver's visor which is mounted in the front vertical plate on the nearside, is of single slitted type. It has a sliding shutter, moving vertically and operated by a handwheel, easily accessible from the driver's position. In addition, the driver has a fixed non-adjustable episcope mounted in his access hatch in the superstructure roof which is aimed forward at 30 degrees to the near side of the tank's longitudinal centreline. A strip of 15 mm plate, of inverted channel section, welded to the hatch cover, affords some protection to this episcope.

It is noted with interest that in this vehicle the apertures over the driver's visor for the 'KFF 2' episcope have been plugged by welding.

In addition to the machine gun sight, the hull gunner is provided with a fixed episcope in the access hatch immediately above him. The instrument is of identical pattern to that in the driver's hatch and is aimed forward at 30 degrees to the offside of the centreline of the tank. All vision slits are fitted with readily removable laminated glass blocks.

6. PISTOL PORTS

A pistol port is provided at 8 o'clock in the nearside turret wall. The port is formed in a heavy circular plate bolted to the turret wall. It may be opened or closed by the rotation of an internal disc with a similar slot.

A detachable ceiling clamp is carried in the vehicle's equipment to render this port watertight for submersion.

7. ACCESS DOORS AND ESCAPE HATCHES

In general the access doors and escape hatches in the vehicle appear to be well-placed and of reasonable size.

There disposition and purpose is given hereunder:

Cupola

A circular hatch with an inside diameter of 18.25 inches is provided for the use of the commander and gunner. The cover is of 15 mm plate and is hinged at approximately 2 o'clock. It is secured by three cockspur latches from the inside and maybe locked from outside the vehicle by a square key operating a separate turnbuckle. A spring-loaded catch is provided to retain the door in the open position. A compensating device consisting of a slotted lever, the spring-loaded fulcrum of which is mounted on the cupola top and a trunnion welded to the door which retains the slotted end of the lever. The whole of this mechanism is externally mounted. A rubber sealing ring is fitted in a recess in the door.

Turret

The loader's access hatch is a rectangular opening 14 × 20 inches in the offside front of the turret. The hatch cover is hinged at its leading edge and is formed by the hot pressing of 15 mm plate. The hatch is secured by four bolts which are placed diagonally on the door and are operated by a central lever. Sealing of the hatch for submersion is achieved by the fitting of a rubber seal and a central clamping screw which applies average to the securing bolts.

A catch is provided to retain the door in a slightly open position. A vertical room formed at the sides and rear of the hatch frame affords some protection when the door is thus adjusted.

Complete closure of the door is delayed by the fitting of an enclosed compression spring on the turret roof. The spring is compressed when a plunger is engaged by an arm mounted on the door.

A circular escape hatch of 15.5-inch diameter is provided at the offside rear of the turret. The hatch cover of 82-mm plate is hinged at 6 o'clock and secured by a heavy vertical bar and two hand screws.

Superstructure

A circular hatch of 19-inch diameter is fitted in each side of the superstructure top plate forward of the turret. These are for use by the driver and the hull gunner. The hatch covers are hinged at their outside edges and their closure is retarded by similar compensating mechanism to that on the cupola hatch, but mounted internally.

A spring-loaded catch is fitted to retain the doors in a half open position. The doors are secured by three bolts operated from a central lever. Three independent clamps are carried in the vehicle equipment for sealing the doors for submersion. A fixed episcope is mounted in each of these hatches (see para. 5 'Observation').

Access to the engine compartment is provided by a rectangular door in the rear engine cover plate measuring 3 feet 8 inches × 3 feet 6 inches. The door is hinged to the rear and is secured by four heavy turnbuckle latches operated by a square key. There are in addition six screw clamps for sealing the door for submersion. These are operated by a key with an internal square. A rubber seal is inset in the frame in which the door is seated. An air inlet slit and a mushroom ventilator are provided in the cover.

Heavy grilled plates are fitted over the radiators and fan assemblies on each side of the engine. These are hinged and secured by recess Allen screws.

8. ENGINE

The engine is centrally mounted at the rear of the tank with the flywheel and forward. Circular rubber mountings which surround the front and rear crankshaft bearings are used. Engine torque is transmitted through the forward mounting.

Maker	Maybach
Model	H.L. 210 P.45
Engine No.	46064
Type	60-degree V 12-cylinder petrol
Rating	650 metric hp (642 British bhp)

The aluminium crank case and cylinder block casting houses a circular web crank shaft in 7 roller bearings. The cylinder liners are of the wet type having two rubber sealing rings, with the usual drain hole between them. At the top, a flange recessed into the cylinder block gives the necessary location and a slight spigot stands up into the combustion chamber. Pistons are of aluminium and are carried on steel connecting rods machined all over and forked to permit left and right banks to share the same journal. An interesting feature of design noted here is that the web of the 'H' section of the forked connecting rod is in line with the crankshaft. The forked rod carries a bearing shell which bears on the full length of the crank pin and receives on its outside diameter the unforked rod from the opposite bank. The big end nuts are separated on their circumference instead of being hexagonal.

The camshaft and all auxiliaries are driven by straight spur timing wheels from the opposite end of the crankshaft to the flywheel, which is of steel, machined all over and with starter ring teeth machined on it. There is no detachable starter ring. A normal torsional oscillation damper is fitted at the timing end of the crankshaft outside the crank case.

The cylinder heads, which are of cast iron, and one to each bank have hemispherical combustion chambers.

Valves

Two valves, one inlet and one exhaust are provided for each cylinder. They are operated by a single overhead camshaft to each bank through the medium of rockers. Each rocker is a steel stamping and is mounted upon an eccentric bush, the rotation of which enables tappet clearance to be adjusted. The bush is locked in the desired position by means of an allotted quadrant attached to it working on a set screw and washer in the rocker pillar. The exhaust valves are sodium cooled, but there are no valve seat inserts.

Carburettors

The aluminium inlet manifold of each cylinder head is mounted in the Vee between the banks. Each mounts two down draught Solex Duplex carburettors, type 52 JFF 2—2U 2046. These carburettors are of the twin choke type with exposed jets.

Governor

In each manifold a longitudinal shaft controlled by the engine governor carries a butterfly opposite each carburettor butterfly, thus completely overriding the driver. The governor is of the centrifugal type driven from the timing gears and incorporated in the drive to the water pump. The inlet manifolds have drain holes to deal with excess wet fuel.

Air Cleaners

Carburettor air is drawn from the engine compartment, having first passed through two centrifugal pre-cleaners fire flexible trunks and thence via a breeches pipe through three oil bath type cleaners which are mounted immediately above the carburettors.

The pre-cleaners are of vertical tube type with tangential intakes at the sides and the outlet in the top. The oil bath cleaners are of orthodox pattern with annular gauze element.

Petrol Pumps

Four Solex mechanical type petrol pumps each incorporating a bowl type filter are mounted at the nearside rear of the engine. An electric pump is provided for priming. A manual priming pump is mounted on the fighting compartment bulkhead and supplies fuel direct to the inlet manifold.

Exhaust

The exhaust manifolds which are mounted on the outside of each bank are of cast iron and each deals with three cylinders. The rear manifold on each side is spigotted into the leading one. A sheet metal cover runs the full length of the engine on each side to provide an air duct for manifold cooling. Two silencers are vertically mounted on the tale plate. Hinged flaps are fitted to their outlets which are normally secured in the open position but closed for submersion.

Fuel Tanks

There are four petrol tanks, 2 at each side of the engine compartment. The top tank in each side is of wedge shape and the lower is rectangular the total capacity of the tank is approximately 125 gallons.

The tanks on each side are coupled, the upper wedge shaped tanks feeding the lower by gravity. The filler caps are accessible on each side by removing a circular bullet-proof screwed cover. An asbestos screen is fitted to the engine side of each rectangular tank.

Cooling

Water—radiators, centrifugal pump and four fans.

Ignition

The cylinder head of each bank carries a 6-cylinder Bosch magneto, driven by a spur pinion and idler from the camshaft timing wheel. These magnetos have an automatic advance and retard device which enables the rotating magnets to flick over in a retarded position below normal engine tick over revs. This produces a fat spark no matter how slowly the engine is turning over. The ignition leads pass through a short-screened hose directly from magneto to cylinder head cover of each bank, thus reducing to the minimum the amount of screening required. Totally enclosed 14-mm Bosch sparking plugs are fitted, one per cylinder.

Starters

Two starters are fitted—one electric and one inertia. The Bosch 24V axial motor is mounted on the starboard side of the engine at the forward end and immediately above it a Bosch hand operated inertia starter, also of the axial type. The hand crank for the inertia starter, is carried in suitable clips on the tail plate, the orifice being covered by a bullet-proof sealing plate when it is not in use.

Accumulators

The accumulator consists of two 12V 150 amp/hrs batteries stowed on the hull floor astride the propeller shaft immediately ahead of the engine bulkhead. They are normally connected in parallel but a series/parallel switch permits a change over to 24V for starting.

Radiators

There are two film type radiators mounted transversely at the rear of the engine compartment—one on the nearside and one on the offside. The radiators are coupled and a common filler cap is provided in the nearside unit. The pressure relief valve is mounted on the offside radiator and a balance pipe maintains equal pressure in the two radiators.

Relief valves are fitted in the water inlet and outlets to the engine to avoid airlocks when external hot water circuit is in use. The capacity of the water system is approximately 16 gallons.

Water Pump

Water returning from the nearside radiator enters the engine cooling system at an oil/water heat exchanger, mounted at the rear nearside of the engine from which a pipe leads to the water pump. The output from the pump is directed into the cylinder block water jacket from whence it is circulated through the cylinder heads. The outlets from the cylinder heads are coupled and from them the water enters the top of the offside radiator, from the bottom of which it is directed to the top of the nearside radiator.

Fans

A twin fan assembly is mounted transversely at each side of the rear of the engine compartment. The fans are of radial flow type and are mounted in aluminium housings bolted to the radiators. A two speed drive is taken off the timing gears and a short universally jointed shaft carries this drive to the fan drive housing which is mounted on the rear plate of the engine compartment. In this housing the drive is split and taken on each side transversely to each fan assembly through universally jointed shafts. An oil pump is mounted on the housing and supplies oil from the fan drive casing to each fan assembly. The level of oil in the housing is checked by means of a dipstick accessible when the engine hatch is open and is replenished through a filling orifice in the fixed portion of the engine compartment cover.

Lubrication

The engine sump is dry and a pressure fed lubrication system is used. The pressure pump draws oil from a canister mounted on the offside of the engine and directs it into a gallery in the crankcase casting, from which it is led off to the cylinder heads and timing gears. The crank shaft receives oil under pressure from a muff which is piped to the pressure gallery. The connection from the oil container to the pressure pump is via oil-ways in the crankcase casting. The scavenge pumps, which are set at opposite ends of the engine, have a common output into the heat exchanger from whence it is returned to the oil canister. The oil capacity is 28 litres (6.1 gallons).

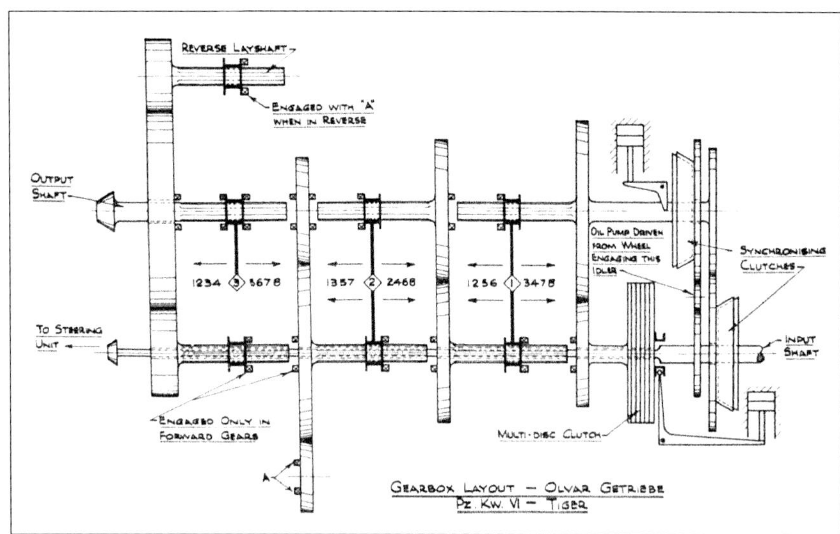

Panzer VI Ausf. E Tiger tank gearbox layout. (*School of Tank Technology*)

9. GEARBOX AND TRANSMISSION

From the flywheel a universally jointed shaft takes the power to the turret base junction which is used as a centre bearing for the propeller shaft by the mounting of a short shaft in it. This shaft has companion flanges and another universally jointed shaft conveys the power to the gearbox input coupling. The output flanges from the gearbox and steering unit are coupled to the final drive assemblies by short shafts which at their outer ends carry the brake assemblies. These shafts are connected to the companion flanges by muff couplings.

The gearbox is manufactured under 'Maybach' licence by Olva-Getriehe and provides eight forward speeds and four reverse speeds with preselected hydraulic engagement. The gears are arranged on a main shaft, lay shaft and reverse lay shaft, although, in fact, both main shaft and lay shafts consist of four short lengths of shaft each carrying a gear and each able to be engaged or disengaged by a dog clutch. The rearmost dog clutches on both main shaft and lay shafts are controlled by selector forks mounted on a common shaft in such a manner that when one dog is engaged the other is free. The movement of the selector forks is controlled by a double acting hydraulic cylinder mounted on top of the gearbox. Likewise, the central pair is operated by another cylinder. The remaining dog clutch on the lay shaft is operated by a third cylinder, but has engagement with a different gear at each end of its travel thus it has no neutral or free position. The remaining dog clutch on the main shaft and the dog clutch on the reverse are operated together by a hand lever, so that in the forward position of the hand lever the dog on the main shaft is engaged and that on the reverse shaft free, with the exact opposite for the rear position of the hand lever, whilst in the intermediate position of the hand lever both dogs are free. Thus for forward drive, once the hand lever has been placed in the forward position, all changes of gear are affected through the operation of the hydraulic cylinder.

The movement of the gearchange lever through its quadrant causes the rotation of a valve which determines the distribution of oil pressure to the appropriate hydraulic cylinder for the ratio required. Side pressure on the gearchange lever then admits pressure to that cylinder and affects the gear change.

In reverse, the procedure is similar but only the four lowest ratios are available. With the exception of the final output gear and the main shaft and reverse shaft gears messing with it, all gears are of helical type.

An extension of the input shaft carries a small bevel for controlling the speed of the steering differentials.

At the input end of the main shaft it is a multi-disc clutch, which can be disengaged by the admission of hydraulic pressure to a cylinder, the piston of which operates a withdrawal fork. The same withdrawal fork is operated by a clutch pedal. A small cone clutch on the input side of the main shaft and the rear end of the lay shaft are geared together and operated by hydraulic pressure giving synchronisation of the lay shaft and engine speeds.

An easily accessible oil filter is provided which serves both gearbox and steering unit which have a common oil level. A filler cap and a dipstick are provided on the gearbox. The oil capacity is 32 litres (7 gallons).

A metal strip on the gearbox cover bears the following figures:

1 2 3 4 ⟨3⟩ 5 6 7 8   1 3 5 7 ⟨2⟩ 2 4 6 8

1 2 5 6 ⟨1⟩ 3 4 7 8

The figures within the diamonds correspond to the hydraulic cylinder of each selector. The figures on the left of the diamonds in each case represent the number of the gear engaged with respective selectors in the forward position. The figures on the right of the diamonds represent the gear engaged with the selectors in the rear position.

The table thus gives the position of each set of selectors for each gear. The overall ratios for the gearbox input flange to the steering unit output flanges, including bevel reduction on the gearbox output shaft are:

8th	.98–1
7th	1.45–1
6th	2.11–1
5th	3.16–1
4th	4.86–1
3rd	7.15–1
2nd	10.2–1
1st	15.4–1

The four ratios of reverse correspond to, but are lower than, the 4 lowest forward gears.

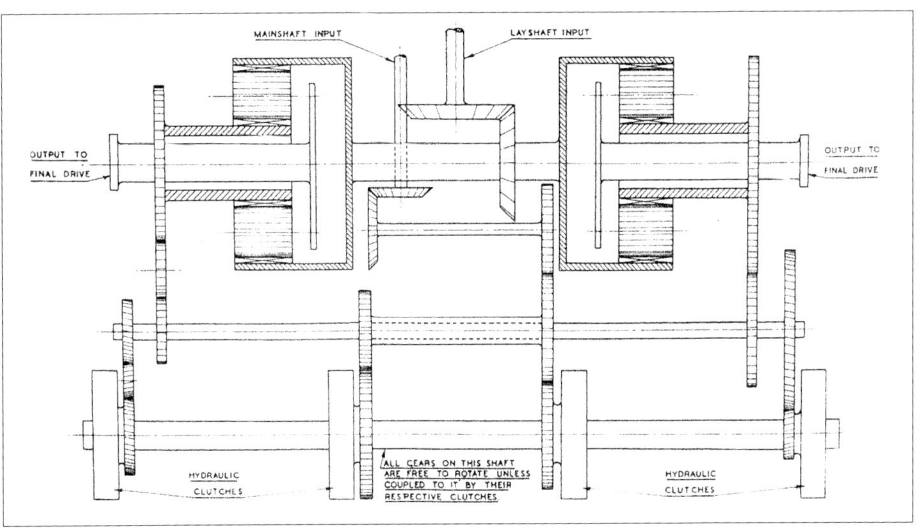

The layout of the steering unit on a Panzer VI Ausf. E Tiger tank. (*School of Tank Technology*)

10. STEERING

From the gearbox the drive is transmitted through a bevel gear on the main gearbox output to a hydraulically operated steering unit controlled by a steering wheel. The transverse bevel shaft so driven carries an epicyclic train at each end. The annuli of the epicyclics are positively driven with the shaft, whilst the planet carriers of each train are integral with the output flanges to the final drive.

Steering is effected by imposing different speeds upon the sun wheels of the epicyclics. The direction and speed of rotation of these sun wheels and selection of right or left hand side is dependent upon the engagement of four hydraulically operated multidisc clutches. These clutches connect to the sun wheels through a two speed lay shaft meshing with a small bevel on an extension of the gearbox input shaft. A choice of two ratios may thus be imposed at will upon the sun wheel of the epicyclic, the annulus already rotating at a multiple of engine speed dependent upon the gear engaged.

When no drive is taken from the gearbox layshaft, i.e. when the gears are in neutral position, a drive is still obtained from the gearbox input shaft via a small bevel and steering unit layshaft. Thus with the engagement of the appropriate steering clutch opposing rotations of the left and right sun wheels are obtained. As the annuli of the epicyclics are positively secured to a common shaft they are unable to rotate in opposite directions consequently the opposing rotations of the sun wheels necessitates opposing rotation of the planet carriers which are integral with the output flanges to the final drive. A natural turn is thus obtained. The overall reduction between the gearbox input and the output to the final drive reduction gear is 117:1.

Oil pressure from a pump is admitted to the required steering clutches through ports in the steering assembly casing, the opening of which is controlled by piston valve. Movement of the piston valve is governed by the driver's steering wheel. In this way to distinct radii of turn are available for each gear engaged, and identical form right and left turn. A mushroom-shaped knob on the gearbox casing operates hydraulically a break on one section of the main shaft, thereby eliminating clutch drag and making the neutral turn more positive.

The tank can also be steered when required by steering levers on each side of the driver which operate the right and left brake assemblies.

11. FINAL DRIVE

The final drive assemblies are bolted directly to the hull from outside and contain 2 stages of reduction:

(a) A straight spur reduction, and

(b) An epicyclic.

The steering unit output shaft drives the small pinion of the spur reduction which meshes with the large pinion. The large pinion is mounted on the same shaft as a smaller pinion, which is the sun wheel of the epicyclic train. The planet carrier mounts the driving sprocket and the annulus is rigidly secured to the final drive casing. The overall ratio is 10.55:1. Each final drive casing, which is a steel casting, has its own drain plug and filler plug, and a third plug which gives the correct oil level. The all capacity is 8 litres (14 pints).

12. BRAKES

On each steering unit output shaft there is mounted at the outer end a brake assembly, the stationary member of which consists of two circular discs held back to back by tension springs and expanded as required by a cam and lever operated by either the brake pedal or the handbrake lever or the appropriate steering stick. The rotating member consists of two cast iron saucers, well ribbed, and bolted rim to rim so as to encompass the stationary member.

Operation of the cam lever separates the brake discs until they bear upon the braking surface of the saucers. After which a limited rotation produces a Servo effect. There is no adjustment for these breaks. The brake is very effective but high temperatures results from prolonged application. Friction surfaces are metal to metal.

13. SUSPENSION

The tank is mounted on solid rubber tyred bogie wheels 31.5-inch diameter carried in crank arms, the opposite ends of which fit into plastic bearings in the hull. Movement of these arms is restricted by torsion bars coupled to them at one side of the tank, anchored to the hull at the other. The suspension arms on the starboard side of the tank are trailing, whilst those on the port side are inclined forward, thus making room for both sets within the hull.

The bogie wheels are so arranged as to carry three tyres per suspension arm, and these are placed singularly and in pairs in such a way that the wheels of the adjustment arms overlap. Thus for eight crank arms on each side of the hull, there is a total of 16 bogie wheels carrying one tyre each and 4 bogie wheels carrying two tyres each, giving a total of 24 tyres, in every case arranged with three per axle. The outer wheel is detached from each axle when the narrow track is used. The bogie wheels are arranged in the following manner on their crank arms, working in each case from the outer edge of the track towards the centre:

	1	2	3	4	5	6	7	8
1st crank arm	Single bogie	–	–	Track horn	Double bogie twin tyres		Track horn	–
2nd crank arm	–	Single bogie	Single bogie	Track horn	–	–	Track horn	Single bogie
3rd, 5th and 7th crank arms as No. 1	Single bogie	–	–	Track horn	Double bogie twin tyres		Track horn	–
4th, 6th and 8th crank arms as No. 2	–	Single bogie	Single bogie	Track horn	–	–	Track horn	Single bogie

The rear idler 27-inch diameter runs between the track horns. The vertical movement of front and rear suspension arms on each side is restricted by rubber blocks (mounted on the hull side). The nipples for lubrication of all of the torsion bar bearings are grouped together and piped to their bearings.

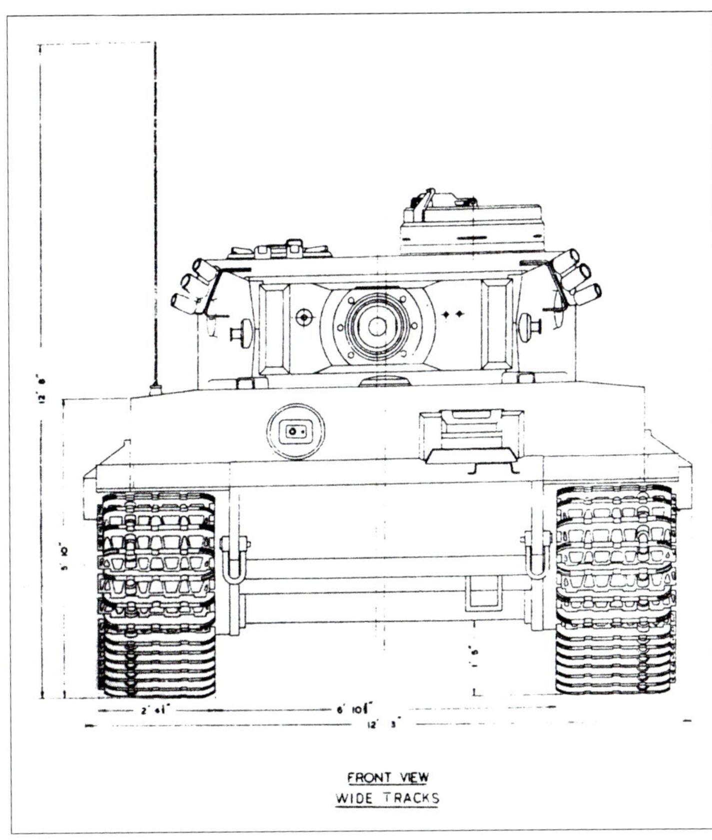

The heavy Panzer V Ausf. E Tiger tank had wide tracks to reduce the amount of ground pressure it exerted. (*School of Tank Technology*)

14. TRACKS

The cast steel track is of orthodox design but of unusual width (2 feet 4.5 inches). A further unusual feature is that the track lugs are offset in relation to the tread, the track pins are spaced at 5.25-inch centres and are retained by spring rings fitted into half round grooves at each end which are countersunk into recesses cored in the track shoe casting. The track shoe consists of a main transverse bar on the track pin centre line with a light well ribbed plate to the next track pin bosses. The inside of the track shoe forms a smooth surface upon which the bogie wheels run. The teeth of the driving sprocket engage circular bosses surrounding the track pin, one set on the inside of the track, the other set on a line between the first and second bogie wheels from the outside of the second suspension arm.

When it is desired to reduce the overall width of the tank to a minimum, a narrow track is fitted. This is identical with the track just described except that the outer portion is removed. The track is thus made symmetrical on the sprocket, the overall width of the track and sprocket being equal.

With the narrow track, only two tyres on each suspension arm were supported and the outer one in each case is therefore removed, together with its hub extension. This results in a material reduction of overall width whilst still retaining a satisfactory suspension and track arrangement. A set of track tools, including spare retaining rings, is carried on a bracket on the rear hull plate.

Track Adjustment

Tensioning of the tracks is provided by the cranked mounting of the rear idler wheels. The draw bolts, by means of which the adjustment is made, are internally mounted and are accessible from outside the vehicle by the removal of a dome-shaped bullet-proof cover at each side of the tail plate. The covers themselves locking the adjustment when in position.

15. INSTRUMENTS AND CONTROLS

The driver's controls comprise:

Steering wheel	Controlling the power steering.
Steering levers	Working on the vehicle brakes (for use only when power steering is inoperative).
Handbrake lever	On the left, operating vehicle brakes.
Foot brake pedal	For right foot operating vehicle brakes.
Clutch pedal	Operating engine clutch mechanically, but with power assistance when engine is running. A hand wheel situated at the driver's right rear provides adjustment.
Accelerator pedal	For operation by right foot.
Starter carburettor	At right rear of driver's seat.
Gear controls	These are described in para. 9 'Gearbox'.

The driver's seat may be adjusted longitudinally, the angle of its back is adjustable and may be lowered to a horizontal position for ease of access or exit.

The instrument panel is mounted on the right of the driver above the gearbox and carries the following:

(i)	A revolution counter recording up to 3,500 rpm (3,000 to 3,500 marked in RED) (1,300 to 2,500 marked in GREEN)
(ii)	A speedometer—calibrated to 100 km/h
(iii)	An oil pressure gauge—calibrated to 12 Kg/cm^2
(iv)	A water temperature gauge-from 40 to 120 degrees C
(v)	Ignition switch and warning light.
(vi)	Lighting switches and fuse boxes.

In the pannier space to the left of the driver is an electrically operated gyroscope direction indicator. This is identical with that found in certain Pz.Kw. IIIs and IVs.

16. ELECTRICAL EQUIPMENT

The accumulator consists of two 12-V barriers with earthed negative. The batteries are carried on the hull floor astride the propeller shaft immediately forward of the engine bulkhead. The battery master switch and necessary junction boxes are mounted on the bulkhead.

The two batteries are normally connected in parallel but are connected in series for operation of the 24-V starter motor by a solenoid operated series parallel switch.

All crew positions are adequately illuminated by individual lighting. Rotary converters and transformers supply the necessary step up in voltage required to drive the gyroscope direction indicator and to supply the wireless system.

The wireless and intercommunication arrangements are of the standard type usually found in German tanks.

No external lamps are present on this vehicle although the wiring and brackets are present. Illumination is provided for the following instruments:

(i)	The graticule of the binocular sight.
(ii)	The bubble of the clinometer.
(iii)	The gyroscope direction indicator.
(iv)	The driver's compartment panel.

17. FIRE FIGHTING EQUIPMENT

In the event of fire in the engine compartment, temperature elements (two above and one each side of the engine) close the electrical circuit of an automatic CTC fire extinguisher mounted on the fighting compartment bulkhead, and illuminates a red lamp in front of the driver. An instruction plate round the lamp says 'When there is a fire in the engine, throttle down immediately to idling speed'. A clockwork mechanism in the fire extinguisher allows a 7 seconds period of operation which will be extended for a further 7 seconds period if the temperature elements have not cooled sufficiently. This process will be repeated until the extinguisher is empty. The warning light goes out as soon as the temperature elements are below operating temperature. The CTC is delivered through four jets situated alongside each heat element and fed by piping from the extinguisher. In the event of electrical failure the extinguisher can be operated mechanically by means of a plunger on top. The extinguisher reservoir has a car type air valve and a 0–10 Kg/cm^2 pressure gauge.

Normal CTC extinguishers are provided on the radiator top covers and on the turret floor, with suitable retaining straps.

18. VENTILATION

A mushroom type ventilator is provided in the hinged engine cover plate. A Sirocco fan mounted at the flywheel end of the engine draws air from the bottom of the engine compartment for cooling. Air is also drawn by this fan from the casing surrounding the gearbox and is fed into ducts surrounding the exhaust manifolds to the point where the manifolds join the silencers. The ducts then convey the air to the suction side of the radiator fan assemblies.

A further mushroom type ventilator is fitted in the top front plate between the driver's and hull gunner's access hatches. This ventilator provides an airflow to the rear of the gearbox and removes fumes caused by firing of the hull machine gun.

An electrically driven fan is mounted in the turret roof above the loader, and expels the fumes resulting from the firing of the turret armament.

19. DEEP WADING AND SUBMERSION ARRANGEMENTS

The vehicle is equipped for a limited underwater performance to a depth of approximately 15 feet. This feature is achieved by the ceiling of the entire tank except for a small compartment on each side of the main engine compartment, containing the radiators.

During submersion air for the engine and crew is admitted through a standpipe mounted above the engine compartment, the top of which is approximately 16 feet above ground level.

The following provision is made to keep the tank watertight for submersion: –

(i). All hatches have rubber sealing rings and screw clamps.

(ii). All vision slits have rubber seatings for their glass blocks and cam operated clamps.

(iii). The ball mounting of the front machine gun has a rubber edged external cover retained by screw clamps.

(iv). The ventilator between driver and hull gunner screws onto a rubber seating.

(v). A pneumatic ceiling ring is provided to render the turret ring joint watertight. The tube is recessed in an annular groove formed in the turret ring and its seating. It is inflated through a valve which projects downwards through the superstructure top plate in the forward corner of the fighting compartment on the nearside.

(vi). The vision openings for the binocular sights are filled by rubber plugs mounted on a hinged plate attached to the sight.

(vii). The turret machine gun opening is sealed with a rubber plug mounted on a wooden rod and expanded in position by rotation of a handle.

(viii). The gun mantlet joint is sealed by means of a rubber lined frame clamped in position. A canvas muzzle cover reduces the entry of water in the barrel and one round in the breech prevents water entering the tank.

(ix). A rubber lined cover fits over the outlet of the turret ventilating fan and is tightened down by six screw clamps.

(x). A plate normally carried on the hull top plate, behind the driver, fits over the main air inlet to the engine compartment and shut it off.

(xi). The subsidiary air inlet to the engine compartment incorporates a sealing plate which screws down onto a rubber seating.

(xii). All engine compartment cover plates have rubber seals.

(xiii). Each length of the extension pipe is rubber sealed so that the only means of entry for air is through the top of the extension pipe.

(xiv). The exhaust outlets have clapper valves, but exhaust back pressure is relied on to exclude water.

(xv). A rubber lined screw clamps seals the machine carbine port.

(xvi). The pannier space is on each side of the engine compartment which housed the petrol tanks, radiators and fan assemblies, are completely sealed from the main engine compartment by a longitudinal vertical plate running the full length. The appropriate pipe connections and fan drive are thus the only connections to the main engine compartment.

At the point where the air ducts pass through from the engine compartment to the radiator compartments, butterflies are fitted which can be closed by a lever on the fighting compartment bulkhead for underwater travel, the same lever operating a third butterfly which allows the manifold cooling air to return to the top of the engine compartment when the other butterflies are closed.

During submersion, water takes the place of air for cooling the radiators greatly simplifying the problem of keeping the engine compartment watertight and the engine cool. The petrol tanks are of course exposed to the water but a cock on the fighting compartment bulkhead changes over the vent pipe so that the tanks are vented into the engine compartment.

In the event of water entering the vehicle in spite of the above arrangements, a bilge pump mounted below the turret prevents it from rising to a level at which it can cause harm. The pump is driven from the rear of the gearbox from the same output as the power traverse.

WHAT HAPPENED NEXT?

The information contained in this and other similar reports were combined to produce an instruction manual to educate army personnel about this new enemy tank. It was printed in January 1944 by the Military College of Science, School of Tank Technology, (STT), Chobham Lane, Chertsey. It was called 'Report on PzKw VI (Tiger) Model H'. Part I of this manual was the general description of the tank. As it carried similar information in the above report this has not been reproduced but what follows are some of the illustrations, diagrams, and photographs contained in the manual.

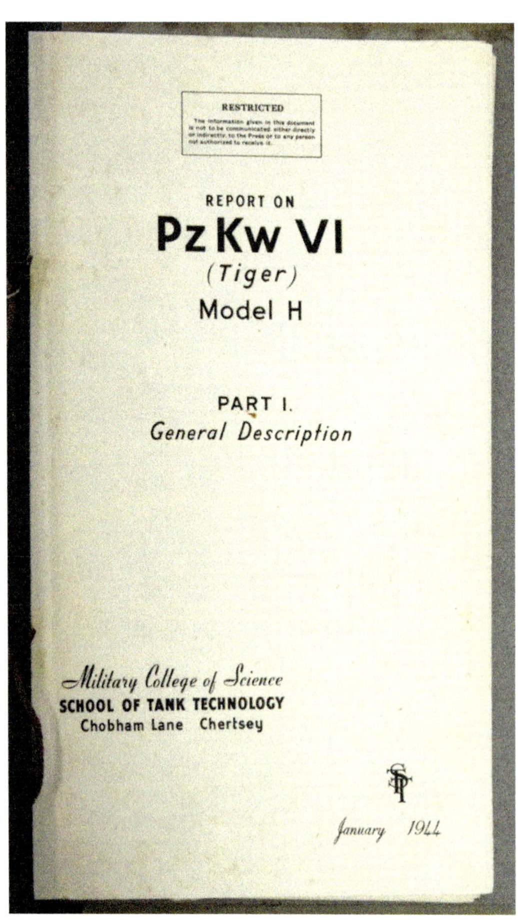

RESTRICTED

REPORT ON

PzKw VI

(Tiger)

Model H

PART I.

General Description

Military College of Science

SCHOOL OF TANK TECHNOLOGY

Chobham Lane Chertsey

January 1944

(STT)

Captured Tiger tank 131 now at the Tank Museum, Bovington. (*STT*)

This is an illustration of a Tiger tank prepared for combat. It has its wide tracks fitted and a debris cover has not been fitted to the gun muzzle. The side track guards are bolted to the hull side. (*STT*)

This is an illustration of a Tiger tank prepared for rail travel. Its wide tracks have been replaced with slimmer transportation tracks. The side track guards have been removed, and the front side stack guards have been unlocked and flipped up on their hinge. The gun barrel has a debris cap fitted over the end of the gun. (*STT*)

This is the three-quarter view of a Tiger tank prepared for combat. It has its wide tracks fitted. A debris cover has not been fitted to the gun muzzle brake. The side track guards are bolted to the hull side. (*STT*)

This is an illustration of a Tiger tank prepared for rail travel from the side three-quarter view. Its wide tracks have been replaced with slimmer transportation tracks. The side track guards have been removed and the front side stack guards have been unlocked and flipped up on their hinge. The gun barrel has a debris cap fitted on the end. (*STT*)

This is an early-production Tiger fitted with a dome-shaped cupola, wide tracks, exhaust silencer/muffler sheet metal covers, rear turret stowage box, and pre-cleaner Feifel air filter system. Notice the hand crank fixed to the rear armour plate. (*STT*)

(*STT*)

(*STT*)

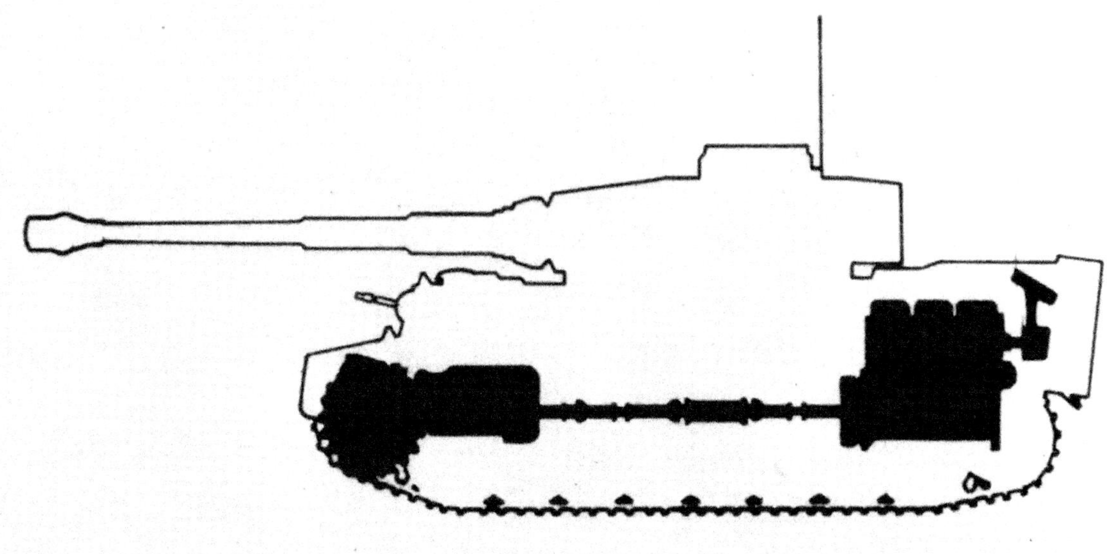

Diagram showing the positions of the engine at the rear of the Tiger and the gearbox and final drive at the front of the tank. (*STT*)

11

THE CAPTURE OF PANZERKAMPFWAGEN VI AUSF. E (TIGER) TURRET NO. 344

British forces knocked out Tiger 344 in Normandy. British 75-mm armed Sherman tanks were suddenly confronted by this Tiger tank around a bend in the village of Fontenay-le-Pesnel. Several rounds were fired at the Tiger, but none penetrated the thick armour. The Tiger's crew bailed out, believing their tank was on fire. A shell had hit the side of the driver's visor, which showered hot white sparks inside the tank. The driver shouted he had been hit and there was a fire. The tank commander gave the order to abandon the tank. As it was in a good condition and drivable, the tank was chosen to be shipped back to Britain and used in live firing trials at the South of England Range in Shoeburyness, Essex.

Tiger tank 344 abandoned by its crew in Normandy.

Two British Sherman tanks drive past Tiger tank 344, abandoned by its crew at the side of the road in Normandy.

Tiger tank 344 in Britain standing next to a Panther Ausf. G.

Front view of Tiger tank 344 in Britain.

Right-hand side view of Tiger tank 344 in Britain.

12

FIRING TRIALS AGAINST PANTHER AND TIGER TANKS, 18–23 SEPTEMBER 1944

Unfortunately, many of the original photographs contained in this report were of poor quality and some were out of focus. The information in this chapter has been transcribed from original wartime documents. The report format and brief notation style has been kept.

DTD EXPERIMENTAL REPORT

AT No. 225
Project Nos. M. 6816A/8
M. 6815A/5

SUBJECT

Effect of anti-tank projectile against Pz.Kw.V. and Pz.Kw.VI tanks.

ORIGIN OF TRIAL

This trial was initiated by D.G. of A., and carried out generally in accordance with the requirements set out under O.B. Trials Nos. AP(A) 189/1/2.

REMARKS

The targets attacked in this trial were the German Panther and Tiger tanks.

Frontal and flank attack was carried out using 17-Pdr. and 6-pdr. on the Panther and 6-pdr on the Tiger. In each case Armour Piercing Capped Ballistic Cap (APCBC) and Discarding Sabot (DS) shot was fired.

Detailed results appear in the report.

It is considered that: –

(a) The chances of disabling either tank appear to be greater from attack directed at the sides mainly owing to the possibility of cordite fire is due to the open storage of ammunition in the panniers.

(b) In most cases penetration of either tank would result in the killing or wounding of members of the crew. In this connection, DS shot appears to be more effective owing to its greater fragmentation.

A.T. Bowden
Assistant Director (Armour)
A.A.M Durrant
Director
17.10.44.
M.110(S)
JFW

DTD EXPERIMENTAL REPORT

AT No. 225
Project Nos: M. 6816A/8
M. 6815A/5
Trial Nos: X798, X799
File Ref: 25/14/4 & 5.

REPORT ON FIRING TRAIL Against Pz.Kw.V and Pz.Kw.VI Carried Out at S. of E. Range, Shoeburyness, on September 18, 19, and 23, 1944

Report			
Compiled by: –	Mr. G.W. Gray	-	DTD Armour Branch
Checked by: –	Major G. Guthrie R.E.M.E.	-	DTD Armour Branch
	Mr. J.B. Sankey	-	DTD Armour Branch
References			
	Section I	-	Object of Trials.
	Section II	-	Target Details.
	Section III	-	Method of Attack.
	Section IV	-	Trial Commentary.
	Section V	-	Summary of Results.
	Section VI	-	Conclusions.
Appendices			
	Appendix A	-	Detailed Results.
	Appendix B	-	Photographic Record.
	Appendix C	-	Sketches.
	Appendix D	-	Plate Hardnesses.
	Appendix E	-	Penetration Code.
Note: –			
	This report must not be reproduced in full or in part without the written authority of the Director of Tank Design		

SECTION I: OBJECT OF TRIAL

To test the effect of various anti-tank projectiles against German tanks Pz.Kw.V (Panther) and Pz.Kw.VI (Tiger) in accordance with Ordnance Board Trial Nos. AP (A) 189/1/2.

SECTION II: TARGET DETAILS

These consisted of two German tanks, one of which was a Pz.Kw.V (Panther) consisting of a hull DTD No. 3041 fitted with the turret DTD No. 3042, and the other was a Pz.Kw.VI (Tiger) DTD No. 3036. Both vehicles were minus engines and stowage. Wooden dummies were used to represent crews. Additional protection to the armour by track links was not given on either vehicle. During the trial the Panther was fitted with plates to simulate skirting.

SECTION III: METHOD OF ATTACK

The vehicles were subjected to the following attack: –

Pz.Kw.V (Panther)
17-pdr DS shot FSC at a range of 1,000 yards.

17-pdr APCBC shot FSC at a range of 1,000 yards.
6-pdr DS shot FSC at a range of 600 yards.
6-pdr APCBC shot FSC at a range of 600 yards.

Pz.Kw.VI (Tiger)
6-pdr DS shot FSC at a range of 600 yards.
6-pdr APCBC shot FSC at a range of 600 yards.

The above attack was carried out generally in accordance with Ordnance Board requirements detailed in their specification for Trials Nos. Ap (A) 189/1/2.

SECTION IV: TRAIL COMMENTARY

In order that the attack could be easily transferred from one vehicle to the other both tanks were in position, and at a suitable distance apart to preclude accidental damage to either vehicle.

For convenience in carrying out the trial, rounds were numbered consecutively irrespective of the target being attacked.

Reference to right-hand or left-hand side of the tanks is relative to the tank crew.

Wooden dummies were used to simulate the crew. Actual rounds were not stowed, therefore an estimate has been made of the probable effect on same.

It should be noted that the Panther was lying 'nose down' approximately 5 degrees and the Tiger approximately 6 degrees. This had the effect of assisting the gun in certain cases and the tank in others. This has been allowed for and the actual angle of the plates from normal, presented to the gun is given in Section V: Summary of Results.

The following are estimated striking velocity which would be obtained over the distances fired.

Gun	Range	Projectile	Estimated Striking Velocity
17-pdr	1,000 yards	Discarding Sabot	3600 f.s.
17-pdr	1,000 yards	APCBC	2600 f.s.
6-pdr	600 yards	Discarding Sabot	3680 f.s.
6-pdr	600 yards	APCBC	2550 f.s.

Pz.Kw.V (Panther)

Tank Front at 10 Degrees to Normal

Firing from a range of 1,000 yards with 17-pdr DS Round 3, struck the glacis plate above the left-hand track after passing through the track guard, holing the glacis 3.5 × 2 inches. Five ammunition racks in the pannier were badly splintered by the shot which broke up. A cordite fire may have been caused by perforation of stowed rounds. The driver would probably have been killed.

Round 5, 17-pdr APCBC from 1,000 yards struck on the horizontal centre line of the cast mantlet passing through the turret and out of the rear quarter side plate. The mechanical damage in the tank was superficial. The commander and gunner layer were killed and the loader wounded.

Round 11, 17-pdr DS from 1,000 yards strike in the final drive housing holed same 1.25-inch diameter. This round would probably have put the tank out of action.

Round 17, 17-pdr. APCBC after grazing 25 yards short struck the glacis plate forcing a plug out 3.25-inch diameter. Superficial damage only was caused in the vehicle. The loader and driver were wounded by fragments.

Tank Right-Hand Side at 31 Degrees to Normal

Mild steel skirting plates fitted.

Plate Thickness Varied Between 0.25 and 0.3125 Inches

Round 18, 6-pdr DS from 600 yards struck between the turret and the hull roof. The hull roof was holed 3 × 1.5 inches. Two ammunition racks were badly splintered, and the turret traverse was jammed due to displaced metal. It is probable that stowed ammunition would have been perforated with consequent cordite fire.

Round 21, also 6-pdr DS from 600 yards, penetrated the skirting and hull side. The mechanical damage caused by the shot inside the vehicle was superficial. The loader and gun layer were wounded.

Round 22, 6-pdr APCBC also penetrated the skirting plate and hull side. This round displaced a wiring terminal bracket from the inside hull wall, destroying numerous wires, and would have cause the engine to stop. The turret platform was also badly damaged and the structure in the area of shot entry severely deformed. The loader was wounded by fragments.

Round 23, 6-pdr APCBC from 600 yards penetrated the sloping pannier side. The shot past into the turret sharing away several rack teeth, then penetrated the engine compartment bulkhead, perforated and entered the main fuel tank, probably causing the tank to take fire. The loader and layer were wounded by fragments.

Round 25, 6-pdr APCBC from 600 yards penetrated the cupola casting, severely damaging internal fittings in the locality. The commander was killed.

Round 27, also 6-pdr APCBC from 600 yards, struck and penetrated the turret side plate and passing across the turret destroyed the fan motor. The shot broke up on the opposite side wall. The commander was probably killed, and the gun layer and loader severely injured.

Pz.Kw.VI (Tiger)
Tank Front at 30 Degrees to Normal

Round 29, 6-pdr DS shot from 600 yards penetrated the upper nose plate, and broke up on the bulkhead behind ammunition stowage bin. The gun layer and driver were severely wounded.

Round 31, 6-pdr APCBC from 600 yards striking the visor plate failed to defeat the plate and gave code D back damage.

Round 34, 6-pdr DS from 600 yards penetrated the visor plate but apart from purely local damage to the driver's hatch locking catch, no other damage could be found.

Round 37, 6-pdr DS from 600 yards also penetrated the visor plate. The shot past through the driver's compartment and fragments struck the roof stiffener causing severe pitting of surface. The co-driver was killed and the tight crew wounded.

Round 39, 6-pdr DS penetrated the visor plate, passed across the fighting compartment and struck the gun elevating shaft bracket. This round would have caused the turret to jam. The commander, co–driver and gun layer were wounded.

Pz.Kw.V (Panther)
Tank Right-Hand Side at 31 Degrees to Normal

Rounds 40 and 41, 6-pdr APCBC from 600 yards penetrated the hull side after passing through the skirting plate. Round 40 caused considerable local structure and wiring damage. Round 41, after striking the engine compartment bulkhead, it severely perforated ammunition, in probable damage to stowed rounds and the subsequent cordite fire.

Tank Front at 10 Degrees to Normal

Round 45, 17-pdr DS from 1,000 yards penetrated the glacis plate, but caused only superficial mechanical damage in the vehicle. The co-driver was killed and the driver was wounded.

Round 46, 17-pdr APCBC from 1,000 yards glancing off the inner edge of track struck the final drive housing previously penetrated by Round 11, and caused the housing to split severely. This round would have stopped the tank.

Tank Left-Hand Side at 30 Degrees to Normal

Round 52, 17-pdr APCBC from 1,000 yards struck and penetrated the hull side, passed through the fighting compartment causing considerable mechanical damage. One ammunition rack was destroyed. With stowed rounds a cordite fire would probably have been caused. The loader was killed and the gun layer and driver injured.

Pz.Kw.VI (Tiger)
Tank Front at Normal

Round 55, 6-pdr APCBC from 600 yards striking between the turret and the hull roof passed down through the roof. The shot entered the hull striking and shearing through a floor cross member. The gun layer was wounded.

Round 56, glancing off the 88-mm gun on to the mantlet passed through the hull roof, and broke up on the bulkhead between the driver's compartment and fighting compartment. The gun layer, loader and driver were slightly wounded.

Round 63, 6-pdr APCBC from 600 yards penetrated the visor plate, carrying away metal from the bulkhead behind the driver, and the hull roof fan ducting.

Tank Left-Hand Side at 30 Degrees to Normal

Rounds 66 and 67, 6-pdr DS from 600 yards penetrated the superstructure side plate. Round 67, broke up on the engine compartment bulkhead, and perforated the engine primer pump casing. The commander and driver were injured.

Round 68, 6-pdr DS from 600 yards striking between Rounds 66 and 67 failed to penetrate the armour giving Code C back damage only. It was noted that the shot shattered.

Round 72, 6-pdr DS from 600 yards penetrated the turret side plate, causing additional mechanical damage within the turret. The commander gun layer and loader was severely wounded.

Round 75, 6-pdr APCBC from 600 yards also struck and passed through the turret side plate causing extensive damage to the turret fixed race ring and shelf plate. Commander gun layer and loader were severely wounded.

Round 76, 6-pdr APCBC from 600 yards struck the base of the turret and scooped down through the hull roof holing same 11 × 7 inches. This shot removed numerous teeth from the traverse rack and entered an ammunition bin on the opposite side of the turret. A cordite fire would probably have resulted. The gun layer was killed and the loader wounded.

Round 80, 6-pdr APCBC from 600 yards struck and passed through the superstructure, pannier ammunition stowage, gun balancing gear, and broke up on the engine compartment bulkhead. A cordite fire was very probable. The commander was severely wounded.

Section V indicates in table form a brief summary of the results.

SECTION V

SUMMARY OF RESULTS

PANTHER HULL DTD No. 3041 TURRET DTD No. 3042

Tank 'Nose down' approx. 5 degrees

Presentation of Tank	Plate Struck	Normal plate thickness and acute angle to normal.	Projectile and Range	Effect on Plate	Effect on fighting capacity	
					Tank	crew
Front at 10 degrees to Normal	Glacis	80 mm at 51 degrees to Normal	17-pdr APCBC at 1,000 yds	Plate defeated Code W	Round 17 nil	Round 17 loader and driver wounded
Front at 10 degrees to Normal	Glacis	80 mm at 51 degrees to Normal	17-pdr DS at 1,000 yds	Plate defeated Code W	Round 45 nil	Round 45 co-driver killed and driver wounded
Front at 10 degrees to Normal	Glacis	80 mm at 51 degrees to Normal	17-pdr DS at 1,000 yds	Plate defeated Code W	Round 3 cordite fire	Round 3 driver killed
Front at 10 degrees to Normal	Final drive housing	80 mm at 51 degrees to Normal	17-pdr DS at 1,000 yds	Casting defeated Code W	Round 11 out of action	Round 11 nil
Front at 10 degrees to Normal	Nose	60 mm at 60 degrees to Normal	17-pdr APCBC at 1,000 yds	Plate defeated Code W	Round 10 nil	Round 10 nil
Front at 10 degrees to Normal	Mantlet	100 mm at 10 degrees to Normal	17-pdr APCBC at 1,000 yds	Casting defeated Code W	Round 5 nil	Round 5 commander and gun layer killed, loader wounded
Side at 31 degrees to Normal	Hull side + Skirting plate	0.3125 or 0.25 inches + 40 mm at 31 degrees to Normal	6-pdr APCBC at 600 yds	Plate defeated Code W	Round 22 out of action	Round 22 loader wounded
Side at 31 degrees to Normal	Hull side + Skirting plate	0.3125 or 0.25 inches + 40 mm at 31 degrees to Normal	6-pdr APCBC at 600 yds	Plate defeated Code W	Round 40 probably out of action	
Side at 31 degrees to Normal	Hull side + Skirting plate	0.3125 or 0.25 inches + 40 mm at 31 degrees to Normal	6-pdr APCBC at 600 yds	Plate defeated Code W	Round 41 probably cordite fire	Bailed out if possible.
Side at 31 degrees to Normal	Hull side + Skirting plate	0.3125 or 0.25 inches + 40 mm at 31 degrees to Normal	6-pdr DS at 600 yds	Plate defeated Code W	Round 21 nil	Round 21 layer and loader wounded.
Side at 31 degrees to Normal	Sloping pannier side	40 mm at 48 degrees to Normal	6-pdr APCBC at 600 yds	Plate defeated Code W	Round 23 fuel fire	Round 23 gun layer and loader wounded. Crew bailed out.
Side at 31 degrees to Normal	Turret side plate	45 mm at 34 degrees to Normal	6-pdr APCBC at 600 yds	Plate defeated Code W	Round 27 nil	Round 27 commander killed. Gun layer and loader wounded.

Side at 31 degrees to Normal	Turret side plate	45 mm at 34 degrees to Normal	6-pdr DS at 600 yds	Plate defeated Code W	Round 18 cordite fire.	Round 18 loader wounded. Crew bailed out if possible.
Side at 31 degrees to Normal	Cupola	45 mm at 34 degrees to Normal	6-pdr APCBC at 600 yds	Casting defeated Code W	Round 25 nil	Round 25 commander killed.
Front at Normal	Visor	102 mm at 4 degrees to Normal	6-pdr APCBC at 600 yds	Plate defeated Code W	Round 63 nil	Round 63 nil
Front at Normal	Nose (upper)	102 mm at 31 degrees to Normal	6-pdr APCBC at 600 yds	Plate wire scoop	Round 61 nil	Round 61 nil
Front at 30 degrees to Normal	Nose (upper)	102 mm at 41 degrees to Normal	6-pdr DS at 600 yds	Plate defeated Code W	Round 29 nil	Round 29 gun layer and loader wounded.
Front at 30 degrees to Normal	Visor	102 mm at 30 degrees to Normal	6-pdr DS at 600 yds	Plate defeated Code W	Round 34 nil	Round 34 nil
Front at 30 degrees to Normal	Visor	102 mm at 30 degrees to Normal	6-pdr DS at 600 yds	Plate defeated Code W	Round 37 nil	Round 37 co-driver killed. Turret crew wounded
Front at 30 degrees to Normal	Visor	102 mm at 30 degrees to Normal	6-pdr APCBC at 600 yds	Plate win Code D	Round 31 nil	Round 31 nil
Side at 30 degrees to Normal	Superstructure	82 mm at 30 degrees to Normal	6-pdr DS at 600 yds	2 Plate defeats Code W.	Round 66 67 nil	Round 67 commander and driver injured
Side at 30 degrees to Normal	Superstructure	82 mm at 30 degrees to Normal	6-pdr. D.S. at 600 yds	One plate win Code C	Round 68 nil	Round 68 nil
Side at 30 degrees to Normal	Superstructure	82 mm at 30 degrees to Normal	6-pdr APCBC at 600 yds	Plate defeated Code W	Round 80 cordite fire	Round 80 commander wounded. Crew bailed out if possible
Side at 30 degrees to Normal	Turret side	82 mm at approx. 30 degrees to Normal	6-pdr DS at 600 yds	Plate defeated Code W	Round 72 nil	Round 72 commander gun layer and loader killed
Side at 30 degrees to Normal	Turret side	82 mm at approx. 30 degrees to Normal	6-pdr APCBC at 600 yds	Plate defeated Code W	Round 75 out of action	Round 75 commander gun layer and loader wounded
Side at 30 degrees to Normal	Turret side	82 mm at approx. 30 degrees to Normal	6-pdr APCBC at 600 yds	Plate defeated Code W	Round 76 cordite fire	Round 76 gun layer killed, loader wounded

SECTION VI: CONCLUSIONS

Pz.Kw.V. (PANTHER)

Front at 10 Degrees to Normal

From 1,000 yards both the 17-pdr APCBC and DS shot will completely defeat the glacis, nose plate, and the gun mantlet (100 mm).

Side at 31 Degrees to Normal

From 600 yards both the 6-pdr APCBC and DS shot will completely defeat the hull side plus skirting, sloping pannier side, and turret side.

Pz.Kw.VI. (TIGER)

Front at Normal

From 600 yards 6-pdr APCBC Shot will defeat the visor plate at 4 degrees to Normal and probably at the natural angle of 10 degrees to Normal. The shot however, fails against the nose plate.

Front at 30 Degrees to Normal

From 600 yards the 6-pdr DS shot will completely defeat the visor plate and nose plate. The 6-pdr APCBC Shot fails against the visor plate. A comparison of the results of DS Round 29 and the APCBC Round number 31 gives a good indication of their relative performance.

Side at 30 Degrees to Normal

Both the 6-pdr APCBC and DS shot from 600 yards will defeat the superstructure, and turret side plate.

Generally speaking penetration of the hull side plates by APCBC and DS shot at angle on either vehicle is unlikely when the shot first passes through road bogie discs.

The chances of disabling either tank appear to be greater from attack directed at the side, mainly owing to the possibility of cordite fire is due to the open stowage of ammunition in the panniers.

The damage effect of the 6-pdr APCBC and DS rounds striking near the base of the turret on either vehicle and turning down through the hull roof, should also be noted.

In most cases penetration of the tanks would result in the killing or wounding of members of the crew. This would seem to be greater with D.S. due to the more extensive breakup of the shot.

G. Guthrie, Major R.E.M.E.

O i/c Armour Trials Section (Armour Branch)

17.10.44.

JDH

APPENDIX A

Trial No. X. 798 & X.799

DETAILED RESULTS

TARGET	ATTACK	OBSERVATIONS
	Pz.Kw.V. (Panther)	
Tank—front at 10 degrees to Normal	Round 1. 17-pdr DSRL Lot 4. Range 1,000 yards	Missed—100 yards short
Tank—front at 10 degrees to Normal	Round 2. 17-pdr DSRL Lot 4. Range 1,000 yards	Missed—200 yards short
Tank—front at 10 degrees to Normal	Round 3. 17-pdr DSRL Lot 4. Range 1,000 yards	Struck on glacis plate above left hand track after passing through guard over front of left hand track. Plate holed 3.5 × 2 inches. Rear Metal off rear of glacis plate in several pieces—total area 8 × 5 inches. Shot shattered. Five wooden ammo racks on left-hand pannier splintered. Driver probably killed.
Tank—front at 10 degrees to Normal	Round 4. 17-pdr APCBC Range 1,000 yards	Missed. Shot passed under tank.
Tank—front at 10 degrees to Normal	Round 5. 17-pdr APCBC Range 1,000 yards	Code. W. Struck on centre line of 75-mm gun cast mantlet, 14 inches left of gun. Mantlet holed 3-inch diameter. Rear Metal off rear of mantlet over area 5-inch diameter. Shot past through turret and came out through left-hand rear quarter turret side plate. Position of the gun trunnion bracket removed. Bracket on the front end of turret sighting binocular cradle broken off. Fragments perforated sheet metal stowage bins on right-hand turret shelf, adjacent exit door. Stowage bins on left-hand turret shelf also damaged. Exit hole in left-hand rear quarter turret side plate 3.5 × 2.5 inches. Commander and gun layer killed. Gun loader wounded. Gun elevation and traverse in working order.
Tank—front at 10 degrees to Normal	Round 6. 17-pdr DSRL Lot 4. Range 1,000 yards	Missed. Grazed 25 yards short and penetrated target board to rear of target.
Tank—front at 10 degrees to Normal	Round 7. 17-pdr DSRL Lot 4. Range 1,000 yards	Missed. Grazed 250 yards short.
Tank—front at 10 degrees to Normal	Round 8. 17-pdr DS Mackie Lot 3. Range 1,000 yards	Struck right-hand track at front topside. Hole 5 × 3 inches in link. First bogie tyre torn away. Five track teeth torn away.
Tank—front at 10 degrees to Normal	Round 9. 17-pdr APCBC Range 1,000 yards	Missed target. Grazed 500 yards short.

TARGET	ATTACK	OBSERVATIONS
Tank—front at 10 degrees to Normal	Round 10. 17-pdr APCBC Range 1,000 yards	Code W. Struck on junction of glacis and nose plate. Metal off glacis plate 3 × 2.5 inches. Hole in nose plate 5 × 3 inches. Flake off glacis plate. Welded joint cracked from shot impact to left-hand side. Side plate to glacis plate and lower nose plate welded joints—cracked total length 18 inches
Tank—front at 10 degrees to Normal	Round 11. 17-pdr DS Mackie Lot 3. Range 1,000 yards	Code W. Struck right-hand final drive casing hole 1.25-inch diameter—3.5 inches from right-hand side plate. Crack in weld attaching housing to side plate 14 inches long. Crack continuing across side plate and on inside under nose for 12 inches.
Tank—front at 10 degrees to Normal	Round 12. 17-pdr DS Mackie Lot 3. Range 1,000 yards	Shot grazed hull roof above driver. Driver's periscope shield removed. Driver's door damaged, metal off 9 × 3.5 inches. Hatch pivot damaged. Numerous bolts from roof hatch frame removed. Driver slightly injured.
Tank—front at 10 degrees to Normal	Round 13. 17-pdr DS Mackie Lot 3. Range 1,000 yards	Struck front outer edge of right-hand track, glancing off front sprocket, front bogie, second bogie, and finally striking third bogie, buckling and tearing rim. Tyre torn severely. Hole in outer disc of first bogie 9 × 4 inches.
Tank—front at 10 degrees to Normal	Round 14. 17-pdr DS Mackie Lot 3. Range 1,000 yards	Struck left hand track shield—removing same. No other damage.
Tank—front at 10 degrees to Normal	Round 15. 17-pdr APCBC Range 1,000 yards	Missed. Grazed 25 yards short
Tank—front at 10 degrees to Normal	Round 16. 17-pdr APCBC Range 1,000 yards	Missed. Holed target board to rear of tank.
		It was noted after this round that either round 15 or round 16 had grazed turret roof, striking fan cowl guard, and removing metal from same 3 × 3 inches. Shield over the gun loader's periscope removed. Turret roof split for 4 inches length behind periscope opening.
Tank—front at 10 degrees to Normal	Round 17. 17-pdr APCBC Range 1,000 yards	Code R. Shot grazed 25 yards short, ricocheted onto glacis plate. Plug out of plate 3.25-inch diameter 8 inches from machine gun mounting. Scoop 8 × 3 inches. Crack in weld attaching machine gun mounting to glacis plate 10 inches long. Part of shot did not penetrate. Gun clamping bracket damaged. Rear Flake off glacis plate 8 × 6 inches in several pieces. Driver's visor opened. Two holes in turret platform 4 × inches and 2-inch diameter. Driver wounded by fragments. Gun loader severely wounded.
Tank—right-hand side at 31 degrees to Normal. (MS Skirting plates fitted one 0.3125 inches thick and two 0.25 inches thick)	Round 18. 6-pdr DS Lot 115. Range 600 yards	Code W. Struck between turret and hull roof. Hole approximately 2-inch diameter. Hole roof holed 3 × 1.5 inches. Rear Two ammunition racks badly splintered. Turret traverse jammed. Gun loader badly wounded.
Tank—right-hand side at 31 degrees to Normal. (MS Skirting plates fitted one 0.3125 inches thick and two 0.25 inches thick)	Round 19. 6-pdr DS Lot 122. Range 600 yards	Struck fourth bogie 6 inches below skirting plate and holed inner wheel disc 3 × 2.5 inches. Shot passed under vehicle and fragments splattered rear bogie on left-hand side.
Tank—right-hand side at 31 degrees to Normal. (MS Skirting plates fitted one 0.3125 inches thick and two 0.25 inches thick)	Round 20. 6-pdr DS Lot 114. Range 600 yards	Struck and holed skirting plate 1.5 × 1.875 inches adjacent fourth bogie. Holed bogie—outer disc and tyre of inner disc. Fragments pitted hull side.
Tank—right-hand side at 31 degrees to Normal. (MS Skirting plates fitted one 0.3125 inches thick and two 0.25 inches thick)	Round 21 6-pdr DS Lot 108. Range 600 yards	Code W. Struck skirting plate above fourth bogie. Holed plate 1.75 × 1.25 inches. Hull side plate holed 2.25 × 1.5 inches—7 inches below pannier side plate. Rear metal off hull side plate 4.5 × 3.5 inches in several pieces. Shot past through turret fan ducting—cutting same. Two perforations 2 × 1 inch and 1-inch square in shield over turret rack on left-hand side. Gun loader wounded in legs. Gun layer wounded in body.

TARGET	ATTACK	OBSERVATIONS
Tank—right-hand side at 31 degrees to Normal. (MS Skirting plates fitted one 0.3125 inches thick and two 0.25 inches thick)	Round 22. 6-pdr APCBC Lot 321. Range 600 yards	Code W. Skirting plate holed 3-inch diameter above fourth bogie Hull side holed 3-inch diameter. Rear Terminal bracket behind impact forced away from wall. Wiring in vicinity severed. Engine would have stopped. Turret platform broken away in vicinity. Gun loader wounded in the legs.
Tank—right-hand side at 31 degrees to Normal. (MS Skirting plates fitted one 0.3125 inches thick and two 0.25 inches thick)	Round 23. 6-pdr APCBC Lot 321. Range 600 yards	Code W. Holed pannier side 3.5 × 2.5 inches adjacent hull roof. Main weld above impact cracked in junction 8.5 inches length. Roof bulged approximately 0.375 inches. Rear Metal off rear of pannier side plate 3 × 2 inches. Shot past into turret rack, breaking off teeth for 4 inches length. Large hole in gun shield adjacent gun seat. Shot past through engine bulkhead into left-hand petrol tank—probable fire. Loader slightly wounded in thigh gun layer wounded
Tank—right-hand side at 31 degrees to Normal. (MS Skirting plates fitted one 0.3125 inches thick and two 0.25 inches thick)	Round 24. 6-pdr APCBC Lot 321. Range 600 yards	Missed tank.
Tank—right-hand side at 31 degrees to Normal. (MS Skirting plates fitted one 0.3125 inches thick and two 0.25 inches thick)	Round 25. 6-pdr APCBC Lot 321. Range 600 yards	Code W. Holed cupola casting 2.75 × 2.5 inches. Roof plate split in vicinity approximately 10-inch length and force down locally 0.25 inches. Rear Metal off behind impact 10 × 5 inches. Bin front on turret shelf adjacent commander badly perforated. Commander's seat perforated and twisted.
Tank—right-hand side at 31 degrees to Normal. (MS Skirting plates fitted one 0.3125 inches thick and two 0.25 inches thick)	Round 26. 6-pdr APCBC Lot 321. Range 600 yards	Code W. Shot struck on rear right-hand lower corner of turret 6 inches above hull roof and on repair patch which was removed. Shot turned it down through hull roof. Rear Welding between shelf and turret wall split for 4 inches length. Turret shelf split for 4 inches at right angles to wall. Hull roof holed 18 × 7 inches. Numerous strikes on engine compartment bulkhead. Various brackets in vicinity of hole broken away or badly damaged. Gun loader severely injured.
Tank—right-hand side at 31 degrees to Normal. (MS Skirting plates fitted one 0.3125 inches thick and two 0.25 inches thick)	Round 27. 6-pdr APCBC Lot 321. Range 600 yards	Code W. Struck turret right-hand side plate forward end 4 inches from top edge. Plate holed 2.75 × 2.25 inches. Roof plate bulged slightly in locality. Protecting ring around the fan cowl lifted 0.375 inches maximum. Weld failed 20 inches in junction with ring. Rear Metal off turret side plate over area 5 × 4 inches. Shot passed across turret destroying fan motor. Opposite wall severely pitted over area 14 × 3 inches. Extensive crack in left-hand rear quarter turret side plate starting from exit hole—Round 5. Commander probably killed. Gun layer and loader severely injured.

TARGET	ATTACK	OBSERVATIONS
	Pz.Kw.VI. (Tiger)	
Tank—front at 30 degrees to Normal	Round 28. 6-pdr DS Lot 114. Range 600 yards	Missed. Grazed 200 yards short.
Tank—front at 30 degrees to Normal	Round 29. 6-pdr DS Lot 115. Range 600 yards	Code W. Struck approximately central on the upper nose plate—hole 1.5 × 1.375 inches. Rear Shot past through gun layer's legs, striking lid stowage bin and impacting on bulkhead behind stowage bin. Gun layer and driver severely injured.
Tank—front at 30 degrees to Normal	Round 30. 6-pdr APCBC Range 600 yards	Code B. Struck glacis plate 8 inches from front edge, glanced onto protection piece in front of visor, and then onto Maine visor plate.
Tank—front at 30 degrees to Normal	Round 31. 6-pdr APCBC Range 600 yards	Code D. Struck on visor plate 9 inches from centre line of ball mounting. Metal off 6 × 4 inches. Welded joint—visor plate to glacis plate—Split in throat 16-inch length. Rear Cracked bulge. Visor plate split from ball mounting hole—horizontally for 6 inches approximately to shot impact.
Tank—front at 30 degrees to Normal	Round 32. 6-pdr DS Lot 113. Range 600 yards	Shot entered she gun hole in gun mantlet. No assessment made.
Tank—front at 30 degrees to Normal	Round 33. 6-pdr DS Lot 114. Range 600 yards	Struck top left hand corner of visor plate 2.5 inches from top and outer edges. Metal off 3 × 3 inches.
Tank—front at 30 degrees to Normal	Round 34. 6-pdr DS Lot 114. Range 600 yards	Code W. Struck 4.5 inches from top edge and 13 inches from outside edge of visor plate. Hole 1.25-inch diameter. Rear Metal off 6 × 3 inches in several pieces. Driver's hatch locking catch damage.
Tank—front at 30 degrees to Normal	Round 35. 6-pdr DS Lot 115. Range 600 yards	Shot struck top edge right-hand side of visor plate. Periscope cover removed from co-driver's hatch. Metal off rear corner of hatch amateur 2 × 1.5 inches. Inner cast periscope housing damaged by fragments passing under hatch. Metal off 3 × 1.5 inches. Clamping spider and one guide lug removed. Wiring in co-driver's compartment severed in several places. Note: hatch was not closed down properly.
Tank—front at 30 degrees to Normal	Round 36. 6-pdr DS Lot 115. Range 600 yards	Code B. Shot struck edge of glacis plate right-hand track ricocheted onto visor or plate. Scoop 3 × 1.5 inches.
Tank—front at 30 degrees to Normal	Round 37. 6-pdr DS Lot 115. Range 600 yards	Code W. Struck visor or plate 7 inches from top—on right-hand side. Crack in visor plate to glacis plate welded joint extended. Rear Plate holed 1.125 inches diameter. Shot past through driver's compartment. Fragments struck roof stiffener and turret platform suspension column. Co-driver killed. Gun layer severely wounded. Gun loader commander wounded slightly in legs.
Tank—front at 30 degrees to Normal	Round 38. 6-pdr. DS Lot 114. Range 600 yards	Scoop. Shot struck hull right-hand side plate at junction with glacis plate. Scoop 5 × 2 inches. Several strikes by fragments of visor plate. Machine gun ball mounting jammed.
Tank—front at 30 degrees to Normal	Round 39. 6-pdr. DS Lot 122. Range 600 yards	Code W. Struck on visor plate 11 inches from centre of ball mounting and 9 inches from top edge. Normal front damage. Visor plate heavily pitted over area 9 × 8 inches. Gun barrel pitted. Rear Metal off 2.5 × 2 inches. Welded support bracket for fittings on the visor badly bent and one fitting perforated over area 6 × 4 inches. Shot past through vehicle and struck bracket supporting turret gun elevating shaft. Numerous small strikes in surrounding area. Turret traverse jammed. Co-driver and gun layer severely wounded. Commander wounded in legs.

TARGET	ATTACK	OBSERVATIONS
	Pz.Kw.V. (Panther)	
Tank—right-hand side at 31 degrees to Normal. (MS Skirting plate fitted)	Round 40. 6-pdr APCBC Range 600 yards	Code W. Shot struck skirting plate above fourth bogie just below pannier and penetrated hull side plate adjacent Round 21. Skirting plate holed 3-inch diameter. Hull side holed 2.75-inch diameter. Internal assessment not carried out.
Tank—right-hand side at 31 degrees to Normal. (MS Skirting plate fitted)	Round 41. 6-pdr APCBC Range 600 yards	Code W. Struck skirting plate above fifth bogie—10 inches below pannier. Hull side holed 3.25-inch diameter. Internal assessment after Rounds 40 and 41. Round 40 struck ribbing above pannier base and side plate forcing same way 7 inches. Length of ribbing completely dislodged. Shot past through metal frame work adjacent turret motor. Wiring severed. Round 41. Metal off hull side plate 6.5 × 6 inches. Plate flaking. Fragments struck engine compartment bulkhead and ammunition bin in locality severely perforated—probable damage to rounds.
Tank—right-hand side at 31 degrees to Normal.	Round 42. 6-pdr APCBC Range 600 yards	Missed. Grazed 500 yards short.
Tank—right-hand side at 31 degrees to Normal.	Round 43. 6-pdr APCBC Range 600 yards	Missed. Grazed 500 yards short.
Tank—right-hand side at 31 degrees to Normal.	Round 44. 6-pdr APCBC Range 600 yards	Shot grazed 30 yards short and struck sixth bogey near ground. Outer disc holed 4 × 2.5 inches. Inner disc holed 6 × 5 inches. Shot passed out to rear of the left-hand track.
Tank—front at 10 degrees to Normal.	Round 45. 17-pdr DS Mackie Lot.3. Range 1,000 yards	Code W. Shot struck on glacis plate 8 inches from side plate. Metal off 8 × 5 inches. Plate holed 2 × 2.5 inches. Rear Metal off 9 × 8 inches. Three radial cracks—10, 18, and 6 inches long. Pitting of roof stiffener between drivers and fighting compartment. Co-driver killed. Driver slightly wounded.
Tank—front at 10 degrees to Normal.	Round 46. 17-pdr APCBC Range 1,000 yards	Shot glanced off inner edge of right-hand track at front and struck final drive housing—splitting same. Sprocket and part of final drive housing forced away 6 inches approximately. Casing metal removed over area 18 × 2 inches. Four track links partially severed maximum damage 11 × 4 inches.
Tank—front at 10 degrees to Normal.	Round 47. 17-pdr APCBC Range 1,000 yards	Missed. Grazed 500 yards short.
Tank—front at 10 degrees to Normal.	Round 48. 17-pdr APCBC Range 1,000 yards	Missed. Grazed 500 yards short.
Tank—front at 10 degrees to Normal.	Round 49. 17-pdr APCBC Range 1,000 yards	Missed. Grazed 100 yards short.
Tank—front at 10 degrees to Normal.	Round 50. 17-pdr APCBC Range 1,000 yards	Shot struck right-hand track further damaging sprocket final drive housing. Sprocket public removed.
Tank—left-hand side at 30 degrees to Normal.	Round 51. 17-pdr APCBC Range 1,000 yards	Struck rear bogie—left-hand side outer disc holed 3.5 × 4 inches the wheel damaged.
Tank—left-hand side at 30 degrees to Normal.	Round 52. 17-pdr APCBC Range 1,000 yards	Code W. Struck skirting plate above first bogie—12 inches below pannier. Plate holed 5 × 4 inches. Rear Metal off 6.5 × 6 inches. Shot passed through fighting compartment severing vertical column supporting turret platform. Wiring junction box on turret floor dislodged and wiring severed. Shot passed to opposite side of hull vertical stiffening plate. One ammunition rack destroyed. Gun loader killed. Gun layer severely injured. Co-driver wounded. Driver probably wounded.

TARGET	ATTACK	OBSERVATIONS
	Pz.Kw.VI. (Tiger)	
Tank—front at Normal	Round 53. 6-pdr APCBC Range 600 yards	Code NFH double hit on the visor plate with Round 61. Rear metal off 12 × 8 inches. Shot past through fighting compartment and holed same 3.5 × 2.5 inches. Right-hand stowage bin on floor of fighting compartment damaged. Rounds probably ignited. Shot probably pass through radiator compartment. Shots struck low right front between turret and roof after striking on hull roof and turret race protecting ring.
Tank—front at Normal	Round 54. 6-pdr APCBC Range 600 yards	Shot struck low right front between turret and hull roof—after striking on hull roof and turret race protecting ring. Ring securing bolts sheared out. Portion of ring lifted 1-inch maximum. Rear Turret shelf broken away over area 10 × 3 inches. Turret probably jammed. Gun layer wounded.
Tank—front at Normal	Round 55. 6-pdr APCBC Range 600 yards	Code W. Shot struck low left front between turret and hull roof. Segment of turret protection ring completely dislodged. Shot turned down penetrating hull roof—3 × 2 inches. Rear Turret probably jammed. Shot entered hull—grazed engine compartment bulkhead and struck cross member on tank floor breaking same for full depth of 5 inches. Shot, less base, found on the floor of tank. Gun layer severely wounded.
Tank—front at Normal	Round 56. 6-pdr APCBC Range 600 yards	Scoop. Shot struck protection sleeve around 88-mm gun, gun mantlet, and then holed hull roof—4 × 2.5 inches. Rear Metal off hull roof over area 8 × 6 inches. Shot struck bulkhead between driver's and fighting compartment. Metal off 12 × 6 inches. Shot broke up causing pitting on structure near floor of tank. Gun layer wounded in leg. Gun loader slightly wounded in legs. Driver slightly wounded.
Tank—front at Normal	Round 57. 6-pdr APCBC Range 600 yards	Shot passed between left hand hull pannier side and sheet metal track guard.
Tank—front at Normal	Round 58. 6-pdr APCBC Range 600 yards	Code B. Struck lower nose plate near junction with upper nose plate. Scoop 4 × 2 inches.
Tank—front at Normal	Round 59. 6-pdr APCBC Range 600 yards	Shot scooped off protection piece in front of driver's visor and then removed entire driver's visor assembly. Rear Retaining tongue for left-hand visor guide broken away found lying on driver.
Tank—front at Normal	Round 60. 6-pdr APCBC Range 600 yards	Code B. Scoop off lower nose plate near left-hand side.
Tank—front at Normal	Round 61. 6-pdr APCBC Range 600 yards	Scoop. Shot struck junction upper and lower nose plate. Scoop 12 × 3.5 × 2.5 inches deep. Crack in weld junction extending toward centre of vehicle for 9 inches and towards right-hand side for 10 inches.
Tank—front at Normal	Round 62. 6-pdr APCBC Range 600 yards	Scoop. Struck junction of glacis and upper nose plate 10 inches from right-hand side. Scoop 6 × 3 × 2 inches deep maximum. Weld cracked from shot impact to right-hand edge 8 inches long.
Tank—front at Normal	Round 63. 6-pdr APCBC Range 600 yards	Code W. Struck central on visor plate 4 inches from top edge. Shot hole 2.25-inch diameter. Top edge set up 0.375 inches maximum. Five cracks in plate adjacent to impact. Visor plate to roof plate welded joint split over 7-inch length in junction with roof and lifted slightly. Rear Metal off 5.5 × 4 inches. Bulkhead between driver's and fighting compartment shot away over area 11 × 5 inches. Fan ducting in hull roof shot away. Base of shot found in engine compartment.
Tank—left-hand side at 30 degrees to Normal	Round 64. 6-pdr DS Lot 114. Range 600 yards	Struck top side of left-hand track and shattered on hull side close to joint with pannier floor.
Tank—left-hand side at 30 degrees to Normal	Round 65. 6-pdr DS Lot 114. Range 600 yards	Shot grazed top front left-hand edge of turret.
Tank—left-hand side at 30 degrees to Normal	Round 66. 6-pdr DS Lot 114. Range 600 yards	Code W. Struck left-hand pannier side 2.5 inches above lower edge.
Tank—left-hand side at 30 degrees to Normal	Round 67. 6-pdr DS Lot 115. Range 600 yards	Code W. Struck superstructure side plate centrally, 10 inches from lower edge. Rear Shot passed through fighting compartment and broke up on engine compartment bulkhead perforated engine primer pump casing and heavily pitting bulkhead. Commander severely wounded. Driver probably injured.

Tank—left-hand side at 30 degrees to Normal	Round 68. 6-pdr DS Lot 114. Range 600 yards	Code C. (Slight). Struck superstructure side plate between rounds 66 and 67. 6 inches above lower edge. Shot shattered. Rear Smooth bulge 3-inch diameter 0.75 inches high displacing metal attachment strip.
Tank—left-hand side at 30 degrees to Normal	Round 69. 6-pdr DS Lot 114. Range 600 yards	Scoop. Struck second bogie, penetrating outer disc and scooped off hull lower side plate, lower edge. Hole in disc 1.75 × 1.5 inches. Metal off lower edge of side plate 3 × 2.5 × 2 inches deep.
Tank—left-hand side at 30 degrees to Normal	Round 70. 6-pdr DS Lot 114. Range 600 yards	Scoop. Shot struck top left-hand forward turret side plate. Metal off 4.5 × 2 × 1 inch deep.
Tank—left-hand side at 30 degrees to Normal	Round 71. 6-pdr DS Lot 114. Range 600 yards	Scoop. Struck driver's periscope shield, and glanced on to front edge of turret base, scooping off metal 7 × 3 × 1.5 inches. Periscope guard metal off 5 × 2.5 inches.
Tank—left-hand side at 30 degrees to Normal	Round 72. 6-pdr DS Lot 114. Range 600 yards	Code W. Struck turret left-hand side plate 2.25 inches below top edge. Hole 1.25-inch diameter. Edge of plate bulged up. Side plate split across to top edge in several places. Rear Metal off over area 2 × 1.5 inches. Welded bracket completely removed from turret roof. Two tubular store beans destroyed. Lever arm and spindle supporting gun breech removed by shot and considerable pitting of surface in vicinity. Commander, Gunner layer and gun loader wounded severely.
Tank—left-hand side at 30 degrees to Normal	Round 73. 6-pdr DS Lot 114. Range 600 yards	Scoop. Struck top forward edge of turret left-hand side plate, removing metal 2 × 2 inches. Shot passed through turret roof, removing metal 3.5 × 2.5 inches. Rear Metal off 3 × 2.5 inches. Welding split badly. Gun loader and gun layer killed. Further damage to lever brackets on gun breach. Shot broke up causing heavy pitting of surrounding bin faces.
Tank—left-hand side at 30 degrees to Normal	Round 74. 6-pdr APCBC Range 600 yards	Scoop. Struck top left-hand edge of superstructure. Scoop 4 × 3.5 × 1.5 inches. Shot shattered on turret side.
Tank—left-hand side at 30 degrees to Normal	Round 75. 6-pdr APCBC Range 600 yards	Code W. Struck 11 inches from base of turret, left-hand turret side plate holed 2.25 × 2 inches. Rear Metal off 3-inch diameter. Shot passed into turret, striking reduction gear for turret traverse, Casing for reduction gear perforated resulting in considerable oil loss. Shot passed across turret, striking turret fixed race ring and shelf plate, forcing away metal over area 5 × 4 inches. Locking bolt for rear escape hatch broken away. Commander severely wounded in body and legs. Gun layer wounded in head and legs. Loader slightly wounded in body and thigh.
Tank—left-hand side at 30 degrees to Normal	Round 76. 6-pdr APCBC Range 600 yards	Code W. Shot struck base of turret, scooped down through hull roof and entered fighting compartment. Roof holed 12 × 7 inches. One turret protecting ring bolts sheared out. Rear Shot recovered from ammunition bin on opposite side of turret. Turret traversing rack sheared removing teeth 12 inches and breaking away hand traverse gear. Considerable perforation of ammunition stowage bins immediately below hole. Gun layer killed, loader wounded.
Tank—left-hand side at 30 degrees to Normal	Round 77. 6-pdr APCBC Range 600 yards	Scoop. Struck rim of second bogie glanced off inner rim of third bogie, and the scooped off left-hand hull side plate. Wheel rims holed 3 × 2.5 inches. Scoop 7 × 4 × 0.5 inches deep.
Tank—left-hand side at 30 degrees to Normal	Round 78. 6-pdr APCBC Range 600 yards	Struck fourth bogie, hold outer disc 3 × 2.5 inches below hub level. Passed through inner fifth bogie disc and passed out under hull of the tank striking sixth bogey rim of right-hand side. Metal off 11 × 4 inches.
Tank—left-hand side at 30 degrees to Normal	Round 79. 6-pdr APCBC Range 600 yards	Grazed top edge of track, approximately central in length of vehicle and struck hull side. Three taper headed bolts securing pannier base sheared out. Scallop welding split for 18 inches, mainly in junction.
Tank—left-hand side at 30 degrees to Normal	Round 80. 6-pdr APCBC Range 600 yards	Code W. Struck 4.5 inches from top edge of left-hand superstructure side plate. Hole 2.25-inch diameter. Rear Shot past through pannier ammunition stowage, through gun balancing gear, and broke up on engine compartment bulkhead. Various fittings in path of shot removed from bulkhead. Commander severely injured in legs.

APPENDIX B

Trial No. X. 798 & X.799

AT No. 225

Pz.Kw.V.—Panther and Pz.Kw.VI.—Tiger

Left-hand rear three-quarter view of Panther tank after attack. Note: Exit hole in left-hand rear quarter turret side plate made by Round 5, a 17-pdr APCBC. (*DTD Materials Division, Armour Branch*)

Right-hand front three-quarter view of a Panther tank after attack. (*DTD Materials Division, Armour Branch*)

Right-hand rear three-quarter view of a Panther tank after attack. (*DTD Materials Division, Armour Branch*)

Right-hand front, three-quarter view of a Tiger tank after attack. Note: This tank has been identified as Tiger 114 of 1/s SS-Pz.Abt.101 that was captured by the British tanks of 'A' Squadron, Sherwood Rangers Yeomanry, 8th Armoured Brigade, outside Rauray near Fontenay-le-Pesnel in Normandy on 26 June 1944. They wanted to use it against their enemy. The 8th Armoured Brigade fox emblem was painted on the front and rear of the tank. The SS-Panzer Battalion unit badge painted over. British High Command ordered it to be transported back to Britain for trials. (*DTD Materials Division, Armour Branch*)

View of right-hand side of Tiger tanks after attack. (*DTD Materials Division, Armour Branch*)

Left-hand rear, three-quarter view of a Tiger tank after attack. (*DTD Materials Division, Armour Branch*)

Panther tank glacis plate holed: Round 3, 17-pdr DS. Range 1,000 yards. Tank front 10 degrees to Normal. Plate at 51 degrees to Normal. (*DTD Materials Division, Armour Branch*)

Panther tank cast mantlet holed: Round 5, 17-pdr APCBC at 10 degrees to Normal. Range 1,000 yards. (*DTD Materials Division, Armour Branch*)

Panther tank final drive housing holed. Round 11: 17-pdr DS at 10 degrees to Normal. Range 1,000 yards. (*DTD Materials Division, Armour Branch*)

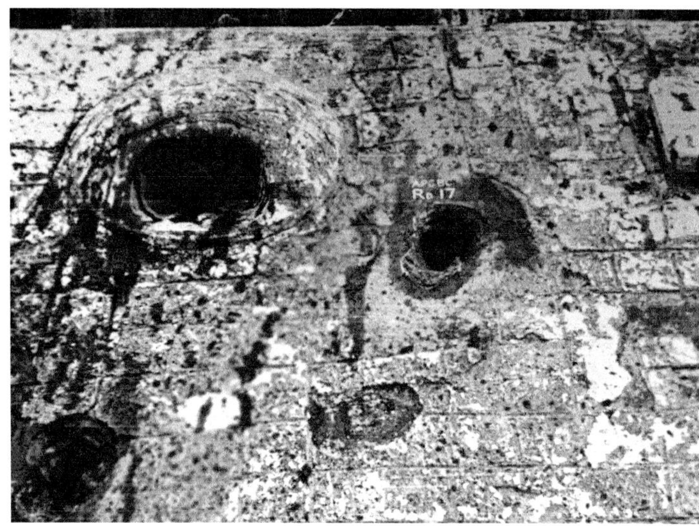

Panther tank glacis plate holed. Round 17: 17-pdr APCBC. Range 1,000 yards. Round 45: 17-pdr DS. Range 1,000 yards. Tank front at 10 degrees to Normal. Plate at 51 degrees to Normal. (*DTD Materials Division, Armour Branch*)

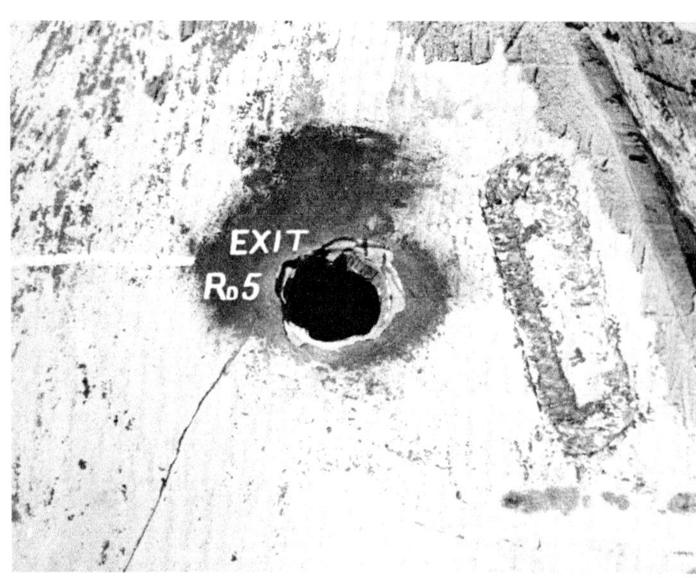

Exit hole in Panther tank turret, left-hand rear-quarter side plate, made by Round 5: 17-pdr APCBC. See Print No. 8. (*DTD Materials Division, Armour Branch*)

Hull roof plate holed—Round 18: 6-pdr at 31 degrees to Normal with hull side. Range 600 yards. Shot scooped off the lower edge of the turret's side plate. Pannier side plate holed—Round 23: 6-pdr APCBC at 48 degrees to Normal. (*DTD Materials Division, Armour Branch*)

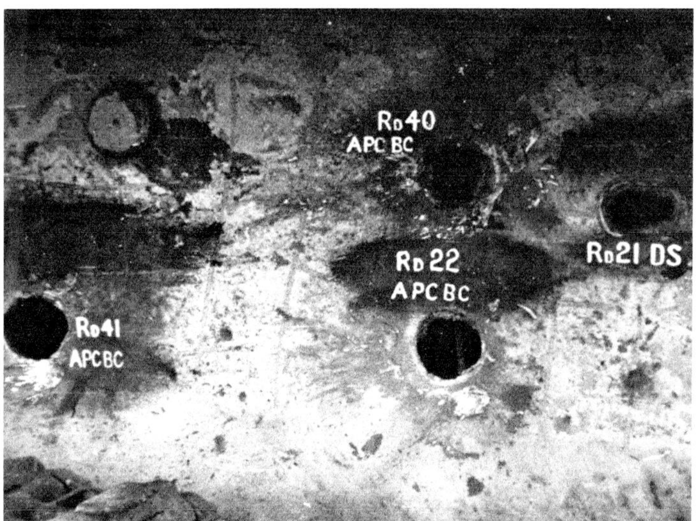

Round 40 and 41: APCBC. Range 600 yards. Shot struck skirting plate above fourth bogie just below pannier and penetrated hull side plate adjacent Round 21. Skirting plate holed 3-inch diameter. Hull side holed 2.75-inch diameter. Internal assessment after Rounds 40 and 41. Round 40 struck ribbing above pannier base and side plate forcing same way 7 inches. length of ribbing completely. (*DTD Materials Division, Armour Branch*)

Round 25: 6-pdr APCBC. Lot 321. Range 600 yards. Holed cupola casting 2.75 × 2.5 inches. Roof plate split in vicinity approximately 10 inches in length and force down locally 0.25 inches. Rear: Metal off behind impact 10 × 5 inches. Bin front on turret shelf adjacent, commander badly perforated. Commander's seat perforated and twisted. (*DTD Materials Division, Armour Branch*)

Round 27: 6-pdr APCBC. Lot 321. Range 600 yards. Struck turret right-hand side plate forward end 4 inches from top edge. Plate holed 2.75 × 2.25 inches. Roof plate bulged slightly in locality. Protecting ring around the fan cowl lifted 0.375 inches maximum. Weld failed 20 inches in junction with ring. Rear: Metal off turret side plate over area 5 × 4 inches. Shot passed across the turret, destroying the fan motor. Opposite wall severely pitted over 14 × 3 inches. Extensive crack in left-hand rear-quarter turret side plate starting from exit hole: Round 5. Commander probably killed. Gun layer and loader severely injured. (*DTD Materials Division, Armour Branch*)

Tiger tank hull upper nose plate holed—Round 29: 6-pdr DS. Range 600 yards. Tank front 30 degrees to Normal. Nose plate 41 degrees to Normal. Note: A 6-pdr APCBC shot (Round 31) failed to defeat the same thickness plate (visor plate), at an angle to Normal, which was more favourable to the gun—i.e. 30 degrees to Normal. (*DTD Materials Division, Armour Branch*)

Tiger tank Round 31: 6-pdr APCBC at 30 degrees to Normal failed to defeat visor plate. (Code D damage) Range 600 yards. Visor plate holed by Round 63: 6-pdr APCBC. Range 600 yards. Tank front at normal. Visor plate at 4 degrees to Normal. (*DTD Materials Division, Armour Branch*)

Tiger tank visor plate holed—Round 34: 6-pdr DS at 30 degrees to Normal. Range 600 yards. Note: the badge under the 34.DS hole that looks like an animal head is the unit badge of the British 8th Armoured Brigade who were involved in the capture of this Tiger tank. The German unit badge under the 33.DS scoop has been painted over but you can just see the leaves of the unit badge of the *schwere* SS-Panzer *Abteilung* 101. (*DTD Materials Division, Armour Branch*)

Tiger tank visor plate holed—Rounds 37 and 39: 6-pdr DS at 30 degrees to Normal. Range 600 yards. (*DTD Materials Division, Armour Branch*)

Panther tank final drive casing split open by Round 46: 17-pdr APCBC at 10 degrees to Normal. Range 1,000 yards. The shot glanced off the inner edge of the track. (*DTD Materials Division, Armour Branch*)

Panther tank skirting plate and hull side plate holed—Round 52: 6-pdr APCBC at 30 degrees to Normal. Range 1,000 yards. (*DTD Materials Division, Armour Branch*)

Tiger tank hull roof holed—Rounds 55 and 56: 6-pdr APCBC at Normal to the front of the tank. Range 600 yards. Round 55 scooped off turret ring. Round 56 glanced off the underside of the gun mantlet. (*DTD Materials Division, Armour Branch*)

Tiger tank turret left-hand side plate holed—rounds 72 and 73: 6-pdr DS at 30 degrees to side of tank. Range 600 yards. (*DTD Materials Division, Armour Branch*)

Tiger tank left-hand side plate holed—Round 75: 6-pdr APCBC at 30 degrees to Normal. Hull roof holed—Round 76: 6-pdr APCBC at 30 degrees to Normal. Range 600 yards. Shot struck base of turret and scooped down through hull roof. (*DTD Materials Division, Armour Branch*)

Tiger tank superstructure side plate holed—Round 80: 6-pdr APCBC at 30 degrees to Normal. Range 600 yards. (*DTD Materials Division, Armour Branch*)

Tiger 114 of 1/s SS-Pz.Abt.101 that was captured by the British outside Fontenay-le-Pesnel on 26 June 1944 and was transported back to Britain for trials. Tiger 114 first went to the British Department of Tank Design, Fighting Vehicle Proving Establishment (DTD FVPE) in Chertsey, Chobham Lane, Surrey. It was used as a test load for a prototype steerable 80-ton trailer built by the Henry J. Coles Ltd. The trailer was designed to carry the very heavy Tortoise assault tank that was being developed. (*DTD Materials Division, Armour Branch*)

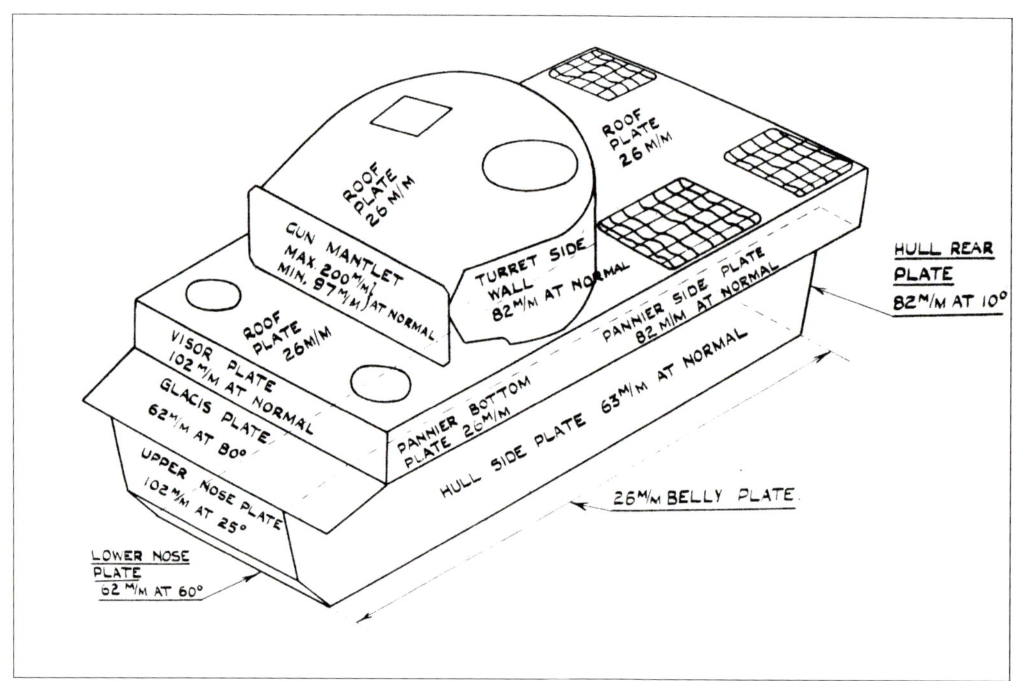

APPENDIX C

Trial No. X. 798 & X.799

AT No. 225

Pz.Kw.V.—Panther

Plate Thickness & Angles

Hull DTD No. 3041

Turret DTD No. 3042

AT No. 225

Pz.Kw.VI.—Tiger

Plate Thickness & Angles

Vehicle DTD No. 3036

APPENDIX D

Trial No. X. 798 & X.799

Plate Hardness

Poldi Hardness at surface on German tanks Pz.Kw.V. (Panther) and Pz.Kw.VI. (Tiger).

Pz.Kw.V. (Panther) hull DTD 3041 and Turret DTD 3042.

Plate	Hardness No.
Glacis	293
Nose	293
Pannier Sloping	295
Hull Side	307 approximate
Mantlet	230
Turret Sideâ	285

Pz.Kw.VI. (Tiger) hull and Turret DTD 3036

Plate	Hardness No.
Visor	230

Upper Nose	220
Superstructure Side	280
Hull Side	280
Turret Side	276

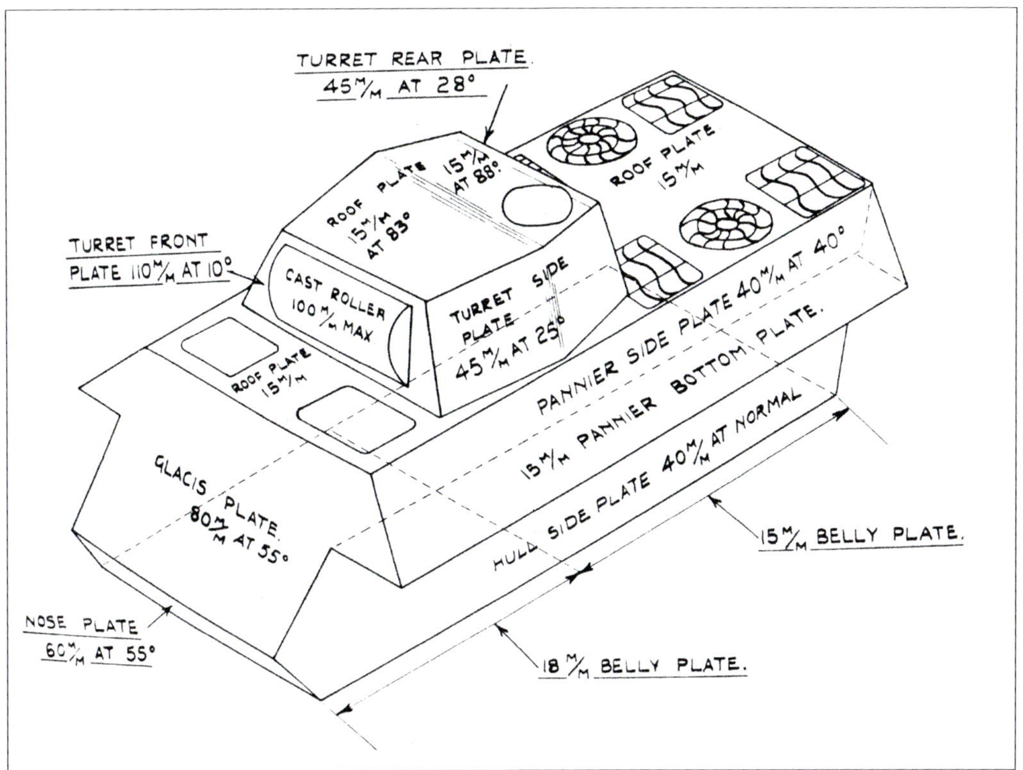

The Tiger 114 of 1/s SS-Pz. Abt. was used to test the ability of the British prototype Henry J. Coles Ltd 80-ton steerable trailer to cope with the loading and unloading of a heavy tank. (*DTD Materials Division, Armour Branch*)

13

PART I: FIRING TRIALS AGAINST Pz.Kw. VI (TIGER) 7–12 MARCH 1945

Unfortunately, many of the original photographs contained in these reports were of poor quality and some were out of focus. The information in this chapter has been transcribed from original wartime documents. The report format and brief notation style has been kept.

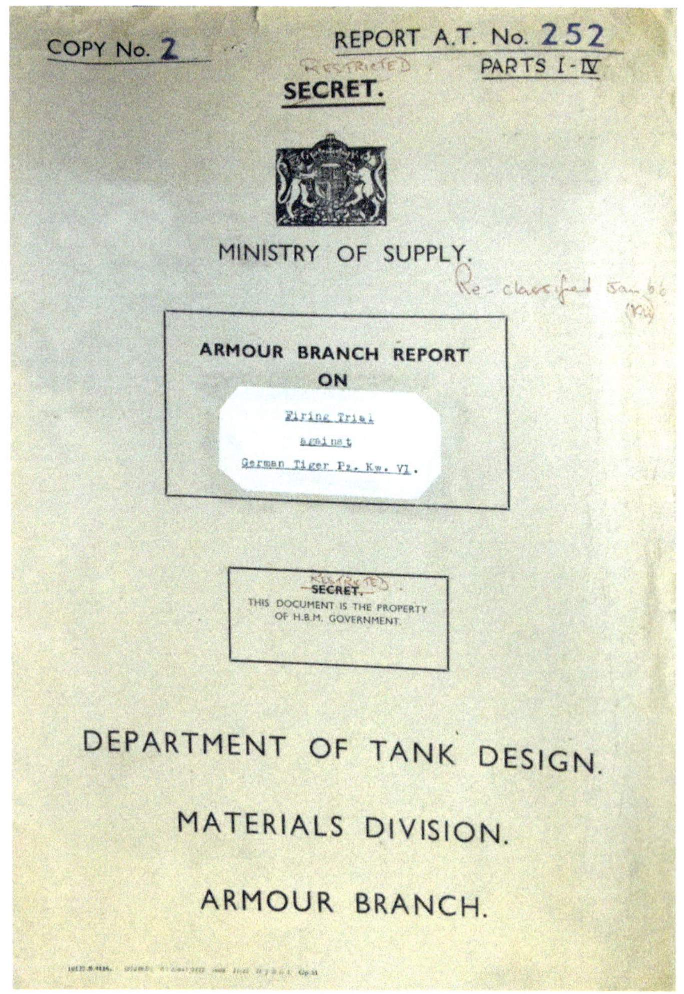

COPY No. 2

REPORT A.T. No. 252

PARTS I - IV

RESTRICTED

SECRET.

MINISTRY OF SUPPLY.

ARMOUR BRANCH REPORT

ON

Firing Trial

against

German Tiger Pz. Kw. VI.

RESTRICTED

SECRET.

THIS DOCUMENT IS THE PROPERTY OF H.B.M. GOVERNMENT.

DEPARTMENT OF TANK DESIGN.

MATERIALS DIVISION.

ARMOUR BRANCH.

The front cover of the report on the firing trials against a Tiger tank, March 1945. (*DTD Materials Division, Armour Branch*)

DTD EXPERIMENTAL REPORT AT NO. 252 PART 1

Project No. M. 6817A/10
Trial No. X. 610
File No. 250/14/4

Report of Firing Trials Against Pz.Kw. VI (Tiger) Held at S. of E. Range, Shoeburyness on 7, 9, 12 March 1945

Present at Trial			
	Lt. Tredinnick	-	S. of E. Range Officer
	Mr. Phillips	-	DTD Armour Branch
	Mr. Gray	-	DTD Armour Branch
	Mr. Wilde	-	DTD Armour Branch
Report			
Compiled by: –	Mr. G.W.Gray	-	DTD Armour Branch
Checked by: –	Mr. J.B. Sankey	-	DTD Armour Branch
References			
	Section I	-	Object of Trials
	Section II	-	Target Details
	Section III	-	Method of Attack
	Section IV	-	Trial Commentary (Small Arms)
	Section V	-	Trial Commentary (Air Burst HE)
	Section VI	-	Trial Commentary (Air Attack AP and incendiary)
	Section VII	-	Conclusions
Appendices			
	Appendix A	-	Detailed Results
	Appendix B	-	Photographic Record
Note: –			
	This report must not be reproduced in full or in part without the written authority of the Director of Tank Design		

SECRET DTD EXPERIMENTAL REPORT AT NO. 252

Part 1

Project No. M. 6817A/10

Subject

Comprehensive firing trial against German Tiger Pz.Kw. VI Model E.

Origin

The series of trials was initiated by the Armour Branch of the Department of Tank Design.

Remarks

The vehicle, hull number 250570, used throughout these trials, was captured in Normandy. The reference number is DTD 3039.

The trial took place in 4 parts, and the weapons and ammunition used were as follows:

Part I	.303-inch rifle	Ball and AP
	25-pdr	HE (Air Burst)
	20-mm Hispano	AP and Incendiary
Part II	6-pdr	APDS and APCBC
	17-pdr	APDS and APCBC
	75-mm	APCBCHE and HE
	25-pdr	HE (Contact Burst)
	PIAT	3.5 lb
	AT Mine	Mk V Standard
Part III	6-pdr	APCBC
	17-pdr	APCBC
	AT Grenade	No. 75 (used as a grenade)
Part IV	AT Mine	Mk V Standard
	AT Grenade	No. 75 (used as a grenade)

Results may be summarised briefly as follows: –

1. From horizontal attack the vehicle is virtually immune to 'splash' from small arms ball.
2. From an angle of 30 degrees, free entry of 'splash' in certain instances is likely.
3. Attack directed downwards at 30 degrees into the water-cooling system louvres will cause perforation of the water tubes.
4. Jamming of the hull machine gun mounting, and visor shutters is possible from small arms AP.
5. Very extensive radiator perforation is likely from air burst HE over the engine compartment, with probable early stoppage of vehicle.
6. 20 mm AP Attack downwards at 30 degrees will also severely damage radiators. Direct penetration into fuel tanks is most unlikely except a strike be made direct on the filler neck. Fuel fires from 20 mm incendiary are unlikely owing to the inferior penetration of this ammunition.
7. Projectiles of 6-pdr calibre, and upwards, striking low on the turret mantlet, will probably scoop, perforate the hull roof and arrest the vehicle. Penetration of the middle third of vehicle side will probably cause a cordite fire, and in the rear third a fuel fire. This is true for a PIAT as well as an AP attack.
8. The armour generally behaved in a manner similar to British machinable.
9. The hull roof is immune to HE up to 25-pdr burst on the turret but such bursts on the turret rear will severely perforate the water radiators.
10. The track on this vehicle is very much stronger than that fitted to Panther, and arrest of the tank by breakage is only likely to occur by the use of charges equal to two British Standard Mk V Mines. Defeat of the hull floor is unlikely except with a much higher charge than was used in these trials.
11. The type of anti-magnetic covering used does not appear to have any marked advantages over that used on British vehicles.
12. From an armour viewpoint the vehicle has few weaknesses.

Full discussion of the above remarks will be found in the body of the report.

A.T. Bowden
Assistant Director (Armour)
A.A.M. Durrant
Director
13.6.45.
M.995(s)

SECTION I

Objects of Trial

1. Determine the degree of immunity of various fitments on the Tiger tank to .303-inch ball and AP attack.
2. To determine the effect of 25-pdr HE. Air burst on the engine cooling radiators.
3. To determine the effect of 20-mm AP. And incendiary on the engine compartment roof, and the engine cooling radiators and fuel tanks.

SECTION II

Target Details

Pz.Kw. VI (Tiger) tank DTD No. 3039 model E complete with tracks, suspension, engine and transmission, but less stowage. Vehicle in running condition. Fuel tanks were approximately a quarter full of petrol.

SECTION III

Method of Attack

1. Small Arms

Various items, fully detailed in Appendix A, were attacked with .303-inch FSC. At angles calculated to give the least resistance to splash entry. .303-inch AP FSC was also used against certain items to obtain a measure of their immunity to jamming.

The following items were missing or disabled, and complete results were not therefore obtainable.

(a) Driver's visor or glass block.
(b) Turret vision slit glass block.
(c) Revolver port plug.
(d) Turret cupola, or glass blocks.

2. Air Burst HE

25-pdr HE Shell (Charge II) TNT. Filled were detonated at heights of approximately 13 feet and 5 feet above the forward louvres, and impositions forward of the engine covers to ensure that maximum zone of fragmentation would be over the single radiator cooling louvres.

3-feet square wooden boards 1-inch thick were used to detonate the shell, and these were slung from a wire rope stretched across the walls of the butt.

3. Air Attack AP and Incendiary

In order to simulate attack from the air, the engine compartment roof and radiator air cooling louvres and fuel tanks were attacked with 20-mm AP and incendiary FSC. From 30 degrees above horizontal.

SECTION IV

Trial Commentary (Small Arms)

Item 1: Hull Machine Gun Ball Mounting

.303-inch ball disclosed only slight markings of the witness card, and in no way affected the function of the mounting.

.303-inch AP temporarily jammed the movement, but this was freed by hand. Further attack effectively jammed the movement.

Item 2: Driver's Visor

Since the glass vision block was missing, the attack had to be confined to the visor in the closed position.

.303-inch ball splash entered along the join between the upper and lower shutters, causing numerous perforations and splash markings.

.303-inch AP directed between the slides completely jammed the motion. With the vision glass in position, the ball splash entry would probably not occur.

Item 3: Turret Escape Door

.303-inch ball splash caused witness card marking from the normal attack, and at an angle of 30 degrees the card was severely torn and marked. Injury to the crew considered possible from angle attack.

Item 4: Turret Vision Slit

Entry of .303-inch ball shattered the already partially damaged glass block, a splinter from which cause one small perforation.

Item 5: Turret Race Ring

There was no indication that .303-inch ball splash penetrated the turret ring, and since a sheet metal guard is normally fitted inside the turret, little if any splash could do harm. The chance of jamming the ring with .303-inch AP is very slight.

Item 6: Driver's Escape Hatch

From an elevation of 20 degrees above the horizontal, .303-inch ball entered and severely perforated the witness card after splitting the rubber joint ring in several places. Wounding of the driver would be certain.

Item 7: Cupola Hatch

Attack from 13 degrees above the horizontal with a .303-inch ball gave no indication of splash entry. It is considered that the design is practically splashproof.

Item 8: Gun Mantlet

.303-inch ball splash directed at the mantlet ends at normal to turret side, entered the turret, tearing and marking the witness card severely. It is probable that wounding of a member of the turret crew would have occurred.

Item 9: Engine Air Louvres

Note: This attack was carried out after the airburst HE, but for convenience is included in this part of the report.

Attack from 30 degrees above the horizontal with both .303-inch ball and AP showed that serious damage to the radiators could be caused, resulting in considerable loss of cooling water. Rounds ricocheted from the grille bars and sloping fuel tank protection plate into the radiators.

No damage was caused to the airflow fans.

This concluded the small arms attack.

SECTION V

Trial Commentary (Air Burst HE)

25-pdr HE Shell (Charge II) was fired from 150 feet range to detonate on wooden boards above the tank in such position that fragments would enter the air intake and exhaust louvres.

Diagram 1 indicates the position for bursting the shell relative to the target. Although it was intended to run the engine for this attack, and every effort was made to do so, it was not found possible without a considerable delay, and the attack proceeded with the tank head on to the gun.

Round 1

Detonating 13 feet above and 4 feet 6 inches forward of the intake louvres, caused extensive perforations to the water-cooling radiators with consistent water leakage at a very fast rate. Loss of water over five minutes was sufficient to cause engine overheating with probable stoppage in a comparatively short time.

The results from this attack were sufficiently convincing and needed no further confirmation from the site.

Round 2

Detonating 5 feet 6 inches above and 1 foot 6 inches forward of the intake louvres, caused even more extensive perforations of the water-cooling radiators. Water leakage was considerably increased and would probably have resulted in the stoppage of the engine quickly. All the evidence required was now provided, and the attack was discontinued.

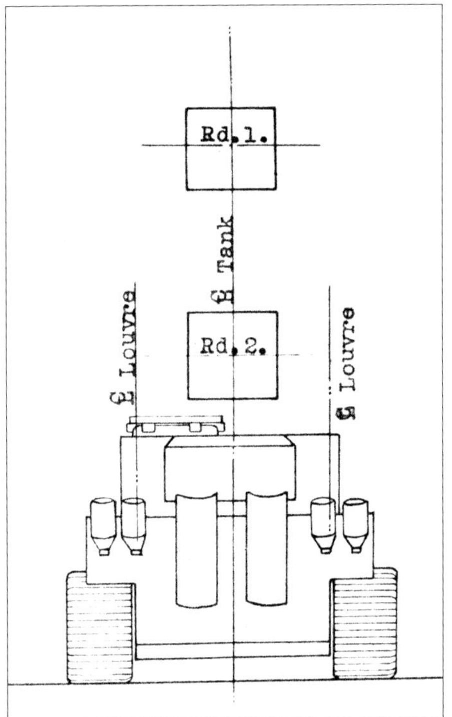

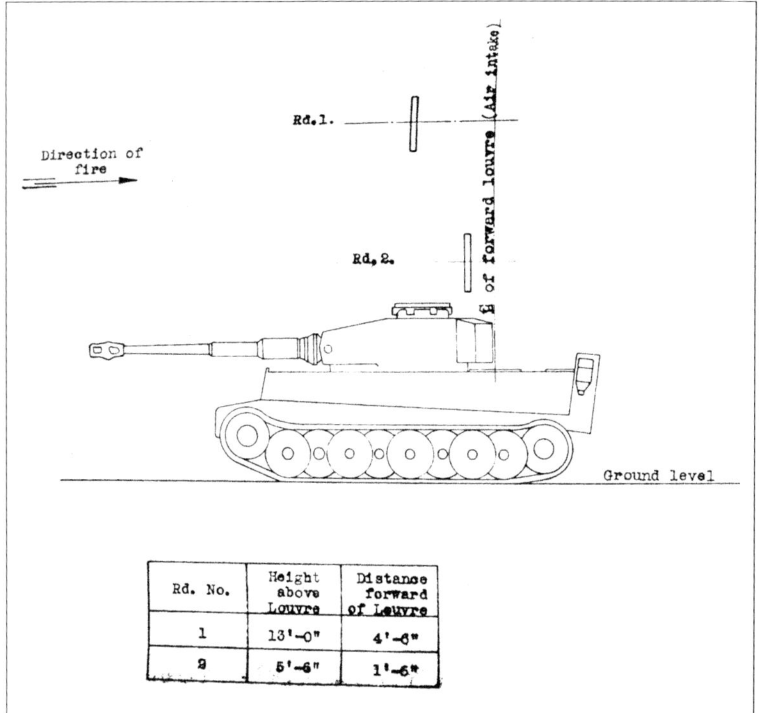

Rd. No.	Height above Louvre	Distance forward of Louvre
1	13'-0"	4'-6"
2	5'-6"	1'-6"

❮ Rear view of Tiger tank. Showing the relative positions occupied by the burster boards during 25-pdr HE air-burst attack. The positions chosen were based on results of previous trials. Round 1: Height above louvre 13 feet; distance forward of louvre 4 feet 6 inches. Round 2: Height above louvre 5 feet 6 inches; distance forward of louvre 1 foot 6 inches. (*DTD Materials Division, Armour Branch*)

❯ Side view of Tiger tank, showing the relative positions occupied by the burster boards during a 25-pdr HE air-burst attack. The positions chosen were based on results of previous trials. Round 1: Height above louvre 13 feet; distance forward of louvre 4 feet 6 inches. Round 2: Height above louvre 5 feet 6 inches; distance forward of louvre 1 foot 6 inches. (*DTD Materials Division, Armour Branch*)

SECTION VI

Trial Commentary (Air Attack AP and Incendiary)

1. 20-mm AP

Attack from 26 degrees above horizontal produced scoops only on the air intake louvre grille, but at 30 degrees above horizontal and slightly to a flank, rounds penetrated one traverse grill bar and broke up on the rear bar, ricocheting into the fans. Round 6 from this attack resulted in the fan hub having metal sheared out 3 × 2 inches, and adjacent vanes partially severed.

The attack was then transferred to the air inlet louvre.

Owing to the numerous perforations in the radiators from air burst, it was decided to place witness cards in front of same to assist in the assessment of further damage.

Two rounds, Nos. 7 and 8, were sufficient to show the vulnerability of the radiators to this form of attack. The witness cards in each case were very severely torn, indicating serious perforations of the radiator water tubes, several of which were located.

Penetration into the fuel tanks would appear possible only through the neck of the outer filler. Round 11 achieved this, passing through the outer neck and striking the inner filler cap, a fragment from which holed the fuel tank 1.25 × 0.5 inches. No fire resulted attempts to strike projections on the engine roof and turned down were not successful; neither was an attempt to jam the turret ring.

2. 20 mm Incendiary

An attack on the fuel tank through the air intake grilles was unsuccessful, due to the falling off in penetration with this type of ammunition. Further perforation of the radiators was caused.

This completed Part 1 of the trial.

SECTION VII

Conclusion

1. Small Arms Attack
Splash (.303-inch Ball)
It is concluded that under normal attack the extent of splash entry is insufficient, with one exception, to cause serious trouble to the crew. This exception was against the end of the gun mantlet at normal, when sufficient splash entered to indicate that a member of the tank crew may have been wounded severely.

Attack from an angle of 30 degrees to a flank show that splash entered freely through the turret escape door, with the probable effect of wounding one or more of the crew.

AP (.303-inch)
It was shown that jamming of the hull machine gun ball mounting, and visor or door, was possible. The jamming of the latter would be much more difficult to release due to the dowel effect.

Jamming of the turret traverse would be unlikely, although core fragments may enter the ring.

2. Air Burst (HE)
The evidence shows that the water-cooling system is very vulnerable to 25-pdr air burst. Extensive damage will result from burst occurring within the range of position used on this trial.

The loss of cooling water would be very considerable, causing overheating and stoppage of the engine in a fairly short time.

3. Air Attack (20-mm AP and Incendiary)
Further damage to the radiators resulted from attack with either AP or incendiary, causing extensive water loss.

Penetration into the fuel tanks is only likely if a strike is made on the small area offered by the filler. Penetration is possible only with AP and not incendiary.

The engine covers are immune to attack and rounds cannot be turned down by striking projections.

It is also doubtful whether the turret can be jammed by this attack.

G. Guthrie, Major, R.E.M.E.
Officer i/c. Armour Trials Section, Armour Branch.
GWG/GB
12.6.14.
M.995(8)
DEF

SECRET

APPENDIX A

Trial No. X.810
Detailed Results
Small Arms

Note: Items numbers and round numbers are consecutive throughout this AT Report.

ITEM No.	DETAIL ATTACKED	ATTACK No. OF ROUNDS	POSITION OF IMPACT	CONDITION OF SPLASH	REMARKS
1	Hull Machine Gun Mounting	10 Rounds .303-inch ball FSC at normal to front of vehicle. Range 10 yards.	10 rounds effective	Slight marking of witness card on left side of mounting for 2.5 inches length.	
	Hull Machine Gun Mounting	10 Rounds .303-inch AP at normal to front of vehicle. Range 10 yards.	2 rounds effective	Witness cards clear.	Ball mounting temporarily jammed, freed by effort.
	Hull Machine Gun Mounting	5 Rounds .303-inch AP FSC at 30 degrees to normal to front of vehicle. Range 10 yards.	4 rounds effective	Witness cards clear.	Ball mounting completely jammed.
2	Driver's visor (closed) (no glass block in position)	15 Rounds .303-inch Ball FSC at normal to front of vehicle. Range 10 yards will stop	15 rounds effective on joints between shutter and sides	Line of splash along full length (10.5 inches) join of upper and lower shutters. Numerous perforations over this length and full width of 1 inch approx. No splash card is fitted.	Motion of shutters unaffected
	Driver's visor (closed) (no glass block in position)	10 Rounds .303-inch ball FSC at normal to front of vehicle	6 rounds effective on joint between sides.		Motion of shutters completely jammed
3	Turret Escape Door	20 Rounds .303-inch ball FSC at normal to face of door. Range 25 yards.	2 rounds effective	Slight splash annulus 14 × 0.5 inches wide adjacent lower left hand sector. To pinhole perforations. Card severely torn around top left hand sector over 11 inches length and marked over 2 feet × 1.5 inches wide.	
	Turret Escape Door	5 Rounds .303-inch ball FSC at 30 degrees to normal to face of door	3 rounds effective		
4	Turret Vision Slit. (Damaged glass block)	5 Rounds .303-inch ball FSC at normal. Range 25 yards	1 round effective.	One small perforation caused by glass splinter.	Glass block shattered.
5	Turret Ring. (Distributed over 2-foot-long arc)	10 Rounds .303-inch ball FSC at normal to arc attacked. Range 25 yards	4 rounds effective	Card clear	Splash did not penetrate ring. Sheet metal guard over turret rack unmarked.
	Turret Ring. (Distributed over 2-foot-long arc)	10 Rounds .303-inch AP FSC at normal to arc attacked.	2 rounds effective	No card fitted	Turret ring still free.
6	Driver's Escape Hatch	10 Rounds .303-inch ball FSC at 20 degrees above horizontal. Range 10 yards.	4 rounds effective	Card severely perforated in many places. Max. area of main perforation 5 × 4 inches. Largest 0.375 × 0.125 inches. Considerable marking over area 5 × 3 inches and 4 × 2 inches.	Rubber joint ring split in several places. Largest split 6 inches long.
7	Cupola Hatch	10 Rounds .303-inch ball FSC at 13 degrees above horizontal. Range 10 yards.	2 rounds effective	Card clear.	Hatch splash proof.
8	Gun Mantlet	10 Rounds .303-inch ball FSC at normal to turret right-hand side. Range 10 yards.	6 rounds effective	Card severely torn perforated over 18 × 7 inches. Severe splash markings. Largest tear 1.5 inches long.	Probable crew wounds.
9	Outlet louvre (right-hand rear)	5 Rounds .303-inch ball at 30 degrees to horizontal. Range 10 yards.	5 rounds effective	Card not fitted	No effect
	Inlet louvre (right-hand forward)	5 Rounds .303-inch ball at 30 degrees to horizontal. Range 10 yards.	5 rounds effective	Splash card (placed in front of radiator) severely torn and perforated over full area.	Indicating that slight perforations were cause to radiator. Damage caused by ricochets from grill and sloping petrol tank cover plates.
	Outlet louvre (right-hand rear)	5 Rounds .303-inch AP at 30 degrees to horizontal. Range 10 yards.	5 rounds effective	Card not fitted	Fans undamaged.
	Inlet louvre (right-hand forward)	5 Rounds .303-inch AP at 30 degrees to horizontal. Range 10 yards.	4 rounds effective	Card severely perforated over full area.	Numerous perforations of radiator resulting from this attack.

Detailed Results: Air Burst HE

TARGET	ATTACK	OBSERVATIONS
Tiger No. 3039 Front-facing and at normal to gun. Burster boards 13 feet above louvres, 4 feet 6 inches, in front of forward intake louvre.	Round 1. 25-pdr HE TNT filled Charge II at normal. Range 100 feet.	10 severe perforations on right-hand radiator. Fragments entered through forward louvre. One survey perforation in left-hand radiator. Fragments entered through forward louvre. Water leaking quickly from 5 perforations in right-hand and one perforation in left-hand radiator. Exhausting fan left-hand side, veins perforated into cases and several on grille. For shell splinters resting on fan housing. Numerous large perforations in rear turret stowage bins. Several strikes on turret roof. Exhaust sheet steel casings perforated in many places. Loss of water over period of 5 minutes considerable.
Front-facing and at normal to gun. Burster boards 5 feet 6 inches above louvres, 1 foot 6 inches, in front of forward intake louvre.	Round 2. 25-pdr HE TNT filled Charge II at normal. Range 100 feet.	Approximately 40 strikes including perforations in right-hand radiator. Fragments entered through forward louvre. 7 strikes on left-hand radiator including perforation. Fragments entered through forward louvre. Several strikes on inlet and outlet grilles both left-hand and right-hand, including strikes on fans. Numerous perforations in rear turret stowage bins. Numerous scoops in turret roof. Further water loss very considerable.

Detailed Results: 20-mm Air Attack

TARGET	ATTACK	OBSERVATIONS
Left-hand rear outlet louvre	Round 3. 20-mm APBE 42 at 26 degrees approximately to horizontal FSC Direction of fire slightly to right flank. Range 10 yards.	Scooped off 2nd traverse grille bar, scoop 1.5 × 0.625 × 0.625 inches and glance upwards of 3rd bar.
Left-hand rear outlet louvre	Round 4. 20-mm APBE 42 at 26 degrees approximately to horizontal FSC Direction of fire slightly to right flank. Range 10 yards.	Scooped off 2nd traverse grille 1.5 × 0.625 × 0.625 inches and glance upwards of 3rd grille and lock. One perforation of fan vane 0.75 inches × 1 foot 4 inches.
Left-hand rear outlet louvre	Round 5. 20-mm APBE corrected to 30 degrees to horizontal FSC range approximately 8 yards.	Penetrated 4th traverse bar and broke up on 5th bar and severely pitted fan hub, and sheared small portion from 1 vane.
Left-hand rear outlet louvre	Round 6. 20-mm APBE corrected to 30 degrees to horizontal FSC Range approximately 8 yards.	Penetrated 3rd vane and passed under 4th vane striking fan hub casing sharing end. Metal 3 × 2 inches, adjacent vanes, partially severed
Left-hand forward inlet louvre	Round 7. 20-mm APBE corrected to 30 degrees to horizontal FSC Direction of fire slightly to the left flank. Range approximately 8 yards.	Shot lodged in 2nd transverse bar. Fragments caused severe tearing and perforation of witness card over an area 20 × 12 inches. Numerous strikes on the radiator.
Adjacent filler cap	Round 8. 20-mm APBE corrected to 30 degrees to horizontal FSC Direction of fire slightly to the left flank. Range approximately 8 yards.	Shot scooped 6 inches off grill. Scoop 0.75 × 0.75 × 0.75 inches. Shot shattered on 7th bar. Witness card severely torn and perforated over area 2 feet 6 inches × 1 foot 6 inches. Largest perforation 2 × 0.625 inches. Many strikes on radiator. Several perforations.
Left-hand forward inlet louvre (direction of fire slightly to the left flank) (adjacent filler cap)	Round 9. 20-mm APBE 42 at 28 degrees to horizontal FSC Range approximately 8 yards.	Shot scooped off 7th and 9th bars and shattered on the filler casting.
Left-hand forward inlet louvre (direction of fire slightly to the left flank) (adjacent filler cap)	Round 10. 20-mm APBE 42 at 30 degrees to horizontal FSC Range approximately 8 yards.	Shot lodged in armour casting surrounding filler tube.
Left-hand forward inlet louvre (direction of fire slightly to the left flank) (adjacent filler cap)	Round 11. 20-mm APBE 42 at 30 degrees to horizontal FSC Range approximately 8 yards.	Code W Shot struck under rim of armour filler cap and turned down inside. Inside. Shot struck in filler cap and shattered. Fragment penetrated tank holding same 1.25 × 0.5 inches.

TARGET	ATTACK	OBSERVATIONS
Left-hand forward inlet louvre (direction of fire slightly to the left flank) (adjacent filler cap)	Round 12. 20-mm APBE42 at 30 degrees to horizontal FSC Range approximately 8 yards.	Scoop 1 × 1 inch on 3rd bar. Shot shattered on 4th bar. No effect on sloping tank cover plate.
Left-hand forward inlet louvre (direction of fire slightly to the left flank) (adjacent filler cap)	Round 13. 20-mm SAP Incendiary Mk IZ at 30 degrees to horizontal. FSC Range approximately 8 yards.	Shot scooped off 3rd traverse bar and broke up on 4th. Further striker on radiator.
Left-hand forward inlet louvre (direction of fire slightly to the left flank) (adjacent filler cap)	Round 14. 20-mm SAP Incendiary Mk IZ at 30 degrees to horizontal. FSC Range approximately 8 yards.	Shot scooped off 9th bar and shattered on 10th. Crack 4 inches long in sloping tank cover plate adjacent to impact.
Engine cover (Hull roof) over engine adjacent to air ducting clamp.	Round 15. 20-mm APBE 42 at 30 degrees to horizontal FSC Range approximately 8 yards.	Scooped off bolts, passing on to roof plate under roof cover. Welding of ducting clamp fractured.
Hull roof above engine adjacent air ducting clamp	Round 16. 20-mm APBE 42 at 30 degrees to horizontal FSC Range approximately 8 yards.	Scoop 1.5 × 0.75 × 0.25 inches deep. Shot past into air duct perforating same 3 × 1 inch.
Junction hull roof and turret edge.	Round 17. 20-mm APBE 42 at 30 degrees to horizontal FSC Range approximately 8 yards.	Struck 1.25 inches above the lower edge of the turret side.
Junction hull roof and turret edge.	Round 18. Junction hull roof and turret edge.	Struck hull roof and scooped under lower edge of turret side plate. Turret not jammed.

APPENDIX B

Small Arms Attack

Before attack: three-quarter front view of the right side of Tiger tank 334. (*DTD Materials Division, Armour Branch*)

Before attack: three-quarter front view of the left side of Tiger tank 334. (*DTD Materials Division, Armour Branch*)

Before attack: three-quarter rear view of the left side of Tiger tank 334. (*DTD Materials Division, Armour Branch*)

Item 1. After attack with a .303-inch ball and AP FSC on machine gun mounting. Note: AP effectively jammed the mounting. (*DTD Materials Division, Armour Branch*)

Item 2. After attack with a .303-inch ball and AP FSC on driver's visor. Note: Dowel effect of AP rounds. (*DTD Materials Division, Armour Branch*)

Item 3. After attack with a .303-inch ball and AP FSC on the turret escape door, at angle. (*DTD Materials Division, Armour Branch*)

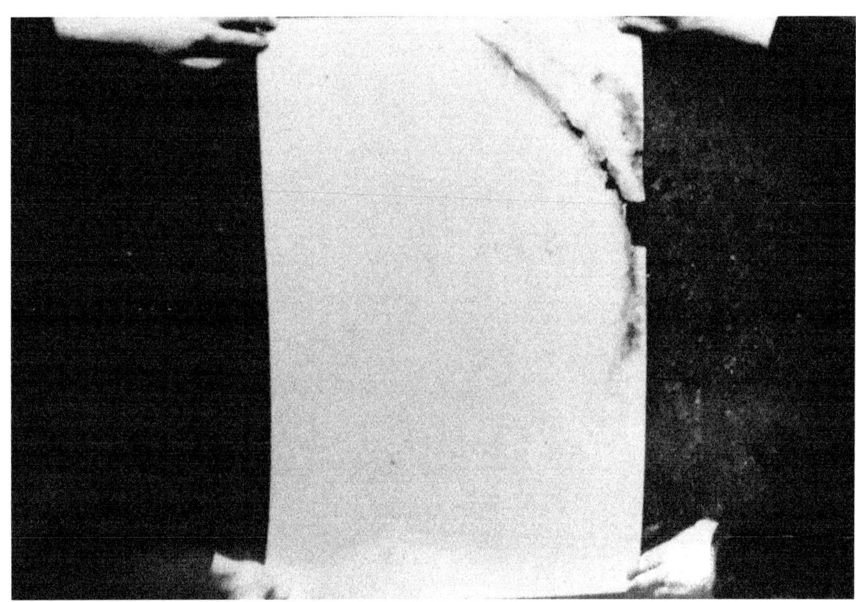

Item 3. Showing effect of witness card from the attack. (*DTD Materials Division, Armour Branch*)

Item 4. After attack with a .303-inch ball FSC on turret vision slit. (*DTD Materials Division, Armour Branch*)

Item 5. After attack with a .303-inch ball FSC and AP on the turret ring. Note: Area attacked indicated by chalk markings. (*DTD Materials Division, Armour Branch*)

Item 6. After attack with a .303-inch ball FSC against the driver's escape hatch, at 20 degrees above horizontal. (*DTD Materials Division, Armour Branch*)

Item 6. Showing effect on witness card from attack. (*DTD Materials Division, Armour Branch*)

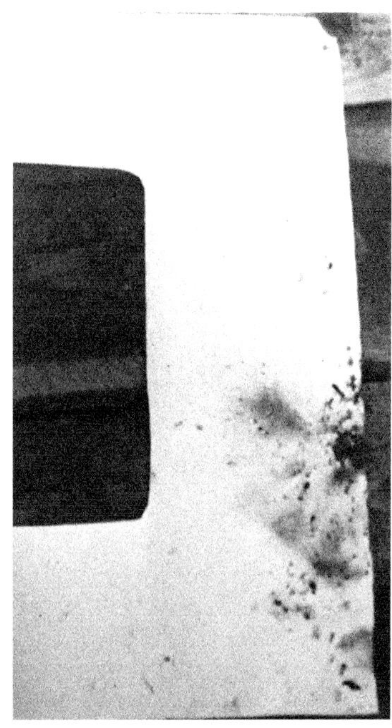

Near right: Item 8. After attack with a .303-inch ball and FSC against the gun mantlet end. (*DTD Materials Division, Armour Branch*)

Far right: Item 8. Showing effect on witness card from attack. (*DTD Materials Division, Armour Branch*)

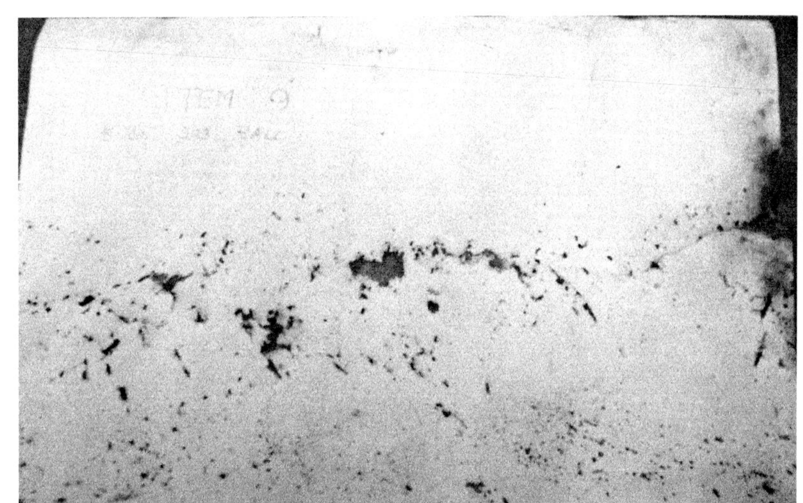

Item 9. Showing effect on witness card from attack on right-side water-cooling radiators with a .303-inch ball and FSC from 30 degrees above horizontal. (*DTD Materials Division, Armour Branch*)

Item 9. Showing effect on witness card from attack on right-side water-cooling radiators with a .303-inch ball and AP FSC from 30 degrees above horizontal. (*DTD Materials Division, Armour Branch*)

Air Burst HE Attack

Showing burster board in position 13 feet above the tank louvres for Round 1: 25-pdr HE. (*DTD Materials Division, Armour Branch*)

After Rounds 1 and 2 (25-pdr HE), showing zone of maximum fragmentation. (*DTD Materials Division, Armour Branch*)

Showing effect of 25-pdr air-burst fragmentation on right-side water-cooling radiator from Rounds 1 and 2. (*DTD Materials Division, Armour Branch*)

Showing effect of 25-pdr air-burst fragmentation on left-side water-cooling radiator from Rounds 1 and 2. (*DTD Materials Division, Armour Branch*)

20-mm Hispano Attack

Showing entry of Round 6 (20-mm AP) through the radiator outlet grille. (*DTD Materials Division, Armour Branch*)

Showing damage caused to exhaust fam casing and vanes by Round 6: 20-mm AP. (*DTD Materials Division, Armour Branch*)

After attack with 20-mm AP. Note: Round 11 penetrated outer fuel fitting cap. See the next photograph below. (*DTD Materials Division, Armour Branch*)

View with grille removed, showing entry of Round 11 (20-mm AP) into fuel tank. No fire resulted. (*DTD Materials Division, Armour Branch*)

Showing effect on witness card from attack on left side water cooling radiator by Round 7: 20-mm AP FSC from 30 degrees above horizontal. (*DTD Materials Division, Armour Branch*)

Showing effect on witness card from attack on left side water cooling radiator by Round 8: 20-mm AP FSC from 30 degrees above horizontal. (*DTD Materials Division, Armour Branch*)

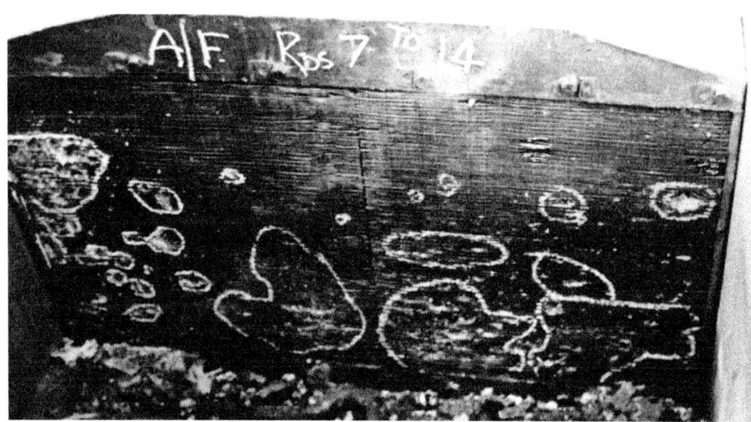

After attack with 20-mm AP, Rounds 7 to 14, against the left-side radiator. Note: the additional damage can be most readily noted by comparing with the bottom photograph on page 158, showing initial damage caused by air-burst. (*DTD Materials Division, Armour Branch*)

14

PART II: FIRING TRIALS AGAINST Pz.Kw. VI (TIGER) 15–22 MARCH 1945

The information in this chapter has been transcribed from original wartime documents. The report format and brief notation style has been kept.

DTD EXPERIMENTAL REPORT AT NO. 252 PART II

Project No. M. 6816A/10
Trial No. X. 811
File No. 250/14/4

Report of Firing Trials Against Pz.Kw. VI (Tiger)
Held at S. of E. Range, Shoeburyness on 15, 16, 19, 20, 21, and 22 March 1945

Present at Trial	Representing	Dates
Capt. Pennycuick	AORG	16th, 20th
Major Harris-Jones	DTD Armour Branch	16th
Major Thompson	DTD Armour Branch	16th
Mr. Turner	DTD. Armour Branch	16th
Miss Lawson	DTD Armour Branch	16th
Mr. Redhead	DTD Welding Branch	16th, 20th
Mr. Swallow	Canadian MHQ	16th
Mr. Ellis	Canadian MHQ	16th
Major Steane	DTD (General Design)	19th
Capt. Turner	Canadian MHQ	19th
Major Shaw	DTD (General Design)	19th
Major Fowler	DTD Welding Branch	19th
Mr Butterfield	DTD Welding Branch	19th
Mr. Arney	AORG	20th
Mr. Weirs	English Electric Company	20th–21st
Mr. Fee	IFV	20th–21st

Lt. Tredinnick	S. of E. Range officer	All Dates
Mr. Phillips	DTD Armour Branch	19th–22nd
Mr. Gray	DTD Armour Branch	All Dates
Mr. Wilde	DTD Armour Branch	All Dates

Report		
	Compiled by:- Mr. G.W. Gray	DTD Armour Branch
	Checked by:- Mr. J.B. Sankey	DTD Armour Branch

References			
	Section I.	-	Object of Trial.
	Section II.	-	Target Details.
	Section III.	-	Method of Attack.
	Section IV.	-	Trial Commentary (6-pdr APCBC and DS)
	Section V.	-	Trial Commentary (17-pdr APCBC and DS)
	Section VI.	-	Trial Commentary (75-mm and 25-pdr HE)
	Section VII.	-	Trial Commentary (3-lb PIAT)
	Section VIII.	-	Trial Commentary (AT Mines)
	Section IX.	-	Conclusion

Appendices			
	Appendix A.	-	Detailed Results.
	Appendix B.	-	Photographic Record.
	Appendix C.	-	Sketches.
	Appendix D.	-	Design Features.
	Appendix E.	-	Penetration Code.

Note:-
This report must not be reproduced in full or in part without the written authority of the Director of Tank Design.

SECTION I

Objects of Trial

1. To determine the general battle worthiness of a Tiger tank against 6-pdr and 17-pdr APCBC and DS, 75-mm and 25-pdr HE.
2. To determine the effect of the PIAT against the vehicle, and in particular against stowed ammunition.
3. To determine the minimum combination of grenades or AT mines required to break the track.

SECTION II

Target Details

Pz.Kw.VI (Tiger) Tank. DTD No. 3039 as used for Trial X. 810, being complete with tracks, suspensions, engine and transmission, but less stowage. Fuel tanks approximately a quarter full of petrol.

Forty 75-mm inert rounds were stowed in panniers, twenty-two on left and eighteen on right side.

Dummies to represent driver and co-driver were in position. Other dummies were not available, but an estimate of the probable effect on the crew is given.

SECTION III

Method of Attack

The target was attacked from a range of hundred and 50 feet with the following projectiles: 6-pdr APDS shot; 6-pdr APCBC shot; 75-mm APCBC shell; 17-pdr APDS shot; 17-pdr APCBC shot; 75-mm HE shell; 25-pdr HE shell; and 3-lb PIAT (Range 40 feet).

The tank was attacked with the front at normal and angle, and the sides at angle, the target being turned to give the required presentation.

Full details of attack and presentation of target are set out in Appendix A.

The attack with AT Mines was carried out on meadowland.

SECTION IV

Trial Commentary 6-pdr APDS and APCBC

1. Nose Plate 24 Degrees (102 mm)

6-pdr APDS

Five rounds were directed at this plate. A strike at a velocity of 3,530 f.s., Round No. 21, gave a complete defeat, and one at 3,298 f.s. a non-defeat. A further defeat resulted from Round No. 22 at 3,390 f.s., But on account of its proximity to Round No. 21 this must be considered an unfair hit. Round No. 21, passing through the nose plate, struck the shield round the final drive and severely wounded the driver. It seems reasonable to expect to arrest the tank head on from a range of about 1,000 yards.

With a length of track fitted (Panther was the only track available) a strike at 3,665 f.s. caused Code C damage, indicating that defeat would occur only at very short range. The attack was therefore discontinued.

2. Turret Side at 40 Degrees (62 mm)

6-pdr APDS

Three rounds produced to non-defeat at striking velocity of 3,160 f.s. and a complete defeat at 3,365 f.s., Round 25.

Round 25 passed through the turret, breaking up on the opposite wall. The wall stowage boxes were severely perforated, and it is probable that the crew in the fighting compartment with all of been seriously injured. The defeat Round 25 represents a range of approximately 1,200 yards.

With a length of track fitted (Panther), it was found that at 40 degrees negligible damage was caused to the turret side at striking velocity is of 3,375 f.s., Round 30, and 3,670 f.s., Round 39, the latter representing a fairly short range. At 30 degrees, Round 32, striking velocity 3,507 f.s., Plate damage equal to Code C was caused.

It is evident even from the rather limited shooting, that considerable added protection is given by track at angle, and that the range for defeat would be short.

A round aimed at the vision slit, striking at 3,159 f.s. 2.5 inches away, splits the world securing the outer cover to the side wall. The inner weld damage was slight and won bolts securing the locking plate was sheared out.

There is little doubt that a direct strike would force the glass block and holder away from the turret wall.

To obtain any data from attack with APCBC, it was considered necessary to attack from a reduced angle.

3. Turret Side at 30 Degrees (62 mm)

6-pdr APCBC

Round 62, given a strike velocity of 2,595 f.s., failed to defeat the plate, and later in the trial the angle was further reduced to 20 degrees when Round 98, giving a similar velocity, did completely defeat the plate. This round entered the turret and destroyed the left-hand side gun buffer. The turret crew would all have been casualties.

A further round to test the roof joint, struck 1.5 inches from the top edge. Although a piece of roof plate 5.5 × 4.5 inches was removed, the main welds, outer and inner, remained intact.

4. Turret Mantlet at 30-Degree Compound Angle (100 mm)

6-pdr APDS

Three rounds, Nos. 27, 28 and 29, gave one defeat Code E, and two non-defeats at striking velocity is of 3,357 f.s., 3,351 f.s., and 3,511 f.s. Respectively. From Rounds 27 and 28 and estimated limit was obtained at 3,354 f.s., Representing a range of approximately 1200 yards.

Round 27, striking in the area of the turret telescope, sheared two bracket holding bolts, but otherwise appeared to do little damage.

5. Turret Mantlet at Normal

6-pdr APCBC

Round 73, striking at 2,398 f.s., 1.5 inches above the lower edge of the mantlet, scooped down through the roof, holding same 7.5 × 4 inches. Considerable damage was caused to the rear end of the gearbox.

Fragments of roof plate were found on the driver's seat. (The dummies, having been badly torn about, had been removed.) The driver would have been killed and other members of the crew may have been casualties.

6. Superstructure at 30 and 20 Degrees (82 mm)

6-pdr APCBC

Round 61 striking at 2,575 f.s. failed to defeat the plate at 30 degrees.

At 20 degrees, Round 96 also at 2,575 f.s. completely defeated the plate. The shot passed across the driver's station, causing damage to the instrument panel. The driver would probably have been killed by fragments.

7. Hull Side Plate at 30 Degrees (62 mm)

6-pdr APCBC

Due to the track and bogies, the space available was limited and advantage was taken to attack the plate in the area offered by a missing No. 8 bogie. Defeat was obtained by the only round possible at 2,534 f.s., The shot entering the fuel tank causing a fire. (The amount of fuel in the tanks had been reduced to approximately 10 gallons.) Owing to the free use of water, it is thought that the plates were unaffected by heat. With the bogie in position, such a result would be hardly possible. Attack through the bogie wheel discs would be unprofitable. Due to the overlapping of the bogies, the spaced wheel discs tend to deflect the shot.

SECTION V

Trial Commentary (17-pdr APDS and APCBC)

8. Turret Side at 50 and 40 Degrees (82 mm)

17-pdr APDS

Defeated the turret side was not achieved at 50 degrees, Round 35 with a striking velocity of 3,511 f.s. causing a severely cracked bulge. With a reduced angle of 40 degrees, Round 36, striking velocity 3,511 f.s., completely defeated the armour. Round 38, 3,172 f.s., Also defeated the turret side, but on checking the point of strike it was found that the angle was 36 degrees.

The internal damage caused by Rounds 36 and 38 was very considerable. Round 36 destroyed, among other items, the small arms stowage bins, which may have resulted in a cordite fire. The indications are that at 40 degrees the turret (without track) would be defeated at 1300 yards range.

17-pdr APCBC

This tack at 50 degrees, Round 54, velocity 3,035 f.s., cause only a cracked bulge. The main roof joint welding was not affected by this attack, but the fuse box flexible fitting welds failed in 3 places. Casualties among the crew were considered unlikely.

At 40 degrees Round 57 was directed at the interlocking joint, striking at 2,984 f.s., Gave complete perforation. The round broke up on the opposite wall. Casualties among the crew were probable.

9. Visor Plate at 41 Degrees CA and 10 Degrees (102 mm)

17-pdr APDS

Attack at 41 degrees (CA) at striking velocity is of 3,427 f.s., Round 48, and 3,602 f.s., Round 49, gave Code C and D damage respectively. Holing of this plate would not be expected above a range of 800 yards.

17-pdr APCBC

Round 55, striking at 2,595 f.s., failed to defeat the plate, but caused some cracking in the main transverse outer weld with the glacis plate. Existing fine cracks were now evident throughout this joint.

Round 56, estimated striking velocity 2,900 f.s., struck on this joint at a point midway between the driver's visor and ball mounting, splits of the world for nearly 5 feet long and opened it a maximum of 0.375 inches. The machine-gun outer housing was forced away from the visor plate 0.25 inches.

The rear lug and wedge giving the interlock feature at the centre junction of the visor and glacis plates was sheared off and found on the turret floor. Casualties to the hull crew would probably have been caused by this round.

With the front of the tank at normal (visor or plate 10 degrees), attack against the roof plate joint at Round 75, striking velocity of 1,905 f.s., sheared out roof metal 9.5 × 6.5 inches and further increased the weld damage caused by Round 74. The shaped hull right side plate joining the visor plate was sheared off level with the pannier, together with the reinforcing angle bar. The hull crew would probably have become casualties.

Round 75 produced a defeat Code R at 1,923 f.s., suggesting that this plate is vulnerable head-on at all fighting ranges.

10. Superstructure Side at 50 Degrees (82 mm)

17-pdr APDS

The results obtained against this plate were very conflicting when compared to a similar thickness plate, i.e. the turret side. Whereas against the turret side plate defeat was not caused at a striking velocity of 3,511 f.s. (Round 35), in this case complete defeat was obtained when striking at 3,131 f.s., Round 50. The plate hardnesses were identical.

Rounds 46, 47 and 50, defeating the plate and entering the pannier stowage, would also certainly have caused cord it fires.

17-pdr APCBC

Rounds 51 and 52, striking at 2,700 f.s. and 2,858 f.s., Produced a non-defeat and defeat Code R, respectively, and the indications are that only at relatively short range would this plate be defeated.

Round 52, striking 8.5 inches below the top edge, sheared out roof plate over an area 36 × 12 inches. This was by far the hardest plate in the tank. Casualties were considered certain, and damaged to rounds would probably have produced a cordite fire.

11. Nose Plate at 48-Degree CA, 24- and 37-Degree CA (102 mm)

17-pdr APDS

Two rounds at 48 degrees, striking at 3,215 f.s. and 3,437 f.s. respectively, failed to defeat the plate, producing Code C damage.

17-pdr APCBC

Attack against the nose plate joint with the glacis at 24 degrees cause further splitting of the main outer transverse weld, but this damage did not materially affect the strength of the structure. Velocities given by Rounds 77 and 79 showed that for head on attack defeat of the nose plate at this angle would be achieved at long range.

Round 94, estimated striking velocity 2,900 f.s. at 37-degree CA, Striking near the hull side, forced the side plate away from the nose plate 0.875 inches. The main welding was severely split by this attack and the mortice joint partly forced out.

12. Turret Mantlet at 40 Degrees (100 mm)

17-pdr APDS

Strikes on this somewhat restricted target produce one fair hit which completely defeated the mantlet at 3,482 f.s., Round 43, passing through a thickened section of the casting, broke up on the right side gun buffer casing.

Further shooting was not possible owing to lack of space. It seems, however that defeat would be likely up to a range of 1,500 yards.

13. Final Drive

17-pdr APCBC (at normal)

Round 83, striking at 2,260 f.s., entered the final drive casing through the right-side track, and would have immobilised the vehicle.

Round 84, also entered the casing at a striking velocity estimated at 2,900 f.s., causing further considerable damage. This round would also have stopped the tank. It is apparent that the vehicle can be arrested by strikes in the final drive at all fighting ranges from normal attack.

17-pdr APCBC (at 30 Degrees)
Round 93, estimated striking velocity 2,900 f.s., passed through the left side track and into the final drive casing. The casing was split open revealing the destroyed epicyclic gearing. Both drive and track were forced away from the hull side 5 inches, resulting in the complete disablement of the vehicle.

The range at which the vehicle could be stopped at this angle could not be ascertained.

SECTION VI

Trial Commentary (75-mm and 25-pdr HE)

75-mm APCBC (M61) at 20 Degrees
Superstructure and Turret Side (82 mm)
Attack against the superstructure and turret sides at full service charge failed to defeat them.

Hull Side (63 mm)
The hull side was defeated by Round 59, also full service charge. This round produced a large flake in 3 pieces from the rear of the armour. The force with which this flake was projected, together with shot fragments, would no doubt have killed the driver and probably wounded the co-driver.

75-mm HE
Turret Mantlet
Round 86, striking the mantlet 17 inches above the hull roof remote from previous damage, extended splits in the hull roof caused by Round 75, and also caused a fresh split branching from it.

It is, however, doubtful whether with any serious damage would have resulted.

Driver's Visor
Round 87 detonated on the visor 8 inches above the glacis. Apart from slight opening of the main outer glacis plate weld the plate was unaffected. The effect on the visor unit was also slight.

Hull Side
Round 90, striking 1 inch below the pannier floor and on the hull side, sheared the floor plate out over a large area. The adjacent track was also completely sheared through, and the local welds were badly split and severe damage was caused to small arms stowage which might have caused a cordite fire.

Hull Rear
Round 91, striking 16 inches above the engine roof, was ineffective against the roof plate, but produced further damage, through fragments, to the radiators.

25-pdr HE
Hull Machine Gun
Round 88, striking on the ball mounting 8 inches above the glacis, further opened the main weld split in the glacis, but otherwise the plate remained intact. The gun clamping bracket was fractured. This attack also loosened the visor housing bolts.

Hull Rear
Round 91, striking the turret rear 14 inches above, failed to defeat the hull roof, but caused numerous further strikes on the radiators.

SECTION VII

Trial Commentary (3-lb PIAT)

Superstructure at 30 Degrees (82 mm)
Perforation of this plate was achieved by Rounds 67 and 68. Both rounds entered the stowage racks and Round 68 severely perforated 3 stowed rounds. A cordite fire would have resulted.

Hull Side at 30 Degrees (63 mm + Bogie discs)
The jet from Round 69 expended its energy in perforating to bogie discs and failed to affect the hull side.

Turret Side at 30 Degrees (82 mm)
Round 70 defeated the plate. The jet passed across the gun loader's station and struck the gun breech and turret wall. Wounding of the crew seriously would probably have resulted.

Visor Plate at 10 Degrees (102 mm)
Round 71 defeated the plate, passing through the gunner's compartment and striking the bulkhead, splattering the area locally. The gunner would probably have been killed.

Nose Plate at 24 Degrees (102 mm)
Round 72 holed the plate, but the back damage was obscured by the final drive. The effect on the crew would have been nil.

SECTION VIII

Trial Commentary (AT Mines)

Track (Left-Hand Side) No. 3 Bogie
One Mark V Standard AT Mine detonated beneath the outer edge of the track, failed to break it. The damage to the track was comparatively slight, a piece being sheared out 2.5 × 2 inches. The bogie discs sustained only slight damage. The total damage was so slight that the tank would continue to run.

Track (Right-Hand Side) No. 5 Bogie
Based on the failure of one AT mine to break the track, Mk 75 grenades (smaller anti-tank mines) were ruled out, and two Mk Vs were used in a similar position, with one mine placed above the other, and wired in parallel.

This attack also failed to break the track, and only slightly greater damage was caused. The tank was not immobilised.

Track (Left-Hand Side) No. 7 Bogie
Still unsuccessful in breaking the track with two mines placed most favourably to the track, i.e. under an outer edge, it was decided to place two mines beneath the track centre, one above the other. This completely severed the track. Temporary stoppage would have been caused, but it is considered that field repair would have been possible.

This concluded the trial.

SECTION IX

Conclusions

1. Vulnerability
This trial (Part II) has shown that the tank can be completely defeated, by all types of AP shot used, although in some instances the range for plate penetration would be comparatively short.

From head on attack arrest of the vehicle is possible by strikes on the lower edge of the gun mantlet from 6-pdr at relatively low velocities which scoop down through the roof. Unlike the Panther which due to its curved mantlet affords a large surface for deflection, the mantlet is flat and therefore the target area is much smaller.

Attack from a flank on the superstructure side by either type of AP or PIAT is likely to be very effective when penetration is made, due to the open ammunition stowage adopted, with liability to cordite fire. The rounds are stowed immediately behind the armour in the area approximately within the centre third of the vehicle length.

The effect of HE up to 25-pdr is comparatively ineffective against the hull roof and glacis plates from detonations approximately 16 × 8 inches respectively above them. Attack from 75-mm detonated on the hull side close to the pannier floor was very effective. It should be noted, however, that the track and bogies give very good cover to this plate and the target is, therefore, very limited. The air louvres are very vulnerable to entry of fragments from detonations on the turret rear, and perforations of radiators with resultant water loss is certain. Reference to sketch sheet 3, Appendix C, illustrates this point.

Unlike previous experience with Panther tanks, the armour plates, with one exception (hull roof plate) did not show any marked tendency to brittleness, and their behaviour generally was not unlike British machinable plates.

2. Armour Quality

The following table gives a list of the Poldi hardnesses, corrected to Brinell figures, taken at the surface of the armour.

The last column indicates the hardness expected, as a result of the examination of recently captured German armour since the invasion, including Panther, Jagdpanther and Tiger.

Armour	Nominal Thickness	Corrected Poldi	Hardness expected
Turret roof	25 mm	290	300–350
Hull roof—front	25 mm	335	300–350
Glacis	60 mm	265	270–310
Vertical sides	60 mm	265	270–310
Turret wall	80 mm	255	260–300
Superstructure near side	80 mm	260	260–300
Superstructure off side	80 mm	255	260–300
Hull rear	80 mm	255	260–300
Visor	100 mm	265	240–290
Nose	100 mm	265	240–290
Mantlet	100–200 mm	280	250–300

The hull number 250570 shows that this tank is one of the most recent Tigers.

Making full allowances for possible errors of the Poldi portable hardness tester, the table reveals a tendency to softer armour in the 60- and 80-mm plates, and they lie within the British range to specification I.T.80E. This German trend to soften their armour was noted on the Royal Tiger, and is probably to avoid the cracking and flaking tendency hitherto met within much of the German armour examined.

In this respect, a certain success has been attained in this tank, as no major cracking or flaking was noticeable on the plates liable to direct attack. The hull roof plate was the only bad case of plate failure, and the hardness of this was of the order 335 Brinell.

3. Liability to Fire

Fuel

The disposition of the fuel tanks immediately behind the superstructure renders them very liable to perforation by defeat of the armour, with consequent risk of fire. This is probably more easily achieved through the superstructure (82 mm) than the hull side (63 mm), as the lower tanks are very well screened by the track and bogies.

Cordite

The only protection afforded to stowed rounds from direct attack is the main side armour. Forty inert HE rounds were stowed in the panniers, distributed either side of the vehicle. Judged from damage to these rounds, there is ample evidence that attack all types of AP may cause cordite fire is from penetration of the pannier sides. Similar results may also be expected from the PIAT when the jet defeats the armour in this region.

Structure

As the trial progressed, it became apparent that the failure, where it occurred in the main welds, constituted an extension and opening of already existing fine cracks. These fine cracks were not generally discernible before the trial, being to some extent screened by the use of anti-magnetic covering.

It is generally considered that the welding behaved well, although in certain instances severe splitting occurred. This however, was usually the result of repeated attack.

Despite the intensity of the attack, the rigidity of the structure remained substantially unimpaired.

Effect of AT Mines

This trial has shown that the Tiger track is considerably stronger than that fitted to the Panther tank. This can be readily appreciated by reference to a scale sketch No. 4, Appendix C, which shows the heavier track section, supported against failure by more and closer pitched bogies.

Two Standard Mk V AT mines failed to break the track when detonated under the outer edge, and it was only when a similar attack was carried out under the track centre that complete breakage occurred.

Anti-Magnetic Compound

The compound used on this tank has been applied to all easily accessible surfaces subject to direct attack, the average thickness being 0.1875 inches. Its behaviour is very little different to our own compounds and can easily be removed by small arms or heavy attack. HE will wipe clean large surfaces.

G. Guthrie, Major, R.E.M.E.
Officer i/c Armour Trials Section.
Armour Branch.
GWG/GB. 13.6.45 M.996(a) MD

APPENDIX A

SECRET

Trial No. X.811

Detailed Results: Heavy Attack

TARGET	ATTACK	OBSERVATIONS
(102 mm) Nose plate (without tracks) (Front of vehicle at normal)	Round 19. 6-pdr APDS Mackie J.M.13 at 24 degrees to normal. Estimate shell velocity 3,300 f.s. Range 150 feet.	Code NFH. Scooped off guard in front of driver's visor and struck lower shutter. Scoop 3 × 1.5 inches. Rear. Shutter operating wheel shattered. Wheel rim laying under driver's seat. Back damage cannot be seen.
(102 mm) Nose plate (without tracks) (Front of vehicle at normal)	Round 20. 6-pdr APDS Mackie J.M.13 at 24 degrees to normal. Shell velocity 3,298 f.s. Range 150 feet.	Code C. Struck 10 inches above lower edge of nose plate. Shot broke up. Rear. Smooth bulge in plate.
(102 mm) Nose plate (without tracks) (Front of vehicle at normal)	Round 21. 6-pdr APDS Mackie J.M.13 at 24 degrees to normal. Shell velocity 3,530 f.s. Range 150 feet.	Code W. Struck 16 inches above the lower edge of nose plate. Rear. Shield round final drive perforated and torn. Driver struck in thigh and severely wounded.
(102 mm) Nose plate (without tracks) (Front of vehicle at normal)	Round 22. 6-pdr APDS Mackie J.M.13 at 24 degrees to normal. Shell velocity 3,390 f.s. Range 150 feet.	Code NFH. Double hit with Round 21. Rear. Damage invisible. Further damage to final drive shield. Driver wounded in left arm.
(102 mm) Nose plate (without tracks) (Front of vehicle at normal)	Round 23. 6-pdr APDS Mackie J.M.13 at 24 degrees to normal. Shell velocity 3,395 f.s. Range 150 feet.	Code NFH. Too close to Round 21. Nose plate holed. Rear. Damage not visible. Driver very severely wounded on body and face. 2 fragments of armour resting on dummy's legs. Largest 3 × 2 inches.
Turret left hand side (without tracks) (Front of vehicle at normal)	Round 24. 6-pdr APDS at 40 degrees to normal. Shell velocity 3,164 f.s. Range 150 feet.	Code C. Struck 7 inches above bottom edge of turret. Rear. Smooth bulge 3.5 × 2.5 × 0.5 inches high.

TARGET	ATTACK	OBSERVATIONS
Turret left hand side (without tracks) (Front of vehicle at normal)	Round 25. 6-pdr APDS at 40 degrees to normal. Shell velocity 3,365 f.s. Range 150 feet.	Code W. Struck 6.5 inches below top edge. Rear. Shot passed into turret, breaking up and causing numerous strikes on opposite turret side, and perforating stowage boxes. Turret roof fitting adjacent gun breech sheared through by fragment. Turret crew probably seriously injured.
Turret left hand side (without tracks) Vision slit (glass block missing) (Front of vehicle at normal)	Round 26. 6-pdr APDS at 40 degrees to normal. Shell velocity 3,159 f.s. Range 150 feet.	Code C. Struck on plate 2.5 inches from edge of vision cover plate welding. Weld split around cover for 18 inches approximately. Shot broke up in hole. Rear. Smooth bulge. Inner weld around the block holder and side wall cracked for 2 inches length. One bolt securing the locking plate sheared out.
Turret Mantlet. Angle 13 degrees of elevation. Turret front at 27 degrees to normal.	Round 27. 6-pdr APDS at 30 degrees (compound) to normal. Shell velocity 3,357 f.s. Range 150 feet.	Code E. (Nose lodged) Struck 6.5 inches above bottom edge and 13 inches from outer edge of mantlet. Rear. Damage invisible. Impact behind telescope bracket. Two bracket securing bolts sheared out. One lying on turret shelf. Telescope may have been damaged.
Turret Mantlet. Angle 13 degrees of elevation. Turret front at 27 degrees to normal.	Round 28. 6-pdr APDS at 30 degrees (compound) to normal. Shell velocity 3,351 f.s. Range 150 feet.	Code D (Sv.) Struck 7 inches from bottom edge. 8.5 inches from outer edge. Shot now lodged. Rear. Cracked bulge. Horizontal crack max. 0.1875 inches open. Another telescope bracket securing bolts sheared out. Bracket now visible. Bolts found on the turret floor.
Turret Mantlet. Angle 13 degrees of elevation. Turret front at 27 degrees to normal.	Round 29. 6-pdr APDS at 30 degrees (compound) to normal. Shell velocity 3,351 f.s. Range 150 feet.	Code D. (Nose lodged). Struck 5.5 inches from outer edge. Casting split from point of impact to top of mantlet 9 inches open, 0.125 inches max. Rear. 3 star cracked bulge. Max. Open 0.1875 inches.
Turret left-hand side with (Panther) track.	Round 30. 6-pdr APDS at 40 degrees to normal. Shell velocity 3,373 f.s. Range 150 feet.	Code B on plate. Track holed and removed bodily. Shot scooped off side wall of turret and passed out through track link. Track entry hole approximately 2-inch diameter. Exit approximately 2.5 inches. Scooped on wall 3.5 × 2 × 0.375 inches deep.
Turret left-hand side with (Panther) track.	Round 31. 6-pdr APDS at 35 degrees to normal. Shell velocity 3,491 f.s. Range 150 feet	Code C (Sv.) Struck extreme end of track, removing metal measuring 3 × 3 inches. Shot entered turret side wall. Nose lodged. Rear. Smooth bulge 3 × 2.5 × 0.375 inches. Turret junction and fuse box adjacent impact and mounted on the flexible strips still intact.
Turret left-hand side with (Panther) track.	Round 32. 6-pdr APDS at 30 degrees to normal. Shell velocity 3507 f.s. Range 150 feet.	Code C. Struck and penetrated track. Metal removed 2.25 × 1.75 inches and entering turret side wall. Shot nose lodged. Point of entry 12.75 inches down from top edge. Rear. Smooth bulge in plate.
Turret right-hand side without track.	Round 33. 17-pdr APDS Mk 1. BTRL at 50 degrees to normal. Shell velocity 3,507 f.s. Range 150 feet.	Code C. Struck 3" above bottom edge of turret. Scoop 7 × 3 × 1.25 inches. Split in outer weld—side to floor plate—6 inches long. Rear. Split in throat of weld securing shelf to side wall behind impact 3 inches long × 0.016 inches max. Roof to floor mounted stowage bin adjacent impact intact.
Turret right-hand side without track.	Round 34. 17-pdr APDS Mk 1. BTRL at 50 degrees to normal. Shell velocity 3,365 f.s. Range 150 feet.	Code C. Struck 12.5 inches above bottom edge. Scoop 10 × 2.25 × 1.75 inches. Rear. Smooth bulge 6 × 2 × 0.375 inches high. Flexible roof to floor strips. In behind bulge, but securing welds intact.
Turret right-hand side without track.	Round 35. 17-pdr APDS Mk 1. BTRL at 50 degrees to normal. Shell velocity 3,511 f.s. Range 150 feet.	Code D. (Sv.) Struck 3 inches below top edge. Scoop 11.5 × 2.25 × 2.5 inches deep. Side plate set up 0.25 inches on edge above impact. Three transverse cracks inside armour plate running into roof weld. Rear. Cracked bulge 7 × 3 × 0.5 inches high. Horizontal crack 2.75 inches long. Vertical crack 1.25 inches. Adjacent roof weld intact. Adjacent roof fitting removed. Fuse box broken away from roof adjacent roof periscope. Roof weld to adjacent flexible mounting strip broken through.
Turret right-hand side without track.	Round 36. 17-pdr APDS Mk 1. BTRL at 40 degrees to normal. Shell velocity 3,511 f.s. Range 150 feet.	Code W. Struck 13.5 inches down from top edge. Hole 2-inch diameter approximately. Crack in outer weld—junction—vision cover to outer armour for about full perimeter. Rear. Welded pad behind impact sheared through and top portion projected into turret. Small arms stowage bins on rear of turret severely torn and perforated. In our face of rear side wall pitted over area 3 feet × 2 inches. Small arms damage would probably have caused a fire. Probably all turret crew would have been casualties. Several turret ring securing bolts at rear now loosened turret gun locking jack knocked out of position by fragment and gun fallen to full depressed position due to absence of cylinders.

TARGET	ATTACK	OBSERVATIONS
Turret right-hand side without track.	Round 37. 17-pdr APDS Mk 1. BTRL at 40 degrees to normal. Shell velocity 3,240 f.s. Range 150 feet.	Code NFH. Struck between Round 36 and vision slit. Weld damage to vision cover plate extended for full circumference. Rear. Vision block housing—left hand half removed and welded pad behind impact partially forced away. Shot past across to rear of turret and fragments marked rear wall of turret over wide area, causing further perforation of stowage boxes.
Turret right-hand side without track.	Round 38. 17-pdr APDS Mk 1. BTRL at 40 degrees to normal. Shell velocity 3,172 f.s. Range 150 feet. Check angle 36 degrees	Code W. Struck 15 inches above bottom edge of turret. Actual angle of strike 36 degrees to normal. Rear. Normal damage. Commander's seat and pedestal on opposite side of turret severely torn and damaged by fragments.
Turret left-hand side without track.	Round 39. 6-pdr APDS at 40 degrees to normal. Shell velocity 3,670 f.s. Range 150 feet.	Code B. Track holed 3 × 2.5 inches. Shot scooped off side wall of turret.
Hull nose plate with track. Front of vehicle at normal.	Round 40. 6-pdr APDS at 24 degrees to normal. Shell velocity 3,655 f.s. Range 150 feet.	Code C. Struck 9 inches down from top edge of nose plate. Track holed 3 × 3 inches. Rear. Smooth bulge in plate.
Turret gun mantlet, right-hand side. Mantlet face vertical angle 13 degrees. Horizontal angle 38 degrees.	Round 41. 17-pdr APDS at 40 degrees (CA) to normal. Shell velocity 3,535 f.s. Range 150 feet.	Code NFH. Scoop off top edge of mantlet and struck machine gun mounting ring on cupola hatch sharing through same and removing one periscope protection cover.
Turret gun mantlet, right-hand side. Mantlet face vertical angle 13 degrees. Horizontal angle 38 degrees.	Round 42. 17-pdr APDS at 40 degrees (CA) to normal. Shell velocity 3,470 f.s. Range 150 feet	Struck 3.5 inches below top edge passing through junction between thick and thin sections and shattered on front turret plate. Top edge of plate set at 0.625 inches. Metal out of the top edge of mantlet 5 × 3 × 1.5 inches.
Turret gun mantlet, right-hand side. Mantlet face vertical angle 13 degrees. Horizontal angle 38 degrees.	Round 43. 17-pdr APDS at 40 degrees (CA) to normal. Shell velocity 3,482 f.s. Range 150 feet	Code W. Struck 7.5 inches up from lower edge of mantlet and entered through corner of thin and thick sections. Rear. Back damage normal. Shot past into turret and struck right-hand gun buffer cylinder. Fragments of shot found on turret shell. Machine gun connecting link dislodged. Section of machine-gun shield torn out.
Nose plate without track. Front of Tank at 40 degrees to normal. Nose plate vertical angle 24 degrees.	Round 44. 17-pdr APDS at 48 degrees (CA) to normal. Shell velocity 3,213 f.s. Range 150 feet.	Code C. 11 inches from bottom edge. 12 inches from right-hand edge. Scoop 7 × 3.5 × 1.5 inches deep. Rear. Smooth bulge in plate.
Nose plate without track. Front of Tank at 40 degrees to normal. Nose plate vertical angle 24 degrees	Round 45. 17-pdr APDS at 48 degrees (CA) to normal. Shell velocity 3,437 f.s. Range 150 feet.	Code C. 8 inches above bottom edge and central on nose plate. Scoop 9 × 3.25 × 1.5 inches. Rear. Smooth bulge in plate.
Left-hand superstructure side plate. (82 mm)	Round 46. 17-pdr APDS at 50 degrees to normal. Shell velocity 3,245 f.s. Range 150 feet.	Code W. Struck 8 inches down from top edge. Rear. Passed through forward pannier 88-mm stowage racks. 3 stowed rounds destroyed. Large fragments passed across turret breaking up on engine compartment bulkhead. Ammunition stowage racks and covers severely torn. Several clip fittings distorted and discharge pipe on engine bulkhead perforated in several places. Also perforations in rear right-hand ammunition stowage covers. Cordite fire may have resulted. Turret crew all casualties.
Left-hand superstructure side plate. (82 mm)	Round 47. 17-pdr APDS at 50 degrees to normal. Shell velocity 3,311 f.s. Range 150 feet.	Code W. Struck 5.5 inches from top edge. Metal sheared out around shot over area 4 × 3 × 0.5 inches. Rear. Shot past through forward stowage rack. One stowed round displaced. Case severely dented. Further damage to racks. Large fragments passed across turret, striking rear right-hand stowage rack tearing away front covers and causing perforations in two stowed rounds. Cordite fire would have resulted. Turret crew all casualties. Further extensive strikes on engine bulkhead and bin fronts.
Visor plate. Front of vehicle at 40 degrees to normal. Vertical angle 10 degrees.	Round 48. 17-pdr APDS at 41 degrees (CA) to normal. Shell velocity 3,427 f.s. Range 150 feet.	Code C. Struck 4 from edge of visor housing. Scoop 8 × 4 × 2 inches deep. Rear. Weld securing visor and hull side split for 12"approximately.
Visor plate. Front of vehicle at 40 degrees to normal. Vertical angle 10 degrees.	Round 49. 17-pdr APDS at 41 degrees (CA) to normal. Shell velocity 3,602 f.s. Range 150 feet.	Code D. Struck 5.5 inches below top edge 12 inches from outer edge. Weld split in junction between roof plate and visor for 17 inches, open 0.0625 inches maximum. Rear. Bulge 5.5 × 4 × 0.5 inches. One horizontal crack. Weld securing visor and hull side—crack extended overall length 16 inches. Inner roof weld immediately above impact shows slight crack in throat 6 inches long approximately.

TARGET	ATTACK	OBSERVATIONS
Left-hand superstructure side plate.	Round 50. 17-pdr APDS at 50 degrees to normal. Shell velocity 3,131 f.s. Range 150 feet.	Code W. Struck 6 inches down from top edge. Rear. Flake off 4.5 × 3 inches in several pieces. Fragments passed through rear left-hand stowage rack damaging noses of two stowed shells. Probable explosion or fire. Stowage racks and bin doors torn and destroyed. Fragments splashed on engine compartment bulkhead causing severe pitting. Turret crew probably all casualties.
Left-hand superstructure side plate.	Round 51. 17-pdr APCBC Mk VIII TNCN at 50 degrees to normal. Estimated Shell velocity 2,700 f.s. Range 150 feet.	Code D. Struck 7 inches from Round 50, 7 inches from top edge. Rear. Weld securing superstructure and roof plate split mainly in junction with roof for 27 inches. Stiffening angle welds with superstructure and transverse bulkhead split for 8 inches. Stiffener forced away 0.5 inches maximum. Further local damage to stowage racks.
Left-hand superstructure side plate.	Round 52. 17-pdr APCBC Mk VIII TNCN at 50 degrees to normal. Estimated Shell velocity 2,858 f.s. Range 150 feet.	Code R. Struck 8.5 inches below top edge of superstructure side plate. Holo 3.5 × 2.5 inches. Shot broke up. Roof plate immediately above impact sheared out over area 36 × 12 inches in one piece. Piece thrown clear of vehicle 15 feet. Weld securing roof to hull superstructure split—forward for 14 inches to visor and rearward 4 feet approximately. Failure in junction with superstructure side. Split in roof plate rearward 27 inches long. Vertical stiffening angle connecting superstructure with transverse bulkhead forced away due to weld failure. Forward stowage rack severely buckled and displaced. Both rounds stowed adjacent to driver lying on driver's lap. Cases separated. Fragments struck driver in and shoulder. Probably killed. Other case found in co-driver's position. Cordite fire would have resulted. Co-driver severely wounded in arm and left leg.
Turret left-hand side	Round 53. 17-pdr APCBC at 50 degrees to normal. Estimated Shell velocity 2,800 f.s. Range 150 feet.	Code C. Struck 9.5 inches above bottom edge of turret. Scoop 9 × 4.5 × 1.75 inches. 2 track lugs shot away. Rear. Smooth bulge 4.5 × 3.5 × 0.375 inches high. Adjacent fuse box supported on flexible mountings unaffected.
Turret left-hand side	Round 54. 17-pdr APCBC at 50 degrees to normal. Estimated Shell velocity 3,035 f.s. Range 150 feet.	Code D. (S1.) Struck 5 inches below top edge. Scoop 7 × 4 × 2 inches deep. To track lugs adjacent—removed. Main outer roof—turret side—weld intact. Two transverse fine cracks in side plate at top edge. Rear. Bulge 7 × 5 × 1 inch high. In a main roof weld intact. Fuse box flexible fittings sheared away in 3 places. Fitting hanging by electrical leads.
Visor plate. Front of vehicle at 40 degrees to normal. Vertical angle 10 degrees.	Round 55. 17-pdr APCBC at 40 degrees (CA) to normal. Shell velocity 2,595 f.s. Range 150 feet.	Code D. Struck 4 inches from centre of bottom weld. Scoop 5 × 4 × 1.125 inches. Outer visor to glacis weld—fine cracks for total length of 18.5 inches in weld metal. Rear. Bulge 7 inches diameter × 1 inch high. Horizontal crack 1 inch long, 0.0625 inches open.
Joint between glacis and visor.	Round 56. 17-pdr APCBC at 40 degrees (CA) to normal. Estimated shell velocity 2,900 f.s. Range 150 feet.	Code D. Struck on visor plate and joint central between driver's visor and ball mounting. Saucer scoop 6 × 4.5 × 3 inches deep. Shot broke up. Machine-gun Housing displaced forward 0.25 inches. Main horizontal weld cracked intermittently in weld and junction for 4 feet 8 inches and open 0.375 inches maximum adjacent impact. Rear. Log in visor and gib securing same to glacis sheared out, found lying on turret floor. Hull fan cowl removed owing to failure of remaining weld, 8 inches long approximately. Machine-gun housing securing bolts slack in threads. Other internal damage not visible.
Turret front and left-hand side plate—interlocking joint.	Round 57. 17-pdr APCBC at 40 degrees to normal. Shell velocity 2,983 f.s. Range 150 feet.	Code NFH. Struck 5 inches forward of Round 25 on lower edge of upper interlocking joint between side armour and turret front. Side plate holed 4.5 × 3.5 inches. Wedge peace behind interlocking tongue forced out of position and fitted welds around all sides of tongue split. Shot passing across turret, struck rear escape door and displacing same for 10 yards, across butt. Bolts securing hinge already sheared. Weld broken by Round 52, now lifted 0.25 inches. Fracture rusty. Rear. Metal off above hole 4.5 × 2 × 1 inch thick. Vertical corner weld broken and hinged back 4 for 2 inches. Main welds appear intact. Opposite wall splashed with fragments. Carbine clip removed.

TARGET	ATTACK	OBSERVATIONS
Left-hand superstructure side plate.	Round 58. 75-mm APCBC M61 shell at 20 degrees to normal FSC. Estimated shell velocity 2,000 f.s. Range 150 feet.	Code D. Struck 8 inches below top edge of superstructure. Scoop 5 × 3.25 × 3 inches deep. Rear. Bulge 5.5 inches diameter, crack 6 inches long. Ammunition rack bars forced forward and badly distorted.
Left-hand hull side plate.	Round 59. 75-mm APCBC M61 shell at 20 degrees to normal FSC. Estimated shell velocity 2,000 f.s. Range 150 feet.	Code W. Struck opposite driver. Plate holed 4 × 3.5 inches. Rear. Flake off 11 × 8 inches in 3 pieces. Fragments entered driving compartment, striking left-hand shock absorber destroying same and killing driver. Surrounding area severely affected.
Left-hand turret side plate.	Round 60. 75-mm APCBC M61 shell at 20 degrees to normal FSC. Estimated shell velocity 2,000 f.s. Range 150 feet.	Code D. Centre of impact 5 inches below vision slot. Rear. Bulge 8 × 5.5 × 1 inch high. Horizontal split 5 inches long, open 0.125 inches maximum. Vision block housing removed.
Right-hand superstructure side plate.	Round 61. 6-pdr APCBC Mk XV TNCN at 30 degrees to normal FSC. Shell velocity 2,553 f.s. Range 150 feet.	Code D. Struck 8.5 inches down from top edge. Scoop 7.5 × 3 × 2 inches deep. Rear. Cracked bulge.
Right-hand turret side	Round 62. 6-pdr APCBC at 30 degrees to normal. Shell velocity 2,595 f.s. Range 150 feet.	Code C. (Sv.) Scoop 6 × 3 × 1.5 inches. Struck 16 inches from top edge, 12 inches from escape hatch. Shot broke up. Rear. Bulge 5 × 4 × 0.3125 inches high. Flexible mounting in vicinity unaffected.
Right-hand hull lower side plate.	Round 63. 6-pdr APCBC at 30 degrees to normal. Shell velocity 2,534 f.s. Range 150 feet.	Code W. Struck 6 inches above bottom edge and immediately above rubber stop block for No. 8 bogie (bogie missing). Shot entered lower right-hand fuel tank. Fire resulted. Rear. Damage not visible.
Right-hand hull lower side plate + 1 bogie disc.	Round 64. 6-pdr APCBC at 30 degrees to normal. Shell velocity 2,574 f.s. Range 150 feet.	Code W. Penetrated 3rd bogie (rough disc) holing same 3.5-inch diameter. Hole in hull side 2.5-inch diameter. Rear. Damage normal. Shot passed to rear of co-driver's seat, damaging gearbox casing, glanced into forward left-hand ammunition stowage.
Right-hand hull lower side plate + closed flange bogies.	Round 65. 6-pdr APCBC at 30 degrees to normal. Shell velocity 2,575 f.s. Range 150 feet.	Code C. Holed 5th bogie wheel discs destroying inner rim of 4th bogie. Rear. Smooth bulge.
Right-hand superstructure side. PIAT projector 6-degree elevation.	Round 66. PIAT Mk 1. Filled RDX at 30 degrees to normal. Range 40 feet.	Scooped off top edge of superstructure. No damage to vehicle.
Right-hand superstructure side. PIAT projector 6-degree elevation.	Round 67. PIAT Mk 1. Filled RDX at 30 degrees to normal. Range 40 feet.	Struck 7.5 inches down from top edge. Entrance hole 0.625 inches diameter. Hole welded up. Rear. Explode jet 0.5 inches diameter entered fuel right-hand stowage racks and struck nose of one stowed round. Round not damaged. Cordite fire unlikely.
Right-hand superstructure side. PIAT projector 6-degree elevation.	Round 68. PIAT Mk 1. Filled RDX at 30 degrees to normal. Range 40 feet.	Struck 11 inches down. Entry hole 0.75 inches diameter. Rear. 3 rounds severely torn and perforated in case, 1 round thrown full into co-driver's position. Cordite fire would have resulted.
Right-hand lower hull side + Bogie wheel. Elevation of projector 6 degrees.	Round 69. PIAT Mk 1. Filled RDX at 30 degrees to normal. Range 40 feet.	Holed 2 discs of 2nd bogie wheel. Area around entry hole badly torn and perforated. Hull side not touched.
Turret right-hand side. Elevation 8 degrees.	Round 70. PIAT Mk 1. Filled RDX at 30 degrees to normal. Range 40 feet.	Struck 5 inches above bottom edge of turret. Entry hole 0.625 inches diameter. Rear. Exit hole in weld junction with side and turret shelf. Jet passed across gun loader's station and splashed on gun breech over area 18 × 15 inches, also on opposite wall. Turret crew probably all casualties.
Front at normal. Visor plate.	Round 71. PIAT Mk 1. Filled RDX at 10 degrees to normal. Range 40 feet.	Struck 9.5 inches down from top edge. Entry hole 0.375 inches diameter. Plate holed. Weld—visor to glacis—crack extended 30 inches to write side and 6 inches to left side. Junction of the main weld glacis and nose plate cracked for 42 inches—apparently old crack—only now visible. Rear. Jet passed across hull gunner's compartment striking bulkhead, splashing area 6 × 4 inches. Hull gunner probably killed.
Nose plate. Hull front at normal.	Round 72. PIAT Mk 1. Filled RDX at 24 degrees to normal. Range 40 feet.	Struck 8 inches below upper edge of plate. Plate holed. Entry hole 0.625 inches diameter. Rear. Damage not visible.

TARGET	ATTACK	OBSERVATIONS
Turret gun mantlet. Lower edge. Front of vehicle at normal.	Round 73. 6-pdr APCBC at 30 degrees to normal. Shell velocity 2,348 f.s. Range 150 feet.	Code W. on roof plate. Struck 1.5 inches above bottom edge. Scoop 2.75 × 2 inches and glanced down and through roof plate below turret ring. Roof holed 7.5 × 4 inches approximately. Rear. Further damage to rear end of gearbox. Fragments of roof lying on driver's seat. Driver probably killed. Other members of crew possibly casualties.
Visor plate—roof joint front of vehicle at normal.	Round 74. 17-pdr APCBC at 10 degrees to normal. Shell velocity 1,957 f.s. Range 150 feet.	Code scoop Struck 3.25 inches below top edge of visor. Scooped 6.5 × 5 inches. Shot scooped upwards. Weld—roof to visor—junction with roof plate shows evidence of old crack and intermittent new crack over length 19 inches and 5 inches over the side of roof plate
Visor plate—roof joint front of vehicle at normal.	Round 75. 17-pdr APCBC at 10 degrees to normal. Shell velocity 1,923 f.s. Range 150 feet.	Code R. Shot base lodged. Struck 4.5 inches down bulging top plate 0.5 inches immediately above impact. Roof plate behind impact sheared out for area 9.5 × 6.5 inches. Weld junction with roof plate now split and extending to Round 74. Roof plate split from front of vehicle indirection of rear for 21 inches approximately. 2 cracks running from roof hole 8.5 inches long and inches long. Main outer weld—visor to glacis—originally cracked by Round 56 now open 0.375 inches maximum and extended for full length of visor. Rear. Hull side plate joining the visor plate sheared off level with pannier together with the reinforcing angle. Inner roof weld with visor split for similar dimensions to outer weld.
Visor plate, near right-hand end. Front of vehicle at normal.	Round 76. 17-pdr APCBC at 10 degrees to normal. Shell velocity 1,853 f.s. Range 150 feet.	Code D. Struck 9.5 inches down from top edge. Petals sheared out. Outer weld—visor plate to right-hand side plate—old cracks opening in junction 12 inches and 5.5 inches long. Rear. Cracked bulge 5.5-inch diameter × 1 inch high. Starting crack 1.25 inches long, 0.0625 inches open.
Nose plate—joint with glacis plate. Front of vehicle at normal.	Round 77. 17-pdr APCBC at 24 degrees to normal. Shell velocity 2,131 f.s. Range 150 feet.	Code E. Struck 5.5 inches from edge of nose plate. Top edge set up 0.375 inches maximum locally. Crack in main weld with glacis now open 0.0625 inches maximum and old crack in junction with nose plate now apparent over 15 inches approximately. Rear. Cracked bulge in plate. Daylight
Nose plate near right-hand end. Front of vehicle at normal.	Round 78. 17-pdr APCBC at 24 degrees to normal. Shell velocity 1,865 f.s. Range 150 feet.	Code C. (Sv.) Struck 14 inches from top, 8 inches from right-hand end. Rear. Smooth bulge.
Nose plate—joint with glacis plate.	Round 79. 17-pdr APCBC at 24 degrees to normal. Shell velocity 2,089 f.s. Range 150 feet.	Code D. (Sv.) Struck 7 inches below top edge of nose plate. Nose and glacis—opened and extended 15 inches approximately. Rear. Cracked bulge in plate.
Turret mantlet	Round 80. 17-pdr APDS at 40 degrees to normal. Shell velocity 3,212 f.s. Range 150 feet.	Code NFH. Double hit with Round 43. Turret casting cracked below impact through to bottom edge. Rear. Fragments entered under right-hand gun buffer. Buffer casing perforated. Numerous strikes in surrounding area.
Turret mantlet	Round 81. 17-pdr APDS at 40 degrees to normal. Shell velocity 3,272 f.s. Range 150 feet.	Code NFH. Struck 4 inches above lower edge of casting removing metal 8 × 5.5 inches. Piece lodged under turret front edge.
Turret right-hand side.	Round 82. 17-pdr APDS at 38 degrees to normal. Shell velocity 2,995 f.s. Range 150 feet.	Code W. Struck 11.5 inches above bottom edge. Rear. Fragments passed across turret causing numerous strikes on opposite wall and further damage to stowage bin.
Right-hand final drive. Front of vehicle at normal.	Round 83. 17-pdr APCBC at normal. Shell velocity 2,260 f.s. Range 150 feet.	Track holed 3.5 inches diameter. Shot entered casing of final drive. Base broken off and lying on track. Nose lodged. Tank immobilised.
Right-hand final drive. Front of vehicle at normal.	Round 84. 17-pdr APCBC at normal. Shell velocity 3,025 f.s. Range 150 feet.	Struck and passed through track and entered the final drive housing. Track sheared out over area 7 × 5 inches. Casing split from entry hole. Round 84 to Round 83. 2 teeth off inner sprocket missing. Metal off 10 × 2 inches. Inner mounting flanges sheared through; oil leaking from casing. Tank immobilised.

TARGET	ATTACK	OBSERVATIONS
Turret right-hand side.	Round 85. 17-pdr APCBC at 38 degrees to normal. Estimated shell velocity 3,025 f.s. Range 150 feet.	Code W. Struck 3.75 inches down from top edge. Side plate set up 1 inch locally. Several transverse cracks in edge of plate. Main outer roof weld intact. One track clamp hinged back due to weld failure. Cracked weld round vision slit cover, now open 0.1875 inches maximum. Rear. Damage normal. Inner weld lifted locally. Crack in junction with roof 12 inches long towards rear. Roof stiffening bar over loader's station sheared out for 14 inches, depth 2 inches. Inner ring under cupola hatch fallen down on turret floor. Remainder of bins on turret rear wall removed.
Turret mantlet right-hand end.	Round 86. 75-mm HE Shell TNT filled PDM.48 Set SQ at normal FSC. Range 150 feet.	Struck and detonated 17 inches above hull roof. Splits in roof plate caused by Round 75 extended to turret ring 1 foot 10 inches. Now split running from above to hull gunner's hatch 2 foot 2 inches long. Roof plate set down 0.25 inches. Other splits open 0.0625 inches. Hull gunner's hatch opened (not locked). Main front weld—roof to visor—crack now 0.0625 inches open.
Driver's visor (closed) for effect on glacis plate.	Round 87. 75-mm HE Shell TNT filled PDM.48 Set SQ at normal FSC. Range 150 feet.	Struck top shutter 8 inches above glacis 5 inches from left hand housing. Protection bar pitted. Surrounding area severely pitted. Glacis plate not affected. Main outer weld—glacis to visor open slightly. Rear. Hand wheel spindle and latch for shutter damaged but still in position.
Hull machine gun ball mounting. Visor plate.	Round 88. 25-pdr HE Shell TNT filled Fuze 119, Cap off at normal FSC. Range 150 feet.	Struck on ball. Ball forced in 0.2875 inches, 8 inches above glacis. Housing set forward 0.3125 inches. Main weld between glacis and visor open now 0.4375 inches maximum. Severe pitting of glacis plate. Weld junction hull side mortice and glacis cracked for 0.5 inches perimeter. Similar effect on left hand side. Main outer weld glacis to nose—crack in junction extended for practically full length. Split in roof caused by Round 84 extended to right-hand hull side 2 feet 6 inches. Rear. Gun clamping bracket—bolted to ball—fractured. All bolts securing housing to visor very loose due to threads stripping.
Right-hand hull lower side adjacent pannier floor.	Round 89. 75-mm HE Shell TNT filled PDM.48 Set SQ at normal FSC. Range 150 feet.	Struck superstructure side 2 inches above lower edge. Track pitted in locality. One small section of track 4 × 3 inches sheared out.
Right-hand hull lower side adjacent pannier floor.	Round 90. 75-mm HE Shell TNT filled PDM.48 Set SQ at normal FSC. Range 150 feet.	Struck 1 inch below bottom pannier plate on hull lower side plate. Pannier floor sheared out over area 18 × 18 inches maximum, narrowest width 5 inches. Main weld securing floor and superstructure side split for 3 feet 9 inches. Failure mainly in junction with superstructure side maximum open 0.25 inches. Pannier floor set down 0.375 inches at outer edge. Two splits in floor plate 11 and 10 inches long respectively. Metal sheared out of track below point of strike 1 foot 10 inches × 6 inches almost completely severing track. Track secured only by one link. Rear. 7 rivets securing reinforcing angle to pannier floor sheared out. Weld securing pannier floor to hull side split 3 feet 6 inches long and several bolts securing reinforcing angle to hull. Lower side loosened. Small arms stowage trays severely buckled and perforated. Possible cordite fire.
Hull rear at normal. Turret rear for effect on hull roof over engine compartment.	Round 91. 75-mm HE Shell TNT filled PDM.48 Set SQ at normal FSC. Range 150 feet.	Struck 16 inches above hull roof. Numerous strikes on hull roof. Hull roof unaffected. 12 strikes in right-hand radiator. 8 strikes in left-hand radiator. Fragments entered through forward grille. Several of each probably caused perforations.
Hull rear at normal. Turret rear for effect on hull roof over engine compartment.	Round 92. 25-pdr HE Shell TNT filled Fuze 119, Cap off at normal FSC. Range 150 feet.	Struck 14 inches above hull roof. Roof door forced up 0.375 inches maximum. 2 locking bolts sheared out. Numerous pitting over roof in the vicinity. Stock pipe aperture with engine compartment—hinged lid forced open. End cover of one magneto blown away. Numerous new strikes on both radiators. Probable water leakage. Aerial bar knocked away.
Left-hand side final drive.	Round 93. 17-pdr APCBC at 30 degrees to normal. FSC. Estimated shell velocity 3,025 f.s. Range 150 feet.	Shot past through track 9 inches from inner edge holing same 5 × 3 inches. 3 track spuds sheared through. Entered final drive housing, shearing casing from point of entry to sprocket wheel inner flanges shot past across housing, shearing out extensive metal on housing adjustment to hull side. Extensive damage to gearing. Part of shot laying in debris. Vehicle definitely immobilised. Sprocket and track forced away from hull side 5 inches.

TARGET	ATTACK	OBSERVATIONS
Nose plate—joint with glacis plate near right-hand end. Vertical angle 24 degrees. Front of vehicle at 30 degrees to normal.	Round 94. 17-pdr APCBC at 36 degrees (CA) to normal. FSC. Estimated shell velocity 3,025 f.s. Range 150 feet.	Code W. Round struck 4.5 inches down from top edge of nose plate and 4 in from hull side. Shot past into hull. Hole 2.5 × 3 inches. Hull side. Away from nose plate 0.875 inches maximum and set up 0.75 inches at top corner. Outer weld between hull side plate and nose plate split for full length 26 inches. Failure mainly in junction open 0.375 inches maximum. Main weld securing glacis and nose plate further opened 0.25 inches maximum top wedge securing nose mortice joint with hull side forced out and lower wedge partially forced out. Front right-hand corner of places lifted 0.5 inches maximum over 6 inches length. Nose plate mortice ceiling welds failed full-length. Armour shield round final drive—weld with hull side failed and shield displaced 1.75 inches. Weld—hull side to glacis failed 22 inches length—junction and weld metal. Inner weld failure is of similar extent. Rear. Metal off 5 × 4.5 inches. Shot broke up inside.
Left-hand superstructure side.	Round 95. 6-pdr APCBC at 20 degrees to normal FSC. Estimated shell velocity 2,575 f.s. Range 150 feet.	Code NFH. Struck 0.75 inches down from top edge. Scoop 3 × 3 inches. Shot glanced off turret side.
Left-hand superstructure side.	Round 96. 6-pdr APCBC at 20 degrees to normal FSC. Estimated shell velocity 2,575 f.s. Range 150 feet.	Code W. Struck 7.5 inches down. Rear. 2 segments off. One segment forced back. Shot passed across driver's station causing further damaged to instrument panel.
Turret left-hand side.	Round 97. 6-pdr APCBC at 20 degrees to normal FSC. Estimated shell velocity 2,575 f.s. Range 150 feet.	Code. Scoop Struck 3.5 inches above bottom edge of turret. Turret shelf metal sheared out 7 × 1 inch. Outer weld split 15 inches long.
Turret left-hand side.	Round 98. 6-pdr APCBC at 20 degrees to normal FSC. Estimated shell velocity 2,575 f.s. Range 150 feet.	Code W. Struck 13 inches above bottom edge of turret side. Rear. Shot entered turret and destroyed left-hand gun buffer. Oil leakage. Turret crew all casualties.
Turret left-hand side to test roof joint.	Round 99. 6-pdr APCBC at 20 degrees to normal FSC. Estimated shell velocity 2,575 f.s. Range 150 feet.	Code. Scoop Struck 1.5 inches down from top edge of side plate. Scoop 3.5 × 2.5 inches from side plate and 5.5 × 4.5 inches from roof. Main outer and inner roof weld is intact.
Item 10. Track (left-hand side). Centre of mine in line with outer edge of No. 3 road wheel.	1 × Mk V Standard anti-tank mine. Top of mine 2 inches below track.	Small pieces of track 2.5 × 2 inches sheared out. One split 1.75 inches long stop track pin and one link forced out 1.5 inches from end. Outer disc of No. 3 bogie split at rim over 6 inches to edge, buckled 1 inch. Hub of wheel at inner disc sheared for more than half perimeter—open 0.375 inches maximum. Crater 8 feet × 7 feet × 2 feet 6 inches deep.
Item 11. Track (right-hand side). Centre of mine in line with outer edge of No. 5 bogie.	2 × Mk V Standard anti-tank mines. Top of mine 2 inches below track. Mines wired in parallel.	Track not severed, but metal removed from outer edge 6.5 × 3.5 inches. 3 spuds sheared through to links at points 4.5 inches approximately from outer edge. Outer rim disc split around lower edge over 11 and forced up locally 4 inches. Tyre split. Inner rim severely buckled—set in 3.5 inches maximum. Two track pins adjustment sheared through 2.5 × 1.75 inches respectively from outer end. Crater size 7 feet × 9 feet × 3 feet 6 inches deep.
Item 12. Track (left-hand side). Centre of mine in line with No. 7 bogie and under centre of track.	2 × Mk V Standard anti-tank mines. Top of mine 2 inches below track. Mines wired in parallel.	Track completely severed. Split in outer disc of No. 7 bogie. Slight buckling of inner inside wheel disc. Vehicle temporarily immobilised. Crater size 7 × 7 × 4 feet deep.

APPENDIX B

Trial No. X.811
AT No. 252 Part II
Pz.Kw.VI Tiger
Structural Attack

Showing point of entry of Rounds 36, 37, and 38: 17-pdr APDS. (*DTD Materials Division, Armour Branch*)

Showing rear demand from Rounds 36, 37, and 38: 17-pdr APDS. The demand is typical of DS. The tungsten carbide core from which ultimately shatters into many fragments. (*DTD Materials Division, Armour Branch*)

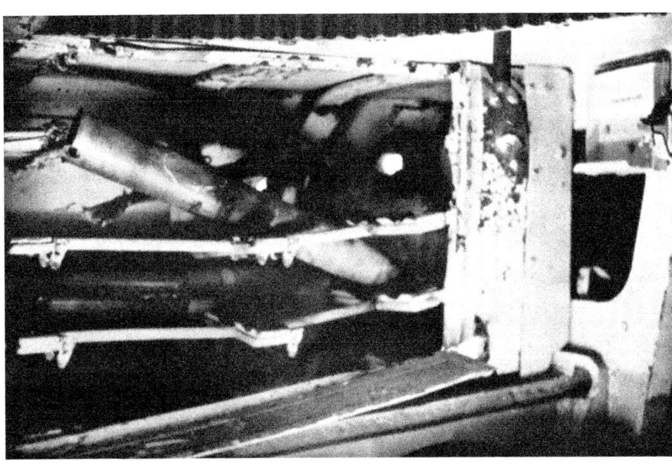

Damage to stowed ammunition by Rounds 46 and 47: 17-pdr APDS. Note: Entry holes of rounds. (*DTD Materials Division, Armour Branch*)

Showing stowage rack on opposite side of fighting compartment struck by fragments from Rounds 46: 17-pdr APDS. (*DTD Materials Division, Armour Branch*)

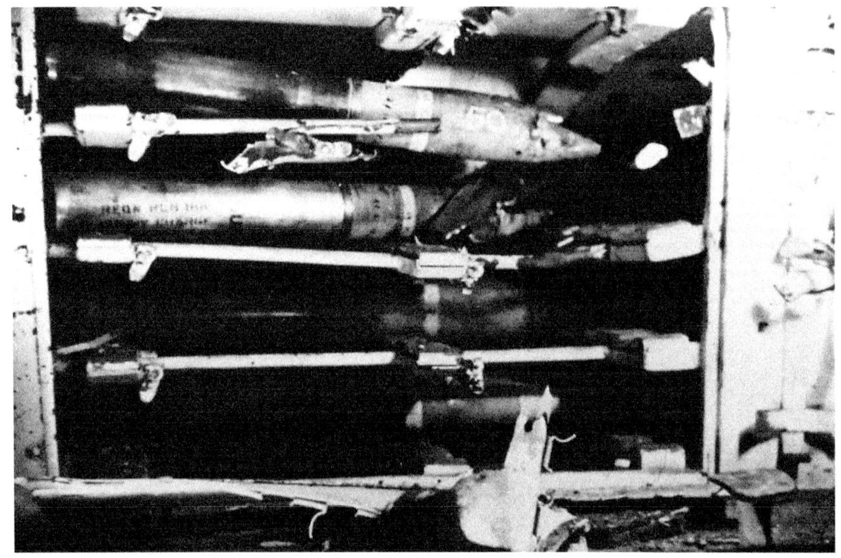

Showing damage to stowed ammunition caused by Round 50: 17-pdr APDS. Note: Entry hole made by round. (*DTD Materials Division, Armour Branch*)

Two stowed rounds damaged by Round 50: 17-pdr APDS. (*DTD Materials Division, Armour Branch*)

Showing the effect of Round 52: 17-pdr APCBC at 50 degrees. Round passed through forward superstructure. Note the roof failure and plate broken out in one piece. (*DTD Materials Division, Armour Branch*)

After Round 52 above, two stowed rounds were found in the driver's position separated from cases. (*DTD Materials Division, Armour Branch*)

Damaged stowed rounds as the result of Round 52. (*DTD Materials Division, Armour Branch*)

Round 56: 17-pdr APCBC striking visor plate near main joint with glacis. Note the main weld fracture. (*DTD Materials Division, Armour Branch*)

Showing lug and wedge forced off rear of glacis by Round 56. (*DTD Materials Division, Armour Branch*)

Showing attack against interlock structure by Round 57: 17-pdr APCBC. The structure remained substantially intact. (*DTD Materials Division, Armour Branch*)

Showing point of entry Round 63 (6-pdr APCBC) in hull side and into fuel tank. Note the start of a fire through the entrance hole. (*DTD Materials Division, Armour Branch*)

Fighting the fire caused by Round 63. A free water supply prevented the plate from overheating. (*DTD Materials Division, Armour Branch*)

Showing damage to stowed rounds by Round 68: 3.5-lb PIAT, defeating superstructure. (*DTD Materials Division, Armour Branch*)

Stowed ammunition destroyed by Round 68: 3.5-lb PIAT. (*DTD Materials Division, Armour Branch*)

Stowing Round 73: 6-pdr APCBC, which scooped off lower edge gun mantlet down through hull roof. (*DTD Materials Division, Armour Branch*)

Showing effect of Round 75: 17-pdr APCBC. Chalk lines indicate the extent of plate cracking. (*DTD Materials Division, Armour Branch*)

Showing extension to splits in roof plate caused by Round 86 (75-mm HE), indicated by chalk lines. Initial split was caused by Round 75. (*DTD Materials Division, Armour Branch*)

Round 83 and 84: 17-pdr APCBC, penetrated into final drive. The vehicle would have been arrested by either round. (*DTD Materials Division, Armour Branch*)

Showing effect of Round 88: 25-pdr HE, detonated on MG ball mounting. Note the fracture of the gun clamping bracket at rear of mounting. (*DTD Materials Division, Armour Branch*)

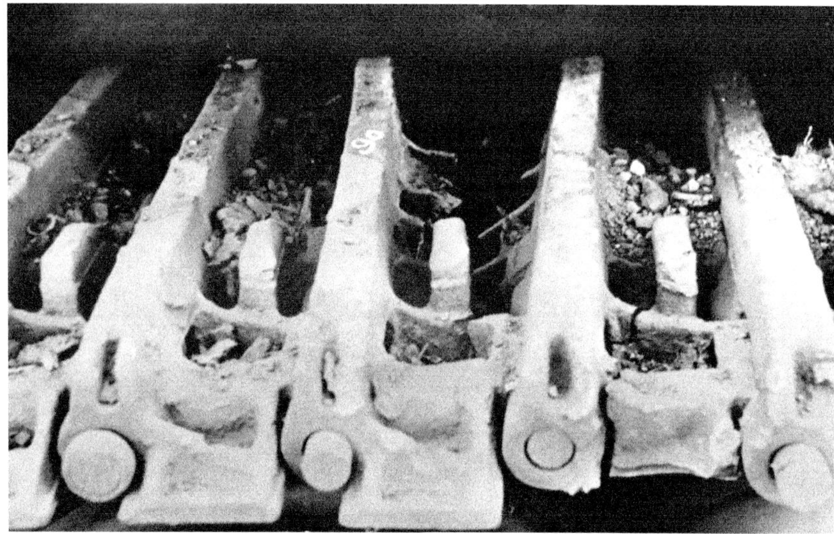

Showing effect on track from the detonation of Round 90 (75-mm HE) on the hull side 1 inch below the pannier floor plate. The track was nearly severed completely. (*DTD Materials Division, Armour Branch*)

Side view showing pannier floor failure due to Round 90 (75-mm HE) detonated 1 inch below. (*DTD Materials Division, Armour Branch*)

View from inside vehicle after Round 90: 75-mm HE. (*DTD Materials Division, Armour Branch*)

Near right: Showing Round 94 (17-pdr APCBC) striking an estimated velocity of 3,025 f.s. to obtain a measure of the ultimate strength of this structure. Although the hull side plate has been forced open, the structure is still immensely strong. (*DTD Materials Division, Armour Branch*)

Far right: Further view showing outer hull side after Round 94. Note the missing mortice wedge at top and weld failure with armour protection ring around final drive. (*DTD Materials Division, Armour Branch*)

Round 98 (6-pdr APCBC FSC) entered the turret and destroyed the left-side gun buffer. (*DTD Materials Division, Armour Branch*)

Effect of Round 99 (6-pdr APCBC FSC) on the turret roof. Note the welding either side of hole is intact. (*DTD Materials Division, Armour Branch*)

Item 10. Showing one Mk V standard AT mine beneath the outer edge of the track before filling in. (*DTD Materials Division, Armour Branch*)

Item 10. Result of detonation of one Mk V standard AT mine shown in Print 29. Note only slight damage to track was caused. (*DTD Materials Division, Armour Branch*)

Item 11. Showing two Mk V standard AT mine beneath the outer edge of the track before filling in. (*DTD Materials Division, Armour Branch*)

Item 11. Result of detonation of two Mk V standard AT mine shown in Print 31. Damage to the track was too small to stop the tank. (*DTD Materials Division, Armour Branch*)

Item 12. Showing two Mk V standard AT mine beneath the centre of the track before filling in. (*DTD Materials Division, Armour Branch*)

‹ Item 12. Result of detonation of two Mk V standard AT mine shown in Print 33. The track was broken through. (*DTD Materials Division, Armour Branch*)

› Item 12. Showing one end of the broken track as a result of Item 12. (*DTD Materials Division, Armour Branch*)

APPENDIX C

Trial No. X.811
AT No. 252 Part II
Pz.Kw.VI Tiger
Sketches: Vehicle DTD No. 3039

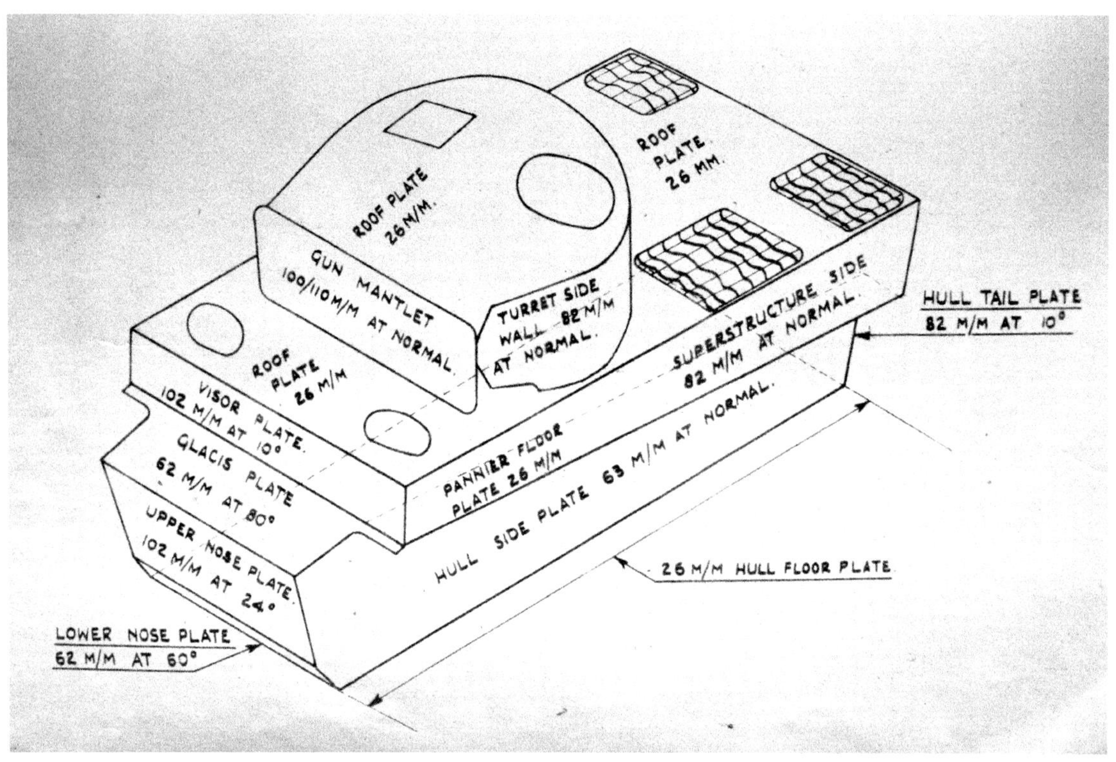

Vehicle DTD No. 3039's armour angle and thickness. (*DTD Materials Division, Armour Branch*)

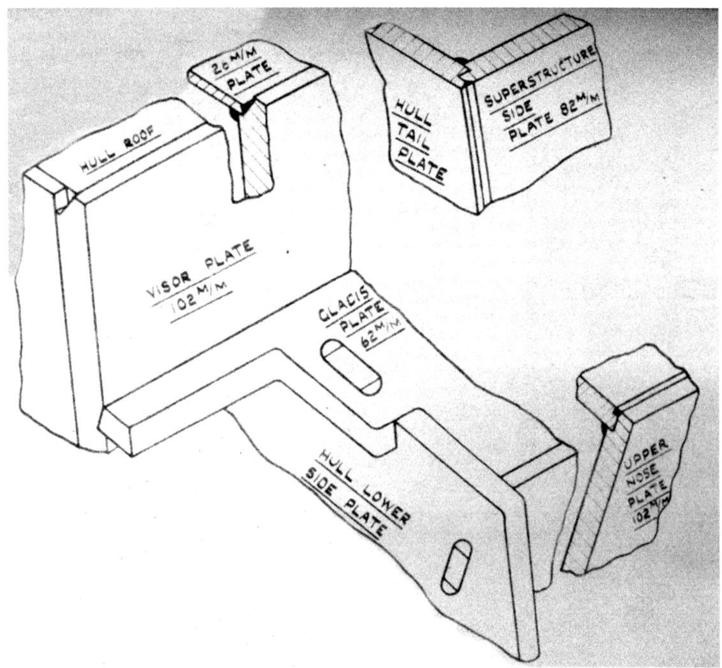

Vehicle DTD No. 3039: details of interlocking and stopped joints and edge preparations. (*DTD Materials Division, Armour Branch*)

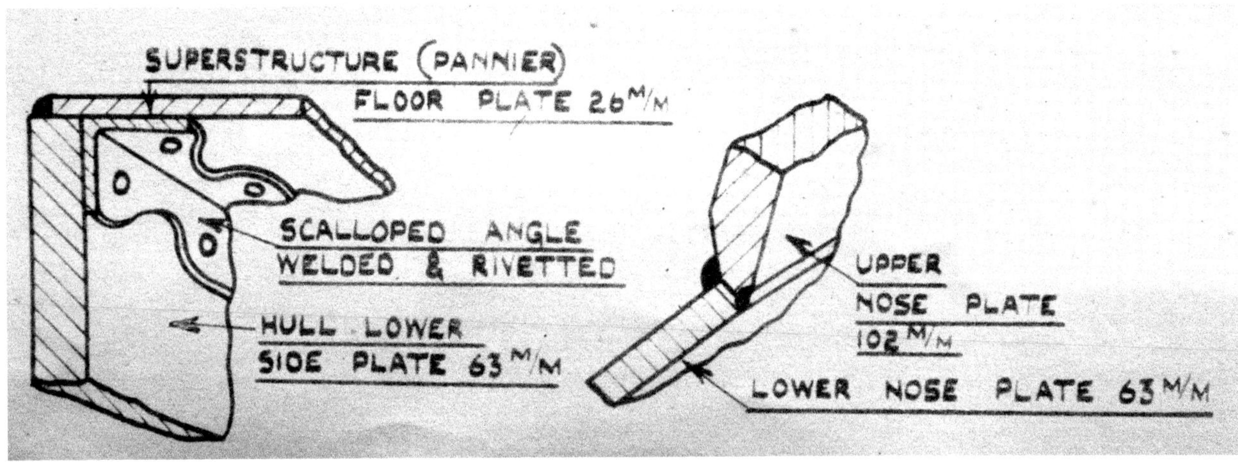

Vehicle DTD No. 3039: details of interlocking and stopped joints and edge preparations. (*DTD Materials Division, Armour Branch*)

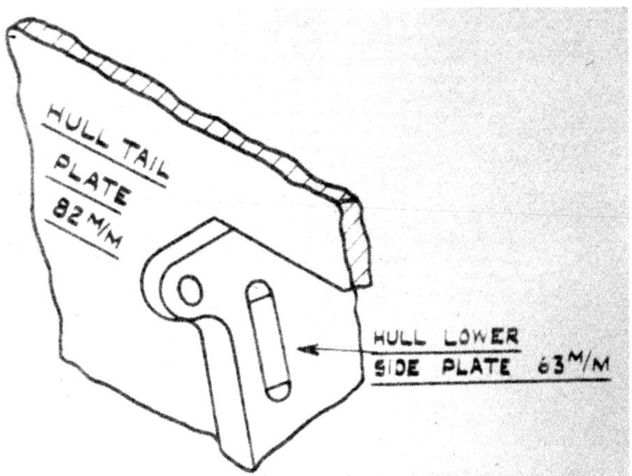

Vehicle DTD No. 3039: details of interlocking and stopped joints and edge preparations. (*DTD Materials Division, Armour Branch*)

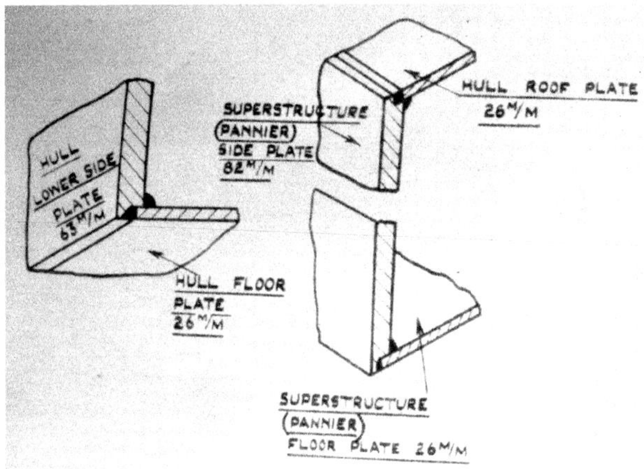

Vehicle DTD No. 3039: details of interlocking and stopped joints and edge preparations. (*DTD Materials Division, Armour Branch*)

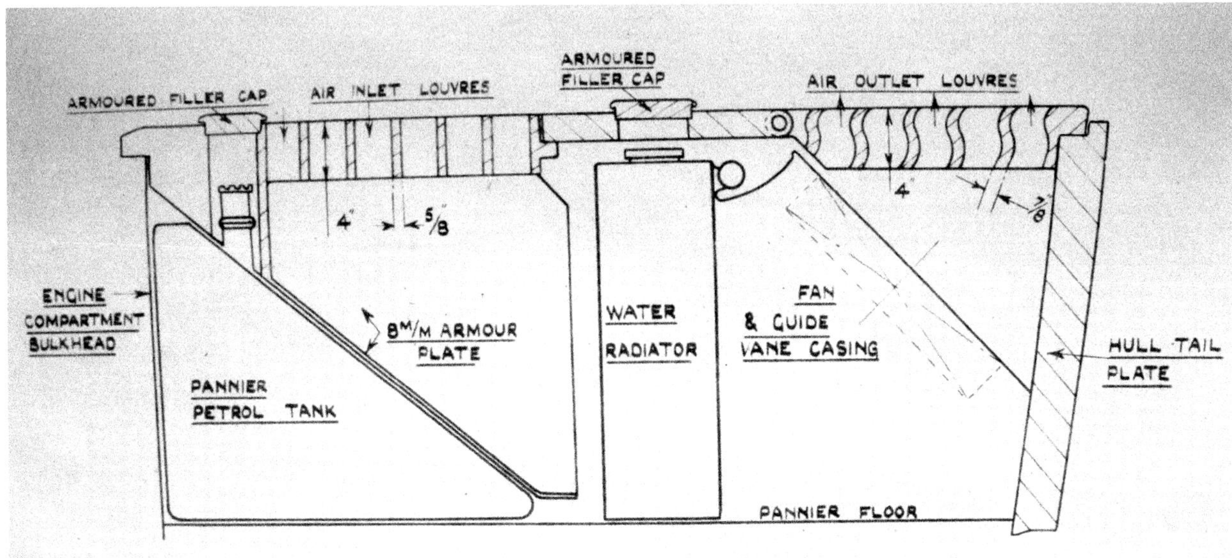

Vehicle DTD No. 3039: diagrammatic view of the layout of the water radiator and petrol tank in the panniers showing the vulnerability of the radiator to fragments entering the air inlet louvres and ricocheting off the 8-mm armour plate protecting the petrol tank. (*DTD Materials Division, Armour Branch*)

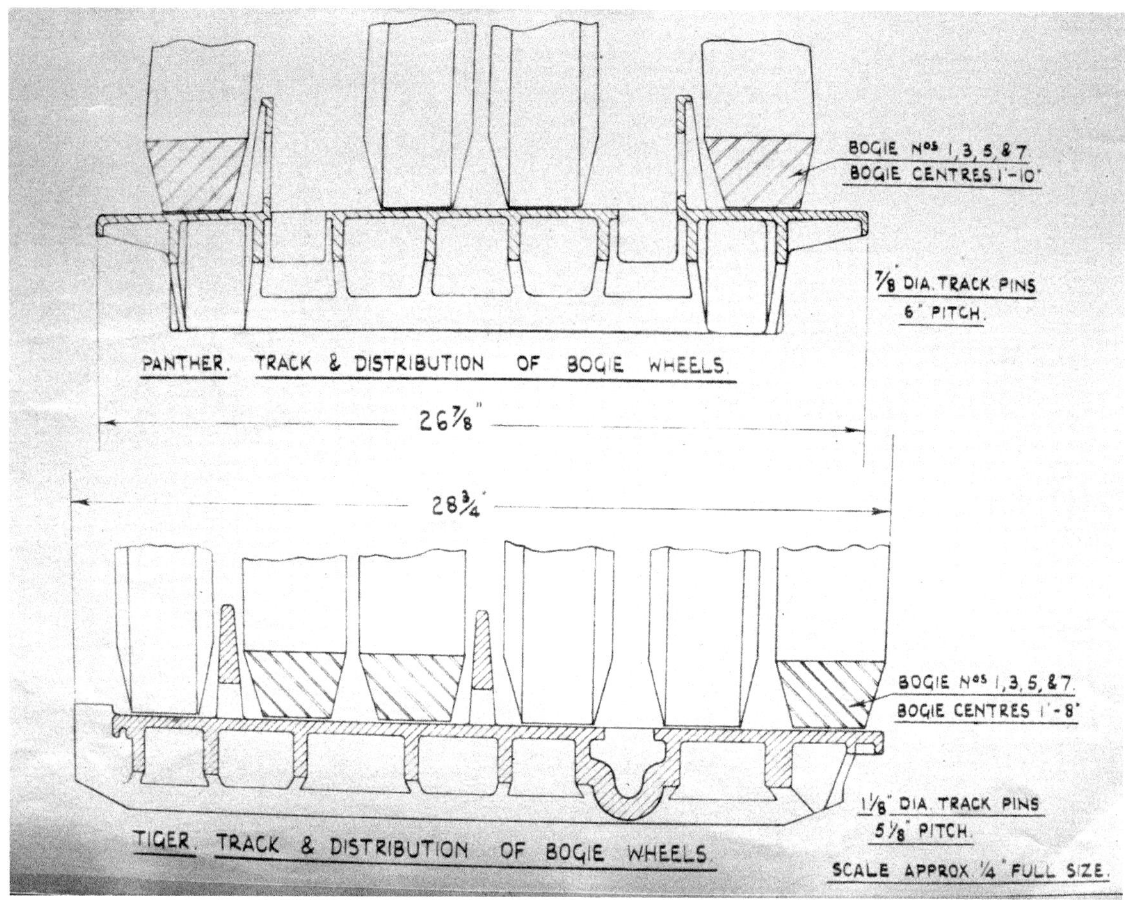

Vehicle DTD No. 3039: diagram showing comparative sections of Tiger and Panther tracks and bogies, indicating the greater section strength and support given by the bogies to the Tiger track against anti-tank mines. (*DTD Materials Division, Armour Branch*)

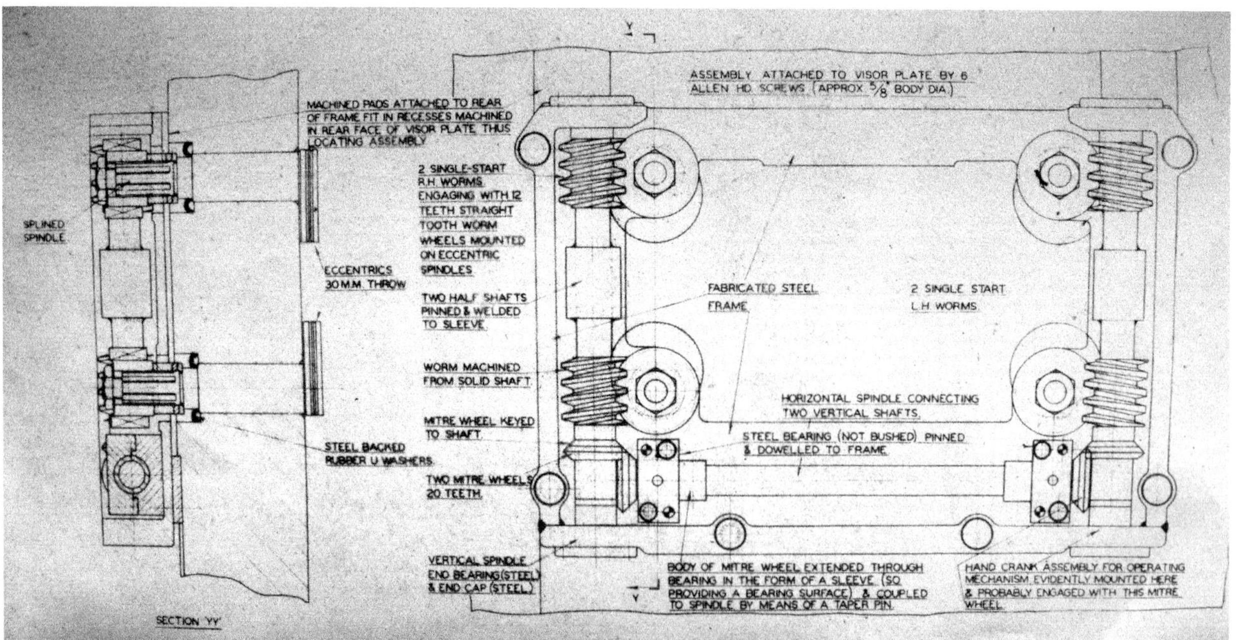

Vehicle DTD No. 3039: detail of operating mechanism for the driver's visor. (*DTD Materials Division, Armour Branch*)

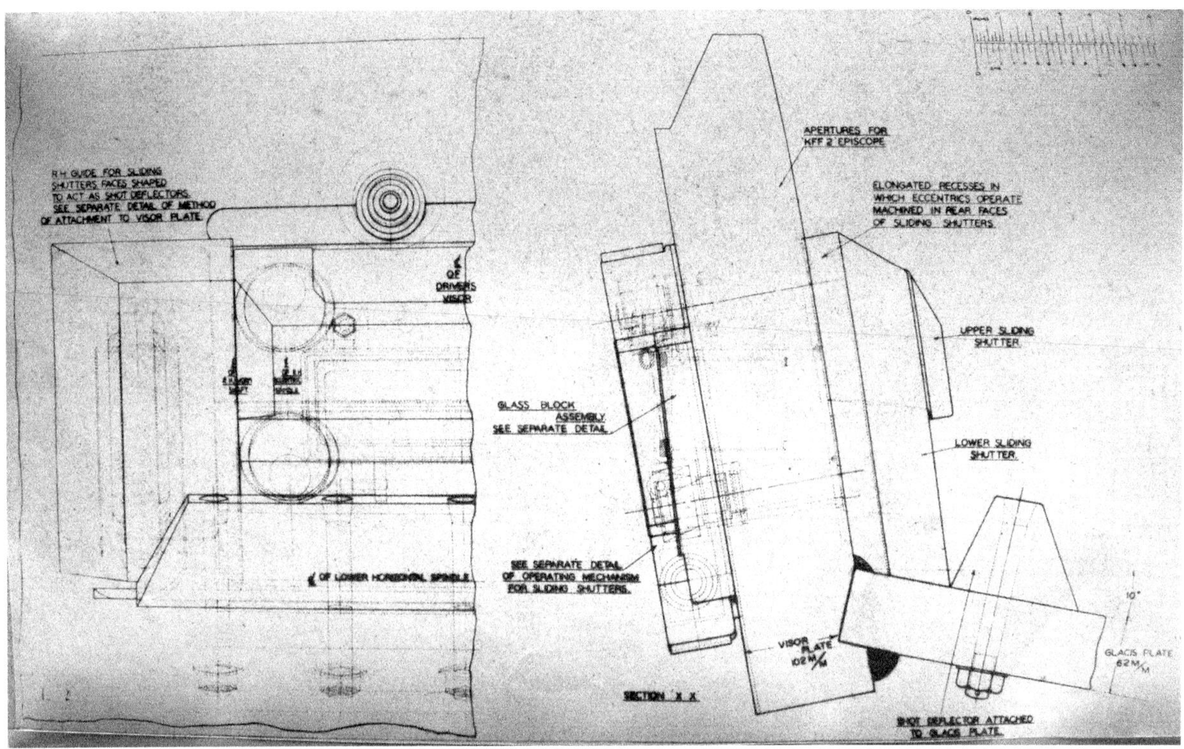

Vehicle DTD No. 3039: diagram of driver's visor. (*DTD Materials Division, Armour Branch*)

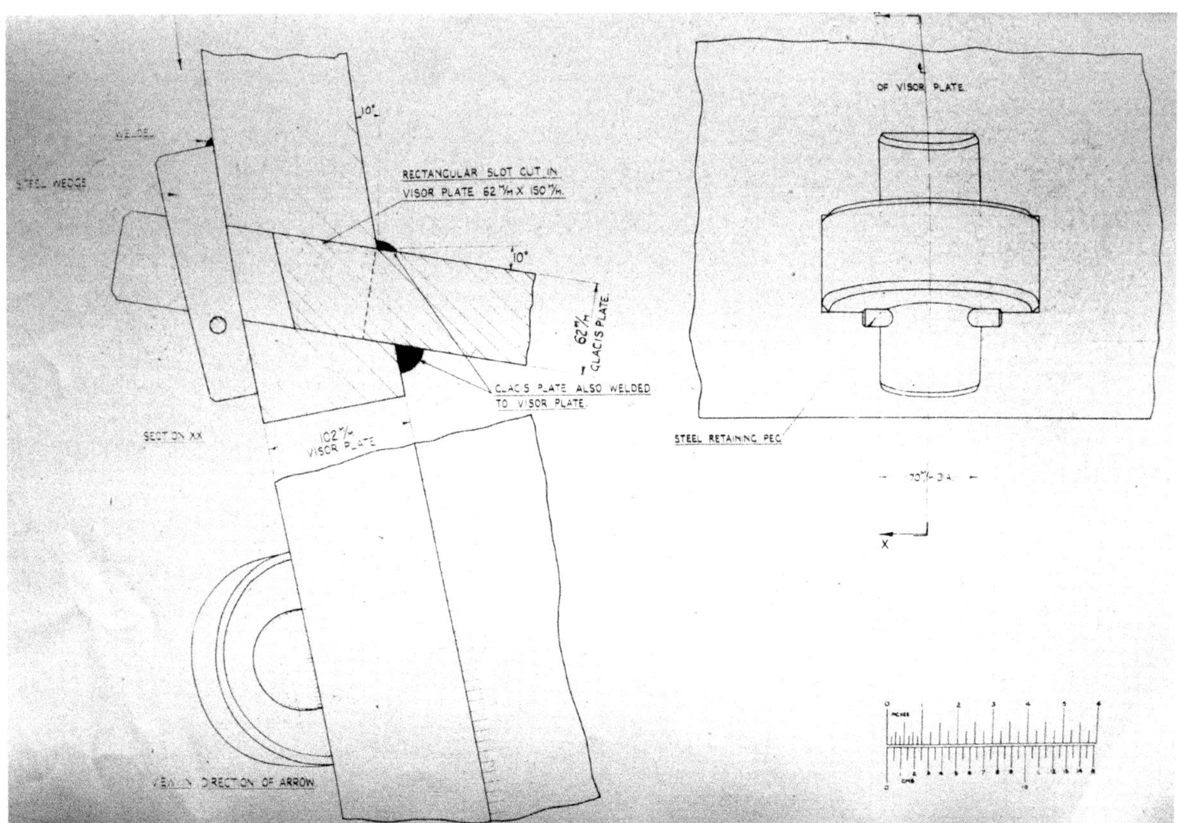

Vehicle DTD No. 3039: arrangement of the auxiliary attachment of the glacis plate to the visor plate. (*DTD Materials Division, Armour Branch*)

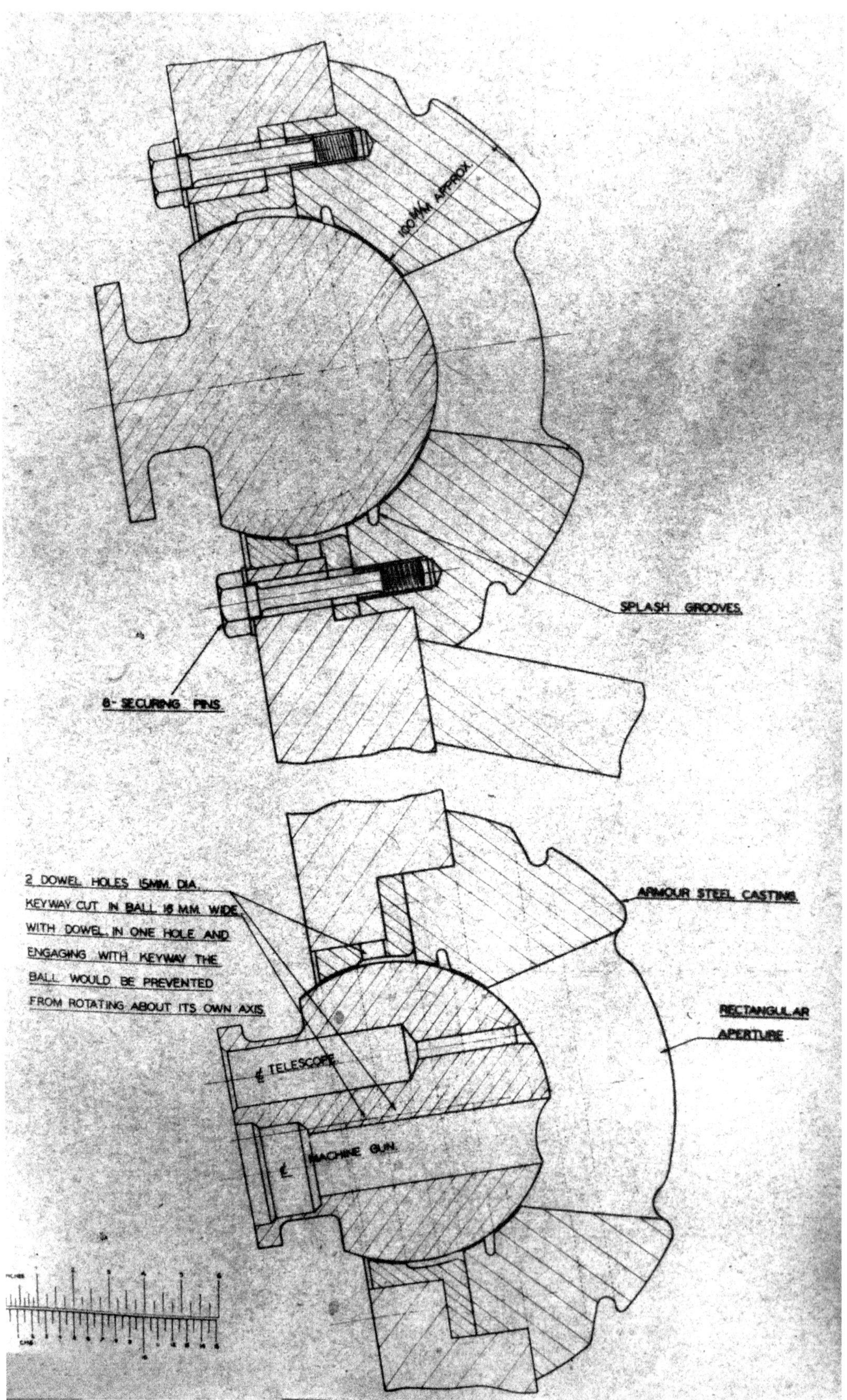

Vehicle DTD No. 3039: hull MG 34 ball mounting. (*DTD Materials Division, Armour Branch*)

APPENDIX D

Trial No. X.811
AT No. 252 Part II
Pz.Kw.VI Tiger
Design Features

Left: Showing interlocking of glacis, nose, and hull side plates. Note the wedge fitted after assembly and welding. (*DTD Materials Division, Armour Branch*)

Below left: Showing interlocking of tail plate and hull side. Note the scalloping welding on the angle bar. (*DTD Materials Division, Armour Branch*)

Below right: Showing interlocking of turret front and side rolled plate. Note the wedge fitted after assembly and welded round. (*DTD Materials Division, Armour Branch*)

Left: Showing turret loader's hatch quick-lock mechanism. (*DTD Materials Division, Armour Branch*)

Below left: Showing driver's hatch quick lock mechanism. (*DTD Materials Division, Armour Branch*)

Below right: Showing turret escape door. Note the simple locking and release mechanism, which is easily operated. (*DTD Materials Division, Armour Branch*)

APPENDIX E

Trial No. X.811
AT No. 252 Part II
Penetration Code

A—slight or no impression.
B—deep impression.
C—deep impression and bulge at the back.
D—deep impression, bulge at the back, and crack or cracks.
E—deep impression, bulge, and cracks or cracks through which daylight can be seen.
R—penetration—core or shot not clean through plate.
W—penetration—core or shot clean through plate.
(l) —following the code letter indicates the core or shot is lodged in the armour.

Ballistic Limit

The figure of merit by which the ballistic quality of a plate is assessed. It is taken as the average of four or more velocities (assessed—two for an estimated figure), usually within a range of 70 f.s., Half of which defeat the armour (E, R, or W) and half of which failed to defeat the armour (B, C, or D).

15

PART III: FIRING TRIALS AGAINST Pz.Kw. VI (TIGER) 23–25 APRIL 1945

The information in this chapter has been transcribed from original wartime documents. The report format and brief notation style has been kept.

DTD EXPERIMENTAL REPORT
AT NO. 252
PART III

Project No. M. 6816A/10
Trial No. X. 812
File No. 250/14/4

Report of Firing Trials Against Pz.Kw. VI (Tiger) Held at S. of E. Range, Shoeburyness on 23, 24, and 25 April 1945

Present at Trial	Representing	Dates
Capt. Wilde	DRAC	23rd
Major Steane	DTD (General Design)	24th
Lt. Tredinnick	S. of E. Range officer	23rd, 24th & 25th
Mr. Gray	DTD Armour Branch	23rd, 24th & 25th
Mr. Wilde	DTD Armour Branch	23rd, 24th & 25th
Report		
	Compiled by:- Mr. G.W. Gray	DTD Armour Branch
	Checked by:- Mr. J.B. Sankey	DTD Armour Branch

References		
Section I.	-	Object of Trial.
Section II.	-	Target Details.
Section III.	-	Method of Attack.
Section IV.	-	Trial Commentary (6-pdr APCBC)
Section V.	-	Trial Commentary (17-pdr APCBC)

	Section VI.	-	Trial Commentary (No. 75 Grenades)
	Section VII.	-	Conclusion
Appendices			
	Appendix A.	-	Detailed Results.
	Appendix B.	-	Photographic Record.
	Appendix C.	-	Penetration Code.
Note:-			
	This report must not be reproduced in full or in part without the written authority of the Director of Tank Design.		

SECTION I

Object of Trial

1. To obtain further ballistic data from the hull and turret of a Tiger tank when subjected to heavy AP attack.
2. To determine the effect of No. 75 Hawkins grenades on the hull and turret roof plates, when placed in contact.

SECTION II

Target Details

Pz.Kw VI (Tiger) Tank DTD No. 3039, hull and turret used in Trial X. 811. The engine, radiators, fuel tanks, and transmission, etc…, have been removed to enable the rear damage to be inspected.

SECTION III

Method of Attack

The target was attacked from a range of 150 feet with 6-pdr and 17-pdr APCBC shot. The tank was attacked with the front at normal and angle, and the sides at angle, the target being turned to give the required presentation. All azimuth angles were read by means of a sighting protractor. Full details of the attack and presentation of target are set out in Appendix A.

The attack against the hull and turret roofs were carried out with Hawkins grenades in contact with roof plates.

SECTION IV

Trial Commentary (6-pdr APCBC)

1. Superstructure Side at 20 Degrees (82 mm)

Two rounds at velocities of 2,146 f.s. gave an estimated ballistic limit of 2,190 f.s. equivalent to a range of approximately 1,750 yards. An estimated W/R limit was obtained from Rounds 100 and 104 at 2,319 f.s. indicating that holing of the plate can be expected at ranges up to 1,350 yards. Owing to limitation of target space, further attack against the turret side was not possible. Since the turret sides were constructed of rolled plate of similar thickness, it is reasonable to expect results from attack similar to those recorded against the superstructure.

SECTION V

Trial Commentary (17 pdr APCBC) Continued

2. Superstructure Side at 50 Degrees (82 mm)

Seven rounds were fired with an estimated ballistic limit of 2,814 f.s. and an estimated W/R limit of 2,864 f.s. were obtained. Those velocities represent practically point-blank range, and it was decided to present the target at the reduced angle of 45 degrees.

3. Superstructure Side at 45 Degrees (82 mm)
Eight rounds were fired at this plate, from which a ballistic limit of 2,607 f.s. was obtained. This figure represents a critical range of approximately 1,000 yards.

Holing of the vehicle from this attack can be expected at ranges up to approximately 900 yards.

It was noted that the bracket between non-defeat and complete defeat of the plates was comparatively small at both angles.

4. Visor Plate at 43-Degree Compound Angle (102 mm)
Three rounds giving striking velocity is of 2,711 f.s., 2,823 f.s., and 2,942 f.s. failed to cause defeat. It is apparent that the plate is immune at this angle.

5. Nose Plate at 24-Degree (102 mm)
Two additional rounds, together with 2 rounds fired during Part II, were sufficient to obtain a ballistic limit of 2097 f.s. A further round enabled a W/R limit to be estimated at 2,140 f.s., representing vulnerability at all fighting ranges.

6. Nose Plate at 37-Degree Compound Angle (102 mm)
Two rounds only were fired. Both rounds defeated the plate, but at velocities representing a very close range. Owing to lack of target space, further rounds at low velocities could not be fired.

SECTION VI

Trial Commentary (continued) AT Grenades Hawkins No. 75

7. Hull Roof Plate (26 mm)
One grenade was placed in contact with the roof and adjacent to the superstructure/roof welded joint, and detonated electrically.

The detonation caused a split in the roof plate 15 inches long locally, and also caused the weld forming the joint with the superstructure side to crack for 16 inches in the weld metal and junction with the roof.

The roof plate was also dished locally, for 0.5 inches over 9 inches.

8. Turret Roof Plate (26 mm)
Two grenades were used for this attack, placed side-by-side, and in a similar relative position, namely, adjacent to the side wall/roof welded joint.

The resulting detonation split the roof plate adjacent to the side wall joint for 22 inches. This split was opened for a maximum of 0.375 inches. A crack 3 inches long was also caused in the weld junction with the side wall, and the roof plate was dished 1.75 inches over 22 × 14 inches. Four rivets securing the loader's hatch mounting were also sheared out and projected into the turret, with consequence probable turret crew casualties.

SECTION VII

Conclusions

Armour
Of the plates directly attacked with AP shot, the majority behaved in a manner very similar to British plates of machinable quality. This is not unexpected since Poldi hardness figures indicate that these plates lie within the hardness range of armour to I.T.80E specification. For details, see Part II, Section IX.

One superstructure side plate did show a tendency to brittleness when Round No. 110 broke a rear area of plate completely away. It is considered that this failure would not occur from isolated rounds, but was the cumulative effects of many rounds, together with joint failure.

The results generally indicate that the ballistic quality is of the armour are comparable with British machinable.

The hull roof plate, not subject to direct attack from AP, did show brittleness, and in places split due to impact. This plate gave a hardness figure of 335 Brinell, approximately 80 points higher than the plates subject to direct attack.

The effect of one No. 75 Hawkins grenade on the 26-mm roof plate caused some plate cracking, but this would not be liable to affect the crew.

Two No. 75 on the turret roof of similar thickness gave increased plate splitting, but again it is not considered that this would harm the crew. Several rivets were shared out of the loader's hatch mounting and projected into turret. These may have caused casualties.

Weld and Structure

Very considerable extension to weld damage was caused in certain instances as the result of repeated attack during the trial, the main failure occurring in the hull roof/superstructure and superstructure/tail plate joints.

It is again pointed out that the weld failure was due to the cumulative effect of continued attack, and normally would not occur.

The structure of the tank under heavy attack proved extremely satisfactory.

G. Guthrie, Major, R.E.M.E.

Officer i/c Armour Trials Section, Armour Branch,

13.6.45 M.997(S) ES.

APPENDIX A

SECRET

Trial No. X.812

Detailed Results: Heavy Attack

TARGET	ATTACK	OBSERVATIONS
Tank No. 3039. Side at 20 degrees. Superstructure side plate. (Right side)	Round 100. 6-pdr APCBC Mk XV.T. (NCN) at 20 degrees to normal. Range 150 feet. Shell velocity 2,386 f.s.	Code W. Struck 5 inches above lower edge of plate, penetrating plate. Shot past through stowage racks, caused further damage, and past fighting compartment, causing further damage to opposite stowage racks.
Tank No. 3039. Side at 20 degrees. Superstructure side plate. (Right side)	Round 101. 6-pdr APCBC Mk XV.T. (NCN) at 20 degrees to normal. Range 150 feet. Shell velocity 2,146 f.s.	Code NFH. (cracked bulge) Struck too close to Round 100. Actual centre distance 4 inches.
Tank No. 3039. Side at 20 degrees. Superstructure side plate. (Right side)	Round 102. 6-pdr APCBC Mk XV.T. (NCN) at 20 degrees to normal. Range 150 feet. Shell velocity 2,144 f.s.	Code D. (S1.) Struck 5 inches from top edge of plate. Cracked bulge. Horizontal crack 2 inches long × 0.016 inches open.
Tank No. 3039. Side at 20 degrees. Superstructure side plate. (Right side)	Round 103. 6-pdr APCBC Mk XV.T. (NCN) at 20 degrees to normal. Range 150 feet. Shell velocity 2,214 f.s.	Code E. (Sv.) Struck 10 inches above the bottom edge. Cracked bulge 5 × 4 × 1 inch. Plug started. Circumferential crack 3.5 inches long × 0.125 inches open max.
Tank No. 3039. Side at 20 degrees. Superstructure side plate. (Right side)	Round 104. 6-pdr APCBC Mk XV.T. (NCN) at 20 degrees to normal. Range 150 feet. Shell velocity 2,252 f.s.	Code R(L). Struck 6 inches down from top edge. Main outer side plate and roof weld split during Part II, now further extended and slightly opened. Rear. Metal off 3 × 3 inches.
Tank No. 3039. Side at 20 degrees. Superstructure side plate. (Right side)	Round 105. 6-pdr APCBC Mk XV.T. (NCN) at 20 degrees to normal. Range 150 feet. Shell velocity 2,146 f.s.	Code D. Struck 9.5 inches above bottom edge. Rear. Cracked bulge 5 × 4.5 inches. Circumferential crack 3 inches long, 0.09375 inches open max.

TARGET	ATTACK	OBSERVATIONS
Tank No. 3039. Side at 20 degrees. Superstructure side plate. (Right side)	Round 106. 6-pdr APCBC Mk XV.T. (NCN) at 20 degrees to normal. Range 150 feet. Shell velocity 2,280 f.s.	Code E. (Sv) Struck 7.5 inches down from top edge. Rear. Cracked bulge 5-inch diameter. Circumferential crack 4 inches long, 0.125 inches open.
Tank No. 3039. Front at 40 degrees. Superstructure side plate. (Right side)	Round 107. 17-pdr APCBC Mk 8T. (NCN) at 50 degrees to normal. Range 150 feet. Shell velocity 2,622 f.s.	Code D. Shot broke up. Struck 9 inches down from top edge. Rear. Cracked bulge 7 × 5 × 1 inch high. Horizontal split running from vertical weld securing engine bulkhead to rear 4 inches open. 0.75 inches max. Vertical weld securing bulkhead split in junction with side plate for 21 inches. Split running into weld junction roof and side plate.
Tank No. 3039. Front at 40 degrees. Superstructure side plate. (Right side)	Round 108. 17-pdr APCBC Mk 8T. (NCN) at 50 degrees to normal. Range 150 feet. Shell velocity 2,610 f.s.	Code C. Scoop Struck 7.5 inches down 7 inches from Round 107. Rear. Smooth bulge 9 × 5 × 0.75 inches high. Split in plate running from Round 107 to top edge for 7 inches, and from Round 107 below and to rear 4.5 inches. Weld split by Round 107 extended and opened. Rear main vertical welds inner and outer with tail plate split for full length alternatively in throat and junction. Weld—superstructure side plate and the pannier bottom split for 8 inches in junction.
Tank No. 3039. Front at 40 degrees. Superstructure side plate. (Right side)	Round 109. 17-pdr APCBC Mk 8T. (NCN) at 50 degrees to normal. Range 150 feet. Shell velocity 2,794 f.s.	Code D. (Sv.) Dent. Shot broke up. Rear. 0.5 × 5 × 1.125 inches high three star cracks 4.25 inches long × 0.0625 inches open max. Superstructure side and tail plate welding now completely split and side plate forced away 1.5 inches maximum at rear end. Base weld with pannier floor split from rear end to engine compartment bulkhead 6 feet 6 inches. Weld failure mainly in throat.
Tank No. 3039. Front at 40 degrees. Superstructure side plate. (Right side)	Round 110. 17-pdr APCBC Mk 8T. (NCN) at 50 degrees to normal. Range 150 feet. Shell velocity 2,849 f.s.	Rear portion of superstructure side plate over an area 25 × 20 inches removed. Plate split from top through Rounds 108 and 109. Shot broke up. Rear. Flake off armour missing from rear of displaced plate. Size unknown.
Tank No. 3039. Near front end at 40 degrees. Superstructure side plate. (Right side)	Round 111. 17-pdr APCBC Mk 8T. (NCN) at 50 degrees to normal. Range 150 feet. Shell velocity 2,524 f.s.	Code C. Struck 10 inches down from top edge. Rear. Smooth bulge 6 inches diameter × 0.375 inches high. Side plate to rear plate weld—old crack in junction opened.
Tank No. 3039. Front at 40 degrees. Superstructure side plate. (Right side)	Round 112. 17-pdr APCBC Mk 8T. (NCN) at 50 degrees to normal. Range 150 feet. Shell velocity 2,834 f.s.	Code C. Struck 6 inches down from top edge. Shot broke up. Rear. Metal sheared out over area 5 × 4 inches in several pieces. Bulkhead supporting angle sheared away. Welding split. Horizontal split from shot hole towards front 18 inches long. Bulkhead split immediately behind impact.
Tank No. 3039. Front at 40 degrees. Superstructure side plate. (Right side)	Round 113. 17-pdr APCBC Mk 8T. (NCN) at 50 degrees to normal. Range 150 feet. Shell velocity 2,894 f.s.	Code D. Struck 7 inches from bottom edge. Plate holed 5.5 × 3.5 inches. Plate split from top to bottom through Round 11? Total length 18 inches. Rear. Shot past through bulkhead to rear of vehicle. Metal off plate 7 × 6 inches. Pannier bulkhead further damaged and welding split.
Visor Plate. Front of vehicle at 40 degrees. Vertical angle of visor 10 degrees.	Round 114. 17-pdr APCBC at 43-degree compound angle to normal. Range 150 feet. Shell velocity 2,711 f.s.	Code C. Scoop off plate onto machine gun outer housing. Shot broke up. Outer housing removed roof plate previously split, further damaged. One-piece removed. Outer housing lying 10 yards in front of vehicle. Main visor and glacis weld further opened. Rear. Smooth bulge 8 × 6 × 0.375 inches high.
Visor Plate. Front of vehicle at 40 degrees. Vertical angle of visor 10 degrees.	Round 115. 17-pdr APCBC at 43-degree compound angle to normal. Range 150 feet. Shell velocity 2,823 f.s.	Code C. (Sv.) Struck above right hand corner of driver's visor. Scoop. Shot broke up. Rear. Main inner roof weld severely split over 2 feet length approximately, running into previous failure. Roof plate set up slightly above impact.
Visor Plate. Front of vehicle at 40 degrees. Vertical angle of visor 10 degrees.	Round 116. 17-pdr APCBC at 43-degree compound angle to normal. Range 150 feet. Shell velocity 2,942 f.s.	Code C. (Sv.) Struck 8.5 inches above joint with glacis. Shot broke up. Rear. Smooth bulge 6 × 5 × 0.75 inches high. Fan ducting behind impact forced away. Splits in main welding split and extended.

TARGET	ATTACK	OBSERVATIONS
Hull roof plate. Left-hand rear quarter forward of air inlet louvre	Round 117. One No. 75 AT grenade. No. 33 electric detonator.	Roof plate dished locally 0.5 inches maximum over 9 inches. Split in plate 15 inches long from edge of blast. Weld split in metal and junction with roof for 16 inches running into cross member supporting radiator louvres.
Turret roof behind loader's hatch and adjacent sidewalls.	Round 118. Two No. 75 AT grenade with No. 33 electric detonators detonated in parallel.	Roof plate dished 1.75 inches over 22 × 14 inches. Split in roof adjacent to side plate joint for 22 inches length, 0.375 inches maximum. Short split in weld junction with side plate 3 inches long. Loader's hatch mounting ring—four rivets sheared out. Rear edge of mounting ring lifted 0.4375 inches maximum.
Tank No. 3039. Superstructure side plate. (Left side)	Round 119. 17-pdr APCBC Mk 8T. (NCN) 3/43 at 45 degrees to normal. Range 150 feet. Shell velocity 2,701 f.s.	Code W. Struck 11 inches down from top edge. Hole 3.75 × 3 inches. Rear. Petal sheared off vertical weld scouring superstructure and tail plate split in junction with side plate for 6 inches.
Tank No. 3039. Superstructure side plate. (Left side)	Round 120. 17-pdr APCBC Mk 8T. (NCN) 3/43 at 45 degrees to normal. Range 150 feet. Shell velocity 2,528 f.s.	Code D. (S1.) Shot broke up. Scoop. Struck 6 inches down from top edge. Plate dished 0.375 inches over 2 feet. Rear. Cracked bulge 7.5 × 5 × 1 inch. Two short vertical cracks.
Tank No. 3039. Superstructure side plate. (Left side)	Round 121. 17-pdr APCBC Mk 8T. (NCN) 3/43 at 45 degrees to normal. Range 150 feet. Shell velocity 2,616 f.s.	Code D. (Sv.) Struck 7 inches down from top edge. Scoop. Shot broke up. Rear. Cracked bulge 6 × 5 × 1.5 inches. Three star cracks maximum open 0.375 inches. Bulkhead angle upright adjacent back damage broken away due to weld failure. Split in vertical bulkhead weld 12 inches long from top edge.
Tank No. 3039. Superstructure side plate. (Left side)	Round 122. 17-pdr APCBC Mk 8T. (NCN) 3/43 at 45 degrees to normal. Range 150 feet. Shell velocity 2,643 f.s.	Code W. Struck 11.5 inches down from top edge. Hole 4.5 × 3.5 inches. Rear. Petals sheared out. Main inner and outer welds securing side and tail plate split for length, open 0.5 inches maximum. Shot past through fan compartment and ricocheted off rear plate and perforated engine bulkhead in several places.
Tank No. 3039. Superstructure side plate. (Left side)	Round 123. 17-pdr APCBC Mk 8T. (NCN) 3/43 at 45 degrees to normal. Range 150 feet. Shell velocity 2,582 f.s.	Code D. Struck 11 inches down from top edge. Scoop. Shot broke up. Rear. Cracked bulge 8 × 8 × 1.25 inches. Two star crack 2 × 0.0625 inches open.
Tank No. 3039. Superstructure side plate. (Left side)	Round 124. 17-pdr APCBC Mk 8T. (NCN) 3/43 at 45 degrees to normal. Range 150 feet. Shell velocity 2,648 f.s.	Code NFH. Too close to Round 121. Plate holed.
Tank No. 3039. Superstructure side plate. (Left side)	Round 125. 17-pdr APCBC Mk 8T. (NCN) 3/43 at 45 degrees to normal. Range 150 feet. Shell velocity 2,613 f.s.	Code NFH. Too close to Round 124. Plate holed.
Tank No. 3039. Superstructure side plate. (Left side)	Round 126. 17-pdr APCBC Mk 8T. (NCN) 3/43 at 45 degrees to normal. Range 150 feet. Shell velocity 2,588 f.s.	Code W. Struck 7 inches above lower edge. Holed 4.5 × 3.5 inches. Side plate forced away 2 inches maximum at rear. Rear. Petals sheared out.
Tank No. 3039. Nose plate. Front of vehicle at normal.	Round 127. 17-pdr APCBC at 24 degrees to normal. Range 150 feet. Shell velocity 2,038 f.s.	Code D. (S1.) Struck 5.5 inches above the upper and lower nose plate joint. Main horizontal weld intact. Rear. Cracked bulge 6 × 5 × 1 inch high. Two short horizontal cracks. Main inner weld—upper and lower nose plate—split locally 7 inches long.
Tank No. 3039. Nose plate. Front of vehicle at normal.	Round 128. 17-pdr APCBC at 24 degrees to normal. Range 150 feet. Shell velocity 2,130 f.s.	Code R(L) Struck 12 inches down from top edge. Rear. Segments off. Nose broke up in fighting compartment.

TARGET	ATTACK	OBSERVATIONS
Tank No. 3039. Nose plate. Front of vehicle at normal.	Round 129. 17-pdr APCBC at 24 degrees to normal. Range 150 feet. Shell velocity 2,150 f.s.	Code W Struck 4.5 inches above joint with lower plate. Shot broke up. Rear. All segments off. Horizontal weld metal immediately below penetration sheared out. Welding either side intact. Peace of shot in fighting compartment.
Tank No. 3039. Nose plate. Front of vehicle at 30 degrees to normal.	Round 130. 17-pdr APCBC at 37 degrees to normal. Range 150 feet. Shell velocity 2,766 f.s.	Code W Struck 4 inches above joint with lower nose plate. Lower plate split 4.5 inches long adjacent to main weld. Vertical split from weld into shot hole 3 inches long. Rear. Metal off 5 × 3 inches. Rear weld metal sheared out 3 inches long. Lower nose plate bowed down 0.75 inches locally.
Tank No. 3039. Nose plate. Front of vehicle at 30 degrees to normal.	Round 131. 17-pdr APCBC at 37 degrees to normal. Range 150 feet. Shell velocity 2,703 f.s.	Code NFH. Struck 6 inches from Round 128. Shot through plate holed. Inspection of vehicle after attack showed that the main welding in the area attacked had failed severely. This was generally considered to be the result of cumulative attack. The right side superstructure plate showed brittle tendencies. Despite the weld and plate failure, it was apparent that the interlocked structure was still very strong.

APPENDIX B.

Trial No. X.812
AT No. 252 Part III
Pz.Kw.VI Tiger
Ballistic Attack

After Round 110: 17-pdr APCBC. The rear end of the right-side superstructure was broken away. (*DTD Materials Division, Armour Branch*)

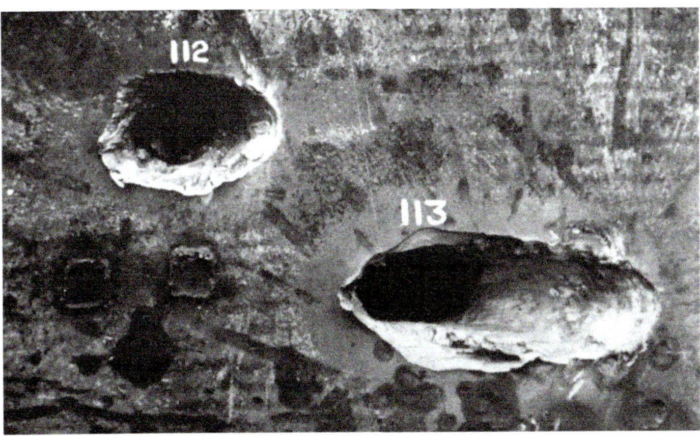

After Rounds 112 and 113 (17-pdr APCBC) on superstructure right side, giving an estimated W/R limit of 2,864 f.s. at 50 degrees. (*DTD Materials Division, Armour Branch*)

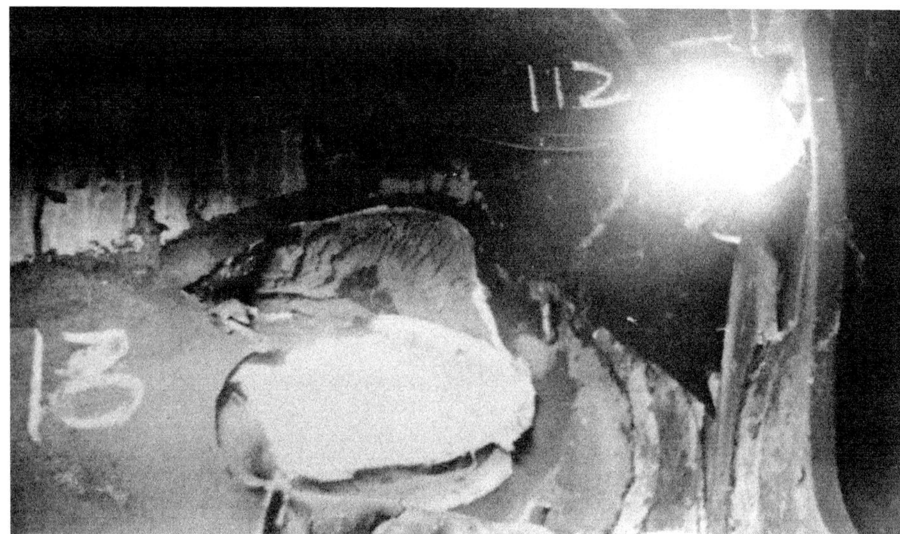

Rear damage from Rounds 112 and 113 on superstructure right side. Note the flaky nature of back damage. (*DTD Materials Division, Armour Branch*)

Showing effect of Round 114 (17-pdr APCBC) on visor plate at 43-degree compound angle. Note the machine gun's outer housing was forced off. Fixing bolts remained in the outer housing. (*DTD Materials Division, Armour Branch*)

Further view of hull roof damage initially caused by Round 75, further increased by Round 114. (*DTD Materials Division, Armour Branch*)

Showing strikes on nose plate by Rounds 128 and 129 (17-pdr APCBC) at 24 degrees, gave an estimated W/R at 2,140 f.s. (*DTD Materials Division, Armour Branch*)

Showing strikes on rear side superstructure by Rounds 108 and 107 (17-pdr APCBC at 50 degrees to normal), and 104 (6-pdr APCBC 20 degress to normal). (*DTD Materials Division, Armour Branch*)

Showing No. 75 Hawkins grenade in position on the hull roof. (*DTD Materials Division, Armour Branch*)

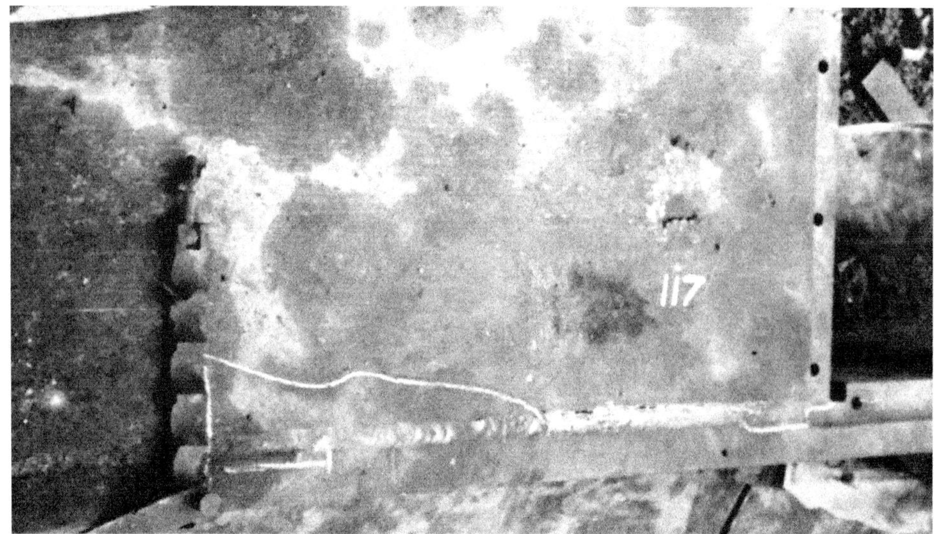

Showing effects of No. 75 grenade. Note the plate and weld split indicated by chalk line. (*DTD Materials Division, Armour Branch*)

Showing two No. 75 Hawkings grenades in position on turret roof. (*DTD Materials Division, Armour Branch*)

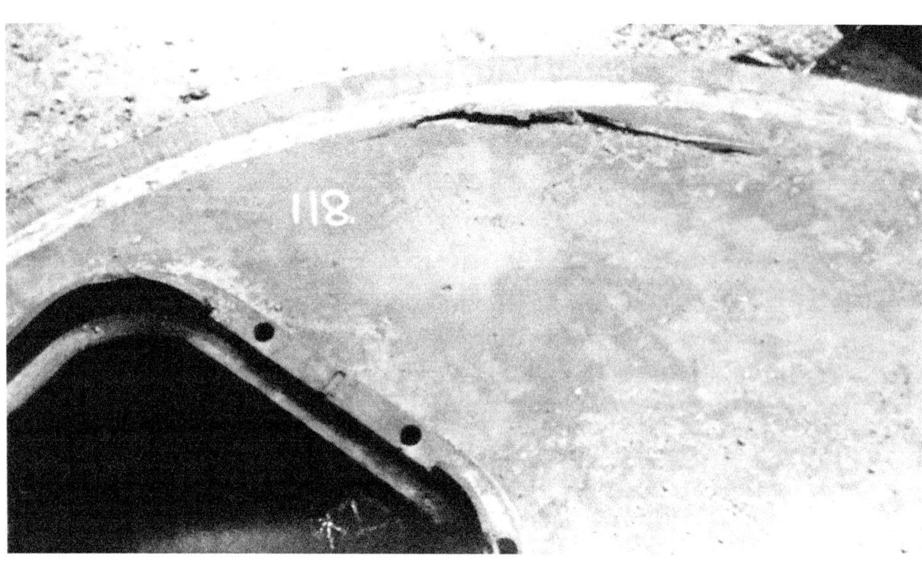

Showing effect of two No. 75 grenades. Note the loader's hatch mounting ring bolt holes from which bolts were projected into turret. (*DTD Materials Division, Armour Branch*)

Showing condition of welding on the rear roof/superstructure after trial. (*DTD Materials Division, Armour Branch*)

Showing condition of welding on the forward roof/superstructure after trial. Note the roof plate failure. (*DTD Materials Division, Armour Branch*)

Showing condition of left side superstructure/rear plate joint after trial. (*DTD Materials Division, Armour Branch*)

16

PART IV: FIRING TRIALS AGAINST Pz.Kw. VI (TIGER) 26–27 APRIL 1945

The information in this chapter has been transcribed from original wartime documents. The report format and brief notation style has been kept.

DTD EXPERIMENTAL REPORT
AT NO. 252
PART IV

Project No. M. 6816A/10
Trial No X. 857
File No 250/14/4

Report of Firing Trials Against Pz.Kw. VI (Tiger)
Held at S. of E. Range, Shoeburyness on 26 and 27 April 1945

Present at Trial	Representing	Dates
Lt. Tredinnick	S. of E. Range officer	23rd, 24th & 25th
Mr. Gray	DTD Armour Branch	23rd, 24th & 25th
Mr. Wilde	DTD Armour Branch	23rd, 24th & 25th
Report		
	Compiled by:- Mr. G.W. Gray—DTD Armour Branch	
	Checked by:- Mr. J.B. Sankey—DTD Armour Branch	

References			
	Section I.	-	Object of Trial.
	Section II.	-	Target Details.
	Section III.	-	Method of Attack.
	Section IV.	-	Trial Commentary
	Section V.	-	Conclusion
Appendices			
	Appendix A.	-	Detailed Results.
	Appendix B.	-	Photographic Record.

	Appendix C.	-	Sketch.
Note:-			
	This report must not be reproduced in full or in part without the written authority of the Director of Tank Design.		

SECTION I

Object of Trial

To determine the degree of resistance of the tracks, suspensions, and hull/floor plate structure, to attack from various anti-tank mines, and 'nests' of No. 75 Hawkins grenades.

SECTION II

Target Details

Pz.Kw. VI (Tiger) Tank DTD No. 3039. Hull and turret, together with tracks and suspensions, as used for Trial No. X. 812. Approximate weight of vehicle, less engine, transmission, etc., 45 tons.

SECTION III

Method of Attack.

The target was attacked with the following AT mines and Hawkins grenades.

(1) Two standard Mk V AT mines, placed one on another

(2) Ten standard No. 75 Hawkins AT grenades in two 'nests' of five, 1 nest above the other.

(3) One box of twelve grenades plus three placed on top.

In each case the charge was buried in undisturbed meadowland, so that a centre line taken through the charge would be immediately beneath the inner edge of the track. The distances from the top of the charge to the track underside was two inches. Reference to the sketch, Appendix C, indicates the position of charge relative to the hull/floor plate structure.

SECTION IV

Trial Commentary

The hull side/floor plate structure was built with a stopped joint secured by inner and outer fillet welds. The floor plate was 26 mm and the hull side plate 63 mm thick.

1. Mines under inner edge of track in line with No. 3 left-hand bogie.

Two standard Mk V mines placed one above the other and detonated in this position, broke the track completely. The final drive casing which had been badly damaged during Part II of this series of trials was broken away. Numbers one and two bogie axles were sheared through and number three outer bogie disc was thrown clear of the vehicle. The hull side/floor plate structure remained intact.

Damage caused to tracks and suspensions would have immobilised the vehicle, but casualties to the crew would probably not have occurred.

2. Grenades under inner edge of track in line with No. 7 left-hand bogies.

This test was carried out for the purpose of comparison with 1.

Ten No. 75 Hawkins AT grenades 'nested' in two rows of five, one row above the other, were detonated in this position. In this case also the track was completely severed. Number 8 bogie axles were sheared through. Number 7 bogie assembly complete with torsion bar was displaced.

Apart from local pitting of the hull floor, no measurable damage was caused to the structure. The suspension failure would in this case also have immobilised the vehicle. Casualties to the crew were considered unlikely.

3. Grenades under inner edge of track in line with No. 7 right-hand bogies.

It was required to know what effect a box of 12 No. 75 Hawkins AT grenades plus three placed on top of the box, would have on an enemy vehicle of this class. One fuse in the top layer of three grenades was wired in parallel with the fuses fitted to three grenades within the box. The resulting detonation completely severed the track. Numbers 5, 6, and 7 bogie assemblies were removed.

Examination of the floor plate indicated a very slight bulging and some surface pitting, but the structure was still intact. The pannier floor plate above the area of blast was split by this attack. Damage to vehicle track and suspensions was very considerable and precluded any possibility of field repairs.

Since the hull structure was left intact, it is reasonable to expect that the crew escaped injury.

SECTION V

Conclusions

1. It is concluded that the effect of the two Standard Mk V AT mines against the track and suspensions of the Tiger when detonated under the inner edge of the track, is such that the resulting damage would arrest the vehicle. Repairs would be of a nature precluding their being made in the field. The effect of blast on the floor plate was negligible.

2. There is very little to choose between the effect of the two Standard Mk V AT mines and ten No. 75 Hawkins AT grenades, the latter caused slightly greater damage. As in 1. the effect on the hull floor was negligible.

3. A box of twelve plus three grenades caused more damage than did either of the charges used in 1 and 2, but failed to defeat the floor plate. The resulting slight bulge would not be likely to cause any injury to the crew.

Finally it is considered that two Standard Mk V AT mines produce results indicating these as being the best mine and least charge required for the purpose of completely immobilising the tank.

It is apparent from results that success against the floor plate could be obtained only with a charge considerably greater than anything used in this trial.

G. Guthrie, Major, R.E.M.E.
Officer i/c Armour Trials Section, Armour Branch,
12.6.45 M.998(S) SCB.

APPENDIX A

SECRET
Trial No. X.867
Detailed Results: Mine Trial

TARGET	ATTACK	OBSERVATIONS
Tank No. 3039. Hull and floor plate structure. Upper inner edge of left-hand track in line with No. 3 bogie. Tank floor to ground level 1 foot 5 inches	Item No. 14. Two Standard Mk V. AT mines (one above the other).Four CE pellets. Two No. 33 detonators in parallel. Mine 2 inches below ground level.	Track completely severed. In a disc of No. 1 road wheel, together with axle, sheared off. Final drive casing and sprocket wheels thrown clear of vehicle. No. 2 bogie axle sheared through. No. 3 outer disc sheared and thrown clear of vehicle. Note: Final drive was already partially severed as a result of AP attack. Hull floor and side plate structure remained intact. No damage to floor plate structure. Several strikes on plate—largest 0.5 × 0.0625 inches deep. Crater size 10 × 9 × 3 feet deep. Vehicle immobilised. Field repair improbable.
Hull and floor plate structure. Under inner edge of left-hand track in line with No. 7 bogie. Tank floor to ground level 1 foot 6 inches.	Item No. 15. Ten standard No. 75 grenades arranged in two layers of five. Four No. 33 detonators in parallel. (Two in top row) (Two in bottom row) Top of grenades 2 inches below ground level.	Track completely severed. No. 7 bogie displaced sideways still on axle. No. 8 bogie axle sheared through. No. 7 bogie discs split and torn. On lifting No. 7 bogie assembly including torsion bar fell out. Floor structure not affected. Slight pitting of plates by fragments. Crater size 12 × 13 × 4 feet deep. Vehicle immobilised. Repair in field not possible.
Hull and floor plate structure. Under inner edge of right-hand track in line with No. 7 bogie. Tank floor to ground level 1 foot 4.5 inches.	Item No. 16. Box of twelve No. 75 AT grenades plus three No. 75 AT grenades on top of box. Four No. 33 detonators in parallel. (one in top three) Top of upper grenades 2 inches below ground level.	Track sheared through and rear lengths thrown over top of vehicle. Bogie assemblies Nos. 5, 6 and 7, completely removed—suspension arms sheared off. No. 7 thrown three yards clear of the vehicle. Top run of track immediately above mine partially sheared. Floor plate—side plate welded joint intact. Vehicle totally immobilised. Floor plate dished 0.1875 inches maximum over 4 feet in length—fore and aft—immediately above detonation. Pannier floor plate split for 6 feet running to split in weld with superstructure side at forward end. Main scallop weld angle front with lower hull side intact. Crater size—12-foot diameter × 3 foot 6 inches deep. Vehicle immobilised. Workshop repairs necessary.

APPENDIX B

Trial No. X.867
AT No. 252 Part IV
Mine Trial

Item 14. Effect of two standard Mk V mines detonated under the inner edge of track in line with No. 3 left-hand bogie. The vehicle was immobilised by this attack. (*DTD Materials Division, Armour Branch*)

Item 14. Further view of damage caused by Item 14. Note the final drive had been severely damaged during part two of trial. (*DTD Materials Division, Armour Branch*)

Item 14. View from front of vehicle, showing No. 1 bogie hub sheared through. Note the floor structure remained intact. (*DTD Materials Division, Armour Branch*)

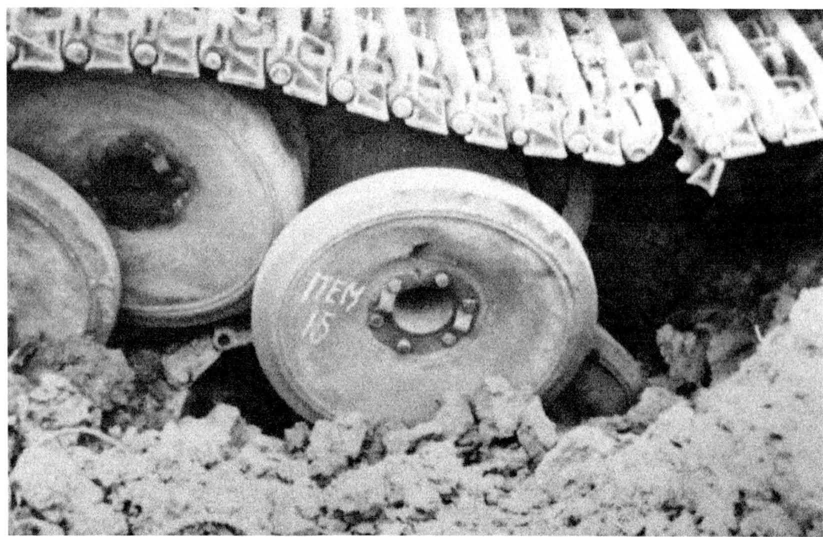

Item 15. Effect of ten No. 75 Hawkins grenades, detonated under the inner edge of track in line with No. 7 left-hand bogie. The vehicle was immobilised by this attack. (*DTD Materials Division, Armour Branch*)

Item 15. Further view of damage caused by Item 15. Note No. 8 bogie has fallen into a crater through a failure of axle. (*DTD Materials Division, Armour Branch*)

Item 15. Showing No. 7 bogie and torsion bar assembly, which came away on lifting the tank. Note the floor structure remained intact. (*DTD Materials Division, Armour Branch*)

Item 16. Effect of one box of twelve plus three No. 75 Hawkins grenades, detonated under the inner edge of track in line with No. 7 right-hand bogie. No. 7 bogie shown in the foreground. The vehicle was immobilised by this attack. (*DTD Materials Division, Armour Branch*)

Item 16. Further view of damage caused by Item 16. Note Nos 5 and 6 bogies in crater. (*DTD Materials Division, Armour Branch*)

Item 16. Close-up of displaced Nos 5 and 6 bogies and partial shearing of top track. Note the floor structure remained intact. (*DTD Materials Division, Armour Branch*)

APPENDIX C

Trial No. X.867
AT No. 252 Part IV
Mine Trial

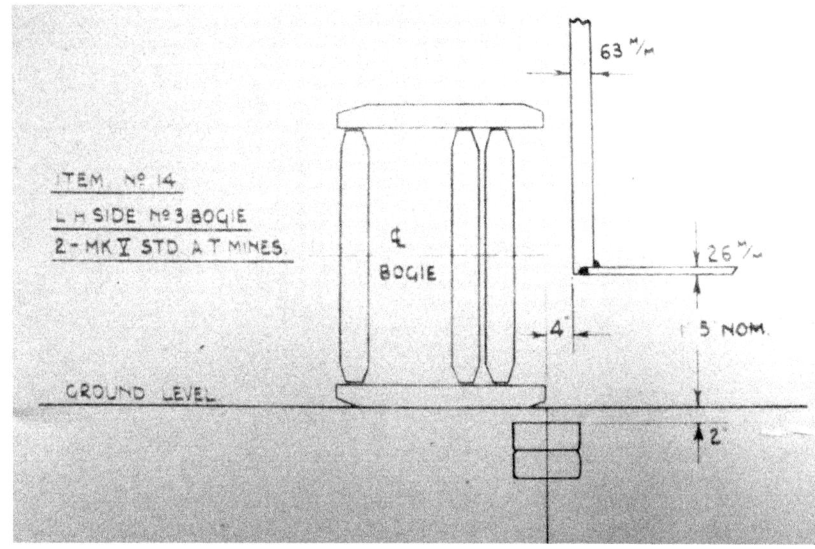

Left-hand side No. 3 bogie. Two Mk V standard AT mines. (*DTD Materials Division, Armour Branch*)

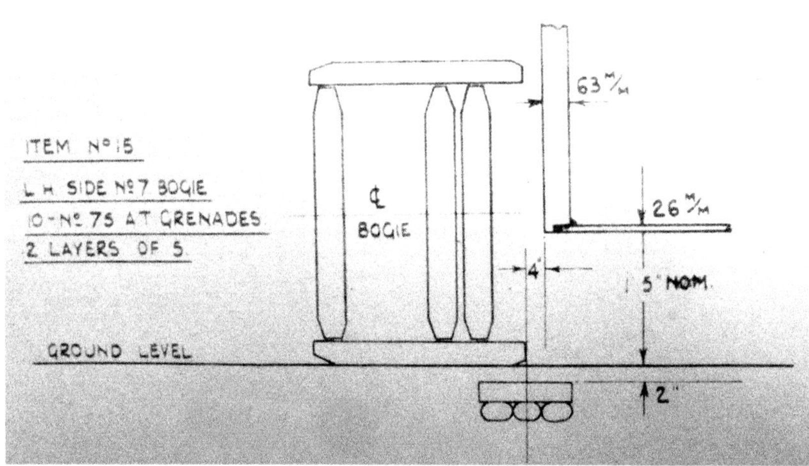

Left-hand side No. 7 bogie. Ten No. 75 AT grenades, two layers of five. (*DTD Materials Division, Armour Branch*)

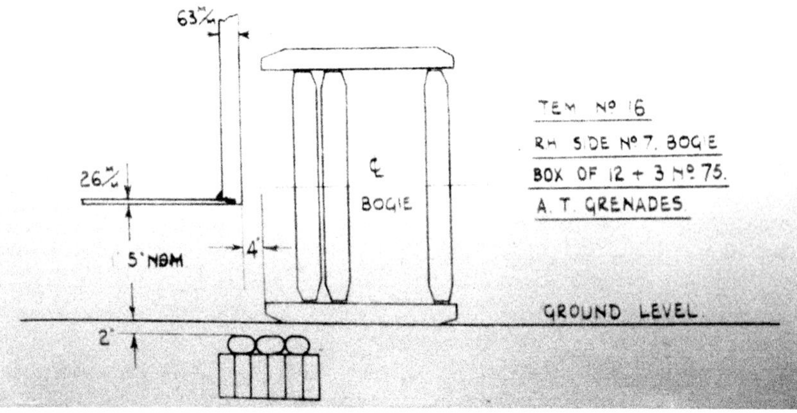

Right-hand side No. 7 bogie. Box of twelve and three No. 75 AT grenades. (*DTD Materials Division, Armour Branch*)

ADDITIONAL COMMENTS (A LETTER OF COMPLAINT)

To G. Guthrie, Major, R.E.M.E.
Officer i/c Armour Trials Section, Armour Branch,
AT Report 252: Pz.Kw.VI (Tiger)

In connection with the above report, I wish to record certain aspects of the findings during this trial and the conclusions drawn therefrom. This is done in a desire to ensure that no feature likely to assist the future development is overlooked, and also since certain omissions from the original report may lead some to believe that insufficient point was made of these features in the report.

I notice on reading through the final reproduction of this report certain omissions from my original statements, which in my view prejudice the value of the results of this trial to no small extent. Very considerable time and thought has been given to this subject, and to find that the data, giving, I submit, most useful information for future guidance, if omitted reduces very considerably the value of one's efforts.

I have been concerned in the trials on both the Panther and Tiger tanks and have had an excellent opportunity to study the behaviour of the main structure against attack. I submit as the result of this opportunity that very serious consideration should be given to the development of Tank hull and turret structures on the lines shown to such advantage in the two German vehicles. With this in view, I intentionally repeated in my original script the value of interlocking in the belief that welding can be considered in a secondary light, and that full advantage should be taken by locking together the armour plates to give the structural strength of the vehicle. This, I think may become even more essential as the thickness of plates increase.

AT252
Cover Sheet

'The design of the vehicle is such that its structural stability is immense. This is achieved by stepped and interlocking joints, and does not depend, except in a secondary way, on welding. However the welding failed generally only after repeated impacts.'

AT252, Part II
Section IX—Conclusions

'It is very apparent that the construction of the vehicle does not rely on welding, and the use made of the principles of interlocking plates and stepped joints ensures considerable stability even when the welding has failed.'

AT252, Part III
Section VII: Conclusions
Welds and Structure

'The structure of the tank proved extremely satisfactory and emphasised beyond question the value of interlocking given by mortice and stepped joints. It was apparent that even when the welding failed over large areas the structure was still extremely rigid, indicating that welding becomes entirely of secondary importance in the construction of this vehicle.'

G.W. Gray
Department of Tank Design, Armour Branch.
GWG/GB 4.7.1945

17

BRITISH ANTI-TANK WEAPONS

An Ordnance QF 17-pdr anti-tank gun without its gun shield and sights, being restored at Adrian Barrell's workshops in Suffolk, England.

THE ORDNANCE QF 17-PDR ANTI-TANK GUN

The 17-pdr gun's full name was Ordnance QF 17 pounder. It was a British tradition to naming their guns after the weight of the shot. The letters QF stand for 'quick firing'. It had a calibre of 3 inches (76.2 mm) and a muzzle velocity that ranged from 2,900 f.s. (884 m/s) to 3,950 f.s. (1,204 m/s) depending on the type of ammunition used.

A towed version was produced, and it was also modified to fit into tank turrets and onto tank hulls to be used as an anti-tank self-propelled gun.

The first 17-pdr prototype was produced in the spring of 1942. With news of the arrival of the heavily armoured Tiger tank in the deserts of North Africa, it was rushed into production. Some of the early production guns built in Glasgow were fitted onto 25-pdr howitzer carriages and called '17pr, Mk 2 carriage'. The communications codename 'Pheasants' was assigned to them. If the Germans intercepted any radio traffic about the gun's arrival, it was hoped they would believe an officer had ordered a delivery of game birds for his dinner table. They first saw action in February 1943.

The next delivery of guns was fitted with their bespoke new gun carriage. They saw service in Sicily and on the Italian mainland. They were very effective. Anti-tank regiment units deployed them in north-west Europe from D-Day until the end of the war.

A 'Pheasant' Ordnance QF 17-pdr anti-tank gun mounted on a 25-pdr gun carriage, in action on the Medenine Front, 11 March 1943.

The Mk I was the first production version of the 17-pdr anti-tank gun. The Mk II was used on the Archer self-propelled gun and the A30 Cruiser Mark VIII Challenger tank. The gun carriage mountings were modified so that it would fit in these vehicles. Initially, the muzzle brake was removed and replaced with a counterweight, but with the introduction of the more powerful APCBC rounds, the muzzle brake was refitted. The Mk III was used by the Royal Navy on landing craft. The Mk IV was adapted to fit in the Sherman Firefly turret. The breech block slid to the side rather than down so as to take up less room. The Mk V version used different gun mounts to enable it to fit into the US-built 3-inch Gun Motor Carriage M10 and replace its 3-inch 76.2-mm M7 gun.

The QF 17-pdr Mk II was fitted into the A30 Cruiser Mark VIII Challenger tank. They were issued to tank regiments equipped with 75-mm armed Cromwell tanks. The A30 Challenger used an adapted Cromwell tank hull so this helped in logistics; the engineers only had to carry Cromwell hull spare parts. Where possible, one Challenger tank was assigned to three Cromwell tanks. It provided a more powerful anti-tank over-watch capability.

The turret had to be totally redesigned to enable the 17-pdr gun to be mounted on the tank hull. It was of a vertical slab armour plate design. To keep the weight of the tank low, the front of the turret armour was only 63 mm thick. The sides were 40 mm thick. The Cromwell tank's turret had 75-mm armour on the front and 60-mm armour on the side. The hull machine gun was removed to provide extra space for the larger 17-pdr shells. Only 200 were built as priority was given to building more Sherman Firefly tanks and the new A34 Comet tank. They saw action in north-west Europe following D-Day.

Over 2,000 17-pdr Sherman Firefly tanks were built. They were issued to tank regiments equipped with 75-mm Sherman tanks, or Cromwell tanks. Where possible, one firefly tank fought alongside three 75-mm Sherman tanks, or three Cromwell tanks. They provided over-watch as they could knock out enemy tanks at a longer distance.

The front half of the longer 17-pdr barrels were often painted a lighter colour to make it appear the tank was only armed with the shorter barrelled 75-mm gun. The Germans quickly realised that the Firefly was a big threat and was the first tank to be targeted if it could be identified.

The 40-inch (1-m) recoil of the towed Mk 1 was too long to work in a tank turret. The recoil system was redesigned. The cylinders were shortened and placed on either side of the gun. On the Sherman Firefly tank, the gun breech now loaded from the left side after it was rotated 90 degrees.

The Sherman Firefly's hull machine gun was removed to enable the larger 17-pdr ammunition to be stored. It still had a coaxial Browning .30-calibre (7.62-mm) machine gun in the turret. Although the turret size was increased with a bustle at the back to house the radio, the armour thickness was not increased apart from an extra 13 mm added to the new gun mantlet. They saw action in north-west Europe following D-Day.

A 17-pdr A30 Cruiser Mark VIII Challenger tank at the Overloon Museum, Holland.

A 17-pdr Sherman Firefly tank at Bastogne Barracks, Belgium.

A 17-pdr self-propelled anti-tank gun, *Archer*, at the Overloon Museum, Holland.

The British 17-pdr self-propelled anti-tank gun Archer entered production in mid-1943, and 655 were built. They entered service in October 1944 and saw action in north-west Europe. In 1942, the British High Command knew they quickly needed a long-range anti-tank gun fitted to a tracked hull that could take on the Tiger tank. It was too big to fit into any of the current British tank turrets then in service. The Valentine tank hull had proven itself to be reliable. Vickers engineers decided to remove the Valentine tank's turret and place the gun behind the driver with the long barrel pointing backwards over the engine deck. The gun crew were protected from small arms fire and shrapnel by a raised, open-topped superstructure.

It was designed as a low-profile ambush weapon. The rearward firing capability was seen as an advantage. It did not have to turn around to retreat. The Archer would back into a position, fire at the target, then drive off at full speed to avoid enemy return fire. This tactic was known as 'shoot and scoot'.

The British Army in the Second World War did not use the American Army term 'Tank Destroyer'. Vehicles like the Archer were called self-propelled anti-tank guns.

The British Army converted 1,100 US-built 3-inch Gun Motor Carriage M10s by replacing its 3-inch (76.2-mm) M7 gun with the more powerful QF 17-pdr gun. This also helped with logistics as ammunition could be sourced from Britain rather than relying on US Army supplies.

They were given the designation 17-pdr self-propelled anti-tank gun M10c Achilles. The letter 'c' indicated that the vehicle was armed with a 17-pdr gun. They saw action with the Royal Artillery and the Royal Canadian Artillery in north-west Europe and took part in the Battle of the Bulge, Ardennes offensive. The gun was enclosed in an open-topped turret.

It was powered by a General Motors 6046 conjoined twin 6-71s diesel engine that produced 375 hp. It has a top road speed of 32 mph (52 km/h) with an operational range of around 186 miles (300 km). It had a five-man crew: commander, driver, gunner, loader, and loaders assistant. Its armour was thin but sloped. It ranged from 9 mm to 57.2 mm in thickness.

A number of other vehicles were fitted with the 17-pdr gun, but these were only prototype versions and did not enter into mass production: Centurion Mk 1, Black Prince, Avenger, AC4 Sentinel, Terrapin 2, Tortoise, Grizzly Firefly, and the TOG.

The 17-pdr tank APCBC (amour piercing capped ballistic cap) round projectile weighed 17 lb (7.71 kg). The complete APCBC round weighed 37.5 lb (17 kg). The 17-pdr tank-mounted gun fired the APCBC round at a muzzle velocity of 2,900 f.s. (884 m/s). Firing range penetration performance trials data show that the 17-pdr APCBC round, when fired at homogeneous armour set at a 30-degree angle could penetrate 140 mm of armour at 500 yards (457 m), 130 mm at 1,000 yards (914 m), 120 mm at 1,500 yards (1.37 km) and 111 mm at 2,000 yards (1.83 km).

The 17-pdr tank APDS (amour piercing discarding sabot) round projectile weighed 7.9 lb (3.58 kg). The complete APDS round weighed 28.4 lb (12.88 kg). The 17-pdr tank-mounted gun fired the APDS round at a muzzle velocity of 3,950 f.s. (1204 m/s). Firing range penetration performance trials data show that the 17-pdr APDS round, when fired at homogeneous armour set at a 30-degree angle, could penetrate 208 mm of armour at 500 yards (457 m), 192 mm at 1,000 yards (914 m), 176 mm at 1,500 yards (1.37 km), and 161 mm at 2,000 yards (1.83 km).

A 17-pdr self-propelled anti-tank gun M10c, *Achilles*, at Bastogne Barracks, Belgium.

THE ORDNANCE QF 6-PDR ANTI-TANK GUN

At a range up to 1.2 km, the British 2-pdr tank gun could penetrate the 30-mm frontal armour of the German Panzer III tanks that were used during the Battle of France in 1940 and all Italian tanks encountered in the deserts of North Africa. This situation changed when the Germans upgraded their tank's frontal armour to 50 or 60 mm. The armour-piercing rounds were no longer able to penetrate that thickness of armour. The British needed a bigger, more powerful anti-tank gun.

A new anti-tank gun was already in development at the Woolwich Arsenal in London. It was called the Ordnance QF 6-pounder (6-pdr) after the British tradition of naming their guns after the weight of the shot. The letters QF stand for 'quick firing'. It had a calibre of 57 mm and a muzzle velocity that ranged from 2,700 f.s. (820 m/s) to 4,000 f.s. (1,219 m/s) depending on the type of ammunition used.

The gun was completed in 1940, but work on the gun carriage design was not finished until 1941. Production started in November 1941, and the first towed version of the 6-pdr entered service in May 1942.

A modified 6-pdr gun was fitted into the Crusader Mk III tank turret. It was also mounted in the turrets of the Valentine Mk IX and Churchill Mk III and IV tanks. The AEC armoured car Mk II was also armed with the 6-pdr anti-tank gun. The Centaur, Cavalier, and Cromwell tanks were designed to be armed with the 6-pdr gun. The Cromwell was upgraded and armed with the Ordnance QF 75-mm gun when it was deployed to the beaches of Normandy in June 1944.

One of the advantages of the 6-pdr was that it could fire a variety of ammunition including HE shells. This was one of the tank crew criticisms of the 2-pdr gun; it could only fire AP rounds. A 2-pdr HE round was developed later but not issued to tank crews.

The introduction of the towed 6-pdr anti-tank gun in the deserts of North Africa meant that crews could once again knock out German tanks. In 1943, the 6-pdr gun crews could choose to load AP, APC, APCBC, and HE shells.

In 1944, the introduction of more sophisticated anti-tank ammunition in the form of the APCR shot and the APDS shot helped increase the potency of the gun.

The first massed produced version was called the Mk 2. It had the shorter L/43 barrel. The 6-pdr Mk 3 was the tank gun version of the Mk 2. The Mk 4 had a longer L/50 barrel and had a single baffle muzzle brake fitted. The Mk 5 was the tank gun version of the Mk 4.

The 6-pdr tank AP round projectile weighed 6.28 lb (2.84 kg). The complete AP round weighed 12.92 lb (5.86 kg). The 6-pdr Mk 3 tank gun fired the AP round at a muzzle velocity of 2,830 f.s. (862.58 m/s). The 6-pdr Mk 5 tank gun fired it at 2,920 f.s. (890 m/s).

The 6-pdr tank APCBC round projectile weighed 7.27 lb (3.30 kg). The complete APCBC round weighed 13.88 lb (6.29 kg). The 6-pdr Mk 3 tank gun fired the APCBC round at a muzzle velocity of 2,580 f.s. (789 m/s). The 6-pdr Mk 5 tank gun fired it at 2,700 f.s. (823 m/s).

The A15, Cruiser Mk VI, and Crusader Mk III were the first tank to be armed with the Ordnance QF 6 pdr anti-tank gun. It had previously been armed with a QF 2-pdr gun. The tank featured Christie suspension, coupled with a relatively powerful V-12 350-hp engine; this gave the Crusader tank greater speed and manoeuvrability compared to others in 1941, especially on flat terrain, as found in the North African landscape. It was built by Nuffield Mechanisations & Aero Ltd.

The 40-mm frontal armour on the early Crusader tanks was strong enough to prevent the early German 3.7-mm anti-tank gun from penetrating its armour. Most Italian tank main guns would also have great difficulty penetrating the Crusader's frontal armour in 1940. The frontal glacis armoured plate was sloped. The sides and rear of the turret were also sloped, but the rear and sides of the hull were vertical and more vulnerable. The arrival of Rommel and his upgraded Panzer III tanks in Africa in January 1941 made the need for a gun more effective than the 2-pdr urgent.

The mounting of the 6-pdr gun into the small Crusader turret led to a complete redesign of the interior. The frontal armour was increased to 2 inches thick (51 mm). Better protection was fitted for the turret mounting and around the ammunition racks. The ventilation system was improved to deal with the gasses and smoke from the new gun. The loader was removed from the crew. His job was now done by the tank commander. Due to limited space, there was only room for fifty of the larger 6-pdr shells compared to 110 for the previous 2-pdr gun. They saw action in Tunisia, Sicily, and Italy.

Valentine Mk VII, IX, and X tanks were initially armed with the 6-pdr gun. In 1941, up-armoured German tanks were used against British and Commonwealth forces in the deserts of North Africa. The early production Valentine tank's 2-pdr gun was no longer effective. Vickers engineers came up with a modified turret design that would accommodate the long-barrel 6-pdr gun. The coaxial Besa machine gun was removed as part of this process.

An Ordnance QF 6-pdr towed anti-tank gun at Adrian Barrell's workshops in Suffolk, England. (*Adrian Barrell*)

The A15, Cruiser Mk VI, Crusader Mk III tank armed with a 6-pdr gun.

This Valentine DD tank is armed with a 6-pdr gun. It is owned and restored by John Pearson.

This Churchill Mk III tank armed with a 6-pdr gun is on display at the Canadian War Museum, Ottawa, Canada.

The Valentine tank was not as fast as the Crusader tank. It was designed as an infantry tank, not a fast cruiser tank. Not being able to fire high-explosive shells against enemy fortifications, machine gun positions, artillery batteries, and soft-skinned vehicles was a negative feature on an infantry support tank. This inability was corrected with the introduction of the 6-pdr gun that could fire HE shells.

The Valentine Mark VIII tank received the British AEC A190 diesel engine. The Valentine Mark IX, an up-gunned Valentine Mark V tank, retaining the US-built GMC 6004 diesel. The Valentine Mark X was virtually identical to the IX, but at the start incorporated the new GMC diesel, and a redesigned turret that reintroduced the coaxial machine gun. They saw action in North Africa, the Eastern Front, North-West Europe, Burma, and Italy. Some were later armed with a 75-mm gun.

The first Churchill Mk I tank rolled out of the factory gates in June 1941. It was designed as a slow-moving, heavily armed infantry support tank that could cross trenches. Officially it was named in honour of the memory of Sir Winston Churchill's seventeenth-century ancestor, Sir John Churchill, 1st duke of Marlborough and not the prime minister. It was intended to replace the Matilda and Valentine infantry tanks.

Churchill Mk III tank was manufactured with a completely new turret and internal configuration to enable the 6-pdr gun to replace the turret 2-pdr gun, used in early versions and to be able to stow the larger 6-pdr shells. The Churchill tank now had the capability of going against up-armoured German Panzer III/IV tanks in North Africa and proved instrumental during the second battle of El Alamein. They also knocked out some Tiger tanks.

THE PIAT

The PIAT was a British infantry shoulder-fired anti-tank weapon that entered service in 1943. The abbreviation PIAT stands for projector, infantry, anti-tank. It is not a Bazooka. That was a shoulder-fired recoilless anti-tank rocket launcher. The PIAT uses a spring not a rocket to propel the armour-piercing shaped charge warhead towards its target.

The PIAT used a spigot mortar system to launch a 2.5-lb (1.1-kg) high-explosive, armour-piercing shaped charge. The round had a propellant filled cartridge in its tail. It was a short-range weapon. To be effective, the soldier had to wait until the enemy vehicle was within 115 yards (105 m), and if he was firing at a heavily armoured tank like the Panther or Tiger, he had to aim at a weak spot where the armour was thinner like the side of the tank.

One of the advantages of the PIAT over the rocket-firing Bazooka was that there was no dangerous backblast or smoke trail that gave away the soldier's position to an observant enemy.

The PIAT had problems. It was hard to cock the weapon as the spring in the spigot mortar system was very stiff. It had a heavy kick. If the user was not pushing the shoulder pad hard against his shoulder, he would get a severe bruise. The barrel had to be looked after and handled with care. It was fragile and could easily get damaged. The most serious problem was that the ammunition was sometimes unreliable. Faulty fuses meant that 25 per cent of the rounds failed to detonate when they hit their target. Accuracy was also a problem.

Men from 1st Canadian Parachute Battalion with PIAT anti-tank weapon in Lembeck, Germany, on 29 March 1945. (*Canadian National Archives*)

Cocking the weapon and loading the initial round took time. The operator was already very close to the enemy and vulnerable to counter-attack if his location was spotted. Although the weapon could be operated by one man, it was usually assigned to two soldiers. The second man carried additional ammunition and loaded the rounds while looking out for additional threats.

The PIAT was first used by British and Commonwealth forces in the invasion of Sicily and later Italy in 1943. They were issued to troops boarding ships destined for the D-Day beaches of Normandy as well as the paratroopers.

It was designed by Lieutenant Colonel Stewart Blacker and enhanced by Major Millis Jefferis. In the factory contract documentation, the PIAT is also described as the 'Jefferis Shoulder Gun' or the 'Jefferis Shoulder Projector'. The weapon was manufactured by Imperial Chemical Industries Ltd and later by various other factories in Britain. The contract record is dated 17 May 1942 and around 115,000 were built during the Second World War. They weighed 32 lb (15 kg) and were 3 feet 3 inches (99 cm) long. The weapon had a muzzle velocity of 250 f.s. (76 m/s).

The PIAT round was a shaped charge. This consisted of a recessed metal cone placed into an explosive warhead, when the round hit the armour plate of a tank, the explosive detonated and turned the cone into an extremely high-speed spike. The speed of the spike and the immense pressure it caused on impact allowed it to create a small hole in armour plating and send a large pressure wave and large amounts of armour plate fragments into the interior of the tank. These sharp jagged hot splinters of metal of different sizes ripped through the flesh of the crew, fuel tanks, radiators, and engines, into ammunition causing fires and explosions.

The round used in the PIAT had a long name—Bomb, HE/AT, Infantry Projector, AT Mk 1. It was put into a trough at the front of the PIAT barrel. When the trigger was pulled, the spring rammed the metal spigot rod into the tail of the bomb, igniting the propellant charge in the tail cartridge and launching it out of the barrel.

The main criticism of the weapon was how difficult it was to initially cock. The shoulder butt of the PIAT had to be placed on the ground. The soldier then had to put two feet on the butt while he turned the weapon to unlock the body and, at the same time, lock the firing pin to the butt. He would then have to bend over and pull the body of the weapon upwards. This had the effect of pulling the spring back until it attached to the trigger and cocking the weapon. Then he had to lower the body of the weapon and turn it to reattach it to the rest of the weapon. You needed strength to operate the PIAT, and you had to be relatively tall.

This procedure did not have to be repeated after firing the weapon. The recoil caused by the explosion of the bomb propellant forced the firing spigot pin backwards onto the spring. This automatically cocked the PIAT, and a new round could be placed in the trough at the front of the barrel.

Replica PIAT used for Second World War re-enactments.

The front gun sight is above the firing trigger and the rear one by the canvas barrel cover.

The front trough section of the PIAT with a round loaded.

Rear PIAT adjustable gun site.

Front PIAT gun site.

THE PIAT VICTORIA CROSSES

Many people believe the PIAT. weapon was a joke and totally useless in combat. Used at close range where there was cover it could be effective. The Victoria Cross medal is only awarded to British and Commonwealth soldiers who displayed gallantry of the highest order.

The London Gazette, Issue no. 36,605, p. 3,273
War Office, 13 July 1944

The KING has been graciously pleased to approve awards of the VICTORIA CROSS to the undermentioned:—

No. 3663590 Fusilier Francis Arthur Jefferson, The Lancashire Fusiliers (Ulverston, Lanes.).

On 16 May, 1944, during an attack on the Gustav Line, an anti-tank obstacle, held up some of our tanks, leaving the leading Company of Fusilier Jefferson's Battalion to dig in on the hill without tanks or anti-tank guns. The enemy counter-attacked with infantry and two Mark IV tanks, which opened fire at short-range causing a number of casualties, and eliminating one PIAT group entirely.

As the tanks advanced towards the partially dug trenches, Fusilier Jefferson, entirely on his own initiative, seized a PIAT and running forward alone under heavy fire, took up a position behind a hedge; as he could not see properly, he came into the open, and standing up under a hail of bullets, fired at the leading tank which was now only twenty yards away. It burst into flames and all the crew were killed.

Fusilier Jefferson then reloaded the PIAT and proceeded towards the second tank, which withdrew before he could get within range. By this time our own tanks had arrived and the enemy counter-attack was smashed with heavy casualties.

Fusilier Jefferson's gallant act not merely saved the lives of his Company and caused many casualties to the Germans, but also broke up the enemy counter-attack and had a decisive effect on the subsequent operation. His supreme gallantry and disregard of personal risk contributed very largely to the success of the action.

The London Gazette, Issue no. 36,849, p. 5,841
Department of National Defense, Ottawa, 19 December 1944

The KING has been graciously pleased to approve the award of the VICTORIA CROSS to:—

No. K 52880 Private Ernest Alvia Smith, The Seaforth Highlanders of Canada.

In Italy on the night of 21/22 October, 1944, a Canadian Infantry Brigade was ordered to establish a bridgehead across the Savio River.

The Seaforth Highlanders of Canada were selected as the spearhead of the attack and in weather most unfavorable [*sic.*] to the operation they crossed the river and captured their objectives in spite of strong opposition from the enemy.

Torrential rain had caused the Savio River to rise six feet in five hours and as the soft vertical banks made it impossible to bridge the river no tanks or anti-tank guns could be taken across the raging stream to the support of the rifle companies.

As the right forward company was consolidating its objective it was suddenly counter-attacked by a troop of three Mark V Panther tanks supported by two self-propelled guns and about thirty infantry and the situation appeared almost hopeless.

Under heavy fire from the approaching enemy tanks, Private Smith, showing great initiative and inspiring leadership, led his PIAT group of two men across an open field to a position from which the PIAT could best be employed. Leaving one man on the weapon, Private Smith crossed the road with a companion, and obtained another PIAT almost immediately an enemy tank came down the road firing its machine guns along the line of the ditches. Private Smith's comrade was wounded. At a range of thirty feet and having to expose himself to the full view of the enemy, Private Smith fired the PIAT and hit the tank, putting it out of action. Ten German infantry immediately jumped off the back of the tank and charged him with Schmeissers and grenades. Without hesitation Private Smith moved out onto the road and with his Tommy gun at point blank range, killed four Germans and drove the remainder back. Almost immediately another tank opened fire and more enemy infantry closed in on Smith's position. Obtaining some abandoned Tommy gun magazines from a ditch, he steadfastly held his position, protecting his comrade and fighting the enemy with his Tommy gun until they finally gave up and withdrew in disorder.

One tank and both self-propelled guns had been destroyed by this time, but yet another tank swept the area with fire from a longer range. Private Smith, still showing utter contempt for enemy fire, helped his wounded friend to cover and obtained medical aid for him behind a nearby building. He then returned to his position beside the road to await the possibility of a further enemy attack.

No further immediate attack developed, and as a result the battalion was able to consolidate the bridgehead position so vital to the success of the whole operation, which led to the eventual capture of San Giorgio di Cesena and a further advance to the Ronco River.

Thus, by the dogged determination, outstanding devotion to duty and superb gallantry of this private soldier, his comrades were so inspired that the bridgehead was held firm against all enemy attacks, pending the arrival of tanks and anti-tank guns some hours later.

The London Gazette, Issue no. 36,774, p. 5,015
War Office, Tuesday 31 October 1944

The KING has been graciously pleased to approve awards of the VICTORIA CROSS to: —

Captain (temporary Major) Robert Henry Cain (129484), The Royal Northumberland Fusiliers, (attd. The South Staffordshire Regiment) (1 Airborne Division) (Salcombe, Devon).

In Holland on 19 September 1944, Major Cain was commanding a rifle company of the South Staffordshire Regiment during the battle of Arnhem when his company was cut off from the rest of the battalion and during the next six days was closely engaged with enemy tanks, self-propelled guns and infantry. The Germans made repeated attempts to break into the company position by infiltration, and had they succeeded in doing so, the whole situation of the Airborne Troops would have been jeopardised.

Major Cain, by his outstanding devotion to duty and remarkable powers of leadership, was to a large extent personally responsible for saving a vital sector from falling into the hands of the enemy.

On 20 September, a Tiger tank approached the area held by his company, and Major Cain went out alone to deal with it armed with a PIAT taking up a position, he held his fire until the tank was only 20 yards away when he opened up. The tank immediately halted and turned its guns on him, shooting away a corner of the house near where this officer was lying. Although wounded by machine gun bullets and falling masonry, Major Cain continued firing until he had scored several direct hits, immobilised the tank and supervised the bringing up of a 75-mm howitzer, which completely destroyed it. Only then would he consent to have his wounds dressed.

The next morning this officer drove off three more tanks by the fearless use of his PIAT, on each occasion leaving cover and taking up position in open ground with complete disregard for his personal safety.

During the following days, Major Cain was everywhere where danger threatened, moving amongst his men and encouraging them by his fearless example to hold out. He refused rest and medical attention in spite of the fact that his hearing had been seriously impaired because of a perforated eardrum, and he was suffering from multiple wounds. On 25 September the enemy made a concerted attack on Major Cain's position, using self-propelled guns, flame throwers and infantry. By this time the last PIAT had been put out of action and Major Cain was armed with only a light 2-inch mortar. However, by a skilful use of this weapon and his daring leadership of the few men still under his command, he completely demoralised the enemy who, after an engagement lasting more than three hours, withdrew in disorder. Throughout the whole course of the Battle of Arnhem, Major Cain showed superb gallantry. His powers of endurance and leadership were the admiration of all his fellow officers, and stories of his valour were being constantly exchanged amongst the troops. His coolness and courage under incessant fire could not be surpassed.

THE BRITISH GRENADE MK 75 ANTI-TANK MINE

These are the instructions given to troops about how to use the Grenade No. 75 Mk 1—insert the open end of the detonator into the open end of the igniter. Then roll the rubber tube on the igniter to cover the joint. This provides a watertight seal. Insert a detonator assembly, detonator end first, into each of the pockets of the detonator holder through the hole in the back of the striker-plate bracket. Bend over the metal tabs, securing the detonator assemblies in the pockets. The red-painted portions of the assemblies should now be visible in the slots of the detonator holders.

The grenade is thrown or placed so that it will be run over. The pressure of the vehicle upon the striker plate will force the strikers through the slots in the detonator holders, crush the igniter tubes, and break the glass capsules containing nitric and sulphuric acid. The action of the acid on the potassium chlorate and charcoal ignition composition produces an immediate flash, which sets off the detonators and explodes the grenade.

In the Grenades No. 75 Mk II and Mk III, the igniters are inserted in their pockets and the tabs bent into place to secure them. When the grenade is run over, the striker pin crushes the glass ampoule and grinds the broken glass and contained igniter composition together, igniting the composition. The resultant flash initiates the detonator, which explodes the grenade.

When the Grenade No. 75 is filled with Ammonal, the designation is changed to No. 75 A. Ammonal is about 80 per cent as powerful as the regular fillings.

The Grenade No. 75 is employed mainly as a land mine for defence against armoured cars, tanks and other vehicles. It will disable light tanks and vehicles and is used principally for hasty minefields. It is often referred to as the 'Hawkins' grenade. They were manufactured by the Self Opening Tin Box Co Ltd, Westerham, Kent. This information is sourced from War Department Field Manual, Corps of Engineers, Land Mines and Booby Traps, FM 5-31, 1 November 1943.

Overall length: 6 ½ inches (16.51 cm)
Width: 3.625 inches (9.19 cm)
Height: 1.875 inches (4.76 cm)
Total weight: 2.25 lb (1.02 kg)
Filling: Nobel's No. 704B, Ammonal, Burrowite, or TNT (all with exploders or C.E. pellets)
Filling weight: 1.75 lb (0.79 kg)
Delay: None
Pressure to fire: 300 lb (136 kg)

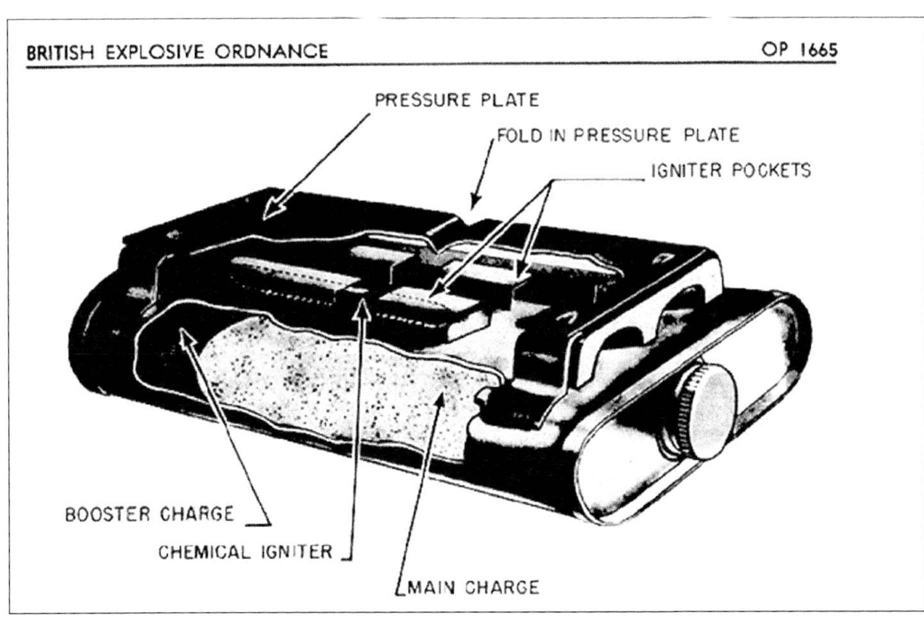

Internal diagram of the British Grenade No. 75 Mk I anti-tank mine. (*War Department Field Manual, Corps of Engineers, Land Mines and Booby Traps, FM 5-31, 1 November 1943*)

❮ Bottom view of a replica British grenade No. 75 Mk II anti-tank mine.

❯ Top view of a replica British grenade No. 75 Mk II anti-tank mine, showing the pressure plate that has to be forced down to explode the mine.

❮ Bottom view of a replica British grenade No. 75 Mk I anti-tank mine.

❯ Top view of a replica British grenade No. 75 Mk II anti-tank mine, showing the pressure plate that has to be forced down to explode the mine.

THE BRITISH MK V ANTI-TANK MINE

The Mk V anti-tank mine consists of three principal components: the loaded mine body, the exploder mechanism, and the mine cover. The cover is fastened to the mine body by three pins, which engage slots provided in three retaining straps attached to the mine body. The mine body is mushroom-shaped and contains a central well for the insertion of the special exploder.

Exploders function on the shear-wire principle. In effect, the exploder is nothing more than a miniature mine. It consists of a fuse body with a well in the top located off-centre for the insertion of a plunger, which is packed separately in the same box as the rest of the exploder mechanism. This plunger is retained by a shear wire. In the side of the exploder body, near the base, is a channel for the insertion of the ampoule cartridge-detonator combination.

The fuse functions when pressure on the mine cover forces the plunger through the shear wire and down onto the ampoule cartridge. The ampoule is crushed, causing a chemical reaction, which fires the detonator. The booster charge, also located in the exploder body, is then detonated, setting off the main charge of the mine.

The mine is used as a defence against armoured cars, tanks, and other vehicles. The mine will break the tracks of light or medium tanks and disable other vehicles.

These were the instructions for assembly and arming of the mine: lay the mine in the ground and remove the cover. Place an exploder in the inverted cover (to keep dust etc. from the plunger) and insert an ampoule, red end first, into the detonator. Fill the open end of the detonator in the hole in the side of the exploder body. Slide the assembly home and seal in place with more luting (sealant). Grease the exploder before inserting it in the fuse well of the mine. Refit the cover.

To neutralise this mine, remove the mine cover without putting any downward pressure on the cover, and then lift the exploder from the exploder well of the mine. Remove the plunger from the exploder. Lift the mine and replace the cover.

Some Mk V anti-tank mines have the letters 'GS' after them. This stands for 'General Service'. Others have the letters HC, which are an abbreviation for 'Higher Capacity'. The two mines are identical in appearance and size. The only difference is that the HC mine has explosives on both sides of the inner wall of the case. This information is sourced from War Department Field Manual, Corps of Engineers, Land Mines and Booby Traps, FM 5-31, 1 November 1943.

Diameter: 8 inch (20.32 cm)
Height: 2 ½ inch (6.35 cm)
Weight: 8 lb (3.62 kg)
Explosive weight: 4 ½ lb (2 kg)
Explosive: TNT
Material: Sheet metal
Fuse: Exploder E.P. No. 1 or No. 2
Pressure required: 250–350 lb (113–159 kg)

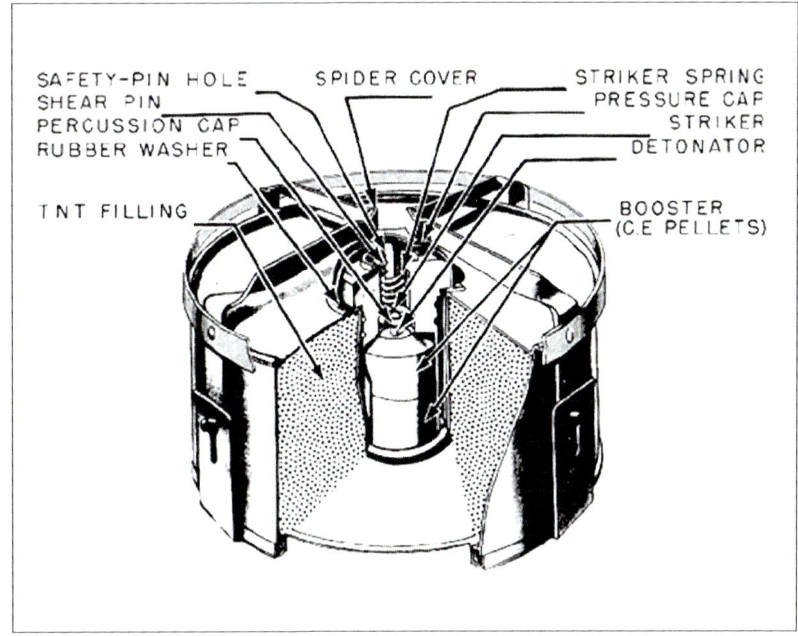

A diagram showing the inside of a British Mk 5 anti-tank. (*War Department Field Manual, Corps of Engineers, Land Mines and Booby Traps, FM 5-31, 1 November 1943*)

‹ A Mk 5 HC anti-tank mine next to a match box to give you an indication of size. (*War Department Field Manual, Corps of Engineers, Land Mines and Booby Traps, FM 5-31, 1 November 1943*)

› A Mk 5 HC anti-tank mine about to be buried in sand. (*War Department Field Manual, Corps of Engineers, Land Mines and Booby Traps, FM 5-31, 1 November 1943*)

Mk 5 anti-tank mines were sometimes called pressure cookers because of the way they looked.

18

BRITISH BATTLE REPORTS

Panzer VI Ausf. E Tiger with turret number 114 knocked out in Normandy.

SECRET—CURRENT REPORTS FROM OVERSEAS NO. 5

THE WAR OFFICE, 3 JULY 1943

Artillery Equipment

The 6-pdr anti-tank gun has been a great success and has destroyed Pz Mk VI Tigers on many occasions. In one action in Tunisia in early February the gunners held their fire until the tanks were 680 yards away. The first two rounds merely nicked the plates, the next two gouged-out scallops of armour, the fifth round went almost through, while the next three penetrated completely and stopped the tank. The first complete penetration was at 600 yards at an angle of impact of 30 degrees from normal, and penetrated through 82 mm of homogeneous armour: the ammunition used was semi-armour piercing solid shot. In the desert, 6-pdr shooting often had to be observed from the flank because the gunners were temporary blinded by the dust kicked up when the gun was fired.

Operational experience of the 17-pdr is still slight. The reasons are that generally these guns have been sited in-depth, and the tank attacks had been broken up by concentrations of HE from 25-pdr field guns, or have been destroyed by the 6-pdrs sited forward. Moreover, little use was made of the 17-pdrs (one round from each of three guns) knocked out three tanks. A little later one gun of the same unit destroyed six tanks, including two Mk VI Tigers, before it was itself knocked out.

Criticisms, that have been made of the 17-pdr are:–

(a) it is a heavy gun for man handling,

(b) the ammunition is bulky for getting forward,

(c) the gun is heavy to tow,

(d) the flash is enormous, and

(e) the dust kicked up is a severe hindrance to observation.

Nevertheless, long range anti-tank fire has undoubtedly come to stay. Tiger tanks appear to prefer to stand off at about 2,000 yards and all agree that the 17-pdr is an absolute first class tank killing weapon.

Our concentrations in the latest breakthrough to Tunis were truly formidable. A highly coordinated, yet simple fire plan enabled infantry commanders to bring down concentrated fire of a very large number of guns onto nominated areas. After the battle 700 German dead were found in one area onto which a concentration had been put down. In this operation the field guns in First Army fired an average of 384 rounds per gun in the first 24 hours after zero—or four rounds more than was fired in the El Alamein battle.

No. 75 Grenades

Experiments Recently carried out in the Middle East show that No. 75 grenades cannot be relied on to cut the track of a PZ Mk VI Tiger tank unless four grenades can be detonated under one track. When a lesser number than four was detonated, the track links were damaged and the pins bent but the tracks remained serviceable. The conclusions reached were that, to make sure of cutting the track, the grenade should be laid either:–

(a) in clumps of four into layers, the top layer overlapping the lower, as a bonded brick work, or

(b) in one layer of four, each grenade being not more than seven inches from the next.

The former method is suitable in open minefields, while the latter is suitable for road blocks or defiles. In either case the grenade should be laid with the long axis parallel to the expected direction of approach of the tank. A single Mk V anti-tank mine is fully effective, and in these trials cut to track pins and shattered three links.

Infantry Weapons and Equipment

PIAT has not been used extensively so far, but is known to have destroyed at least one Pz Mk VI tank.

Tank Gunnery

Up to the time of the battle of El Alamein the 75-mm tank gun was almost invariably fired from hull-down positions over open sites. The intense and prolonged firefight of the October battle, however suggested the possibility of indirect fire from tanks in turret down positions, only the tank commander's head showing above the forward crest. This practice met with immediate success, for the tanks obtained good results both with shot and shell, while at the same time attracting far less fire to themselves.

The next step was to try out a simple form of indirect HE shooting by the troop. A straightforward procedure was worked out under which one tank was forward observing, and degrees scale was marked on the inside of the other tanks to enable the crews to lay their guns parallel by aiming either at a distant object or onto the controlling tank.

Since the battle of El Alamein this type of shooting has been used with much success, and has now become the normal procedure in Eighth Army. It has proved of particular value in the advance in attacks against weak enemy rear guards, for it has been found that a concentration of HE from a troop of Sherman tanks, moving near the head of the Vanguard, will often dispose of located enemy anti-tank guns in less time than would be needed for deployment of a proportion of field artillery.

In this type of shooting, it is essential that the observing tank should be in a direct, on nearly direct, line between the troop and the target, and that such shooting should be restricted to a troop basis. Any attempt to introduce observation from the flank to fire a squadron as a battery, inevitably leads to complications of procedure, and so of training, and would entail the use of artillery instruments which could be carried on a tank only with difficulty.

EXTRACT FROM REPORT TO HQ SECOND ARMY FROM COL A. G. COLE, DD OF A (NO. 20 WTSFF)

APPENDIX 'E' TO 21 ARMY GROUP RAC, LIAISON LETTER NO. 2

The extract is of tank action near Rauray between 27 June and 1 July 1944 (Operation Epsom).

Sherman: 75-mm Guns

4. Lt Fern engaged a Panther side on with his 75-mm and APC. It was moving about 12 mph at 80 yards range and he brewed it up with one hit through the vertical plate above the back bogie.

He saw his squadron commander engage a Tiger (previously examined by us) on the road. At 120 yards the Tiger was head-on. The 75-mm put three shots on it and the crew bailed out without firing. He put in three more. The tank brewed up. Four shots had scooped on front plates, one had taken a piece out of the lower edge of the mantlet and gone into the tank through the roof. And one had ricocheted off the track up into the sponson. At another Panther he had fired five shots with HE. The enemy made off without retaliation.

5. Sgt Dring started out south from Fontenay-le-Pesnel with his 75-mm and fell in with a Panzer Mk IV tank which he shot through the driver's visor. It brewed up and the crew bailed out. Range 200 yards.

Next he fell in with a Tiger at 1,000 yards. The Tiger fired while Dring was reversing, but missed. Dring then pumped five shots in without further retaliation. The last one hit the driver's periscope and the crew bailed out. (This tank is believed to have been recovered for shipment to UK).

Next he came on a Panther at the crossroads. This he got with one shot with APC in front of sprocket and the crew bailed out. Hit at normal and at about 500 yards range. It brewed up.

Next he took on Tiger at 1,400 yards just outside Rauray. He fired six shots, of which four hit and the last one brewed up. The troop Commander thought he had missed it and only hit the wall behind. Sgt Dring's next shot brought the sparks and the remark, 'You don't see a brick wall spark like that'. This tank has been seen and is much shot up. It now has one scoop in front of vertical plate, five penetrations in rear, for strikes with no penetration in rear, plus a scoop and one plate of engine hatch smashed.

Finally to the east of Rauray he took on a Panzer Mk IV at 1,200 yards, fired two HE ranging rounds and then one AP through the tracks which went in and finished it.

NORMANDY 1944: MEMORIES OF TIGER TANK COMPANY LEADER RICHARD FREIHERR VON ROSEN

In June 1944, the three Companies of the German Heavy Tank Battalion 503 (s.Pz.Abt.503) were equipped with Panzer VI Ausf. E Tiger tanks. They had been withdrawn from the Eastern Front, to the Ohrdruf Troop training depot in the Harz mountains, for rest and recuperation after months of fighting. At full strength, the Battalion consisted of 45 tanks. On 6 June 1944, the Allies attacked the beaches of Normandy on D-Day.

On 7 July 1944, orders came through that the Battalion was to be sent to Northern France. It was to provide armoured reserve and be attached to Panzer Regiment 22 (Pz.Rgt 22) of the 21st Panzer Division (21 Pz.Div), LXXXV Armeekorps in Normandy.

The s.Pz.Abt.503, No. 3 Company leader Richard Freiherr von Rosen, had three platoons under his command. Each platoon normally consisted of four Tigers but mechanical problems could reduce the number of tanks available for combat.

Rosen records in his memoirs that he was awoken at 5 a.m., 11 July 1944, by a dispatch rider with orders to advance to the French town of Giberville. The British armour and Canadian infantry had broken through the German frontline between Curerville and the factory complex at Colombelles, east of Caen.

Upon arrival a number of British Sherman tanks were spotted in a defensive position in a cluster of houses below the town of St Honorine, north of Giberville. These belonged to 148th Royal Armoured Corps (RAC). Rosen gave the order to advance. One platoon would rush ahead whilst the other two provided covering fire. After a few hundred metres that platoon would stop and opened fire whilst the other platoons caught up. One of the platoons would then continue the advance under the covering fire of the other two platoons. Each tank reported being hit by enemy fire but none of the shells did serious damage. The British tanks put down a smoke screen and retreated. Rosen recorded finding eleven knocked out Sherman tanks and five destroyed anti-tank guns (these were 17 pdr AT guns belonging to 61st Anti-tank Battalion).

On 18 July 1944, 3 Company, s.Pz.Abt.503, occupied a defensive position around the villages of Emieville, Cagney and Maneville. Between 5.45 a.m. to 8.30 a.m. three waves of Allied bombers dropped thousands of bombs in the surrounding area in preparation for the Allied Operation Goodwood attack. Many of the company's Tigers were lost: some receive direct hits and were completely destroyed; others were flipped over or onto the side when a bomb exploded nearby. The Battalion suffered many casualties and fatalities. Only eight tanks were left in an operational condition out of the original twelve.

Rosen survived but his Tiger tank, under which he was sheltering, did not. When he inspected his tank, he saw that 'the thick armour plate over the engine at the rear of the Panzer had been deformed as though hit by a bomb that had failed to explode: upon examination we established that the cooling unit had been damaged by blast. My Panzer was therefore not combat worthy, and I had to change vehicles again'.

19

PANZERKETTEN (GERMAN TANK TRACK CLASSIFICATION SYSTEM)

The Tiger tank's thinner railway transportation tracks were called *Verladekette* Kgs 63/520/130 (fast-running track for motor vehicles, steel castings of all alloys, with rotating bolts, type 63, width 520 mm, spacing 130 mm).

German tank and armoured tracked vehicle's metal tracks were given different designations. This helped identify the type of track link required when ordering spare parts. These abbreviated code names were designated in the following order:

construction type
material used
connection between links

For example, the Panther Tank's tracks were called Kgs 64/660/150 (fast-running track for motor vehicles made, steel castings of all alloys, with rotating bolts, type 64, width 660 mm, spacing 150 mm).

The Tiger tank's standard tracks were called *Marschkette* Kgs 63/725/130 (fast-running track for motor vehicles made, steel castings of all alloys, with rotating bolts, type 63, width 725 mm, spacing 130 mm).

The Tiger tank's thinner railway transportation tracks were called *Verladekette* Kgs 63/520/130 (fast-running track for motor vehicles, steel castings of all alloys, with rotating bolts, type 63, width 520 mm, spacing 130 mm).

CONSTRUCTION TYPE CODE LETTERS

K: fast running track for motor vehicles (unlike agricultural tractors)
S: Six-wheeled track for multi-axle driven vehicles
Z: tracks for halftrack vehicles
L: tracks for agricultural tractors
P: test tracks (roadway)

MATERIAL USED CODE LETTERS

g: steel castings of all alloys
p: forged steel, drop forged steel
b: sheet steel
t: malleable cast iron
d: duraluminium
ge: cloth fabric
s: silumin

CONNECTION TYPE CODE LETTER

no letter: normal bearing. (Bolt and bush without lubrication)
s: rotating bolts
w: roller bearings (with lubrication and sealing)
gu: rubber seals
b: rotating bushing

THE NUMBERING CODES

Type
Width
Spacing

The exception to the rule is track Gg 24/660/300; this is thought to be a designation indicating a test version.

The Tiger tank's standard combat tracks were called *Marschkette* Kgs 63/725/130 (fast-running track for motor vehicles, steel castings of all alloys, with rotating bolts, type 63, width 725 mm, spacing 130 mm).

20

THE BUCKET

The rear of a Panther tank showing the bucket handle secured to the towing bracket.

For years, people have been asking what is the bucket used for that hangs from the back of German tanks, including the Tiger tank. This wartime instructional pamphlet shows that it was intended to be a fluid receptacle when the crew maintained the vehicle. A bucket is a very useful piece of equipment and can be used to carry water, wood, coal, eggs, and sand. It is ideal for thinning camouflage paste and holding whitewash when a spray gun is not available. If it was clean, the crew could also use it to wash their underclothes and socks. They could also use it to hold water to throw over their heads to get the soap/shampoo out of their hair.

VORARBEITEN—PREPARATION

1. Clean the tank.
2. Drain enough fuel so that the three upper fuel tanks are empty. Then it is possible to remove the middle fuel tank without fuel loss. The fuel drain cock is on the right lower hull. First loosen the 5 nuts of the flange. Open conical valve. Before opening put a bucket below to avoid fuel spill.
3. Drain the coolant.
4. Turn the battery's main switch to off and disconnect battery.

Sonderwerkzeug

Motoraufhängevorrichtung K 7677 81
(MM 225354 2)

Vorarbeiten

1. Pz Kpfw reinigen.
2. Kraftstoff so weit ablassen, daß die 3 oberen Kraftstoffbehälter leer sind. Dann kann der mittlere Kraftstoffbehälter ohne Kraftstoffverlust ausgebaut werden.

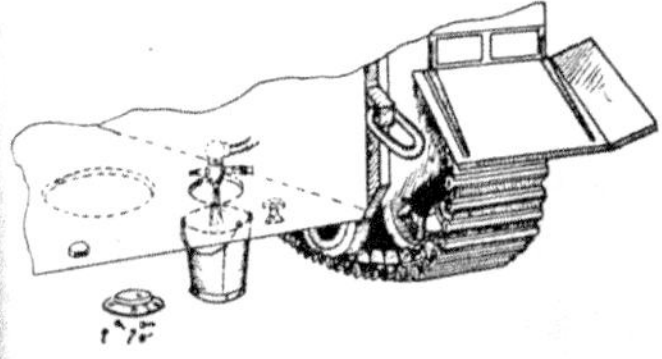

Kraftstoffablaßhahn befindet sich rechts am Heckunterteil. Zuerst die 5 Muttern des Flansches lösen. Das Kegelventil öffnen. Vor dem Öffnen Eimer unterstellen, um Kraftstoffverluste zu vermeiden.

3. Kühlwasser ablassen.
4. Sammlerhauptschalter auf „Aus" stellen und Sammler abschließen.

Ausbau des Motors

1. Sicherungen der Schrauben des Teleskoprohres mit Flachmeißel aufbiegen und Schrauben mit

Second World War German tank crew instructional leaflet.

Early-production Tiger tank with a bucket attached to the rear of the tank. (*German Archives*)

Late-production Tiger tank issued to 102 sch.Pz.Abt in Normandy 1944 with two buckets attached to the rear of the tank. (*German Archives*)

21

SURVIVING PANZER VI TIGER TANKS

Always phone the museum or local town hall to see if the tank is still there before driving to the location as tanks move. That may seem a silly statement, but tanks change locations. Some are sold or temporarily transferred to other museums. Some are withdrawn from public view to enable them to be restored or undergo maintenance. Some tanks are on military bases (Fort Benning in the USA) and may not be open to the public. The Patriot Park Museum in Kubinka is sometimes closed to non-Russian visitors during special exhibitions. There are several new Tiger I construction projects around the world. They are using original parts from different knocked-out Tiger tanks that have been dug up on old battlefields. The most advanced projects belong to the Australian Armour and Artillery Museum, Hoebig Collection, and the Wheatcroft Collection.

FORT BENNING, GEORGIA, USA

This Tiger I is part of the U.S. Army Armor & Cavalry Collection (US AACC) at Fort Benning, Georgia, USA. It belonged to the German 501st Heavy Tank Battalion (s.Pz.Abt. 501) and had the tactical number '712' painted on the side when it was captured intact in Tunis in May 1943 after German forces surrendered.

Its hull number is 250031. Tiger 1 production started with hull number 25001. It was a very early production model. It initially saw service with the second company of s.Pz.Abt. 501 in August 1942. They were posted to North Africa, arriving in January 1943, to join the *Afrika Korps* commanded by Field Marshal Erwin Rommel.

The tank's turret has a different production number to the hull number. They are normally the same. The turret number is 250034. The reason for this is not known. A different turret could have been fitted at the factory or the turret became damaged later and was replaced with a turret from another vehicle that had a damaged hull.

The s.Pz.Abt.501 suffered a lot of battle casualties. What remained of the 501st was attached to the s.Pz.Abt.504 for combat operations in mid-March 1943. This was because the 501st did not have enough tanks to conduct independent operations. The s.Pz.Abt.501 still existed as a unit in North Africa until the surrender.

Tiger 712 was shipped to the US Army Proving Ground in Aberdeen, Maryland, for testing and evaluation. Sections of the armour were cut away to enable it to be used as an educational exhibit, to allow soldiers under training and visitors to see into the fighting compartment. During the Vietnam War, it was moved outside the main engineering building and left in a field along with other captured Second World War armoured vehicles. Metal plates were placed over the holes in the armour in an effort to stop the rain from getting inside the tank. In 1989, it was loaned to the Auto & Technik Museum in Germany. It then spent some time in the Wheatcroft Collection in Britain and was returned to America in 2012. The U.S. Army Armor & Cavalry Collection is kept on an army base that is not open to the public. Its primary role is to be a teaching aid to new classes of American tank crewmen. The public are allowed to see the collection of tanks on special 'Open House' days that are announced on their social media profiles.

MUSÉE DES BLINDÉS, SAUMUR, FRANCE

This surviving Tiger tank is on display at the French Museum of Armour (Musée des Blindés) in Saumur, France. Tiger 221 originally had the tactical number 114 on its turret when it was part of the 1st Company, 102th SS Heavy Tank Battalion (1/s.SS-Pz.Abt. 102). On 19 August 1944, three Tiger tanks were retreating to the north-west. They encountered a British anti-tank gun battery ambush position covering the road they were using. Tiger tank 114 was the third tank. The lead Tiger managed to pass the guns without damage and continued along the road at full speed. The second tiger tank, number 241, managed to open fire on the British positions but received two direct hits. That tank's radio operator and driver were badly injured. Tank 114 was following the second Tiger 241 too close and collided with the rear of the second tank at full speed. The dent in the upper front of the Saumur tiger is the result of the collision with the other Tiger tank.

It was later issued to 2nd Company of the SS Heavy Panzer Battalion 102 (2/s.SS-Pz.Abt. 102). This Tiger fought near Cauville-sur-Mer in Normandy and was abandoned by her crew after a mechanical breakdown. The tank was recovered and repaired. She was recommissioned into the Free French Army at Colmar with the 2nd squadron of the 6th Cuirassiers Regiment. It took part in the fighting retreat all the way back to Germany.

After the war, six German Panther tanks and this Tiger tank were used in the French 6e *régiment de* Cuirassiers Squadron Besnier, based in Treve, Germany. When the regiment left Treve in 1960 for Indochina (Vietnam, Laos, and Cambodia), they transferred the German tanks to the French tank builder AMX (Atelier de Construction d'Issy-les-Moulineaux)'s tank development centre in Satory, where they were used for testing. In 1965, they were transferred to a little military museum, and then in 1968–70, they were transported to the French Musée des Blindés in Saumur. It is believed that the number 221 painted on the turret was on the instructions of the first museum director in the early 1980s as it was the number on the first Tiger tank he saw. The next time it is repainted, the original numbers 114 will be put back on.

The tank's hull number is 251114. It has late-production features like the dome-shaped commander's cupola, metal-rimmed wheels, and a single hole in the gun mantlet on the left of the main gun for the monocular gun sight. It is fitted with thinner transportation tracks. The sidetrack guards are missing. Add the Musée des Blindés in Saumur to your list of places to visit. www.museedesblindes.fr

TANK MUSEUM, BOVINGTON, ENGLAND

Tiger 131 in the arena at the Tank Museum, Bovington, during the Tiger Day event. (*Ian Wilcox*)

The Bovington Tiger 131 was captured in North Africa. On 21 April 1943, the 48th Royal Tank Regiment, which had just arrived in Tunisia from Britain and had virtually no combat experience, was going into action against German *Afrika Corps* for the first time. They were backed up by an infantry battalion as they attacked the hills.

Lieutenant Peter Gudgeon was commanding one of two troops of Churchill Mk III tanks that day. He recorded:

> As we advanced towards our objectives, we could see no sign of the enemy, but suddenly my fellow troop leader's tank erupted in an enormous explosion. Before I had a chance to locate the source of this shot my Churchill tank was hit by a shell that passed through the front armoured plate, right through the fighting compartment and into the engine setting it on fire. We bailed out under heavy German machine-gun fire and were lucky to escape with only minor injuries. The crew of the other Churchill tank were all killed immediately.

Both tanks had been knocked out by 88-mm shells fired by Tiger tank 131, which was later found abandoned in the hills of their objective. What happened to the crew of the Tiger tank is a mystery. Normally, when a tank has to be abandoned because of mechanical problems, it would be destroyed to save it from falling into the hands of the enemy. This Tiger tank was found intact.

The 504th Heavy Panzer battalion's war diary simply states, 'Crew members of tank 131 abandoned tank in panic after two harmless hits from a Churchill'. The hits from the Churchill tank were anything but harmless. The tank was subject to several direct hits. The most damaging—a 6-pdr shot—was the one that hit underneath the gun, hitting the gun mantlet and finally lodging itself in the turret ring. This caused the turret to jam into one position, effectively making it unable to fight. This damage can still be seen on the tank today.

This shell also split the welding on the top of the tank and shattered the radio. It could also have injured the driver and the front hull machine-gunner. With the injured crew unable to call for assistance, it would be quite understandable to see why the crew panicked and failed to destroy the tank. They would have seen advancing British Churchill tanks and infantry coming towards them only 50 yards away and they were unable to fire back.

The British had been fighting Tiger tanks since January 1943. Three months later, this was the first time they could get close up and examine this German beast of the battlefield. The tank was immediately sent to Egypt where it was examined by technical officers, senior officers and VIPs including Winston Churchill and King George VI. It was then shipped to England for testing and evaluation.

The Tank Museum, Bovington, has special events called 'Tiger Days' where you can see Tiger 131 being driven around the Museum's arena. Check their website for details: tankmuseum.org

VIMOUTIERS, NORMANDY, FRANCE

The Vimoutiers Tiger south-east of Caen in the middle of the Normandy countryside needs a lot of restoration work. It is rusting away and its paintwork needs redoing. It has late-production steel-rimmed wheels and a cast metal dome-shaped commander's cupola. There are lots of external and internal parts missing. There is no engine or gearbox inside. The most noticeable missing external parts are the front and side track guards and the rear twin exhausts. Lots of parts have been removed over the years.

To find this Tiger, set your Sat Nav to Vimoutiers, Avenue du Marechal Leclerc. This is the D979. When your Sat Nav indicates you have arrived, keep driving east out of town up the hill. The Vimoutiers Tiger is about 1 mile outside of the town in a layby on the left on a stretch of the D979 road that does not have a name.

It is in an impressive, commanding location. As you come around a bend halfway up a long hill, you see the Tiger looking down on your position from near the top of the crest of the ridge. If you were an Allied soldier and saw that in 1944, you would need a change of underpants.

On 19 August 1944, several German tanks from mixed units, including the Vimoutiers Tiger I, were making their way to get refuelled at the Army fuel dump set up in the Chateau de l'Horloge. They had to make a detour along the Vimoutiers–Gace road.

They were trying to escape the encirclement of the Falaise pocket. A number of the panzers ran out of fuel on that road, before they got to the chateau and had to be abandoned. These included a Panzer III, a number of Panzer IVs, three Tiger I tanks, and a King Tiger. It is believed that around 60 German tanks were abandoned around the rolling hills and rich dairy farmland that surrounds Vimoutiers during the last days of August 1944. Most were cut up after the war by scrap-metal merchants.

The Vitmoutiers Tiger ran out of fuel. Tiger tanks are very thirsty beasts, and going up and down all the limestone hills did not help its fuel consumption. It ground to a halt in the middle of the road. It was too heavy to push off or tow to the roadside using a smaller tank.

The crew placed the demolition charges they had been given on the engine cover and along the turret. The explosives caused the armoured covers on top of the engine to buckle The turret was jammed by the second explosion.

When the Americans liberated the town of Vitmoutiers the disabled Tiger tank was deemed to be causing a traffic obstruction. A US Army bulldozer was used to push it off the road to enable the essential supply lorries to reach the ever-moving front.

French scrap-metal merchant M. Morat purchased the Tiger tank. He took out the transmission but left it sitting on the northern side of the road in a ditch, with its gun pointing menacingly up the road at passing vehicles.

For over thirty years, it was left to rust and get covered in moss. Local children would play on this once deadly weapon of war. It became a local landmark.

Mr Morat's sister inherited the Tiger when he died. She did not want it and sold it to a scrap-metal merchant in Caen. It was too heavy to be towed away and the company arrived on-site with oxy-acetylene metal cutting tools with the intention of cutting it up piece by piece and transporting it away to a smelter in Caen.

A local resident saw what was happening to the town's historic landmark and was horrified. He contacted the mayor of Vimoutiers and with the help of a French Normandy D-Day historian, Eddy Florentin, an emergency purchase of the tank on behalf of the town of Vimoutiers was authorised by the Paris War Office.

In October 1975, the work of restoring the Tiger tank began with its removal from its ditch. This was not an easy job as it was so heavy. The turret was removed to lighten the load. It then took two very large powerful JCB tractor units to pull it out of its resting place for the past thirty years.

All the hatches were welded shut. The armour plating was treated for rust and re-sprayed a desert yellow as a base colour. The turret was then refitted. The additional colours of the Tiger tank's camouflage scheme were added to match the original pattern and colours found on the tank before it was restored.

It was initially just placed in a gravelled area by the side of the road near where it was found. Today it takes pride of place in a lawned lay-by, with a parking space on a raised plinth.

The Vimoutiers Tiger I tank is in the middle of Camembert Cheese Country. After you have looked at the Tiger, set your Sat Nav to the village of Camembert. Visit the Camembert Museum and see how this famous cheese is made then afterwards go to the shop on the other side of the road for free cheese tasting. For the tank enthusiasts, you have to search for the Camembert Cheese label that has a Renault FT tank on the front that was stuck on cheeses supplied to the French troops at the front in the First World War.

PATRIOT PARK, KUBINKA, RUSSIA

This is a *Befehlstiger* I—the command version of the Tiger I. Its *Fahrgestell nummer* is 250427. It was captured in January or February 1944. It was transported to Kubinka for trials in February 1944. The tank was put on display at the Kubinka Tank Museum for many years and has now been moved to the new Patriot Park Museum, which is also in Kubinka, Russia. The tank was painted with the markings of the heavy tank battalion s.Pz.Abt.505. The Patriot Park Museum website is en.patriotp.ru.

LENINO-SNEGIRI, RUSSIA

This surviving Tiger tank was in service with the Heavy Panzer Battalion 510 (s.Pz.Abt.510) when it was captured near the village of Sinyavino, which was part of the Leningrad (St Petersburg) front. It was transported to a tank proving ground near Nakhabino, north-west of Moscow in Russia, for examination and firing trials. It later became a 'hard target'. In the 1970s, Yuri Nikitin found it abandoned in a swamp area at the edge of the now-abandoned firing range, among some lend-lease Sherman tanks, a German Panther tank, and some Soviet tanks. It was put on display in the Lenino-Snegiri Military History Museum in the open with other military vehicles and equipment. The museum is 26 miles north-west of Moscow. It has late production steel-rimmed wheels and cast metal dome-shaped commander's cupola. The gun barrel is a reproduction.

USA PRIVATE COLLECTOR

This Tiger I tank was for many years displayed at the *Deutsches Panzermuseum* (German Tank Museum) in Munster, Germany. It was removed from public display by its owner in November 2017 and sold to its new American owner for his private collection. The tank was rebuilt using many different parts from Tiger tank wrecks found at a number of post-war scrapyards around Europe. They were welded to an empty hull with about 10 per cent fresh new steel. It was given the nickname of the Frankentiger. Just like Frankenstein's monster, it is made up of parts from different bodies. The wheels and gun barrel came from the Kurland area in Latvia. The tracks were reproductions. It was constructed by *Monsieur* Hoebig who owned the Trun scrapyard in Normandy. It did not have an engine or gearbox fitted while it was on public display.

THE AUSTRALIAN ARMOUR AND ARTILLERY MUSEUM

(*Bob Barlow/US AACM*)

The Australian Armour and Artillery Museum (AAAM) have built a late-production Tiger 1 tank from original parts found on various battlefields. If you visit the Great Barrier Reef on a trip to Australia, make sure you add the AAAM in Cairns, Northern Queensland, to your schedule.

22

REPLICA TIGER TANKS

Each year, Second World War historical re-enactment groups in Europe and America entertain crowds at military vehicle shows. The people involved are volunteers who have a love of history and want to pass their passion on to others. They spend lots of money purchasing and restoring old vehicles as well as finding original or replica uniforms to wear.

Vintage wartime vehicles are hard to find and extremely expensive. Some vehicles are beyond the financial means of re-enactors. There is also an argument that the very rare tanks should be kept in a museum for future generations to see and not driven around an arena where they could get damaged through continual use.

Finding spare parts is a big problem. Fabricating a replacement part is difficult and very expensive. This is why re-enactors use replica tanks built on the hulls of Cold War tanks and armoured personnel carriers. These are a lot cheaper to purchase. Spare parts are reasonably priced and more easily sourced. These vehicles are not constructed to museum replica standards. They are built to be used and give the public an impression of what warfare in the Second World War looked like.

Many people on social media say negative things about replica tanks. They point out that the wheels are wrong or the tracks are not wide enough. They totally miss the point. They expect to see a wartime Tiger or Panther tank racing around the arena. They are too expensive and precious to be used in this way. This is why replica tanks are used instead. The volunteers and individual owners who spend hours of their free time operating and looking after these replica tanks should be thanked and congratulated at every opportunity and not criticised.

Every tank museum would like to have a Tiger tank on display. Not enough survived the war. Most were cut up for scrap metal. Some museums have commissioned the building of static full-sized models, so they can tell the story of tank development and what happened on the battlefields of Europe and North Africa. Others have built working replicas that can be driven past the attending crowds during their annual 'Tankfest' shows.

The above two photographs of a Tiger tank replica being used in a Second World War re-enactment display were taken in England at the Military Oddessy show in 2002. It is now on display at the Museum of American Armor, 1303 Round Swamp Rd, Old Bethpage, NY 11804, USA.

AUSTRALIAN ARMOUR AND ARTILLERY MUSEUM

(Australian Armour and Artillery Museum)

The superstructure and turret were fabricated for the Hollywood film *Fury*. The hull and running gear were from a Soviet Cold War T-55 tank. The support arms/torsion bars are from the T-55, but the road wheels are from a M110 self-propelled gun. It is powered by a Scania V8 truck engine with a T-62 transfer case connected to the front drive sprockets. This is why the sprockets are 200 mm higher than they should be. It is drivable and used during special events at the Australian Armour and Artillery Museum (AAAM) is in Cairns, Northern Queensland, Australia.

MUSEUM OF AMERICAN ARMOR, OLD BETHPAGE, NEW YORK, USA

(*Museum of American Armor/S. Biegler*)

This Tiger replica is owned by Nassau County, New York (a suburban municipality some 35 miles east of Manhattan), but operated by the Museum of American Armor. The museum's website is museumofamericanarmor.org.

Carl Marklew-Brown used a Cold War Soviet T-55 tank hull to build this Tiger tank replica. Carl owns a company called C&C Military Ltd in Ludgershall, Buckinghamshire, England, which specialised in fabricating props and providing military vehicles for the film industry. It regularly appeared and military vehicle events in England. It was sold to the Global War Museum in Munkedal, Sweden, and later loaned for a short period to the Arsenalen, the Swedish Tank Museum near Stockholm. It appeared in some films including *Dead Snow II* but was then sold and shipped to America. Add the Museum of American Armor to your list of places to visit if you go on holiday to the north-east coast of the USA.

DEUTSCHES PANZERMUSEUM, MUNSTER, GERMANY

(*Deutsches Panzermuseum*)

The owner of the Tiger tank loaned to the *Deutsches Panzermuseum* decided to sell it to a private owner in the United States of America. This left the German Tank Museum without a Tiger tank. They commissioned the construction of a full-size late production Tiger I replica. It does not have any internal features as it is just designed for static display. The attention to detail is precise and very realistic. Add the *Deutsches Panzermuseum* to your list of places to visit.

SECOND WORLD WAR ARMOR

(*WW2 Armour*)

This Tiger tank replica was constructed for the Second World War Hollywood film *Saving Private Ryan*. It was put together in England using a Polish-built T-34-85 hull. A new superstructure and turret were added to make it look like a Tiger tank. In the film, during the final bridge assault scene, a 'sticky bomb' is attached to the tank and explodes. It also starred in the HBO Second World War television series *Band of Brothers* during the battle sequence set in Holland where it engaged a British tank column in the episode 'Replacements'.

At the conclusion of its Hollywood career, this tank was sold to a private collector who then sold it to another collector. It eventually made its way to northern Maryland, USA. It was crewed by a few groups and could be seen at a variety of military vehicle shows throughout the mid-Atlantic region. Then the original T-34-85 engine seized up, and the tank sat for a few years in a field near Gettysburg, PA.

The American historical re-enactment group called 'Treadheads' obtained the vehicle and started restoration work. The tank was brought back to running status and made appearances at Second World War-related events in Pennsylvania and Massachusetts. In 2019, it was sold to the Florida based 'WW2 Armor', another re-enactment group that likes to bring their 'museum' of restored and replica vehicles to the public, at military history shows around the country. WW2 Armor are giving the tank a complete refurbishment that will allow them to continue using the Tiger tank replica for many years to come.

THE IRISH TIGER TANK REPLICA

A full-size Tiger tank is not the normal thing you expect to see, surrounded by farmland, 76 km south-west of Dublin. In his spare time, fireman Eddie Coleman has built an early production Tiger I replica. Construction started in 2014. Originally, the Tiger tank was going to be built as a static prop for a friend's Airsoft competitive spherical plastic projectile shooting site (a bit like paintball but without the paint). Eddie always had a keen interest in German armour. As the project continued, he became hooked on trying to make it as authentic-looking as possible. Eddie went to France to visit the surviving Tiger tanks at Vimoutiers in Normandy and the Musée des Blindés in Saumur to take measurements and photographs. He researched and found detailed plans for the hull and turret.

This full-scale replica project had now progressed from an Airsoft prop to a private model making mission. It was still going to be a static replica made of wood and steel. A lot of the material was second hand. He had a friend who worked at a recycling centre and gave him sheets of stainless steel from old industrial cookers and fridges. Steel angle irons were welded together to provide strength to the construction. The cut stainless steel sheets were fixed to the plywood hull.

Eddie had decided early on in the project that the tank was going to be as close to the original as possible. He chose to build an early-production Tiger that had the rubber rimmed road wheels and drum-shaped commander's cupola. The main reason for this was that this style of road wheel would be easier to fabricate than the later metal-rimmed version. It took him nearly a year to make a full set of road wheels, two idler wheels, and two front sprocket wheels to the correct width and diameter. He then moved on to building the hull and turret in his back garden by the side of his garage workshop.

When it is finished, Eddie initially intends to keep it on display on his property so he can enjoy his creation.

(*Eddie Coleman*)

BARRANDOV FILM FACTORY, CZECH REPUBLIC

During the Cold War, there were restrictions in Eastern Europe as to what films could be produced. There were no restrictions on films about the Great Patriotic War and the Soviet fight against Nazi Germany. Movie companies like the Barrandov Film Factory based in Prague commissioned the construction of Tiger tank replicas built on readily available surplus T-34-85 tanks. Some of these tanks were sold to private collectors as curiosity pieces, movie props, or to be used in Second World War re-enactments.

MUSEUM ON THE DEMARCATION LINE

A Tiger I replica built on a T-34-85 tank hull, is on display at the Museum on the Demarcation Line, Shtahlavska 337 in Rokycany, Czech Republic, as noted by Pavel Medek.

HOTEL CORRADO TIGER REPLICA

The Hotel Corrado in Akce Střelnice in the Czech Republic has its own Tiger replica. It is built on a T-34-85 tank hull.

CZECH BREWERY TIGER REPLICA

This Tiger I replica built on a T-34-85 tank hull, is now owned by the Brewery Inn, Maxmilián Šimek in the Czech Republic. It was built for the 1978 Czech movie *Osvobození Prahy* (*The Liberation of Prague*).

RUSSIAN FILM PROP TIGER REPLICA

This Tiger I replica was built in Russia as a film prop for Mosfilm Studios. Its construction was commissioned for the film *White Tiger*, but a decision was made not to use it. Instead, the producers decided to use a visually inaccurate hybrid armoured fighting vehicle to represent a 'ghost' panzer. The original replica is now in private ownership in Russia. Unlike most of the other Eastern European replicas, this tank was built using parts from a Soviet T-55 tank and MTLB multi-purpose fully amphibious auxiliary armoured tracked vehicle.

(Mosfilm Studio)

PANZER GROUP SOUTH, TENNESSEE, USA, TIGER REPLICA

(HCM Associated Enterprises Ltd)

This Tiger I replica was built by Harold Marillier and his team at the HCM Associated Enterprises Ltd workshop, situated 30 miles south of central London. The donor tank hull was a Chinese Type 69 main battle tank. I have included this photograph of Harold with members of his team standing in front of the finished tank to give a better perspective on how large the Tiger Tank was. In May 2020, it was shipped to the Second World War historical re-enactment group called Panzer Group South, based in Tennessee, USA.

BIBLIOGRAPHY

Von Rosen, R. F., *Panzer Ace*
Jentz, T. L. and Doyle, H. L., *Panzer Tracks No. 6 Schwere Panzerkampfwagen*
Jentz, T. L. and Doyle, H. L., *D.W. to Tiger I: Design, Production and Modifications*
Fletcher, D., *Tiger! The Tiger Tank: A British View*
Winner. J., *Tiger I and Tiger II from the Bundesarchiv Volume 1*
Winner, J., *Tiger I and Tiger II from the Bundesarchiv Volume 2*
Schneider, W., *Tigers in Combat I*
Schneider, W., *Tigers in Combat II*

OFFICIAL REPORTS, PAMPHLETS, AND FIELD MANUALS

Department of Tank Design, Materials Division, Armour Branch Report No. M6816A/4 No. 1.
Department of Tank Design Experimental Report AT No. 225 Project M.6816A/8
Department of Tank Design Experimental Report AT No. 225 Project M.6815A/5
Department of Tank Design Experimental Report AT No. 252 Project M.6817A/10
Department of Tank Design Experimental Report AT No. 252 Project M.6816A/10
(National Archives, Kew, London WO 194/744)
Illustrated Record of German Army Equipment 1939–1945, Volume III: Armoured Fighting Vehicles. (MI10)
Intercept HW1/1251 National Archives, Kew, London
Intercept HW1/1415 National Archives, Kew, London
Intercept HW1/35998 National Archives, Kew, London
Intercept HW1/1668 National Archives, Kew, London
Intercept HW1/1169 National Archives, Kew, London
War Office Secret Cipher Telegram 1/65667
National Archives, Kew, London WO 1970/275
National Archives, Kew, London WO 194/1434
MI10/A/3008
MI10/A/M/3028
MI10 A/535 April 1943 H.I.6
MI10 A/545 Jan 1943 H.I.6
MI10 A/600 March 1943 H.I.6
MI10 A/601 March 1943 H.I.6
MI10 summary No. 49, Appendix A
MI10 summary No. 94/4
MI10 summary No. 97
MI10 summary No. 99
RA/0/2/5 Feb 1943
STT/10/2 Jan 1943
School of Tank Technology PzKw VI (Tiger) Report No. 19
Secret Cipher Telegram 1/65667 Oct 1942
The London Gazette Issue no. 36,605, p. 3,273; issue no. 36,849. p. 5,841; and issue no. 36,774, p. 5,015.